SUCCESSFUL
CATERING
SECOND EDITION

IOI IOI **SUCCESSFUL**

CATERING
SECOND EDITION

BERNARD R. SPLAVER

A CBI Book
Published by Van Nostrand Reinhold Company
New York

A CBI Book
(CBI is an imprint of Van Nostrand Reinhold Company Inc.)

Copyright © 1982, 1975 by the Culinary Institute of America

Library of Congress Catalog Card Number 81-12223

ISBN 0-8436-2219-9

Printed in the United States of America

Published by Van Nostrand Reinhold Company Inc.
115 Fifth Avenue
New York, New York 10003

Van Nostrand Reinhold Company Limited
Molly Millars Lane
Wokingham, Berkshire RG11 2PY, England

Van Nostrand Reinhold
480 La Trobe Street
Melbourne, Victoria 3000, Australia

Macmillan of Canada
Division of Canada Publishing Corporation
164 Commander Boulevard
Agincourt, Ontario M1S 3C7, Canada

16 15 14 13 12 11 10 9 8 7

Library of Congress Cataloging in Publication Data

Splaver, Bernard R.
    Successful catering.

    Includes bibliographical references and index.
    1. Caterers and catering. 2. Quantity cookery.
I. Title.
TX911.S64   1982   642'.4   81-12223
ISBN 0-8436-2219-9   AACR2

CONTENTS

FOREWORD

The key to successful catering is a combination of many important components, all necessary in order to take on and successfully complete a catering function. An individual must possess the proper culinary background, a thorough knowledge of wines and spirits as well as table service, a definite desire to serve and please people, and, above all, the unique organizational skill that brings all these important components together.

Catering, which is often done off premises, requires a great deal of logistical understanding and much organizational talent. These qualities are absolutely essential in order to prepare and serve the food and beverages according to the high standards for which we must always strive. This book in particular addresses the many important facets and details which one must take into consideration in order to become a successful caterer. It is not enough to just be able to prepare the food and serve it; one must have a good sense of timing, organization, personal relationships, an understanding of equipment and sanitation, and a feel for what the proper arrangement for the various functions may represent.

In addition, the reader may find the recipes listed in this book not only interesting, but also extremely helpful in the preparation of catered functions. The author pays great attention to the many necessary details that make a successful catering function and provides a sound guideline and approach for any type of catering one may have in mind.

Ferdinand Metz
President, Culinary Institute of America

PREFACE

For many years I have lectured, counseled (for the U.S. Small Business Administration), and participated in workshops in the food trade.

The number of persons with expertise in cooking, but ignorance of the ancillary requirements, who enter, or contemplate entering the catering profession is alarming. In many cases, grief and financial losses could have been avoided if guidance had been given or thorough research done. Few know that they can cater without capital risk by becoming accommodators! Many persons have suffered disaster because of inadequate or improper insurance. They did not know that products insurance is the most essential coverage in the industry.

Solutions to the perplexing problems of the catering industry are given in *Successful Catering,* Second Edition. The answers are not theoretical, but have been garnered from operators who overcame the problems successfully. This book details the various types of equipment used to guarantee safe food production, preservation, storage, and transport. It also presents a proven method for properly determining the type of service equipment and the amounts of each unit available or truck-packed for transport, which will save the caterer from the embarrassment of missing equipment or short portions.

Other helpful devices in this book include a list of French culinary terms that may be used to enhance menu presentation and an extensive inventory list of foods to help the operator establish an individualized, permanent referral list. A list of fifty food additives will be beneficial to all food processors, but particularly to those involved in kosher catering.

Every attempt has been made to present the information in a realistic light. The pluses and minuses reflect actual experience. Catering is a prestigious and profitable profession, and if this book makes it easier for qualified persons to enter and *remain* in this most interesting field, I will have achieved my purpose.

CHAPTER ONE

GETTING STARTED

Going into business for yourself is not a move to be taken lightly. Further, the highly specialized skills and professionalism needed in a catering business, and particularly in social catering, are unlike those required in a retail business. For example, for a retail establishment the factors of location, traffic count, parking, and competitive outlets are vital considerations. Effective merchandising displays, advertising, reasonable prices, and good service must be evaluated to attract and retain customers. In social, off-premises catering, many of these considerations are of minor importance. *Exposure for identity* is the primary goal of social catering—it is the way to get new business and keep it. Potential customers or clients want to know who you are, what you have done and can do, and how well and consistently you perform. (The reader is advised to send for the booklet entitled, *Checklist for Going Into Business* SMA#71, available from any field office of the Small Business Administration.)

Another goal is to know your territory! It would be foolhardy to incur the expense of establishing a commissary (a place where food is prepared, and stored or shipped) or setting up a food preparation and service area without making a thorough and objective analysis of the community's need for your services. The results could be wasted time, unnecessary and expensive equipment, and a depletion of necessary cash.

There are ways to avoid such wasteful, frustrating, and traumatic experiences. Take time to evaluate your personal qualifications and the catering potential in your community.

EVALUATING YOUR QUALIFICATIONS

A self-evaluation should enable you to determine if you are qualified and sufficiently prepared to meet the heavy demands of the catering business. To assist you in this effort, take the following quiz.

1. Do you have a basic knowledge of food and beverages? Knowledge of food naturally is a prime requisite. Do you know how to get full value from the food you purchase or prepare? Do you have access to direct and/or alternate sources of supply? Are you personally capable of upgrading your type of presentation should your business develop such a pattern? A basic knowledge of alcoholic beverages is desirable; a fuller knowl-

edge of wines is a real asset. Wine consumption has increased dramatically and people are more knowledgeable as to origin, care, and presentation. You must be as well informed.

2. Are you familiar with various types of foodservice? Can you prepare a basic, elaborate, or classical buffet? Can you set up an attractive and appropriate salad bar? Can you arrange a small or large banquet with the finesse generally associated with such an affair? How knowledgeable and adept are you with American, French, or Russian table service? Can you produce a clambake, barbecue, or picnic for a large number of people? Can you present flaming spectaculars? You could be called upon to provide any one of these presentations.

3. Can you, personally, make the foods you wish to feature? Assuming that you have the most capable cooks, chefs, and bakers, could you immediately and skillfully substitute for any one of them? Can you attractively alter oven-ready or bag-cooked convenience items so that they have the appearance and taste of on-premises prepared foods? Do you have ready access to substitute preparation and kitchen service crews?

4. What aesthetic abilities do you possess? Do you have the talent to arrange food artistically for various types of presentations (preplated, dinner, or buffet)? Can you drape tables and "show" areas? Do you have some concept of harmonious color combinations? Can you arrange flowers, if necessary? Can you make fruit, vegetable, tallow, or ice carvings? This is a marvelous area for self-expression and visible proof of your individuality.

5. Do you have a basic understanding of mathematics? You must know how to check invoices, figure discounts, determine costs, and compute weight losses in production. You must also be able to figure wages, sales, and inventories, and reconcile bank statements. Other necessary skills include estimating the amount and type of help needed, based on anticipated number of guests or on dollar volume. Finally, you must be able to set cost controls for areas where outlays are excessive. These essential skills are integral components in estimating and submitting bids.

6. Will you be able to establish and maintain good working relations with your employees while maintaining authority and control? Do not become emotionally or socially involved with your employees; do not grant special favors or share privileged knowledge; and do not play favorites or show partiality to one or a group of employees. A caterer must, at all times, be above reproach. Aloofness is not necessary and should be discouraged, but a sense of dignity, founded on your abilities, and business propriety are.

7. Are you familiar with foodservice equipment and its proper maintenance and care? If minor malfunctions occur, can you make temporary repairs? Can you replace compressor belts or worn washers, unplug a clogged drain, or make firm electrical connections in a socket or plug? Do you know the proper safety precautions for electric, gas, and electronic equipment? You should be able to establish and supervise schedules for the inspection and maintenance of all equipment.

8. Are you a good mixer and comfortable with people? In this profession, you encounter people from all walks of life. You must be comfortable with people and with crowds. You must be gracious and sincere in providing service. You must always be aware that you are responsible for and involved with the conduct of an affair, and you must refrain from socializing with guests, no matter how close your relationship.

9. Are you familiar with prevailing rules of etiquette and social protocol? The caterer is viewed as an authority on such functions as weddings, confirmations, and showers, just to name a few. Thus, to complement your own knowledge you should possess some good

reference books on etiquette, as well as reliable periodicals focusing on bridal functions, gourmet foods and wines, and entertaining in general.

If you are catering to religious or ethnic groups, you must be knowledgeable about the customs and traditions involved with ceremonial meals. You must be familiar with dietary disciplines. Above all, try to develop a reputation as a trusted counselor to whom clients can come for ideas, information, and advice.

10. Are you by nature a "cool" individual? Can you take command in a crisis? Can you handle emergencies, sudden illness, guest misbehavior, collapsing tables, hot food spills, or fire? If someone is choking do you know what to do? Can you treat scalds and burns? Do you know how to obtain and use an inhalator?

11. Are you physically able to cope with the demands of catering? In the foodservice field, a great deal of physical ability and energy is required to arrange tables and chairs, push dollies, move furniture, carry dishes, tableware, and pots and pans of food, and to clean up (when one's energy quotient is the lowest). Do you have the stamina for such hard work, as well as for the long and irregular hours? Do you recover quickly from fatigue?

12. Do you have the money? Not only do you need money to set up a commissary and/or dining facilities, but you must purchase supplies, pay for basic installations, and meet the rent, utility, and insurance bills. Your cash reserve must be sufficient to enable you and your family to live comfortably and pay personal and home expenses until your business shows a profitable return. This is extremely important. Based on U.S. Chamber of Commerce statistics, the primary causes of business failures are undercapitalization and poor management: ninety percent of these failures

occur within two years of startup. DON'T BE A STATISTIC.

These twelve questions reflect the realistic conditions and situations that one encounters in a career of catering and foodservice. They were not framed to scare or dishearten, but rather to make you aware of the realities that will confront you.

ANALYZING CATERING POTENTIAL IN YOUR COMMUNITY

After carefully evaluating your personal qualifications, your next step is to survey the catering potential in the area you wish to service. A careful examination of the locale should help you develop insights about prospective customers as well as knowledge of the area's economic strengths and weaknesses. Data can be gathered from several sources.

Check the local Bureau of Vital Statistics or Bureau of Records for the number of marriages, births, and deaths. (The last item is important because many religious/ethnic groups use caterers for wakes or postfuneral meals, or to send foods to bereaved families.) To determine if there is a pattern of increase or decrease in any of these statistics, you should look at records going back at least three years.

Visit the offices of every club, church, temple, or synagogue in your area to learn the number and types of social gatherings held in their facilities. Many of these institutions rent their social halls to the public for various functions.

Find out which fraternal and social organizations have clubrooms or halls with kitchen facilities that they use not only for themselves but rent for public use. Such groups include the Grange, American Legion, Veterans of Foreign Wars, Knights of Columbus, Knights of Pythias, Masonic Lodges, Elks, Odd Fellows, and Volunteer Firemen. Some may even grant you exclusive or special privileges to cater in or from their premises for special financial arrangements. (Note: There are religious, social, or civic organizations that have lovely foodservice facilities, but forbid the use of alcoholic beverages, which limits their usability.)

Local Chambers of Commerce will gladly furnish valuable statistical data to help you forecast present and future potentials.

Consult the nearest office of the United States Small Business Administration and ask for an appointment with a representative of the Service Corps of Retired Executives (SCORE). This service is free and available throughout the country. You can discuss your plans with them (all information is held confidentially), and their advice and expertise will be of great value to you. Incidentally, SCORE offers valuable help in administrative, technical, and financial problems even if you are already in business. SCORE can assist in securing additional start-up money or in refinancing your indebtedness. The Small Business Administration does not always give direct loans, but it can assist or guarantee bank loans when the applicant has had difficulty with banking institutions.

The Small Business Administration is particularly helpful to women because of previous discrimination and, as of January 1980, there were special funds available to help in business ventures. Minority groups also will find the SBA extremely helpful. The National Economic Development Association (NEDA), with offices in strategic cities throughout the country, was established especially to help minority groups. The location of the nearest NEDA office can be secured from the SBA. All these services are free. They are listed in the telephone directory under UNITED STATES GOVERNMENT.

If the population is predominantly ethnic or of a particular religious persuasion, it would be a good idea to research the customs and traditions of these groups. Consult their local leaders about the community's needs and the amount of cooperation they would give you. You might even consider developing your business to cater to their special needs. This would certainly give you an advantage over any competition.

SELECTING SERVICES

After appraising your personal qualifications and the catering potential within the community, then determine the type(s) of service you can offer. There are various types of catering—industrial, institutional, wagon or van, on-premise, off-premise, and accommodator. Since we are concerned with social catering, the categories of interest are on-premise, off-premise, and accommodator.

On-Premise Catering

In this type of business, the caterer has his or her own banquet hall with attached kitchen. On-premise catering can have a free-standing facility or single-purpose building devoted exclusively to the production of parties, banquets, etcetera. Or it can be the food and service facilities of a church, club, or organization. It can also be an integral component of a motel or hotel restaurant, owned and operated by individuals or a unit of a chain. The beginner should *never* plan, build, or buy a single-purpose building and business of this kind unless totally qualified in every area of catering and financially secure. (See chapter 10 for more information.)

Lending institutions are hesitant to lend money for single-purpose buildings and, therefore, may require higher interest rates. You might be forced to go to venture capital companies that charge even higher rates and require a share in your business.

Off-Premise Catering

Here, the caterer has or owns the commissary kitchen, a storeroom for all the equipment, and sometimes even garages for trucks and cars. *The caterer always brings the complete service to the customer.* The affair may be at a private home, a club, church, synagogue, or factory; it could be a tent party for a wedding, a store opening, or any type of outdoor affair. Off-premise catering therefore requires special equipment for packing and transporting both food and related service ware. You need equipment for the proper and safe transport of perishables in hot weather; you need the proper equipment to heat or cook food, if it is not readily available at the party area. (It is advisable to rent such items if there is only occasional need for them.) The off-premise caterer must be resourceful and prepared to improvise. Preparation and service areas may be less than ideal. (See chapter 9 on off-premise catering.)

Exclusively off-premise caterers have an advantage—they are not saddled with the considerable expense of furnishing, equipping, and maintaining a dining area. However, as all of their business is mobile, they must purchase expensive equipment to transport safely the food prepared in the commissary. They must use refrigerated trucks (where required by health code statutes) or equipment that maintains perishables at safe temperatures. There are also the hazards of weather and distance to consider.

The scheduling of help must account for the extra time required to travel to and from the affair. An off-premise caterer must be aware of all of these factors and all costs must be reflected in his charges. A small additional percentage for unforeseen factors, such as truck breakdowns or towing, equipment losses, and the high incidence of breakage due to transportation, must also be included.

Accommodator (In-Home Cooking and Serving)

Accommodators, whose service represents an important and profitable branch of catering, are persons with particular skills in cooking, baking, and/or serving. (See chapter 8 on accommodators).

ESTABLISHING YOUR BUSINESS

Civic, fraternal, social, and religious organizations usually have program committees or chairpersons whose duties are to engage speakers, performers, demonstrators, professionals, and entertainment for their meetings. The more interesting, the more well-known, the more unusual the presentation offered at the meeting, the greater the interest and the larger the attendance. If you can present a program on such subjects as food education, food presentation, or food logistics, by all means contact the Lions, Rotary, Chamber of Commerce, and others and offer to speak at a meeting. Notices of their meetings are listed in local papers and frequently mentioned on radio and TV. The speaker's profession, background, and topic are all part of the information disseminated through the media, resulting in free and valuable advertising.

If you are uncomfortable with large groups, try the smaller church or social organizations. Offer to give demonstrations on making hors d'oeuvre, baking or decorating cakes, carving fruits and vegetables, making tea sandwiches, or creating table arrangements. You could also talk on the proper care and handling of knives, or even give a lesson in napkin folding. Prepare one or two of your specialty dishes. Be thoroughly prepared and bring everything necessary for the presentation. Do not plan a program longer than 40 minutes. You don't have to be an orator or a Dale Carnegie graduate to make an effective and well-received program. If you have the skill and dexterity for the demonstration, your words will flow easily. If you are a member of an organization, serve on the program or refreshment committees so that you can aid in the planning or be responsible for the entire presentation. But never undertake anything that you cannot perform with excellence!

DEVELOPING A MARKET

Frequently, beginners are impatient. Anxious to get started and into full swing, they do not allow sufficient time to become established in the community or to accumulate the necessary cash reserves. In social catering, which is based primarily on personal services and personal abilities, this haste can be disastrous. The community must be fully acquainted with the caterer's capabilities and talents. In fact, the more well-known and distinctive the services, the more frequently the community will seek him out.

One excellent way to establish a reputation initially is to approach organizations in the community and offer your services as an accommodator for upcoming events (free for the first time or at a nominal rate). If your offer is accepted, your skill and professionalism (or lack of it) will become apparent. Because most committee members or groups are amateurs, your superior technique and abilities will stand out. If you present a better cooked, better tasting meal or a professional-looking buffet, or offer quicker, more efficient and effective table service, your ability will be recognized.

As the individual responsible for this impressive performance, you will be remembered and sought after for future affairs. People attending the function will be impressed and request your name and other pertinent information for future reference. In this manner, you can gradually build your reputation for ability, integrity, and dependability—three of the most vital attributes of any successful caterer.

Advertising

Another effective way to reach clients is to advertise. Once you know what you want to advertise and whom you want to reach, you must select the advertising medium that will reach them most effectively. Because of the local nature of your operation, you will find that newspapers and radio spots are most effective. If you decide to place six or seven lines in your local "Want Ad" section under "Services Offered," you may be able to compose an effective ad yourself. Personnel at the newspaper office will often help. Rates are related to circulation and vary according to the number of lines purchased over a period of time. If you want to reach wider markets through TV, billboards, or transportation signs, then seek professional help. In this case, locate an advertising agency in your immediate community. As a neighbor, you will receive:

1. expert ideas as to the marketability of your services
2. local opinion regarding the status of your establishment
3. advice on the use of rural or suburban newspapers, or radio stations, to obtain the greatest coverage from your advertising budget, and
4. good will from the agency, as well as the potential business it can generate.

You will receive requests and solicitations for advertising from all types of organizations, including social groups, schools, churches, and fraternal societies. Friends and relatives may make these requests also. In order to maintain good public relations you may be reluctant to turn them down. However, these costs should be considered as donations or contributions, not an advertising expense.

Newspaper ads can be elaborate or simple, but they must be inviting. Give just enough information to whet a customer's interest and to establish the caterer's name with the public. See examples of newspaper ads below and Figure 1.1.

THE EXTRA HAND—Assist or full charge, cooking, baking, serving in homes or for organizations. HERM SCHWARZ—880-9640

ETHNIC FAVORITES—European, Far East, Asiatic and African foods that will be talked about. Prepared in your place or ours. Authentic decorations to complement choice of foods. HANNAH'S CATERING SERVICE—914-6100

Signs. Flyers, throwaways, brochures, and letters can be extremely effective, but they are expensive. The cost of expert design and production can exceed the proposed budget and

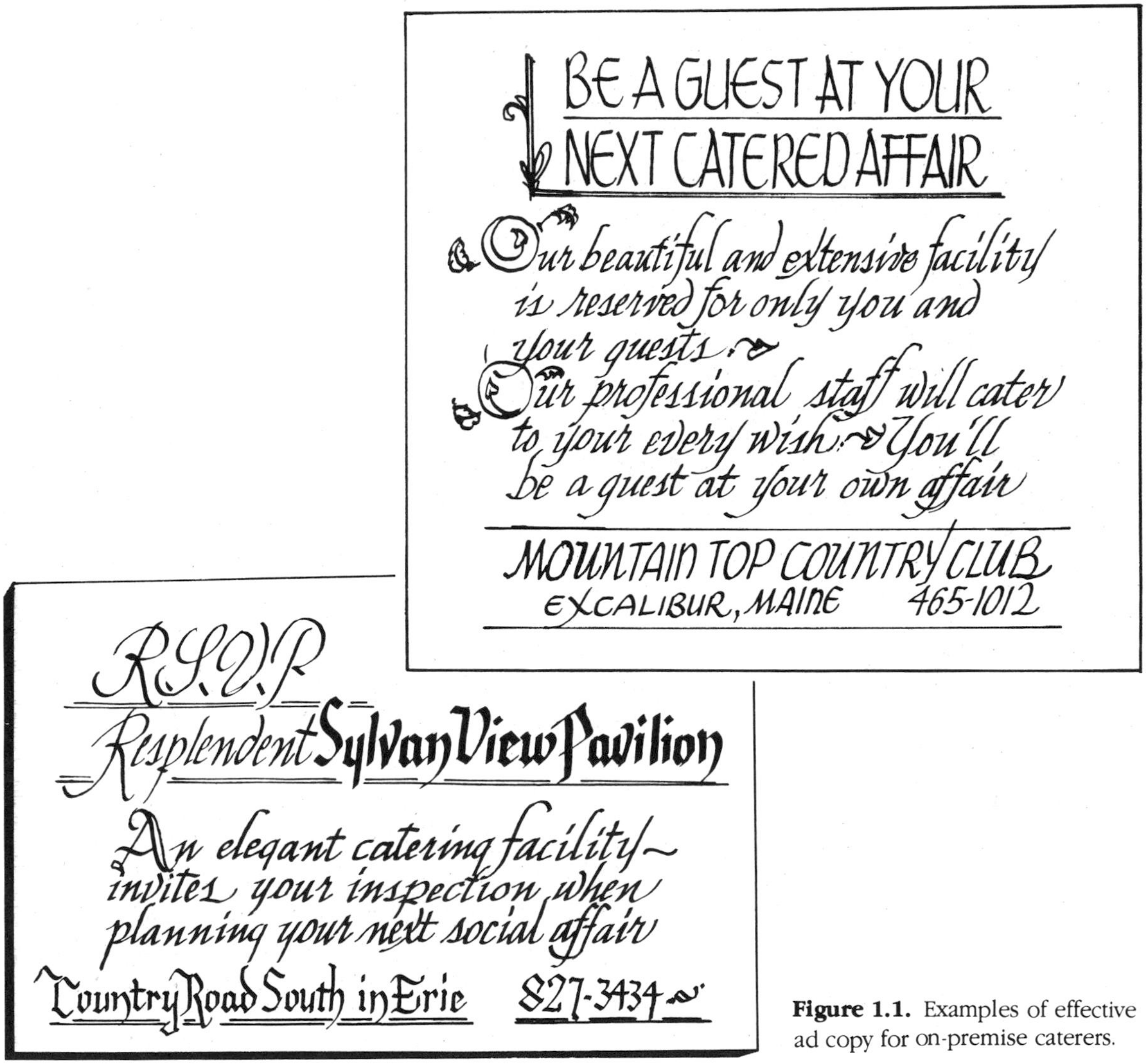

Figure 1.1. Examples of effective ad copy for on-premise caterers.

returns will be minimal compared to the expenditure. TV and radio advertising should not be attempted without professional help.

Signs are an efficient and effective communication tool. Signs present an image of your business—they tell people who you are and what you are doing, and they help people find you. Signs are the most direct form of visual communication. They can be the main device for directing people to your place of business, particularly if your commissary or catering hall is not in a high rent or high traffic area. Compared to all other media, they are the most available and the most practical, and the resultant exposure is probably the cheapest of all advertising media. A sign maker should also be chosen with a great deal of care—the better the design and execution, the greater the message impact. Remember that exterior sign placement may require permission from the local zoning authority.

Other Resources

Contact local business people who provide services related to social functions. Bridal shops, florists, photographers, orchestras, and printers may be willing to supply leads for prospective customers. This, of course, is a two-way street; you must be prepared to reciprocate by providing them with leads.

Read the society pages of newspapers for engagement announcements. Then write a note of best wishes and congratulations to the young lady or call her. Describe your facilities and offer your expert help with her future plans. Stress that there is no obligation attached to a consultation. Be sincere in your offer of help and, regardless of whether or not it is accepted, you will gain immeasurable goodwill.

From newspapers you can also learn about upcoming plans for testimonials, special luncheons, reunions, bowling banquets, fraternity gatherings, or fund-raising affairs. Since many of these articles deal with future events, plans may not be finalized and the options are wide open. It could be advantageous to contact the person mentioned in the news item and promote your services.

If your local newspaper has a Food Editor, try to arrange an interview to discuss your special abilities. You might submit a favorite recipe or even be the subject of a feature story.

Community Involvement

Society affiliations, participation in civic affairs, serving on committees, involvement in popular causes, and even limited and nonpartisan political activities, can be valuable in generating reciprocal benefits. An association with Red Cross or Civil Defense to offer your expertise in times of emergency will serve a twofold purpose—it will fulfill the obligation of a sincere, concerned citizen and will result in favorable publicity that could enhance your image.

Learn a lesson from the large multinational companies that insist their local representatives become civically involved to keep their name projected favorably.

SEEKING PROFESSIONAL HELP

The operation of any business in this competitive economy, large or small, involves the rights of buyers and sellers, landlords and tenants, creditors and debtors, employers and employees, and other groups. The complexities and volume of these laws make it impossible to know all the lawful opportunities and rights, as well as the liabilities. Therefore, a specialist is needed, namely a lawyer. A lawyer provides four basic services—checking, advising, guiding, and representing. Legal services should not be acquired only for emergencies. Emergencies can be avoided if legal counsel is consulted in the first place.

Legal services are particularly desirable and essential in business organization, property acquisition, money borrowing, tax planning, employer-employee relations, litigation, credit problems, and securing the proper licenses and permits from regulatory bodies and other governmental agencies.

A lawyer can advise as to whether the business should be formed under sole ownership, or as a partnership or corporation. For example, under sole proprietorship, possible losses incurred in the start-up years could be used to offset other income. As the business grows and profits increase, the owner could decide to incorporate, or obtain a tax advantage by selling shares in the business to the public. At the same time, this would reduce any personal liability for possible business losses. As management responsibilities increase, a partnership could ease the personal load. Legal contracts must then be drawn as to the responsibilities of each partner and the sharing of profits. Consult your attorney regarding federal and state laws on wages, employees' hours, workmen's compensation, unemployment compensation, and any applicable fair employment legislation.

Legal service is available from bar organizations or local law schools either free or at a minimal charge.

It is also essential to hire an accountant. In addition to obtaining your state sales tax and Internal Revenue identification numbers, the accountant can also set up, organize, and properly maintain your financial records, making certain that they fully comply with all governmental regulations and laws, and can pass regular and unannounced inspections by local, state, or federal auditors.

Although the services of a professional accountant (as well as an attorney) are usually expensive, they are a wise investment. The accountant who is expert in business-financial matters will ensure that you take advantage of all tax and business deductions to which you are entitled. As a result, you will save financial resources by not paying unnecessary monies for taxes.

In addition to completing all necessary tax forms or helping you with them, an accountant will immediately recognize the danger signals of overrides or underrides on all expenditures, and help you institute the necessary controls to keep them within the prescribed ratios.

LEGAL CONSIDERATIONS

Zoning

Your physical plant, whether an on-premise or off-premise catering facility, is subject to proper clearances from the local Zoning Board. Since local requirements and the classifications assigned to catering establishments differ, have your attorney look into these ordinances.

Local ordinances may impose restrictions on where you can locate your business. They may also require provisions for employee and guest parking, but prohibit truck storage and/or truck parking. They may prohibit any sort of business activity on Sundays or holidays, or they may prohibit truck traffic within specified hours (say between 11 P.M. and 7 A.M.), thus severely restricting delivery or loading. This could be a crippling blow to your scheduling.

Garbage collection may also be covered by local ordinances. For example, if outside garbage collection areas are prohibited, you may have to develop an alternate plan, probably refrigerating your garbage. These ordinances should not be taken lightly nor circumvented. Even if the local authority is lax, there is certain to be a civic or ecological group that will bring pressure to have these ordinances enforced. Your attorney should instruct you thoroughly regarding all ordinances so that you can comply with them. Failure to do so can impair your reputation and lead to expensive litigation.

Licensing

After meeting zoning specifications, you must then secure the necessary licenses, particularly the license of your local Board of Health. A Board of Health license is mandatory. Without it, you will not be permitted to operate or offer your services to the public. Local boards vary as to how they classify a catering business. Your establishment might be considered a commissary, a restaurant, or a food-processing plant. However, determining the proper type of license to apply for should be a carefully considered decision and one made with an eye to the future. Select a license that will permit flexibility, allow for business growth, and provide broader privileges, such as retailing. This will allow prepared food to be sold for off-premise consumption, or baked merchandise to be sold either at the wholesale or retail level. Some states require a special license if milk or other dairy products are kept on the premises, either for on-premise consumption or for the preparation of food. The small additional fee incurred at the outset is well worth the expense—it can eliminate the time-consuming red tape and even greater cost of applying for a different or auxiliary license at a later date.

During this same period you will be contacted by other municipal officials to make certain that you meet additional requirements. Consequently, fire, building, plumbing, and electrical inspectors will visit your premises to check required safety precautions. It is not necessary to contact these inspectors as they will be notified by the Zoning Board.

Insurance

The advice of both your attorney and accountant will be invaluable in selecting the insurance you must and should carry. There are essential areas for insurance coverage and there are coverages that are desirable, but not absolutely necessary. There are also coverages for employee benefits. Check all your requirements with an insurance agent. For detailed insurance information, contact your local Small Business Administration office and ask for Small Marketer Aid #148.

First, you must recognize the risks to which you will be exposed. Follow the guides for buying insurance economically, and seek professional advice.

Insurance has many positive advantages as well as the negative one of avoiding losses. Used correctly, it can contribute to your success by reducing the uncertainties under which you operate. Insurance premiums are the price paid for freedom from worry about economic losses from conditions outside your control. It can improve your bank credit since it keeps your business going when an insured peril interrupts operation. The potential benefits of a good insurance program should not be overlooked.

There are five kinds of essential insurances: fire insurance, liability insurance, automobile insurance, workers' compensation insurance, and products insurance.

Fire Insurance. Basic fire insurance can be extended to cover additional perils, such as, windstorm, hail, smoke, explosion, vandalism, and malicious mischief, at a small additional cost.

Comprehensive coverage on all policies is suggested as it includes all-risk contracts that offer the broadest available coverage for the money. Special protection, other than a standard fire insurance policy, is needed to cover the loss by fire of accounts, bills, currency, deeds, evidence of sales, money, and securities.

Liability Insurance. Due to the abnormally high settlements made by juries in liability cases, it is advisable to secure the maximum your business will permit. Most liability policies, in addition to covering bodily injuries, now cover personal injuries such as libel and slander, if these are specifically insured.

NOTE: Because off-premise caterers always work in other people's property and in their care, they may be held responsible for fire and general liability unless the caterer's policy *specifically* mentions that they are covered by fire legal liability insurance!

Automobile Insurance. Five or more automobiles under one ownership, and operated as a fleet for business purposes, can generally be insured under a low-cost fleet policy. This covers both material damage to your vehicle and liability to others for property damage or personal injury. The higher the deductibles, which are available in any amount, the greater reduction there can be on premiums.

Most states require liability insurance or proof of financial responsibility. You may also be able to purchase uninsured motorist protection to cover your own bodily injury claims from someone who has no insurance, even if your state does not have "no fault" insurance. Personal property stored in an automobile and not attached to it (merchandise being delivered) *is not covered* under an automobile policy.

NOTE: When an employee uses his own car on your behalf, you could be legally liable, even if you don't own a car or truck yourself.

Workers' Compensation Insurance. Common law requires that an employer: (1) provide employees a safe place to work, (2) hire competent fellow employees, (3) provide safe tools, and (4) warn employees of an existing danger. If the employer fails to provide the above, under both common law and workers' compensation laws, he is liable for damage suits brought by an employee. Not all employees are covered by workers' compensation laws; the laws vary from state to state.

Products Insurance. Do not attempt to operate your business unless you are fully covered by products insurance. This will protect you in case a foreign object is found in your food or in case contamination of foods processed by you causes illness. Also, if a foreign object is found in foods processed by someone else, but served by you, you could still be sued. However, if you are covered by products insurance, your insurance carrier will protect you and perhaps take action against the manufacturer of the product.

Desirable Coverages. The following types of insurance coverage, although not absolutely essential, can add greatly to the security of your business. These coverages include business interruption insurance, crime insurance, glass insurance, and rent insurance.

Business interruption insurance covers fixed expenses that would continue if a fire shut down your business. These expenses include salaries to key employees, taxes, interest, depreciation, and utilities, as well as the profits you would lose. This type of policy can also provide payments for costs incurred in reopening your business after a fire or other insured peril; it can also indemnify you if your business is suspended because of failure or interruption of the supply of power, light, heat, gas, or water furnished by a public utility company.

Crime Insurance. Policies will pay only if there are visible marks of forced entry. This policy will also pay for loss of property or equipment due to force or violence on or off the premises. This insurance is imperative for off-premise caterers.

Employee Benefit Coverages. Insurance coverages can be used to provide health insurance, group life insurance, group health insurance, disability insurance, and retirement income.

Emphasis has been made on insurance in this chapter because of the reality of the many risks connected with social catering. Wishful thinking or an "It can't happen to me" attitude won't lessen or remove the possibilities that a ruinous misfortune may strike. Before purchasing any insurance, decide what perils to insure against and how much loss you might suffer from each. Cover your largest loss exposure first. Use as high a deductible as you can afford. Seek professional help and review your insurance program periodically to prevent duplication. Investigate package plans that might give you adequate protection at a more reasonable rate.

CHAPTER TWO

SETTING UP A KITCHEN

If after objective study and careful analysis you find that you wish to take full advantage of the additional opportunities that exist in the market you have created, you may be ready to establish a commissary/kitchen.

In setting up such a business, be prepared for a shakedown period during which operations, cost patterns, and systems for performing functions will evolve gradually. This period can be chaotic and frustrating. Emerging business patterns may differ markedly from what you had anticipated and for which you had planned so carefully. And since this particular period can also be very costly, you, the expanding caterer, must be adequately prepared and financially able to cope with many unforeseen difficulties.

While careful planning is essential, no scientific formula exists to assure a hand-in-glove fit. But do not be discouraged. In time—with considerable attention to and objective evaluation of all factors—your business should become a very smooth-running operation.

GENERAL FACILITIES PLANNING

While careful attention must be given to budgetary considerations, equal attention should also be given to equipment costs. From an economic standpoint, the purchase of high-quality equipment is a sound move. In addition to giving superior performance, it will, no doubt, lessen the possibility of breakdowns and high repair costs.

In planning your operation, allow adequate space for shipping and receiving areas. This includes space for a 4-foot by 8-foot table, which will be most helpful for assembling items to be packed and transported to jobs.

The production area should be physically separated from other areas and have as little cross-traffic and interference as possible. Dishwashing facilities should be close to the glass, silver, and china storage areas. Linens and miscellaneous dry foods must be stored in a well-ventilated place and away from pipes. *Never put anything directly on the floor.* Use standard or improvised pallets to keep all merchandise at least 8 inches off the floor. Flour, sugar, rice, potatoes, and onions should be stored in covered containers. Before refilling these containers, make certain that each is spotlessly clean.

A Checklist for Facility Requirements

1. Check all floors, walls, and ceilings for cracks, holes, and peeling paint. *(Do not use lead-based paint in any area.)*

2. Check for possible fly and/or insect infestation. Have all doors and windows properly screened.

3. Have adequate lighting. With fluorescent lighting, cool white bulbs should be used because other shades tend to give food an unattractive appearance. Lighting fixtures should be easy to reach and to clean.

4. Check natural ventilation. In planning your kitchen, carefully consider placement of ovens, ranges, steam kettles, etcetera, so that the mechanical exhaust units above them will be able to operate at peak efficiency and not have too long a "drag area."

5. When planning exhaust hoods above cooking areas, be certain they include automatic fire-fighting equipment.

6. Carefully plan the placement of all equipment. Allow sufficient aisle space so that refrigerators, freezers, and ovens can open to their full swing and to allow room for food trucks and dollies. (A comparatively easy way to plan this is to make a scale floor plan using graph paper. Cut out templates—paper patterns scaled to the size of your equipment—and arrange the most effective layout. [See Figure 2.1.] Blueprint and architectural supply stores may have preprinted templates of kitchen equipment or measurements are available in equipment catalogues.)

7. The commissary kitchen should have more square footage than an on-premise banquet kitchen. The number of stoves needed, ovens, re-cons, fryers, or steam units will depend on the type of menu offered and the volume of business anticipated. The concern in this type of kitchen is for space. Besides the space needed for food production, there must be space for counting, organizing, packing, storing, and shipping.

8. Be certain that the lavatory space is sufficient to meet the local ordinances.

9. If possible, arrange to have one sink for exclusive use by the chef, another for utility work, and a third for pots. Your local Board of Health may also require installation of a special hand sink in the kitchen.

10. Dishwashing, receiving and storage, and packing areas should, if at all possible, be separated from, but within easy access to, the kitchen.

11. Allow sufficient parking space for your employees.
NOTE: It is unwise to establish a kitchen in a building where you must use an elevator either to enter the kitchen or to go from one department to another.

Plan for Deliveries

In planning facilities, all factors involved in the delivery of food and equipment to off-premise jobs are important. Keep in mind that certain streets may be restricted to truck traffic during certain hours and that trucks may be prohibited in residential areas. Therefore, you will have to use other routes.

You may also have to adjust your pattern for school bus routes and in locations where schools, factories, office buildings, stadiums, and other recreational/amusement areas could cause traffic jams.

Be aware of road construction and detours. If uncertain, check with State Police or the local automobile club. Also listen to local radio reports; many give traffic information that could be important, particularly in bad weather.

Always allow plenty of time for deliveries. Give your driver sufficient traveling money for emergencies, additional gas, or tolls. He should also have enough money to pay for minor repairs and be supplied with the names of reputable service stations with towing facilities in the areas where he travels. *He should always know where* YOU *will be and how he can get in touch with you.*

It might be advantageous to install a mobile phone in your trucks, as well as in your lead car. Shortwave communications may also be of value.

Put a "Hide-a-Key" in a place known only to you, on each vehicle that you own. Keys can get

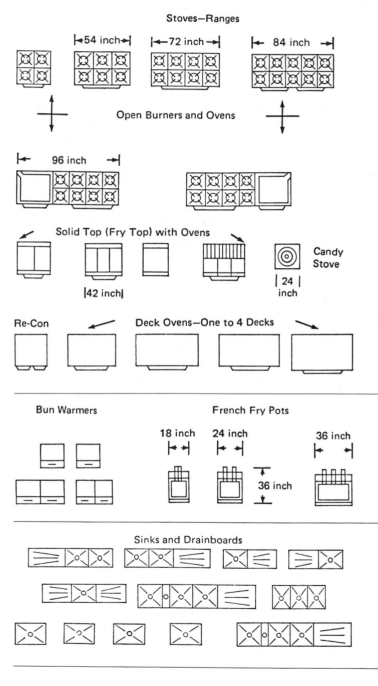

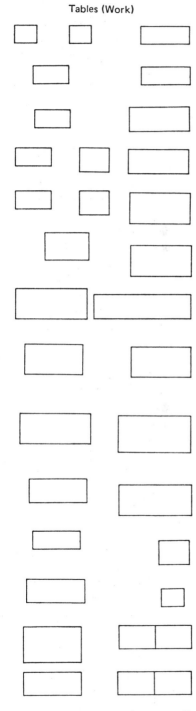

Tables (Work)

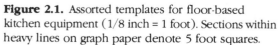

Figure 2.1. Assorted templates for floor-based kitchen equipment (1/8 inch = 1 foot). Sections within heavy lines on graph paper denote 5 foot squares.

(continued)

Figure 2.1. (continued)

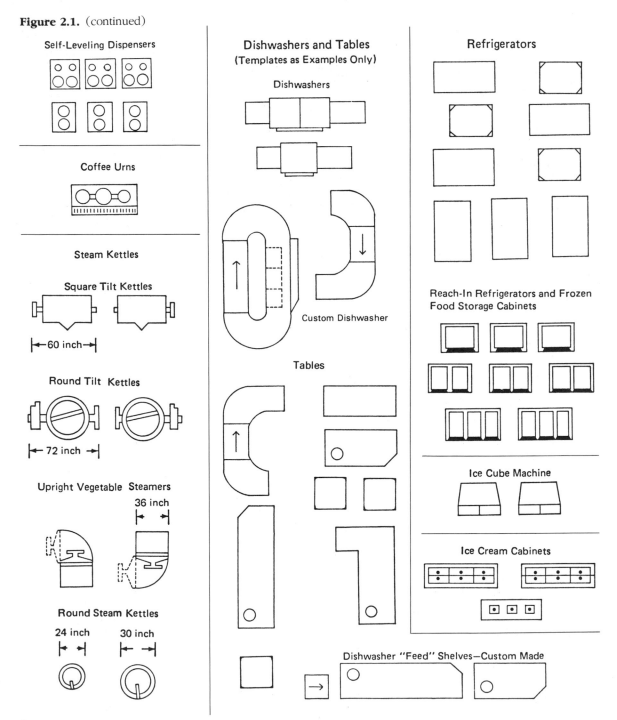

Self-Leveling Dispensers

Coffee Urns

Steam Kettles

Square Tilt Kettles

|←—60 inch—→|

Round Tilt Kettles

|←— 72 inch —→|

Upright Vegetable Steamers

36 inch
|←   →|

Round Steam Kettles

24 inch   30 inch
|← →| |← →|

Dishwashers and Tables
(Templates as Examples Only)

Dishwashers

↑   ↓

Custom Dishwasher

Tables

↑

→

Dishwasher "Feed" Shelves—Custom Made

Refrigerators

Reach-In Refrigerators and Frozen Food Storage Cabinets

Ice Cube Machine

Ice Cream Cabinets

SCALE: 1/8 INCH = 1 FOOT

**Walk-In Reefers—
Freezers (with shelves)**

SCALE: 1/8 INCH = 1 FOOT

lost or misplaced, so it is a good idea to know where one set is at all times.

Kitchen Design and Layout

According to the American Gas Association, kitchen design is characterized by a departmental layout. The criteria for the departmentalization is as follows:

1. the grouping of tasks of similar nature
2. the maximization of labor utilization
3. the maximization of equipment utilization
4. the minimization of interdepartmental traffic
5. the grouping of equipment that requires similar utilities, especially ventilation, and
6. the maximization of sanitary conditions.

As a result of evaluation of these criteria and experience, the following departments would typically be found in a foodservice installation.

Receiving

Dry storage

Refrigerated storage, including frozen foods

Meat preparation

Vegetable preparation

Salad preparation

Main cooking

Short order cooking

Bake shop

Ice cream

Pot washing

Serving area

Dish washing and dish storage

Dining area

Miscellaneous areas (office, employee facilities, miscellaneous storage, and ice manufacturing).

This list is primarily a guide. Some installations will not contain all these departments. It depends on the size of your outfit, or on the extent to which you purchase and process raw materials or buy "convenience prepared" foods that fit into your standards. These departments can be discussed in any one of several ways. Logistically, one should consider the flow of food from receiving through preparation, production, and service— whether on- or off-premise—and also consider such related supporting departments as offices, dishwashing, pot washing, and sanitation. If packaged food is to be sold, consider packaging requirements. If all food is to be served on-premises and you anticipate a substantial volume of business, then you should use banquet carriers and dish carriers and your planning should provide for storage. If your business will be off-premises then check into the various types of dish and food carrying equipment that are available and purchase the sizes and type appropriate to your needs.

Receiving. Receiving is one of the most important areas in your entire installation. It is the function of this department to verify that purchasing standards and quantities are met by thoroughly checking items that are delivered. Weights and counts must be verified, and any short count or short weight must be noted on the delivery slip and countersigned by the delivery person immediately. Reject any part of or the entire shipment if it is not up to specifications. The receiving department can also function as the shipping department for off-premise caterers.

Every receiving department must have the following equipment. (1) A scale, preferably with a large dial, of 500 pounds capacity with quarter-pound graduations. (2) A table for counting rather than weighing some items. It is also extremely useful for small packages and "on spot" examinations of fruits and vegetables. These tables should not exceed 5 by 8 feet for easy reaching. This same table can be used for assembling shipping items for off-premise catering. (3) An office standup desk or shelf for checking packing slips, etcetera. (4) Trucks (hand or platform) to move goods. (To avoid injury to the receiving clerk, insist that nothing be carried that can be put on wheels.)

Dry Storage. When planning your installation, safeguard your dry storage from: (1) deterioration, (2) adverse temperature or temperature changes, (3) adverse moisture or moisture changes, (4) pilferage, and (5) dust, dirt, insects, fire, or other damage.

The following equipment is usually found in storerooms:

1. Shelving, preferably of metal or heavy duty wiring.
2. Platforms or skids. No food may be stored directly on the floor. Platforms should be constructed or merchandise should be kept on skids.
3. Portable bins, plastic or metal being the most satisfactory. Some have attached wheels that allow for ease in cleaning and moving the bin to other departments.
4. Valuable items storage cabinet. This should be a separate, locked storage cabinet for the safekeeping of expensive foods or equipment essential for storeroom operation. Records and files of the storeroom clerk may be kept here.
5. Communication equipment such as a telephone is a must. An intercom is equally important and possibly a TV screen to monitor activity in the area.

Refrigerated Storage. In many installations, refrigerated storage takes place at several points from receiving to service. In small installations, all refrigerated storage may be served by the same refrigerator. Larger installations will provide separate refrigerators for meats, dairy, vegetables, and fish, plus a separate freezer (usually a walk-in). The size of these separates is determined by the volume used and the frequency of delivery.

Unnecessarily large refrigerators waste valuable energy and increase operation costs. The size of the freezer one needs depends on the extent that frozen fruits, vegetables, beverages, and meat are involved in your type of food operation. When a facility is in an outlying district, or when extra delivery charges are made for small quantities or deliveries are infrequent, then the storage facility requirements are much greater.

Shelving for refrigerators must be either heavily plasticized or made of aluminum, stainless, or chrome. They must be easy to clean.

All refrigerators and freezing units must be equipped with thermometers mounted near the access openings. An alarm device should be attached to signal when required temperatures are exceeded.

EQUIPMENT

Every caterer should consult the professional help that is available from equipment and supply houses and/or from the local gas and electric companies. The kitchen is the heart of your facility and it must be planned and designed to secure maximum service from each installation. Your criteria must be guided by the tasks each unit is expected to perform. The placement of each unit is also crucial as you must consider step-saving and traffic flow. Another critical consideration is the element of proper ventilation.

Investigate equipment that requires minimum maintenance and effort to keep clean.* Out of all the basic styles of ranges used in commercial kitchens, it would be advisable to purchase only heavy-duty units. They are considered a wise long-term investment because they can withstand rough and continuous usage. They also withstand the strain of heavy cooking utensils and the added weight of their contents. Their energy quotient, whether gas or electric, is so much greater than standard ranges that processing quantity foods can be accomplished in less time and with less labor.

As a beginning caterer with limited funds, you may consider purchasing used equipment. *Do not*

---

*The reader is advised to consult *The Complete Book of Cooking Equipment,* 2nd ed., by Jule Wilkinson (Boston: CBI Publishing Co., Inc., 1981).

purchase used equipment just because it seems to be a bargain. If it does not fit your needs exactly, do not buy. If used equipment is available, make certain that: (1) it is a standard make; (2) replacement parts are available locally; and (3) all parts and areas function properly. Also consider the additional costs of delivery and setup, and whether you have any recourse in the event of dissatisfaction (new equipment normally includes delivery and setup), and then decide if you are really getting a bargain.

Whether your equipment is new or used, make certain that it meets standards set by the National Sanitation Foundation, American Gas Association, and Underwriters Laboratory.

Scales

The importance of having and *using* accurate scales cannot be overemphasized.

Every item purchased by weight *should be weighed upon receipt* and compared with the weight stated on the original invoice. Therefore, your receiving department must have either a platform scale or a spring scale with a large round dial for easy reading. (See Figure 2.2.)

A portion scale should also be an integral part of your kitchen equipment; and you should insist that it be used. This practice will assure portion control, and properly portioned foods create customer satisfaction because of their uniformity when served.

Food Storage

Dry. The dry-storage stockroom should be dry, well ventilated, out of direct sunlight, and maintained at a temperature of 55°F. to 65°F. Since too cold (freezing) or too warm temperatures can damage canned goods, a good wall thermometer should be placed in a prominent place, and checked regularly to prevent wide temperature fluctuations.

Dry-storage shelves ought to be at least eight (8) inches off the floor and made of metal. They should be arranged to: (1) provide "first-in, first-out" distribution; (2) allow maximum circulation

Figure 2.2. Left: portable beam scale has capacity up to 1,000 pounds. Right: receiving scale weighs up to 250 pounds, but can be of greater capacity.

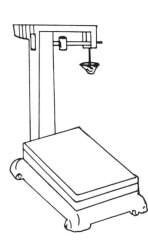
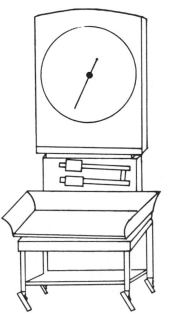

of air; and (3) avoid high stacking of such items as cereal, flour, and sugar.

Refrigerated. Perishable foods require storage at 38°F. to 40°F. in refrigerated cabinets. In selecting refrigeration units (refrigerators or frozen food cabinets), give prime consideration to the interior.

No matter what the type—reach-in, roll-in, or walk-in—each unit should be evaluated by how well it meets basic requirements for:

1. *Good air circulation.* Does the unit have multiple cold air outlets to cool quickly and uniformly under maximum loading? Does it have adequate space and can you easily reach most inside areas? These are important questions because improper or inadequate air circulation can cause freezing and/or food spoilage.
2. *Humidity.* Relative humidity, which is an important consideration, should be maintained at 80 to 85 percent to keep food from drying out.
3. *Temperature.* The refrigeration system components and how they are assembled affect efficiency and economy.
   a. The compressor or pump which circulates the refrigerant at a determined pressure is controlled by the temperature needs of the cabinet interior. There are two types of compressors—standard and high torque. To utilize optimum capacity and to meet sudden high-power demands, it is preferable to have high-torque compressors.

   The following popular "reach-in" refrigerators, for example, *should not* have compressors with a horsepower rating *less than* that stated:

Cabinet Size	Horsepower Rating
19.7 cu. ft.	1/4
36.5 cu. ft.	1/3
45.5 cu. ft.	1/3
71.8 cu. ft.	1/2
96.5 cu. ft.	3/4

   b. The condensor, which cools the refrigerant, should be located in an easily cleanable place, and one where it will be exposed to air. Ease of access will encourage regular cleaning which is necessary. Dust and dirt accumulations prevent proper air circulation; this can cause overloading of the compressor and lead to a breakdown.
   c. Fiberglass and polyurethane are both good insulating materials but today most manufacturers use polyurethane because it can result in a much stronger construction when properly done. The effect of proper insulation, however, can be diminished due to air leakage through seams and door gaskets.
   d. While most commercial units are equipped with thermometers, readings refer to the air within the cabinet and not the product. To get a more accurate reading of the unit's efficiency, insert thermometers into glasses of water or into vegetables or fruits placed in different areas of the cabinet.

   For further protection, install a battery-operated alarm system with visual or audible signaling devices for either or both high and/or low temperature warnings.

4. *Sanitation.* A cabinet that is difficult to clean is a potential health hazard.
   a. Reach-in cabinets should have few interior seams and *preferably* none. Interior construction must be coved all around.
   b. Shelves should be zinc-covered, anodized aluminum, stainless steel, or chromed, as well as adjustable and removable. They should have a minimum of corners, extrusions, and few crossings in shelves, shelf standards, clips, trays, or pan slides because they collect spillage which, if not adequately cleaned, can lead to bacteria growth and mold.
   c. Walk-ins should have tight and durable junctures to reduce the possibility of food spillage, and debris forming under and between panels.

5. *Adaptability.* Refrigeration equipment must be evaluated not only on its food preservation

function, but also for its contribution to other kitchen operations. For instance, tray slides are designed for 18- by 26-inch baking pans or 14- by 18-inch cafeteria trays. Thus, salads, desserts, and other pre-portioned foods can be prepared in advance, put in a pan or tray, and stored in the refrigerator. The items are more accessible, and the capacity of the unit is more fully utilized.

However, be sure the refrigerator door has safety grip handles rather than the latch type to eliminate the chance of clothing catching on the latches.

What is popularly called a freezer is really a *frozen food storage cabinet*. Its basic use is to store at 0°F. those foods that are already frozen. Although foods can freeze at 0°F., the use of these cabinets for freezing foods in quantity for future use results in unsatisfactory quality, and is potentially dangerous.

There are some combination units available that store refrigerated foods on one side and frozen foods on the other. But this type of unit is generally not practical for the catering kitchen. A frozen food storage cabinet should be a separate unit having easy-to-open doors.

Self-defrosting units are slightly more expensive to operate but because they operate without temperature fluctuations, they offer more product protection. Also, this unit does not need frequent shutdown for removal of ice build-up. Although exterior and interior features of frozen food cabinets are similar to refrigerators, their compressors are at least twice as large.

True (air blast) freezers are not essential unless you produce in large quantities for long-term storage, or operate a frozen food carryout business. When used properly and by following proper technical procedures, a blast freezer will produce professionally frozen products. However, compressors on blast freezers are ten times larger than those of refrigerators, and, consequently, are more costly to operate.

Cooking Equipment

There are six basic methods that are employed in commercial cooking, and a specific unit of equipment for each method. Some units incorporate two methods in a single design. Each method is self-contained, operates independently, and is totally effective for its intended purpose. For instance, a stove with open top grates, or with a French-type or solid plate surface, will have a fully functional and thermostatically controlled oven(s) underneath.

The six cooking methods are: (1) surface cooking; (2) top and bottom cooking ovens; (3) griddling—full solid surface cooking with heat controls for each quarter of the assembly; (4) immersion cooking—deep fat frying; (5) radiant cooking—broiling (broiling units can be free-standing or mounted over ovens); and (6) steam cooking (becoming more and more popular because of its versatility. Practically all models can be purchased with built-in steam generating units requiring no remote source of steam supply.)

The main cooking battery, in most instances, is the heart of the kitchen. It requires the largest equipment investment within this area, and reflects the largest operating expense due to the highly skilled labor required and the high cost of utilities. Be aware of your potential needs so that you do not make an excessive investment for large capacity, high operating cost units, or acquire inadequate, insufficient cooking facilities.

If you are outfitting a commissary devoted exclusively to off-premise food preparation, then you may only need a single broiler or a salamander (a small broiler mounted over an oven that saves valuable floor space). This unit would be used for top browning or marking. (It is poor culinary practice to parbroil steaks, chops, or poultry, and oven-finish them later off premises). For a banquet hall kitchen, it might be advisable to install a battery of broilers.

Deep fry kettles (immersion cooking) have limited use in most commissaries—a two-basket

Figure 2.3. An excellent battery of cooking equipment: hot top, open top, griddle, deep fat fryers, char broilers, and convection oven.

unit would be more than sufficient—but a banquet hall kitchen might require a battery of fryers.

Ranges. There are two basic styles of ranges used in commercial eating establishments, heavy duty and restaurant or cafe type.

The restaurant or cafe type is lighter in construction and not usually intended for batteries (each one is a complete unit by itself).

The author recommends heavy-duty ranges because, as mentioned earlier, they withstand severe usage, cook large amounts of foods, and can withstand the weights of heavy cooking utensils and their contents. They have greater gas inputs resulting in shorter food preparation times.

Heavy-duty ranges may have a solid hot top, a set of open top burners (grate top), or a solid griddle for frying. Beneath these tops there is usually an oven for roasting or baking. You can special order a skeleton range with shelves and storage cabinets in place of the oven.

Heavy-duty ranges usually have double-deck high shelves that also function as flueways to carry off the combustion products from the oven and top shelf burners. Heavy-duty ranges can be grouped together with *spreader plates* to provide additional working surface between ranges. Heavy-duty range sections are from 29 to 37 inches wide, and 24 to 42 inches deep. They are available in stainless steel, black and gray Japan finish, and porcelain enamel finish in black or a color.

Range Ovens. These ovens are below the cooking tops, and are used mainly for roasting. They are also available in separate units and can be constructed in pairs, one above the other, known as double-deck range-type ovens. The oven space ranges from 13 to 15 inches in height to permit roasting large cuts of meat. Oven volume varies from 5.4 to 6.3 cubic feet and can handle as much as 130 pounds at one time.

Deck-Type Ovens. Deck or peel ovens, constructed in sections, have special baking (7-inch) or roasting (12-inch) decks that can be combined in any desired arrangement. Decks may be supplied with hearth tile for special baking purposes. Each oven has an individual temperature control, and added value is obtained if each of the decks has removable shelves.

Convection Ovens or High Velocity Forced Air Circulation. This oven offers the most up-to-date design for baking and roasting for commercial purposes. The rapid circulation of air, due to a motor-driven fan unit, permits food to be cooked on multiple racks rather than on a hearth. The full oven space can be utilized and production greatly increased. This oven is equally efficient for both baking and roasting, and you should seriously consider the acquisition of such a unit.

Most caterers will find it to be the most frequently used unit.

Recent models have improved oven heat retention because of more effective insulating materials, including stainless steel doors. Additional features are the cook and hold controls (Market Forge model 2400 HE) that offer the convenience of advance starting of roasts and the potential economy of off periods. Meats are automatically held at serving temperature after the cooking time is completed. These ovens can be mounted on stands or in cabinet bases, and double stacked. Gas models are available with pilotless ignition.

Pizza Ovens. This type of oven is made especially for the production of pizzas. As pizza baking is done within minutes, this unit is built to generate up to 700°F. Much higher input burners are required to make up for the heat loss due to constant door openings for loading and unloading. This is really a single-purpose oven, and not likely to be needed by traditional caterers.

Revolving Tray or Reel Ovens. Large volume caterers will find this type of oven beneficial to their operations. The unit is really a large chamber with two revolving spiders (similar to a ferris wheel), mounted on a longitudinal axis, with flat trays suspended between them. Food is loaded on these trays as they appear opposite the door opening. Heat loss at this point is kept to a minimum by built-in diffusors that prevent the heat from escaping.

Salamanders and Heavy-Duty Broilers. The salamander is really a miniature broiler and is mounted above the cooking surface of the heavy-duty range. They can be mounted in pairs to provide additional broiling capacity. They have practically every feature of the heavy-duty broiler including ceramic radiants. They are particularly valuable in limited areas because they require no floor space.

In large volume banquet or on-premise catering establishments, a heavy-duty broiler can be a valuable production tool. In area, it occupies the same space as a heavy-duty oven. The burners are equipped with ceramic radiants to provide the intense uniform heat that is so essential for mass production. Infrared burners are available for very high production requirements. Some models have overhead ovens, heated by the burners in the broiling compartment, that are integral to the unit. They serve as warming compartments, precook chambers, and finishing ovens and greatly increase the broiler's capabilities.

Steam Cooking. The tremendous design advancements in steam-cooking equipment make it advisable to consider this equipment in your kitchen design. Quantity cooking can be achieved in less time and with better results. Valuable vitamins and minerals, so often lost in other methods of cooking, are retained as is the color. It is almost impossible to burn or scorch foods.

Steam cooking saves time and the cost of lost products, and eliminates the messy job of cleanup.

Every piece of steam-cooking equipment is now available with self-contained, steam-generating facilities that require minimal connecting expense. One of the most popular units is a tilting skillet that comes in 23- and 40-gallon sizes. There is also a 10-gallon and lesser capacity, hand-tilted skillet for minimal requirements. These versatile skillets increase kitchen productivity by boiling, steaming, braising, sauteeing,

Figure 2.4. Electric convection oven. Note the number of shelves for multi-pan capacity.

Figure 2.5. Self-contained table top steam cooker.

simmering, grilling, stewing, and pan-frying—all in a single unit.

There are compartment steam cookers that cook foods in standard cafeteria pans, eliminating the need for transfer and cleanup. Different foods, such as, poultry, seafoods, eggs, rice, pasta, and vegetables, can be cooked in separate pans simultaneously. These units outperform full sections of range tops in cooking capacity and energy savings.

Chinese Cook Stoves. For particular styles of cooking in the kitchen and bakery (for example, candy stoves), there are stoves that meet the desires of any chef who wishes to cook exotic foods in a native manner. Chinese cook stoves, most effective for preparing ethnic foods, develop abnormally high temperatures and incorporate the use of woks as the vessel in which the food is prepared. (Woks are bowl-shaped utensils, usually of black steel.) These stoves are heated from underneath by a high intensity gas flame and have heat-retentive ceramic walls, resulting in rapid food preparation. This is the most satisfactory method of preparing stir-fried foods of every nature.

Microwave Ovens. Although their uses are limited, some caterers may consider the purchase of a microwave oven crucial. They are convenient and effective for heating small amounts of hors d'oeuvre, thawing limited portions of frozen food, baking a dozen potatoes, or heating, at maximum, the contents of two 9-inch dinner plates.

They can be of value at house parties where the contents of ceramic casseroles have to be heated. But as they do not top brown, the desired aesthetic appearance may not be achieved.

Since the unit weighs approximately 150 pounds and uses household current, some off-premise caterers take one along on their jobs. On-premise caterers might find a microwave beneficial in emergencies, for example, quickly heating a few portions that may be short at a banquet.

When purchasing a microwave, make certain that it is fully approved and carries a minimum two-year guarantee against "burn out."

Kitchen Ventilation

A good kitchen ventilating system must be engineered for full efficacy. Some local fire and health authorities require hood and duct design before granting a permit.

No two conditions are alike. Many factors must be considered. Air intake or replacement source, and its effect on the surrounding area, and the most effective method of exhausting heat and grease-laden vapors must be planned. Exhaust ducts from kitchen hoods must be independent of any other ventilating system. This sometimes requires expensive and complicated duct work, frequently (according to need) extending outside a building and above the roof.

Exhaust hoods are intended to capture as much of the odors and heat as possible and to contain them until the integral fan takes over and exhausts them. The fan may be a propellor, mush-

Figure 2.6. Wall-mounted hood showing basic components (automatic fire-fighting equipment not shown).

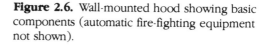
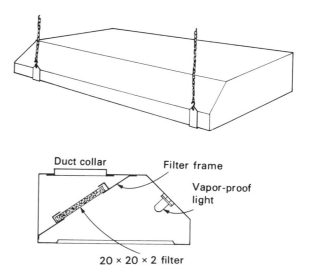

Duct collar

Filter frame

Vapor-proof light

20 × 20 × 2 filter

room, or centrifugal type. The National Fire Protection Association requires that all hoods be equipped with grease filters. Grease filters must fit tightly, against each other and against the holding frame, to prevent the exhaust air from bypassing the filter and depositing grease on the hood. Grease filters should be readily accessible to permit regular cleaning and replacement.

Improper venting of water heaters in kitchen areas, or ineffective venting in the dishwashing area, can adversely affect the proper functioning of a kitchen ventilating system.

Island-type cooking battery installations are particularly susceptible to cross-drafts and require special attention. Aprons may have to be attached to deflect the draft. If an adjoining dining room is airconditioned, improper kitchen venting can cause an overload of the system and waste valuable energy.

The National Fire Protection Association (Standard #96), and local authorities having jurisdiction, require that all hoods be equipped with a fire-extinguishing system of inert gas, dry chemical, or fine water spray. An auxiliary hand-held extinguisher must be accessible nearby.

In addition to standard motor controls for the fans, sensors must be installed that will automatically shut down the fan in the event of overheating or burnup.

All electrical installations must be in accordance with the National Electrical Code (NFPA #70). It may be possible to conserve energy by rerouting the kitchen heat to heat water or limited areas.

Some standard references are:

Design of Kitchen Ventilation Systems, U.S. Public Health Service, Atlanta, Georgia.

Guide for Kitchen Ventilation Systems, Virginia Department of Health, Richmond, Virginia.

National Fire Protection Association (Standard #96—Ventilation of Restaurant Cooking Equipment), Boston, Massachusetts.

Sinks

A sink must be provided for the chef to rinse out utensils and perform the various washing and water-obtaining operations necessary to his work. A separate sink is required for pot washing, and another sink of two or three compartments is needed for general kitchen use in food preparation. A separate handwashing sink is now mandatory in many localities. Sinks are subject to abuse and, consequently, should be constructed of 14 to 16 gauge stainless. Corners and edges should be rounded and seams should be eliminated where possible to prevent harborage of harmful residue. Unless there are unusual space configurations or protrusions, you may be able to purchase fully fabricated units with a 10-inch splash and sized drainboards.

Perforated swill guards with removable standard overflow should be considered an essential adjunct to a sink purchase. Heavy duty faucets are a wise investment to replace the commercial type normally furnished with an installation.

Small volume operators who cannot afford a mechanical dishwasher are advised that gas and electric heaters can be installed *under* a sink unit to convert it into an operational dishwasher. Baskets for dish immersion are available, as are hang-on thermometers that indicate when the desired temperatures have been reached.

Refrigeration

A refrigerator must be considered and chosen as a part of the overall food-handling system. It is one of the most important pieces of equipment in the commissary or banquet kitchen. Refrigerators are available to suit any specialty phase of the industry and to fit any space. There are reach-in, reach-through, undercounter, walk-in, and various other models.

Their function, of course, is to aid in the preparation of food by retarding the growth of molds and bacteria. Internal changes that make food less nutritious, unpalatable, and unsafe are likewise retarded by proper refrigeration.

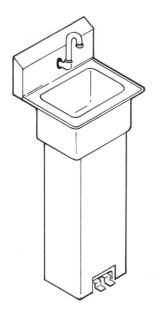

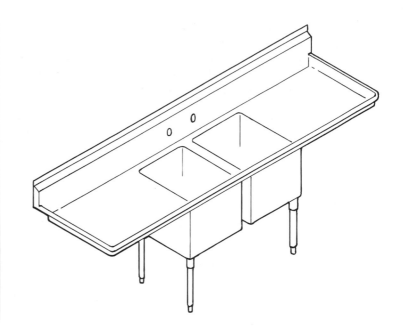

Figure 2.7. Foot-activated hand sink. Manually operated faucets are acceptable and satisfactory.

Figure 2.8. Two-section sink with equal right and lefthand drainboards. Note rounded corners for easy cleaning.

The best refrigerators lose their efficiency when food is packed too closely, preventing the proper circulation of *inside* cooling air.

Outside air circulation is equally important to allow the compressor to function properly and effectively. The placement of the refrigerator should take into account convenience as well as the accessibility of good outside air, which is often the difference between adequate and good refrigeration.

Coolers. Walk-in coolers can be made to any size, in single or multisection units, using modular panels. They can be made for outdoor stationing entirely, or for partial outdoor stationing with the entrance indoors. There are exterior and interior ramps that allow easy access for wheeled food carriers and sealed glass windows for interior observation.

Light switches and thermometers are usually built into the door frames. Reach-in service doors that provide access to smaller shelves are available and should be considered as they will prevent the considerable cold air loss that occurs each time the large entrance door is opened.

The standard inside height is 7 feet 6 inches, with optional heights to 8 feet 6 inches, and 10 feet 6 inches. Depths are standard at 5 feet 10 inches (normally 6 feet), and in 11½-inch increments. The most effective insulation is 4 inches of high density polyurethane, foamed-in-place insulation. The entire door opening should be protected by anticondensate heaters (to prevent condensation and frost formation) for easy opening.

Walk-in Freezers. Walk-in freezers have practically the same specifications as refrigerators. However, they are equipped with heavier com-

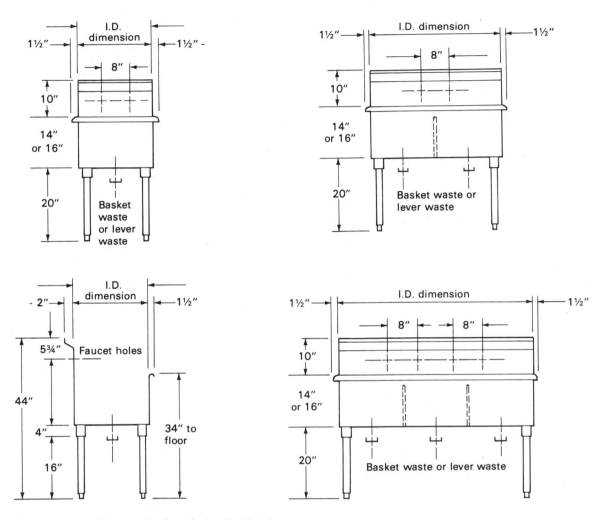

Figure 2.9. Pre-fabricated sink with detailed height dimensions. Individual sink widths may vary.

pressors and condensors, and air curtains to minimize cold air escape.

Refrigerators. Reach-in or reach-through re-frigerators are available in one, two, or three sections. Most have self-contained compressors and range from ¼ to ½ horsepower. Comparable sizes in frozen food units have condensing units of ½, ¾, and 1 horsepower.

Approximate capacities are: single door—21.7 cubic feet; two door—47.8 cubic feet; and three door—72.9 cubic feet. (Specific models may vary slightly.) Cabinet exteriors are stainless, aluminum, or bonded vinyl colors on steel.

Cabinet interiors of the better models are seamless (for easier cleaning) and are aluminum, stainless, or silver white vinyl on steel. None of these units require special wiring as they operate on 115 volts, 60 cycle single phase. No plumbing connections are required.

Blast Freezers. What we commonly refer to as a freezer is really a *frozen food storage cabinet.* Its basic use is to store (at 0°F.) those foods that are already frozen, and the common practice is to use this unit to freeze foods for future use. This can be a potentially dangerous practice as the time required to reduce the product to a safe temperature and frozen state allows for some deterioration.

If you contemplate preparing and freezing house specialties or takeout foods, you should investigate the advantages of a blast freezer. Used properly and in conjunction with the proper technical procedures of recipe formulation and food preparation, you can produce a professionally frozen product.

Preparation Equipment

Food Cutter or Buffalo Chopper. This is one of the most versatile machines in any kitchen. It chops onions, potatoes, celery, and other vegetables, from coarse to extra fine, depending on the time of operation (in seconds).

It is excellent for chopping chicken, shrimp, tuna, eggs, liver, and other salad bases. It will make bread crumbs using either fresh or stale bread. It can produce properly sized potatoes and corned beef for hash.

A meat grinder head can be attached that will save the purchase of a separate motor. A vegetable slicer (for coleslaw, etc.) can also be attached for high speed dicing of fruits and vegetables, and cutting French fries. Because of its versatility and long, trouble-free life, it is one of the scarcest pieces of equipment to acquire secondhand.

Mixers. This is an essential machine for every food preparation establishment. There are bench models available in 5- to 20-quart capacities; floor models are available that process anywhere from

Figure 2.10. Walk-in freezer with self-contained compressor. Also available with remote compressors. Compressors may be weather shielded for outside placement.

20 quarts to as much as 140 quarts. A floor model, 20-quart mixer (adapters are available to take a 12-quart bowl) can handle the mixing needs of a fairly large volume establishment. Paddle attachments of every type, and for any purpose, are available. They are the: (1) flat beater; (2) wing whip; (3) wire whip (standard heavy duty); (4) dough hook; (5) pastry knife; and (6) sweet dough arm.

Vegetable Peeler. This machine is used mainly for potatoes. However, because of the availability of convenience packed potatoes in every desired

Figure 2.11. Counter top and floor-placed mixing machines. Note dolly for easy moving of large bowl and contents.

Figure 2.12. Left: food chopper, commonly called Buffalo chopper, with facility for attaching a meat grinder, vegetable slicer, etc. Right: gravity-feed electric slicing machine in use.

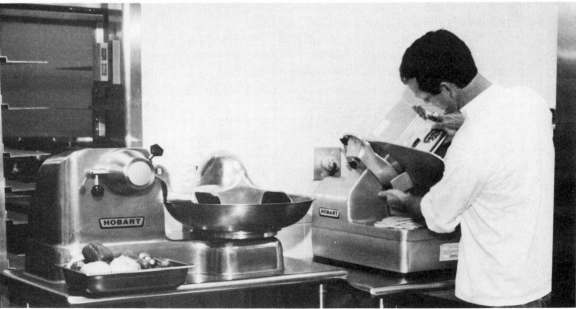

form, and the difficulty of obtaining help for this chore, this machine is not considered essential.

Slicer. A slicer is essential for every kitchen. The most satisfactory type is the manual, gravity angle-feed with a 12-by-12-inch carriage and an 11¾-inch knife that will slice large roasts, etcetera. The knife should be of solid stainless steel. A top-mounted sharpener is available on most models. An automatic stacking model is not recommended except for a high volume operation.

Kitchen Work Tables

Kitchen work tables come in standard 30-inch widths and 34-inch heights. Overall lengths range from 4 to 10 feet. The tops should always be of polished stainless steel (14 to 16 gauge), with turned or rolled down edges and welded and polished corners.

The tops, as well as the undershelf, should be reinforced and sound deadened. The undershelf can be eliminated to allow clearance between the legs for storage bins, either fixed or mobile. If undershelves are provided, they are usually of galvanized steel. This finish will eventually wear away and corrosion will necessitate their being refinished or covered with another material, which can cause a sanitation problem. Lighter gauge stainless undershelving can be ordered and, in the long run, its extra cost will be vindicated.

The legs of steel tubing, with adjustable feet, generally have a gray hammertone finish that will never present a cleaning problem. Legs of polished stainless are standard in special model tables. Casters are available, as are drawers and a back splash. A common complaint about the drawers is that they eventually become a catch-all.

Stainless steel chef's tables are available with built-in, deep-drawn sinks (can be ordered with sinks on either the right or left sides).

Maple tables are outlawed in many parts of the country because it is practically impossible to comply with maximum sanitation require-ments. Besides steel, there are plastic composition table tops that are very satisfactory.

Dishwashers

There are many factors that should determine the purchase of a specific type of dishwasher. Unlike other equipment that becomes operational when plugged in, a dishwasher requires a connection to an energy source (electric and/or gas). It also requires an attachment for water inlet from a water heating unit, and quite frequently from a self-contained or auxiliary booster unit. A direct connection to a waste or sewer outlet is also necessary.

A good installation requires a prewash unit and waste disposer. Soiled dish tables and clean dish tables have to be fabricated individually for each installation. They must often be designed to fit around columns and other obstructions.

A dishwashing system is actually engineered for each facility, depending on the space available, the volume of business, the layout, the traffic flow, the amount and type of food soil and the length of time it will remain on the dishes (from completion of dining time to conveyance to washing area), and the relative hardness of the water.

The amount of required floor space is determined by the combination of various lengths at the loading and unloading ends. Dishwashers may have straight-line feeding or angle-feeding or return. All are equipped with automatic controls for wash, dwell, and rinse. Some models have to be fed manually, opening the door to insert the racks. Closing the door automatically starts the cycle for rinsing, washing, and sanitizing. At the completion of the cycle, all power is terminated and the door has to be opened once again for removal and reloading.

There are larger, fully automatic models in which the racks are engaged at the entrance by arms that convey them through a flexible strip curtain, through the entire wash cycle, and then discharge them at the opposite end.

Plastic dishware is not processed satisfactorily in conventional machines. High temperature, high velocity, blower-dryer units must be installed to dry such dishware quickly.

The heat generated by dishwashers can present a problem. But expensive exhaust ducting can often be avoided by installing a condensor over the dishwasher. This unit exhausts the dishwasher vapor, condenses it, and releases the air back into the dishroom.

Flight-Type Machines. This unit is similar to the rack conveyer machine but *rack filling is completely eliminated.* Instead, dishes are placed on an endless belt constructed of rubber, plastic, or composition "fingers" that hold dishes in place as they pass through the prerinse, rinse, and wash cycles. Upon completion, dishes are removed and placed directly on dish trucks or storage shelves, which is very economical and effective for large operations.

Structurally, there are so many options available that you can virtually design your own dishwasher. (See Figure 2.13.)

Water Heaters. An adequate hot water supply is absolutely essential for proper dishwashing. While hot water may be available from the primary system, it must be boosted in temperature to the minimum 180°F. required for sanitizing.

If feasible, a booster heater should be installed under the dishwasher or placed not more than five (5) feet away. This unit, which can be either the instantaneous or automatic storage type, guarantees that the proper water temperature will always be available on demand.

Racks and Tables. Dish racks normally are not supplied with dishwashing machines. Needs vary since different sized dishes, cups, glasses, and supremes may be used in each operation. For example, if you want the racks to be stored with the dishes, cups, or glasses in them, different structural designs may be required.

Dish tables for the entrance or exit areas of the machine must also be purchased separately. They should be large enough to allow for proper rack loading and for clean stacking and packing.

The tables should be made of heavy gauge stainless steel or fiberglass. Make certain *they are tightly fitted into the machine at entrance and exit areas.* Improper fit will result in dangerous, wet, and slippery floors.

Slanted overhead shelves for holding cups, glass racks, and other odds and ends should be on either side of the dish tables. A small drain should also be at one end or the other of the shelves.

If space permits, provide two soaking sinks— one for silver, the other for dishes. These are particularly useful to the off-premise caterer, since many affairs offer no dishwashing facilities, and food will dry on the dishes. If space does not permit fixed sinks, two (2) large, heavy-duty plastic tubs will be adequate.

Waste Disposers. A garbage disposer is usually part of the dishwashing layout because it can be a valuable time and labor saver.

Depending on the complexity of the dishwashing system, the disposer can be inserted under the prerinse sink, or in a special trough with running water.

Before investing in a disposer, consider the following:

Is the disposer's design rugged enough to take all scraps?

Does a local code prohibit the use of disposers because of sewerage problems?

Is the electrical supply adequate or will fuses blow as soon as both it and the dishwasher are turned on?

Does it have a reversing switch? This is very handy when the disposer gets jammed or clogged.

Since it will be used with and around water, are electrical controls properly safeguarded so that no danger exists for the operator?

FLIGHT TYPE—ENDLESS BELTS
6600 to 9000 dishes per hour
STANDARD WIDTHS—25 in.; EXTRA WIDE—30 in.

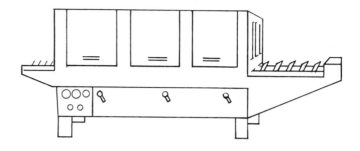

RACK CONVEYOR TYPES

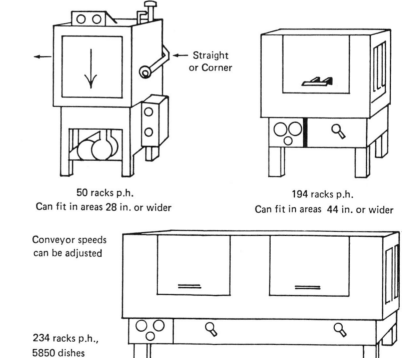

← Straight
or Corner

50 racks p.h.
Can fit in areas 28 in. or wider

194 racks p.h.
Can fit in areas 44 in. or wider

Conveyor speeds
can be adjusted

234 racks p.h.,
5850 dishes

Figure 2.13. Dishmachines can all be built to individual specifications, making combinations endless.

Finally, who is responsible for service and warranty on the unit?

A disposer can also be useful in the preparation area. However, when considering need, determine the type of food products used, that is, fresh or processed. If the former are used, then obviously there will be a lot of peelings and other waste, which can be conveniently thrown into the disposer.

Dish/Utensil Storage. Whatever means are used to store dishes and utensils, do not overlook the cleaning and sanitizing performed in the washing operation. Generally, the most desirable system is one that requires the least amount of handling between the time utensils are washed and their next use, and provides maximum protection for cleanliness. For this reason, storage of *uncovered* utensils in a cupboard is not recommended.

If possible, portable carts should be used in the dishwashing area so that sanitized and dried items can be stored quickly. The items can be protected by a sanitary cover until needed, at which time the cart can be wheeled to the proper place and uncovered.

Portable carts are available in various sizes/types to meet any requirement. However, selection should also be based on ease of maintaining sanitation for both the utensils and the cart; durability of material used; size in relation to portability; and type of casters and whether they have locking devices.

Cleaning Equipment

A heavy-duty, tank-type vacuum cleaner with a 10- to 12-foot flexible hose is an invaluable tool. It can be used for hard-to-reach areas behind ranges and other pieces of equipment.

The vacuum cleaner should be used frequently to keep refrigerator coils from plugging up with dust, which can reduce the unit's efficiency. It is also effective for the superficial cleaning of filters.

There are tank-type, liquid absorption vacuum machines that do an excellent job in cleaning quarry and asphalt tile, concrete, and similar surfaces.

Small Tools/Utensils

The exact type of small tools, pots, and pans that you will require is impossible to forecast. But as business develops, your needs will become evident.

However, all kitchen utensils should be regular *institution ware* of either standard or heavy-duty gauge construction. While the initial cost is high, this ware is more durable than lighter weight

housewares. Porcelain or enamelled ware should be avoided as it chips and stains easily.

Today, many utensils having nonstick coating are on the market. They resist abrasion of metal spatulas and spoons and, so, are virtually scratch-proof and easier to clean. However, for certain types of cooking, especially those requiring the "crusts" of cooked particles to make a tasty sauce or gravy, this type of cookware is ineffective.

One of the most versatile and valuable utensils is the "squarehead," a heavy-duty aluminum roaster, approximately 18 by 20 by 7 inches. You should purchase the roaster with heavy-duty flat covers that can also be used as heavy-duty grills. Besides holding substantial quantities of foods (approx. 42 quarts) to be heated on the range or in the oven, squareheads stack beautifully in refrigerators and trucks.

Vacuum pots, airtight transfer containers—call them what you will—are 3- to 10-gallon capacity containers useful for storing and transporting foods. By virtue of their construction, they effectively retain heat or cold for 24 hours or more.

Attractive in appearance, they can often be used on the buffet table as coffee, tea, and/or punch dispensers, or for transporting and dispensing ice cubes. Moreover, when kept clean and shined, these metal units are more pleasing to the eye than those made from synthetic materials.

CHECK LIST FOR SMALL TOOLS/UTENSILS (Not Including Knives)

BRAZIERS—5 to 24 qt.

CAN OPENERS—heavy-duty manual or heavy-duty electric (with additional gears and cutters for replacement)

CAST IRON SKILLET—to 14 in.

CHINA CAPS—fine or coarse

CLEAN-UP EQUIPMENT—brooms, brushes, mops, squeegies, buckets, pails

COLANDERS—1 to 16 qt.

COMMERCIAL DUTY BLENDERS—for pureeing, vegetables, etc.

DISH OR SALAD PANS—14 to 40 qt.

DOUBLE BOILERS—(can be improvised by using available pots, etc.)

DREDGES—for sprinkling sugar, cinnamon, etc.

FOOD STORAGE CONTAINERS—round and square, from 1 qt. up, made of metal or plastic

FOODMILL—grinder/foodmill

FRY PANS—6 to 14 in.; treated with non-stick coating, from 8 to 14 in.

FUNNELS—⅜-in. to 1½-in. opening or higher

GARBAGE CONTAINERS

HEAVY DUTY FOIL

HOT FOOD SERVICE PANS—approximate size: 12 by 18 by 2½ in.

ICE CREAM SCOOPS—assorted sizes and shapes

MALLET—of solid aluminum, used to break down fibers or flatten meat

MEASURES—1 cup to 4 qt., aluminum, stainless steel, or plastic but *not glass*

MEAT SAW/CLEAVER—for flattening purposes; *do not chop bones with cleaver*

MIXING BOWLS—1½ to 12 qt.

PIANO WIRE WHIPS—assorted sizes

PORTION SCALES—1 to 16 oz. capacity, to achieve uniform individual portions

RECEIVING SCALE—absolutely a must and *to be used constantly*

ROAST AND BAKE PANS—(Squareheads) with a heavy-duty cover that can also be used as a grill; approximate size: 18 by 21 by 7 in. high

ROASTING PANS—standard weight and heavy-duty from approx. 12 by 20 in. to 17 by 26 in. (Check your ovens for largest size they will hold.) Purchase some half-size roasters also.

RUBBER COMPOSITION CUTTING BOARDS —to be used whenever necessary

PLASTIC SELF-SEALING WRAP

SAUCE PANS—1½ to 10 qt.

SAUCEPOTS—4 to 24 qt. (Larger sizes are available but they are too awkward and difficult to handle.)

SCOOPS—for bulk flour, sugar, rice, etc.

SHARPENING STONES—to keep knives constantly sharp

SHEET PANS—approx. size: 18 by 26 in. (Mobile racks to store these will be helpful.)

SKIMMER—6½ in.

SOUP LADLES—2 to 10 oz.

SPOONS—wood; solid, slotted, and perforated

STOCKPOTS—with or without faucets and from 24 to 40 qt.

STRAINERS—to 5 qt.

THERMOMETER—one for roast beef; another for candy, jelly, or frostings

TONGS—7 to 10 in.

UTILITY PANS—2 to 10 qt.

WAXED PAPER

Commissary Kitchen Equipment

A commissary kitchen requires more tables so that pans and pots and trays can be packed with the required amount of food needed for a particular affair. If the commissary is preparing for more than one party, then separate tables, holding racks, and cabinets may be needed for each affair. There must be room for in-kitchen storage of these racks and cabinets. Aisles and areas must be wide enough to allow for unobstructed and free movement of these conveyances either to the refrigerator, the freezer, or the truck.

Volume productions require walk-in refrigerators and freezers with ramps. Then cabinets, tray racks, and dollies can be rolled in, saving double handling. This also reduces the possibility of mix-up and damage to pre-portioned items.

The scheduling of food production differs from on-premise catering, where food is served directly to the diner as soon as it is finished in the kitchen. Off-premise caterers sometimes have to

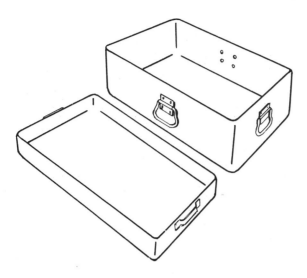

Figure 2.14. Roast and bake pans: (left) "square head" and cover, (right) roasting pan with lock-in cover. Eliminates transferring and is excellent for storage and transport.

finish off on the job. To avoid transferring foods from the original roasting or baking pans to other pans for shipping, it is recommended that you purchase roasters and bakers *with covers* as illustrated. They are not only timesavers, but their solid surface tops permit stacking for storage or transport.

There are also tote boxes with covers that can be commissary-packed and stacked safely and securely.

There are holding units that are so technologically perfect that they maintain uniformly controlled temperatures and prolonged quality control during transport. If there is a disconnect of several hours, these carriers are capable of reconstituting the food to the original kitchen-fresh goodness. Such features eliminate value judgments on the part of employees by keeping the food at the degree at which it was programmed.

Cold food cabinets, which incorporate all the features of the hot cabinets, but with opposing temperature extremes, are a wise investment. They could eliminate the need to purchase or rent a refrigerated truck. Board of Health inspectors will approve efficient self-contained refrigerated units.

There are so many sizes and models available, you should consult your equipment dealer. Factory representatives trained to solve problems of food transport are available to talk with you.

Platform Trucks, Dollies, and Racks

Equipment such as platform trucks and rack dollies will save time, ease work loads, and take the strain out of handling heavy stock, supplies, and equipment. As morale aids they demonstrate a concern for employees involved in the expedition of work functions. They are also an element in your favor should an injury claim arise because of heavy lifting or moving—you have provided the means to prevent such injury!

An investment in rack dollies for stacking and conveying cups and glasses results in greater productivity because a dolly can hold many more units than a person can carry. Dollies can be moved with ease for distances with minimum exertion and fatigue. (Note: Cups should always be packed in cup racks and should never be nested. Nesting results in a high incidence of breakage and roughening of cup rims, which can result in mouth injury and transmit germs more readily.)

Dollies are also available to carry large stock pots, maintain heavy pails used in cleaning, and move large, filled garbage cans.

Open Tray Trucks. These trucks are versatile and can save steps and time in any system. They can hold tray-prepared foods or raw foods processed in one area, be moved into a walk-in, or be moved to another area for finishing or serving. They can also be used as portable shelving.

Enclosed Tray Trucks. Most tray trucks take up no more than 24 by 34 inches of floor space, with a height not exceeding 72 inches, and carry up to twenty trays. They are invaluable in pre-traying all types of food. For buffet presentations, they allow the showpieces to be completed in the kitchen or commissary and taken to the area of service, either on or off premises.

Portioned foods, hors d'oeuvre, pastries, and tall layer cakes can be transported great distances in these with minimal damage to finished surfaces. They reduce packing time by eliminating the search for special containers. Good housekeeping is maintained because the food is under cover and in one place.

Insulated trucks will keep foods at the required safe cold temperature for hours if a unit such as a Koldkeeper (Cres-cor product) is placed in the truck.

Tray trucks are constructed of stainless, and easy to keep clean; colored vinyl can be bonded to match any desired decorative scheme.

Dish Dollies. Considerable time and labor can be saved by removing dishes from the dishwasher and storing them directly on dish dollies. This eliminates double handling in shelving, and removing and transporting to the point of service.

Dollies can hold as many as 240 11-inch dinner plates. They are only 32 inches high, and the outside dimensions rarely exceed 24 by 40 inches. Some models have self-contained ele-

ments that keep dishes hot until service time—a valuable feature for operators concerned with proper and meticulous service.

Fully enclosed models prevent dust and dirt penetration and are excellent for off-premise catering. Open models are more practical for on-premise catering. (Factory furnished dust covers are available.)

High or Low Roll-in Racks. Open sided, roll-in racks are a great convenience in any kitchen or bake shop. Full size roasting and baking pans can be placed in them directly from the ovens to cool off. Adjustable shelves allow for vertical packing and stacking. They can be rolled into walk-in refrigerators or freezers and will fit into sectional roll-in or roll-through refrigerators and freezers manufactured by the following companies: Foster, Glenco, Hobart, Puffer Hubbard, Schmidt, Traulsen, and Victory.

Bake Shop

Different types of baking facilities can be set up in foodservice establishments. As most establishments do not produce their own bread and/or rolls, limited equipment is needed for pastry production.

The tremendous achievements by large commercial specialty bakeries in producing fine quality baked goods, and the advancement in freezing techniques, have almost eliminated the need for bakers in some establishments.

The following limited facility equipment is necessary if you decide to incorporate a baking department in your kitchen:

bake oven
proof box
fryer
mixer
scale
pastry stove

tilting kettle (could be table mounted)
portable bins for storage
work tables, polyurethane or marble top
work tables, stainless
spice bins
sinks and drainboards

racks for proofing and cooling
landing table
storage facilities for flour, sugar, and sifting equipment, refrigerator and freezer storage, and dough retarding refrigerators.

CHAPTER THREE

SANITATION

It is both your moral and legal obligation to set up and maintain high standards of sanitation for your place of business.

If you are an off-premise caterer, you must be even more acutely aware of these responsibilities because you work in many different locations. Not only must your commissary and kitchen conform to rigid standards set by the U. S. Public Health Service Code, National Sanitation Foundation, local Boards of Health, and other regulatory bodies, but your transporting facilities (packaging, equipment, vehicles) and food-serving areas must also meet these stringent standards.

As an off-premise caterer, you are constantly exposed to a great many potentially unsatisfactory conditions. For example, if serving an affair in an infrequently used facility, you must have the area thoroughly and meticulously cleaned before bringing in equipment and/or food. Also, you must carefully and vigorously check the location for insect or rodent infestation.

Moreover, as a *professional,* you must have the courage to refuse to serve any affair that will be held in an area where there is a possible health hazard, or from which there is a danger of carrying insect/rodent contamination back to your own premises.

PERSONNEL

Personal and personnel cleanliness cannot be overemphasized. Most municipalities require that food workers be examined by health authorities, and carry a health card certifying that that individual is "licensed" as a food handler. It is for your protection, and in your best interest, that you enforce this regulation.

Also, remember that the individual in charge of the dishwashing operation and responsible for proper sterilization, is one of the most important people in your entire organization. Thus, it is a prime responsibility to engage a person *who knows and accepts this responsibility and is conscientious in fulfilling it.*

Since improperly and inadequately washed dishes, glassware, and silverware can be a source of infection with often serious consequences, this person's value to your organization must never be minimized. Furthermore, his/her responsibility should entail not only sanitation of eating ware, but also machine maintenance, and proper storage of all equipment once it has been properly sanitized.

The selection of a responsible individual to head such a department is a wise and excellent investment. But to guarantee yourself a dependable, conscientious, and competent employee, be sure to offer this person a salary commensurate with the responsibility.

CLEANING

Definite cleaning schedules must be established for: floors, counters, cabinets, sinks, stoves, ovens, broilers, steam jackets, refrigerators, freezers, walls, and windows.

Containers used for transporting food must be easily cleanable metal or plastic, so they can be cleaned and *sterilized* after each service. They should also have tight fitting covers. If such covers are not available, heavy aluminum foil is an effective substitute. Original plastic bags *should never be reused* for carrying or covering foodstuffs.

Boil or steam out all gas burners at least once each week. Drip pans should be lined with heavy foil to catch overflows and to make cleaning easier.

Steam cleaning is fast and much more effective than other conventional methods. But if permanent steam lines are not available, investigate the possibility of buying one of the small, "fixed," portable steam generators currently on the market.

PROPER SANITATION IS BENEFICIAL

Since careless operations and lack of cleanliness can lead to damage claims against your business, you should place as much emphasis on sanitation standards as you do on food quality and cost control. Moreover, proper sanitation: (1) saves money; (2) saves time; (3) aids safety; (4) improves food quality and service; and (5) projects a favorable public image for both management and personnel.

A Money Saver
Properly maintained and used utensils and equipment last longer.

Foods stored, refrigerated, prepared, and served according to sanitary rules prevent waste, enhance quality, improve appearance, and increase customer acceptability.

The danger of food poisoning, with its consequent cost to management, is minimized.

A Time Saver
The sanitary way is the *right* way and experience has shown that the right way is both the best and the quickest way.

Consistent practice in proper sanitary methods has proved this.

An Aid to Safety
Regular mopping times and proper methods reduce the possibility of falls caused by wet, slippery floors.

Similarly, when floors are kept clean, employees avoid the risk of slipping on spilled food.

Correct methods of handling sharp knives, dishes, glassware, and silverware reduce the danger of cuts and subsequent infection.

Strict adherence to sanitary procedures also prevents transmission of illnesses commonly associated with foodservice.

A Way to Improve Food Quality and Service
In addition to preventing the service of contaminated food, safe food and clean equipment and utensils ensure truly appetizing food flavors.

Sanitary service is *correct* service. Make sure your employees realize this, as it will help them develop the confidence, poise, and pride inherent in quality service.

And remember, high quality food and service are the bases for building a successful catering business.

A Way of Projecting a Favorable Public Image
A clean, sanitary establishment always creates a favorable atmosphere. Your customers are certain

to notice appearance and the use of correct serving methods by trained foodservice workers.

The goal of a good sanitation program is to prevent food-borne illnesses, food poisonings, and food infections.

The following edited list of food protection suggestions, taken from *Sanitation for Foodservice Workers*,* will be helpful in eliminating food contamination and spoilage.

1. All food purchases should be made from sources approved by local, state, and/or federal health authorities and protected from contamination/spoilage during handling, packaging, storage, and while in transit.
2. Shellfish, meat and meat products, poultry and poultry meat products should be purchased from properly inspected sources and so stamped or tagged.
3. Use and serve pasteurized fluid milk and fluid milk products only. Dry milk products may be reconstituted if used solely in and for cooking purposes. Serve milk and fluid milk products for drinking purposes in the individual containers in which they were packaged at the milk processing plant.

   Serve cream, whipped cream, or half-and-half either in original containers or from an approved dispenser.

PREVENTING CONTAMINATION OF FOOD

1. Wash and scrub all vegetables carefully, but especially those to be used in salads or eaten raw because they may contain residuals from chemical sprays.
2. Examine canned food for bulges, dents, leakage, and other distortions prior to use. Open cans having either an odd odor or an unusual appearance should be inspected immediately by you or some other responsible person.

*Treva M. Richardson and Wade R. Nicodemus, *Sanitation for Foodservice Workers*, 3rd edition (Boston: CBI Publishing Co., Inc. 1981).

3. Custard- or cream-filled pastries must be refrigerated *immediately* or, if time is short, quick-chilled in a freezer before serving. But, whenever practicable, test with a thermometer to make certain center is cooled. (Note: custard items cannot be rebaked.)
4. Refrigerate sandwiches containing potentially hazardous food, such as, egg, ham, poultry salads, and similar fillings.
5. Cook pork until well done (150°F. or above in center of mass). Test with meat thermometer.
6. Thoroughly cook all foods, stirring and mixing frequently to assure that heat is uniform throughout.
7. After preparation, do not allow food to remain at room temperature for any length of time before serving. Temporary holding periods are at 45°F. or below, or 140°F. or above.
8. Test the temperature of food on steam tables to be certain it is not below 140°F.
9. Heat leftovers thoroughly; do not merely warm. Keep leftovers for one day only and *never* mix them with fresh food to "extend" supply. Remember that ground, minced foods are especially subject to contamination because much of the food is exposed during the grinding process.
10. Correct washing and sanitizing of dishes, eating utensils, and all equipment or surfaces that come in contact with food are absolutely essential for proper protection.
11. Use small, shallow pans to refrigerate food rather than one large, deep container. For storage purposes, pans three or four inches in depth are suggested.
12. Chemicals, sanitizers, and other cleaning materials should not be kept in food preparation areas. All cleaning materials and tools should be stored in a cabinet used especially for that purpose. Also, do not wash scrub mops in dishwashing or pot sinks.
13. Hands and arms should be washed thoroughly before beginning work, after coughs

or sneezes, after handling soiled dishes and utensils, and after cleaning or handling poultry or raw meat.

14. Cover food in the kitchen to protect it from droplet infection, flies, dust, etcetera.
15. Never put a spoon used for tasting back into the food.
16. Keep fingers away from mouth, lips, face, and soiled surfaces.

Do not handle foods that can be picked up with tongs, scoops, forks, or spoons. Avoid mixing salads and ground meat with the hands, and never work with food if you have a sore, boil, or infected cut on your hands or arms.

In some areas, foodservice workers wear disposable plastic gloves while preparing or dispensing such foods as cooked meats used in sandwiches, hamburger patties, wieners, bread, buns, cookies, vegetable sticks, and fresh fruit.

However, merely wearing gloves does not guarantee a sanitary situation, and management and employees should not get a false sense of security or relax their alertness on required sanitation procedures.

When making sandwiches, a disposable plastic glove can be worn on the hand that touches cooked meat, but should *not* be worn on the hand holding a knife or operating a slicer. Furthermore, workers must understand and follow carefully the safety rules for using the slicer guard and picking up the cooked meat.

If sandwich making is temporarily interrupted, the plastic glove should be discarded and a new one put on when work is resumed.

If worn for a long period, plastic gloves—like hands—can become contaminated. For example, hands can brush against the hair, rub the eyes, scratch the nose, or be wiped on soiled towels.

It is suggested that disposable plastic gloves be discarded when they become cut, punctured, or obviously soiled. The safest

procedure is to change them frequently when continuously preparing or dispensing foods. Similarly, plastic gloves should be changed immediately after the worker has handled raw poultry or meat.

17. Store food above the floor.
18. Do not smoke while preparing food.
19. Refrigerate milk and milk products at all times.
20. Milk containers, bottled drinks, and fruit juices kept cold in ice should never be covered by melting ice water. The reason is simple—if ice water penetrates the containers, the contents could become contaminated.
21. Preparation and work tables should be cleaned frequently with a germicidal detergent solution.

SEWAGE CONTAMINATION

1. If possible, overhead drainage pipes should not be located over work tables, refrigerators, or places where unprotected food is stored. If they are, sheet metal drip pans should be suspended below them to catch condensation and sewage drippings, particularly at joints. Unprotected food should never rest on the floor where it would be subject to contamination from overflow or flooding.
2. A refrigerator should drain through a trap to the open and then into the sewer. There *must not* be a direct connection to the sewer.

RODENT AND INSECT INFESTATION

1. All outside openings must be sealed to prevent the entrance of rodents.
2. Remove rodent nesting places.
3. Protect food by keeping it in covered containers.
4. Use only approved insecticides.
5. Inspect all produce in bags and crates for roaches and other pests.

6. Seal pipe openings, cracks, and crevices.
7. Eliminate insect breeding places.
8. Put garbage in closed metal containers with tight fitting lids.
9. If possible, use a trash compactor.
10. *Practice good housekeeping and be eternally vigilant!*

SUCCESSFUL ATTITUDES

The success of any sanitation program, however, depends largely on the attitudes and actions of the entire catering staff. Management must instill in employees the realization that good sanitation practices are essential not only to their health, but also to the people who purchase their services. Plant sanitation and personal cleanliness are an integral part of good food production and service, and both require constant vigilance by employer and employee.

In planning and implementing your sanitation program, provide for good supervision and employee training. Many excellent sources of information are available to aid in the development of such a program. Local health department sanitarians can be of great help, as can your State Health Department. Its library will provide listings of movies and other materials offered by various governmental health agencies.

Another excellent source of information and advice is the Center for Disease Control, U.S. Department of Health, Education and Welfare, Public Health Service, Training Program, Community Services Training Section, Atlanta, Georgia 30333.

Several well-known manufacturers of food-service industry equipment and supplies have produced visual aids on sanitation routines for their products. These clear, practical depictions of correct procedures are worth viewing by both management and personnel. Ask your dish machine and detergent field technicians for information.

Write the Environmental Health Committee, Single Service Institute, 250 Park Avenue, New York, New York 10017 for copies of its posters, handbook, and other printed material.

You may also contact: The International Sanitary Supply Association, 5330 N. Elston Avenue, Chicago, Illinois 60630. A variety of worthwhile sanitation material is available to customers of member firms.

The National Restaurant Association, Educational Materials Center, 1 IBM Plaza, Suite 2600, Chicago, Illinois 60611 has available a list of food sanitation material developed by its organization.

The National Sanitation Foundation, P.O. Box 1468, Ann Arbor, Michigan 48106 has published *A Reference Manual of Food Service Sanitation Educational and Training Materials* that any owner or manager would find very helpful. It is available at a moderate cost.

SANITATION INSPECTIONS

Local and state Boards of Health make constant and unannounced inspections at all food establishments. The following are areas of concern that will be scrutinized:

1. *Foods*—Food must come from approved sources, and be wholesome and unadulterated (game must be legal and USDA inspected). Original containers must be properly labeled and identified.
2. *Food Protection*—All potentially hazardous food must be kept in temperature controlled areas, during storage, preparation, display, service, and transportation. There must be adequate facilities to maintain product temperature. Frozen food must be thawed properly. Potentially hazardous food must not be served. Food containers must be stored off the floor. Food handling must be minimal. Food-dispensing utensils must be properly stored. Toxic items must be properly stored, labeled, and used.
3. *Personnel*—Personnel with infections must be restricted.

4. *Cleanliness of Personnel*—Personnel must have handwashing facilities, clean outerclothes, and effective hair restraints. Good hygienic practices should be used, and smoking restricted.

5. *Equipment and Utensils* (design, construction, and installation)—Food contact surfaces must be properly maintained (avoid illegal use of wood butcher blocks or other porous substances). Counter surfaces must be clean. Nonfood contact surfaces should be properly installed and maintained. Single service articles should be properly stored and dispensed, and *not reused.* Dishwashing facilities, both hand and mechanical, must be of approved design, adequately constructed, properly installed, and maintained.

6. *Cleanliness of Equipment and Utensils*—Pots must be properly cleaned and free of grease and carbon accumulation. Use only clean sponges, toweling, etcetera. All wash and rinse water must be clean and the proper temperature. Thermometers must be integral to all mechanical washing facilities. Use only approved chemicals.

7. *Water Supply*—Source must be adequate and safe. Hot and cold water must be under pressure.

8. *Sewage Disposal*—Provide for proper disposal of waste water and sewage, particularly for septic tanks.

9. *Plumbing*—Must be properly installed, approved, and maintained, with no cross connections, back siphonage, and/or backflow.

10. *Toilet Facilities*—Must be adequate, convenient, and accessible. Must have self-closing door; all necessary fixtures must be provided and in good repair and clean.

11. *Handwashing Facilities*—Suitable hand cleaners and sanitary towels or approved hand drying devices must be provided, along with tissue and waste receptacles.

12. *Garbage and Rubbish Storage and Disposal*—Use an adequate number of approved containers, covered, rodent proof, and clean; store in approved area. Rubbish rooms must be properly constructed and enclosed, and must be disposed at approved frequency.

13. *Vermin Control*—There must be no evidence of insects or rodents. Extermination control may be scheduled or as needed. Proof of last exterminator's visit should be available. Outer openings must be protected against entrance of insects and rodents.

14. *Floors, Walls, Ceilings*—All floors must be constructed as required, in good repair, and clean. Floors must be properly graded and drained as required. Floors and walls should be properly junctured and covered. Mats must be removable, clean, and in good repair. All attachments to walls and ceilings must be properly constructed, in good repair, and clean. Dustless cleaning methods must be used and cleaning equipment properly stored.

15. *Lighting*—All lighting must be adequate and fixtures must be clean.

16. *Ventilation*—Preparation, storage, and related areas must be free of steam and smoke odors. All room and equipment hoods must have ducts vented as required.

17. *Dressing Rooms and Lockers*—All rooms must be adequate, all facilities clean, and lockers provided.

18. *Housekeeping*—Establishment and premises must be free of litter, insect or rodent harborage, and unnecessary articles.

19. *Laundry*—Clean and soiled laundry must be properly stored.

20. *Animals*—No live birds, turtles, other animals or pets are allowed, except police guard dogs.

Sanitation inspectors will score each area and give demerits where warranted (see Figure 3.1). A final rating and grading will then be given to be displayed in a conspicuous area of the establishment. Violations, unless hazardous and flagrant, are allowed corrective action within a reasonable length of time.

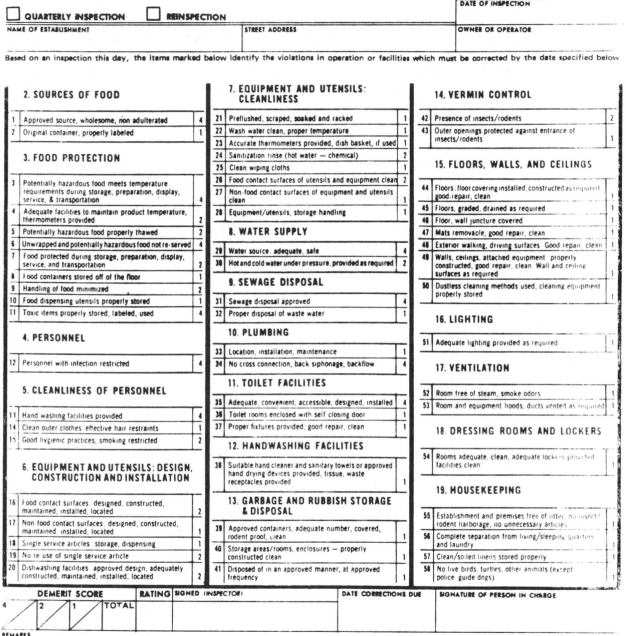

Figure 3.1. Board of Health inspection report form.

Careful and constant attention to all of the above areas should result in excellent working conditions.

Board of Health inspectors *are not* 9-to-5 workers. They are authorized to make inspections any time they feel public health is in jeopardy or for due cause. There are "on-spot inspections," not only in food preparation areas but in service areas of on-premise caterers, and there are inspections of "on-job" performances by off-premise caterers.

Many localities now have ordinances that do not allow out-of-town caterers to serve in any public facility without first registering with the local Board of Health. These ordinances were brought about by pressure from local restaurants, hotels, and health authorities because of the frequency of mass salmonella and other food-borne illnesses directly traceable to improperly prepared food served by inexperienced, unqualified, and careless personnel, who had minimal knowledge of proper sanitary precautions to be taken in food preparation, refrigeration, and the holding of foods at proper temperatures.

More and more areas in the country require a Food Handlers Card, issued by the Board of Health. Card carriers can be employed in the handling or serving of food. Employers who disregard this law are subject to substantial fines. All food establishments, regardless of their classification, must be approved by the local Department of Health, and must comply with applicable state and local laws.

IOI IOI

CHAPTER FOUR

CATERING PERSONNEL

The type of personnel you employ often make the difference between success and failure. Therefore, it is essential that you find suitable employees and place them in the appropriate jobs.

To do this, you must know what work has to be done, how it should be accomplished, and what skills are required for each job. Armed with this information, you can then determine the kind of individual best suited to the job, the training needed, and a fair wage.

The number and type of employees needed are determined by the type of service offered and the size of the facility. You, the *caterer,* are responsible to the client and are required to provide everything agreed on in the contract. You book the job, write the contract, work out the menu, arrange and supervise all details of the affair, and assume responsibility for your employees and their on-the-job activities.

A Secretary/Office Worker is needed by the moderate-sized or high-volume catering operation to handle paper work and office records.

The Maintenance Crew needed depends on the size and type of the catering business.

SOURCES OF EXTRA HELP

The menu and type of service to be used for a function determines the personnel required. Sufficient personnel must be provided to set up, serve, and clear tables within a reasonable period of time. While your basic crew will be able to handle most affairs, there will be times when additional workers will be needed.

Undoubtedly, many sources of part-time skilled kitchen help are available in your area. Approach chefs/cooks in local hospitals, nursing and retirement homes, and public and private schools about their interest in and availability for part-time work. Many chefs in these facilities work a five-day week and would welcome an opportunity to make extra money.

For less skilled help—drivers, packers, prep and "on-the-line-people"—the Post Office is an excellent source of dependable part-time workers. These civil servants are honest, intelligent, dependable, and accustomed to working in all kinds of weather and conditions; many are also skilled drivers.

To "break into" this source, talk to your mailman who, in all likelihood, will be glad to help. He may advise you to ask the postmaster for permission to post a notice on the bulletin board or, if permitted, may do it for you.

Teachers are also a good source of extra personnel. However, teaching is now more lucrative than it once was, so it may be difficult to meet or compete with the pay scale.

Remember that you, the caterer, are responsible for the actions of your employees, whether they are full-time, part-time, or temporary. Select the right people for the job and be sure the employee knows what the job is and how you want it performed.

UNIFORMS

Clean, crisp, attractive uniforms make a good impression on clients and staff members as well. Uniforms must be spotless, so provide your kitchen staff with extra sets of whites when they are to serve off-premises.

Chefs, cooks, and kitchen personnel should also be in whites—white shirts, coats, and aprons. (Gray denim work pants are acceptable in some areas.) Hats are a MUST for all kitchen workers.

Busboys should wear white or colored jackets. Waiters' uniforms are available in traditional and contemporary colored models. The uniform for the waitress has traditionally been a black or gray dress with white apron, collar, and headband. However, colored uniforms are seen more and more frequently today, especially for informal affairs.

Linen rental houses stock a wide variety of uniform accessories. Such service is not unduly expensive and assures a clean and uniform staff appearance—an asset in creating a good impression.

DETERMINING PERSONNEL REQUIRED

The banquet manager or individual operator must study and analyze the menu to determine how many employees are needed. The type of service requested is most crucial, as is the skill of available employees.

American Service

The rule of thumb is that food preplated in the kitchen or served preplated from banquet carrier—and distance from kitchen—requires one server for twenty diners. (Simple "basic-four" meals can increase the server's allocation by at least one-third.)

French Service

This type of service from gueridons is a slower and more elegant production; a capable server can give ten guests satisfactory service. The assistance of a busboy and captain at certain points in the service may be required, depending on the item being served. Frequently, two servers will team up to care for two tables of ten each. Such cooperation should be encouraged as the service will be faster, more competent, and certainly more impressive. Guests are more aware of the physical presence of two people simultaneously engaged in the process of preparing or combining foods to give them pleasure. There is some excitement in this process as it gives the diner, no matter how blase, a feeling of importance and an awareness of the generosity of the host in providing this luxury.

Russian Service

This service, too frequently and mistakenly called French service, is a system of serving food from a hand-held, attractively arranged tray of silver or polished stainless steel. This type of service requires personnel of inordinate skill. The server must hold a tureen of hot soup in one hand and ladle the liquid directly into the guest's cup or bowl with the other. He or she must be able to balance a tray of food with one hand and skillfully serve the guest with the other hand. This must be done without allowing the tureen or tray to come in contact with any table guest and without spilling or dripping. In a crowded dining area, the completion of this type of service without incident is a tribute to the personnel involved.

Additional Service Personnel

A good busboy can competently assist with twenty guests. The actual number needed is determined by house policy or standards.

Sommeliers, or wine stewards, may or may not be needed, depending on the character of the affair, whether the types of wines to be served have been predetermined, or whether decisions (and sales) will be made at tableside.

Captains and headwaiters required are determined by the duties expected of them. Will they function exclusively as administrators for their stations or will they be involved in actual table service and to what extent?

The kitchen brigade required depends on many variables, including the prepreparation and the amount of finishing-off necessary. Will the kitchen be involved with more than one party at the same time? Will any kitchen help be required to participate "up front" during the reception? Will cooks and chefs be assigned to carve or flambe in the dining room?

Scheduling and assigning help must be done with concern for providing the patron prompt and efficient service. The amount and the type of employees needed can sometimes be determined from past records of similar situations. Union regulations, where applicable, must be complied with. Guest satisfaction must not be sacrificed by chancing an understaffing. But it is also prudent not to overstaff, as salaries and benefits can cut deeply into profits.

FOODSERVICE OCCUPATIONS

Maitre d' Hotel

The *maitre d'hotel* is the chief administrator of all dining areas. The term *head waiter* is equally applicable and interchangeable. He is responsible for staffing and training all dining room personnel, making out their work schedules, and handling reservations.

His immediate superior is the manager. As the kitchen is an extension of the dining room, or vice versa, there must be ongoing communication and cooperation with the chef, with whom he must meet daily. The manager often joins them.

The maitre d' must make certain that all accoutrements for party service, such as, linens, silverware, glassware, and china, are available and "on the ready" in the necessary quantities, and in the areas and at the time required. He delegates a considerable amount of his responsibilities to the captains.

Captains are responsible for certain sections and/or a certain amount of tables serviced by waiters. In addition to the table service, waiters are assigned such side work as checking condiments, linen inventory, silver maintenance, etcetera.

There are no set rules as to the number of captains and waiters needed—it depends on the type and the luxuriousness of the service. Union houses may have contractual stipulations. Some set the *maximum* of one server per twenty guests!

Busboys assist in setting up, serving water, clearing, and cleaning up. One busboy can service twenty guests.

The Kitchen Brigade

Kitchen duties vary in practically every establishment due to size, volume, and the character of business.

Professionally, each staff member has a title and the obligatory work identified with the title. However, conditions may require additional duties; the broiler cook may also be responsible for the fry and roast stations. Responsibilities are also incumbent on capabilities.

The kitchen brigade is headed by the chef, who is responsible for all food preparation of the establishment. Because of professional organization insistance and government encouragement, the term *chef* is no longer a whimsical appellation. The title must be earned and, after passing examinations, one is entitled to use the initials C. E. C. (Certified Executive Chef) after his name.

A chef may also have one of the following titles: Executive Chef, Head Chef, Chef Steward, or Working Chef.

Executive Chef. This term is used in large establishments employing a full staff. In addition to writing the menus, the chef coordinates all kitchen activities. He has regular meetings with the manager and the department heads responsible for food service—the Purchasing Agent, Maitre d'Hotel, and Wine Steward. It is his responsibility to see that all food, including bakery, is prepared in accordance with the standards of the establishment.

Sous Chef. The sous chef reports directly to the chef, and is responsible for the physical condition of the kitchen and the supervision of personnel. He must pass judgment on the food before the chef approves it.

Chef Steward. A chef steward is a chef who also does the food purchasing, which may require occasional absences from the kitchen. The chef steward can also act as meal hour and banquet service supervisor.

Working Chef. In smaller establishments, a working chef not only cooks but supervises all kitchen activities.

Chef de Partie. The title denotes a person in charge of a particular department, such as soups and sauces or a fry station.

Banquet Chef. This chef is responsible for all stations assigned banquet work. All trays and showpieces for a buffet, and its setup, are his responsibility.

Second Cook. In large establishments, the second cook is responsible for all soups, stocks, roasts, etcetera. The title is interchangeable with sous chef.

Broiler Cook. This employee is in charge of *all* broilings of meat, fish, en brochette foods, etcetera. Frequently, a second cook may be required to cover this station in addition to his own.

Fry Cook. This cook is in charge of all immersion cooking, as well as the surface frying of eggs, pancakes, fritters, and crepes. Frequently, all vegetable processing is included in his duties.

Swing Cook, Roundsman, or Relief Cook. This person is conversant with and capable of manning each station as the occasion requires (due to days off, sickness, etcetera). He must follow the routine of the one he replaces, and likewise do the advance work, such as ordering the necessary supplies for continuity.

Garde Manger (Cold Meat Department). This employee's responsibilities include the making of all salad dressings and cold sauces, and the preparation of all meat, fish, vegetable, and seafood salads, and fruit displays. He prepares and decorates all cold food platters for buffet service and makes all appetizers and sandwiches, when necessary. Ice carvings and tallow or butter modeling are his responsibility—the garde manger hopefully is endowed with artistic talent. At a buffet presentation, the cold food offerings allow greater opportunities for exquisite design and spectacular display. This area is the center of attraction.

Pastry Chef or Baker. This chef makes all cakes, cookies, pies, puddings, French and Danish pastries, breads, rolls, and muffins. Ice cream and sherbet are also products of this department, as are other dessert items, such as, baked apples, stewed pears, trifles, etcetera. Ornamental pieces of sugar and dough are produced here. At times talented bakers also carve ice and tallow pieces.

Butcher. In large establishments, the butcher breaks down primal cuts into service orders. Smaller establishments have little use for this skill as pre-portioned and oven-ready products are readily available and are frequently cheaper to purchase than to process.

Fish Butcher. This profession is little used or entirely eliminated in kitchens since seafood packers have developed product portioning to rigid specifications. This development is not only convenient but it permits highly accurate costing.

TRUCK PACKING

If schedules permit, it is to the caterer's advantage to have the truck packed with nonperishables at least a day in advance of the party. When the loader is free of the tension of meeting departure schedules, he can be much more accurate and effective in loading.

The packer should be given the menu, in addition to the packing list, so that he will be alert to omissions on the list. For example, if there will be a reception or pass-around items, and cocktail napkins are not listed, the packer might recognize the omission. The packer should alert the manager or owner when equipment inventory is at a low level.

The truck must be packed in a sequential manner. The equipment needed first at the destination should be packed last. The items must be securely wedged to prevent shifting or sliding. The weight must be evenly distributed—overloading on either side can cause the truck to overturn when making a sharp turn. Excess weight over the axles can cause tire blowouts or cause the axle or springs to snap.

Heavy containers must not be placed on top of light packages; cardboard containers should not be set directly on the floor of the truck as they could disintegrate if wet.

Food should be the last item loaded and, even though properly protected by built-in temperature controls, it should not remain there longer than necessary.

When loading or unloading, *never, never* place equipment or packaged food, even temporarily, on a grassy area, especially in the summer. Ants and other insects will magically appear and swarm over the contents.

SAMPLE JOB RULES AND REGULATIONS

The following is a list of rules and regulations, company policies, and grievance procedures. They should be read carefully, and any section that is not clear should be discussed with your superior.

A. PERSONAL STANDARDS FOR EMPLOYEES
 1. All employees must report to work on time at the place and time scheduled. In case of illness or other valid reason, notify your superior.
 2. Employees must never sign another employee in or out, or punch another employee's time card. Employees *must be in uniform* at the start of the shift. You must sign or punch in or out *at the start of your schedule* and *at the end of your schedule,* not necessarily when you arrive or leave.
B. PERSONAL BEHAVIOR ON THE JOB
 1. Meals are to be eaten only at the time and place assigned. No food is to be eaten at any other time, except for required tasting.
 2. Smoking is permitted only in designated areas and should not be done for at least a half hour before serving guests.
 3. Chewing gum is not permitted while on duty.
 4. Telephone calls of a personal nature are not to be made during time of duty. Emergency calls will be accepted by your superior.
 5. Accidents must be reported at once to your superior, no matter how insignificant you may think them to be. Because many accidents can be prevented, extreme care should be exercised at all times.
 6. Newspapers or other literature should not be read or passed around by any em-

SAMPLE RESPONSIBILITY AND DAILY WORK SCHEDULE FOR A RESTAURANT EMPLOYEE

Salad and Sandwich Maker

Job Description: Prepares fresh fruits, lettuce, celery, and other vegetables, salads, cocktails, salad and sandwich plates, and other cold dishes; makes sandwiches for short orders or in quantity; prepares tea, coffee, and other beverages; slices cold meats and cheeses; and keeps preparation and storage space and equipment clean and orderly.

Hours: 9:00 A.M. to 6:45 P.M. Day off—Monday.

Work Schedule:

9:00 A.M. — 9:10	Change to working clothes, personal grooming, and handwashing.
9:10 A.M. — 9:30	Requisition and obtain needed food supplies and do any minor cleaning prior to beginning food preparation.
9:30 A.M. — 11:30	Prepare and properly store fruit and vegetable salad plates, sandwich plates, cocktails, and cold side dishes as shown on menu.
11:30 A.M. — 12 N	Set up prepared plates for serving and make coffee. Prepare hot tea set up; check availability of other beverages.
12:00 N — 1:30 P.M.	Make sandwiches to order, replace salad items sold out, and assist with other serving duties as directed by the chef.
1:30 P.M. — 2:30	Lunch and rest period.
2:30 P.M. — 2:40	Check to make sure all perishables not served are properly refrigerated.
2:40 P.M. — 3:30	Light cleaning of food preparation equipment and area, and special cleaning work indicated on following schedule.
3:30 P.M. — 5:30	Preparation and storage for serving of dinner salads and cold side dishes. Preparation of coffee, tea, and other beverages on menu.
5:30 P.M. — 6:00	Cleaning of salad area tables, stationary equipment.
6:00 P.M. — 6:45	Supper and off duty.

Special Duties:

Tuesday — Remove all food and thoroughly clean salad refrigerator.

Wednesday — Clean salad table, shelves, and drawers.

Thursday — Thoroughly clean beverage service area.

Friday — Thoroughly clean sandwich-making equipment, toaster, grill, table.

Saturday — Remove all food and thoroughly clean salad refrigerator.

Last Saturday each month — Inspect all equipment and appliances for defects in mechanical condition, wiring, etcetera, and report any unsatisfactory conditions to the manager in writing.

First Tuesday each month — Check for completion of routine monthly maintenance on equipment and for repair of any defects noted. Submit completed form to the manager.

Note: In the event of operating emergencies or special events, the manager may request special temporary assignments for all employees.

ployees during the time of service or within view of guests.

7. *No food raw or cooked* is to be removed from any area. Bones for dogs or other pets may be saved and packed *personally* by your superior, and only at his discretion and convenience.

8. Each employee is responsible for the cleanliness of his or her own working area as well as any other assigned area. Notify your superior immediately if your area has been left in an unsatisfactory manner by the employee preceding you.

9. Any problems or complaints that you may have should be taken up with your superior, and not with a fellow employee. If your superior does not correct the situation, or give you the satisfaction that you feel you are entitled to, you then have the right to appeal to the manager or owner.

10. Be courteous, cheerful, and helpful to customers, guests, and fellow employees at all times. The guests or customers are your reason for being here. Compliments by any guest, written or oral, in regard to a specific employee or the group, will be noted and brought to your attention individually or publicly posted on the bulletin board. Complaints about an individual will be handled in private, and kept strictly confidential unless they are serious enough to affect the whole crew.

C. GENERAL APPEARANCE AND HYGIENE

1. Wash hands thoroughly before handling or serving food.
2. Bathe or shower daily and use an effective deodorant that is not highly scented.
3. Keep hands away from face or hair at all times while on duty.
4. Do not eat while on duty—only at the time of mealbreak.
5. *Smoking is absolutely prohibited in any food preparation and foodservice area.*

6. Brush teeth frequently and use an antiseptic mouth wash.

7. Do not chew gum or chew on match sticks or use toothpicks, etcetera while on duty.

8. Wear clean undergarments at all times. Undergarments absorb perspiration and give off an offensive odor even though one bathes daily.

9. Cover pimples and minor eruptions with effective medication that is not obvious or medically scented.

10. Injuries, cuts, or bruises of any kind, no matter how minor, sustained while on duty, must be reported to your superior immediately.

11. Employees with coughs, colds, or other communicable infections must report to their superior, and are permitted to work only at his discretion. Employees with a fever *will not be permitted to work.*

12. Spitting is not only forbidden by law, but can lead to immediate discharge.

13. No one will be employed unless he or she carries a current and valid health card, if the local law so provides.

D. PERSONAL BELONGINGS

1. Jewelry—no jewelry and rings may be worn except as below:
   a. small, plain earrings may be worn; no earring exceeding one-half inch in diameter will be allowed.
   b. Wedding bands may be worn, as well as school graduation rings, providing they are not too massive (discretion of superior). Rings with society emblems, or rings set with semiprecious or precious stones, are not permitted.
   c. Fine neck chains will be permitted but must not have a pendant of any kind, except a medal of religious significance. It must then be pinned to the undergarment and *never allowed to hang free.*

d. Ankle bracelets are forbidden.

2. Pens, pencils, or thermometers must not be carried in the breast pocket unless securely clipped. Keeping a writing instrument in the hair or behind the ear is forbidden.

3. Cigarettes, matches, combs, keys, etcetera cannot be carried in the breast pocket.

E. UNIFORMS—WOMEN

1. Cooks and bakers—white uniforms with long or short sleeves, and white bib apron; other food production workers must wear designated uniform and apron.

2. Sweaters—only white, washable sweaters may be worn and only with the permission and discretion of the supervisor.

3. Medium or low-heeled shoes (white where mandatory) of the oxford type should be worn. They should be polished, comfortable, and give good support. Clogs are not permitted while on duty.

4. Stockings and pantyhose must be worn at all times. They must be clean, natural-tone, full length, plain seam or seamless, and in good condition. Ankle socks are not permitted.

F. GROOMING—WOMEN

1. Hair—hair nets must completely cover the hair. Hair sprays are not to be considered as a replacement for hair nets.

2. Hands and nails—hands should be washed frequently and always kept away from the face and head. Fingernails should be short, clean, and neatly manicured. Colorless nail polish is permitted.

G. UNIFORMS—MEN

1. Chefs, cooks, and bakers—traditional double-breasted or special house issue of coats with appropriate sleeve lengths. Chefs' hats mandatory at all times; appropriate neckerchief. White or checkered trousers must be worn in conjunction with a bib or bar apron.

2. Food production workers or "on-the-line" persons—white coat or shirt with long sleeves or short sleeves; white cloth or paper hat. Trousers white or checkered, as permitted by chef.

3. Dishwashers, pot washers, porters—blue, gray, or white shirt with short sleeves; trousers to match; paper hat.

H. GROOMING—MEN

1. Hair—hair must be covered with a hat at all times. Wash hair frequently.

2. Beards (where permitted)—beard must be carefully trimmed and short. Beard masks can be required. Always keep hands away from beard.

3. Hands and nails—hands should be washed frequently and fingernails must be kept short and clean. (It is suggested that a nail brush be used each time the hands are washed.)

I. LOCKER AND REST ROOM FACILITIES

1. Lockers, where provided, must be kept clean and neat. All clothing must be stored in the locker and not underneath or on top.

2. Food and beverages of any kind *must not be kept* in the lockers, even temporarily.

3. Valuables or large amounts of money should not be brought to work.

CHAPTER FIVE

GUEST SERVICE EQUIPMENT

Service ware includes all equipment used by you in serving guests—china, flatware, buffet service, linens, disposables, portable equipment, and other special items.

CHINA

The first rule to remember in buying china is to not buy closeouts or discontinued patterns. Because of their low price, they seem tempting, but it is very poor economy. Obviously, when it is necessary to replace broken dishes or to increase your stock due to business expansion, the original pattern may not be available. You will then be compelled to purchase an entirely new set of dishes. If you do not, the use of assorted shapes, sizes, and patterns may well discourage a client who is considering your services. Also, standardization in dish weight, design, and shape lead to greater efficiency in washing, handling, stacking, and storing.

The function of china should be considered from the following standpoints: (1) serviceability; (2) durability; and (3) beauty. The heaviness or thickness of china is often assumed to be the only criterion for its serviceability. This is not always

so since employees are prone to be less careful in handling heavy dishes.

The weight of dishes, when stacked one on top of another, tends to rub off the glazed surface with which they come in contact. Also, when the dishes are stacked, the weight, in transport, can cause shock waves, and may result in a greater number of cracked and broken dishes. (When packing for transport or storage, never stack more than 20 to 24 dishes high.)

Cautiously consider the purchase of any dishes with raised patterns. Raised surfaces chip more easily, and can also be dust and dirt traps that require more attention in cleaning.

Medium-weight dishes are much more practical, and generally considered more aesthetic. Dishes of this weight, when packed in transporting racks, add up to less weight per rack. Rolled-edge dishes are definitely a plus because the rounded edges act as "bumpers," reducing chippage and breakage.

It is obvious to caterers, that guest service dinnerware must be considered the package in which the menu is presented. It must be considered "table-top" merchandising. Properly presented, it can create an ambience that will be recognized by the patron and exemplify your service as distinctive and original. There are countless shapes and theme patterns that are available in open stock, so your choice can appear custom ordered.

Appearance, of course, is a basic consideration. Practicability follows. Are the sizes functional to your operation? One of the most objectionable features of any food offering, is crowding on the plate. Foods must not run into each other and there must be sufficient room to allow for cutting without food rolling off the edges.

China is the generally accepted medium in meal presentation and no substitute has as yet been found for its elegance. Newer products have been developed that have their proper place in certain services. Plastics, oven-proof and fireproof serviceware with lead-free glazes, can be

safely used in microwave ovens. They can also go directly from freezer to oven and then to point of service. They are excellent for French soup, marmites, or shirred egg dishes.

Pot pies, pasta, rarebits, and similar foods in individually controlled portions, are effective when presented in bake-and-serve dishes. Large capacity earthenware casseroles are very effective for family-style and buffet service.

If you wish to have your personal logo or monogram a part of the china pattern, it should be incorporated in a pleasing decoration, and not appear as an obvious bit of advertising.

In selecting dinner plates, consider the 10¾ inch (brim to brim) size. An adequate "show plate" to use as a base for starter courses at banquets, and a satisfactory meal-presentation plate, it is large enough to present the food course with-

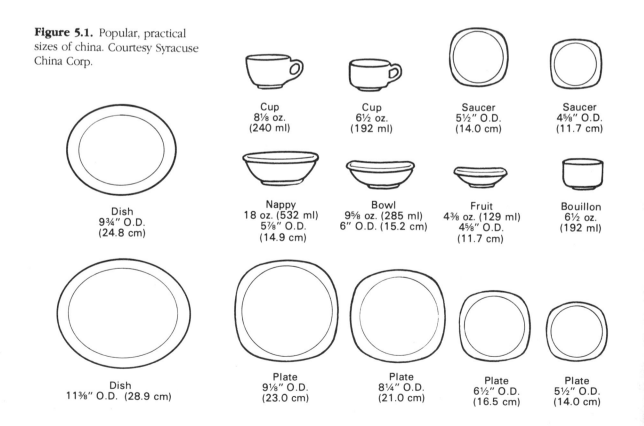

Figure 5.1. Popular, practical sizes of china. Courtesy Syracuse China Corp.

Cup
8⅛ oz.
(240 ml)

Cup
6½ oz.
(192 ml)

Saucer
5½" O.D.
(14.0 cm)

Saucer
4⅝" O.D.
(11.7 cm)

Dish
9¾" O.D.
(24.8 cm)

Nappy
18 oz. (532 ml)
5⅞" O.D.
(14.9 cm)

Bowl
9⅝ oz. (285 ml)
6" O.D. (15.2 cm)

Fruit
4⅜ oz. (129 ml)
4⅝" O.D.
(11.7 cm)

Bouillon
6½ oz.
(192 ml)

Dish
11⅜" O.D. (28.9 cm)

Plate
9⅛" O.D.
(23.0 cm)

Plate
8¼" O.D.
(21.0 cm)

Plate
6½" O.D.
(16.5 cm)

Plate
5½" O.D.
(14.0 cm)

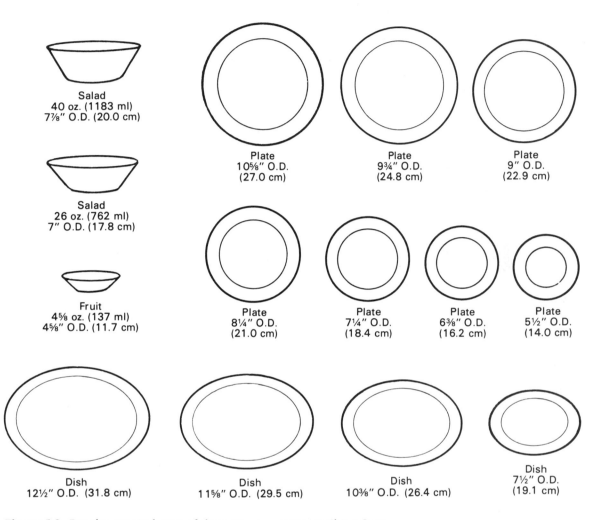

Figure 5.2. Popular, practical sizes of china. Courtesy Syracuse China Corp.

out crowding, giving a desirable impression of spaciousness. For "oversize" beef cuts or pasta presentations, you may use the 12¾ inch steak platter.

Coffee cups come in various shapes and sizes—low cups, high cups, tea cups, and mugs. Many mugs are footed which not only makes them graceful in appearance, but allows them to be used without saucers. Cup sizes range from 4½

ounce (the after-dinner or demitasse size) to 7, 7¼, 7½, 7¾, and 8¾ ounce capacity.

Coffee and bouillon cup handles are not molded with the cup, but are applied separately during the manufacturing process. Check these handles very thoroughly. Will they be able to withstand the abuse that comes in packing and delivery? (When packing cups, do not nest them. Cups should be packed as a single layer in in-

| 6¾ oz. | 6⅞ oz. | 8¼ oz. | 7 oz. | 7 oz. |
| (199.6 ml) | (203.3 ml) | (244.0 ml) | (207.0 ml) | (207.0 ml) |

Figure 5.3. Five popular styles of mugs.

dividual racks.) Give thought to purchasing bouillon cups without handles rather than the standard two-handled bouillon cup. When one handle of a bouillon cup is broken, you might just as well discard the cup.

Do cup bases have separately attached rings, or are the bases an integrally molded part of the cup? Is the base of the ring fully glazed, or is it rough? A rough ring can become a magnet for dirt, and this will make cleaning very difficult.

GUIDE TO PURCHASING DISHES

Ideas vary as to the type and quantity of dishes needed, depending on the mode and scope of service, dishwashing facilities, availability of dishes for reordering, reserve inventory that is feasible, and the funds that are available. However, the following suggested list of basic quantities required for serving 100 guests may be helpful:

Basic Dish Requirements For 100 Guests

Dinner plates	250
Underliners or salad plates	300–400
Bread and butter plates	300–400
Platters (optional)	50–100
Cups and saucers	300–400
Bouillon cups	200–250
Fruit dishes	250–300
Grapefruit dishes	200–250
Soup bowls	125–200
Sugars and creamers	50 sets

STAINLESS STEEL FLATWARE AND SERVING PIECES

Stainless steel equipment is acceptable in most establishments today. However, it should be quality stainless, a metal that has good feel, substance, and body. Pattern details should be articulated and finished off, not just "punched out" as is sometimes the case.

Reputable silver manufacturers have lines of stainless ware comparable in price to their silver line. The advantage of stainless ware over silver is, of course, the upkeep. Polishing and burnishing are practically eliminated. As stainless ware is harder than silver, it shows fewer signs of abuse.

Basic Flatware Requirements Per 100 Guests

125 Dinner knives	125 Fish forks
125 Luncheon knives	125 Dessert forks
125 Butter knives	125 Round bowl
125 Cocktail forks	soup spoons
125 Dinner forks	250 Teaspoons
125 Luncheon forks	125 Iced teaspoons
125 Salad forks	125 Dessert spoons

You may, on occasion, resort to cheap stainless ware and be justified in using it—for example, to serve a large outdoor party where flatware may be carried off or inadvertently discarded. In such instances, *heavy-duty* disposable plasticware could also be used. But plasticware or other disposables *should not be used without the full knowledge and consent of your client.*

Serving Pieces

The type of service offered will determine what you need. However, for general service, you must have a good supply of the following:

Large Serving Spoons
Cold Meat Forks
Salad Tongs/Large Salad Forks and Spoons
Cake Knife/Servers

Chafing Dishes

You will want to stock an assortment of chafing dishes in different shapes and sizes for various buffet needs. Available in round, oval, and oblong shapes; in sizes ranging from two (2) quarts to eight (8) quarts, and larger; and, in a variety of metals (silver, stainless steel, and combinations of copper, brass, and aluminum), they add a decorative note to your buffet.

Trays

Select heavy-duty metal, plastic, or fiberglass utility trays for use by waiters, cooks, and bartenders. For serving hors d'oeuvre and for the buffet, there should be more elaborate round, oval, and oblong trays to complement the food.

Tea/Coffee Service

To cater "teas" and "coffees," you will need: (1) a silver or stainless tea service (tea server, hot water

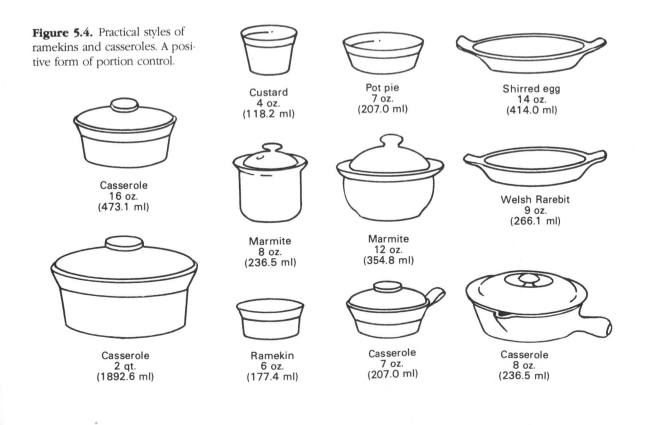

Figure 5.4. Practical styles of ramekins and casseroles. A positive form of portion control.

Custard
4 oz.
(118.2 ml)

Pot pie
7 oz.
(207.0 ml)

Shirred egg
14 oz.
(414.0 ml)

Casserole
16 oz.
(473.1 ml)

Marmite
8 oz.
(236.5 ml)

Marmite
12 oz.
(354.8 ml)

Welsh Rarebit
9 oz.
(266.1 ml)

Casserole
2 qt.
(1892.6 ml)

Ramekin
6 oz.
(177.4 ml)

Casserole
7 oz.
(207.0 ml)

Casserole
8 oz.
(236.5 ml)

Figure 5.5. Supreme rings and insets. Effective for iced foods and liquids.

Figure 5.6. Serving trays and tureen for Russian service.

pot with warming unit, creamer, sugar bowl, and matching tray); and (2) a silver or stainless coffee serving urn with a self-contained heating unit, and matching creamer, sugar bowl, and tray to add a touch of elegance to the tea/coffee table.

Polished silver pitchers have long been used in foodservice operations for serving coffee and tea to seated guests. However, although decorative, they are heavy to handle and are not insulated. You may prefer lighter-weight insulated pitchers with heat-resistant handles.

Candelabras

Candelabras can add an elegant touch or be the focal point of a buffet or head table. They are available in assorted sizes and styles. The quantities, sizes, and styles you need will be determined by the type of service you offer.

GLASSWARE

A social caterer requires a large and varied supply of glassware to meet the various demands of service and to replace the breakage. The type and number of glasses required depends on the ser-

vice offered. However, the following list may be helpful as a basic guide:

Types of Glassware Required

3- to 5-ounce Juice glasses
8- to 10-ounce Water tumblers or goblets
12-ounce Iced tea glasses
Supreme glasses/liners
Relish trays
Parfait glasses
Compotes for candy, nuts, petit fours
Creamers and sugars
Sherbet glasses
Champagne glasses
Wine glasses
Ash trays

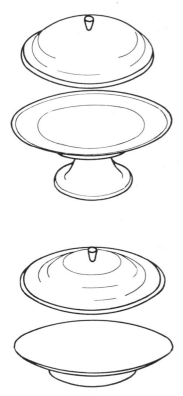

Figure 5.7. Chafing dishes and coffee samovar. Chafing dishes are available with sectioned insets.

Figure 5.8. Comports and covers for Oriental service.

Glassware has emerged as an important component in merchandising food and beverages. There is such a vast array of styles, shapes, colors, weights, and sizes that the potential for practical use of any one unit is literally overwhelming.

The basic function of glasses, that is, to hold liquids only, is obsolete. Glasses are an aid in portion control, in merchandising a house beverage, and a distinctive way of serving fruit or seafood entrees. They add style and showmanship to bar offerings and to the presentation of spectacular desserts, and they can add materially to the income picture.

Caterers, both on- and off-premise, have developed an aspect of promotion that is subtle and ongoing. They offer their individualized house drinks and special desserts in large volume, footed hurricane glasses, 12½-ounce brandy glasses, or oversized parfait glasses, with the business name *etched or imprinted.* And guests are allowed *to take them home.* This unusual container then becomes a souvenir, a topic of conversation, and a medium of advertising! The basic cost should be absorbed in the price of the meal, or a portion charged to advertising.

The decision to purchase a wide variety of glassware to be used for special services, should hinge on a number of factors. First, consider the practicality of the service. Will it be too time consuming to prepare using this type of glass? Will it present a problem in washing or sanitizing? Will storage be a problem? Will it be necessary to purchase special containers for safe packaging and transport? Will fragility lead to a higher incidence of breakage?

Figure 5.9 shows examples of the variety of glassware available.

LINENS AND NAPERY

A beginning caterer will probably find it best to rent linens rather than make an immediate cash outlay for cloths. The disadvantage is that you are always at the mercy of the laundry service. And most are unable to furnish the array of colors so paramount to exciting presentations.

As a result, you may be forced to compromise on quality, and, on occasion, have to accept patched, mold-stained, torn, or improperly folded and ironed cloths and napkins. Also, by renting linens, your offerings will be the same as other caterers who use the same service; thus, you will not have that "linen edge."

Owning your own linens has certain advantages. You can choose your own colors, quality, and sizes. (Most laundries supply 72-inch by 72-inch cloths as standard for 54- and 60-inch round tables. The drop [i.e., amount of cloth that hangs down from the table] of this cloth on a 54-inch table is adequate, but the drop on a 60-inch table is skimpy.)

Rental laundries use the 72-inch by 72-inch size because bolts of tablecloth material generally come in standard 72-inch widths. If you wish to order cloths made up in larger sizes, it will cost more but the aesthetic value may be well worth the extra charge. A generous cloth could provide an added feature of your catering service that your competitor cannot match.

The synthetic polyester fabrics used today, by many companies making tablecloths and napkins, are of such fine quality that they can be used at the most elegant affairs. Many are spot and stain resistant and flame-retardant and, if handled as directed, require no ironing, which is a tremendous boon to many foodservice operators.

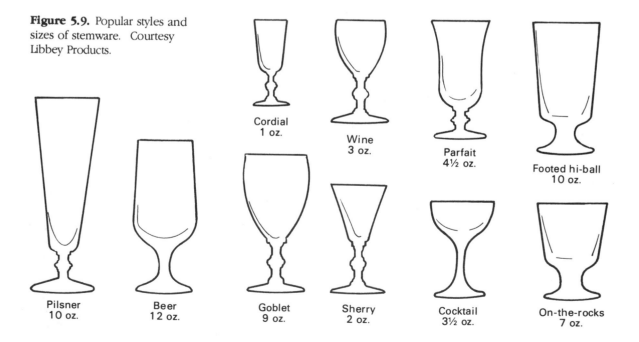

Figure 5.9. Popular styles and sizes of stemware.   Courtesy Libbey Products.

Cordial
1 oz.

Wine
3 oz.

Parfait
4½ oz.

Footed hi-ball
10 oz.

Pilsner
10 oz.

Beer
12 oz.

Goblet
9 oz.

Sherry
2 oz.

Cocktail
3½ oz.

On-the-rocks
7 oz.

Fitting Cloths to Tables

CLOTH SIZE	TABLE SIZE
44 inches by 44 inches	Bridge table or cocktail tables
54 inches square	44 inches to 50 inches bridge or round
64 inches square	48 inches to 54 inches round or square
72 inches square	60 inches round
81 inches by 81 inches	72 inches round
90 inches by 90 inches	84 inches round
110 inches by 54 inches	Rectangular 30-by-96 inch tables used for *banquets* or *buffet*

Furthermore, servicing or laundering these synthetics may not require commercial laundry service.

These quality products can be professionally laundered and finished in isolated areas of any food establishment. It only requires room for a washer-dryer and enough room for soiled and cleaned linen storage. The size of the washer-dryer depends on volume. A small mangler would enhance the appearance of the finished product. This equipment could save the cost of carrying a large inventory. It could also avoid crisis situations caused by delayed linen deliveries. The cost of equipment and installation would be self-liquidating through the elimination of commercial laundry costs.

In selecting tablecloths, it will help to know the cloth sizes that fit various tables.

The following list of service equipment is a guide to help you determine your needs. All of the items can be rented.

LINEN
White - Gold - Blue - Red - Yellow - Brown
Cloth 90 inches Round
Cloth 72 inches Square for Round Tables
Cloth 54 inches by 120 inches
Cloth 54 inches by 54 inches
    White - Yellow - Brown
Napkins
White - Gold - Blue - Red - Yellow - Orange - Brown
Umbrella Tablecloth Yellow
Drapes; Room Dividers (w/Stanchions)

Tableskirts, Dacron
Overlays

PLATFORMS OR STAGING
Sections 6 feet by 3 feet
(Dual Height 16 inches or 32 inches)
Stairs

PUNCH BOWLS—FOUNTAINS
Glass 8 quarts w/Ladle
Silver w/Tray & Ladle, 10 quarts
Plastic w/Ladle, 8 quarts
Plastic w/Ladle, 13 quarts
Beverage Fountains
2 Gallon
4 Gallon

SILVER SERVICE
Butter
Candy
Cake Stand
Chip and Dip
Celery
Olive
Gravy Boat
Jelly w/Crystal
Shrimp
Vegetable with Cover
Casseroles, 3 quarts
Ice Buckets
Wine Cooler
Sugar & Creamer
Bridal Knife
Coffee Server, 10 cups
Coffee & Tea, 5 Piece set

Water Pitcher
Samovar
32 Cups
80 Cups
Silver Tray
Bread
Round
Oval
Oblong, 14 inches by 18 inches

SPEAKERS' STANDS (Podium)
Floor Model
W/PA System
Table Model w/PA System

STAINLESS STEEL
Marmite (25 Cups)
Relish (3 Sections)
Lazy Susan
Bowls, Mixing, Salad, Punch
   8 quarts
   13 quarts
   30 quarts
Bread Trays
Oval Trays
   12 inches by 16 inches
   15 inches by 21 inches
Wine Coolers

STOVES—Propane
4 Burner w/Oven
2 Burner (Tabletop)
   w/French Fryer
Pot Boiler

TENTS—Prices on Request
Green and White Nylon
Striped Panels
   20 feet by 20 feet (Seats 40)
   20 feet by 40 feet (Seats 80)
   20 feet by 60 feet (Seats 120)
   30 feet by 30 feet (Seats 90)
   30 feet by 45 feet (Seats 135)
   30 feet by 60 feet (Seats 180)
   30 feet by 90 feet (Seats 270)
7-foot Wide Canopy to Match
Gazebo 10 feet by 13 feet

MISCELLANEOUS
Aisle Standards
Aisle Ropes (Red or Gold)
Blackboard w/Stand
Bread Baskets
Bridal Arch
Clam Steamers
   Small
   Large
Cocktail Shaker Sets
Crystal Ball w/Lights
Kneeling Bench
Lap Trays
Salad Bowl w/Stand
Fork & Spoon, all wood
Salad Bowl, wood tone, individual
Shower Umbrella
Smoke Stands
Stock Pots (Aluminum)
   20-32 quarts
   40-60 quarts
   80-100 quarts
Waiters' Trays

CHAIRS, Folding
Gold metal frame; foam cushioned seat and
   back in red or gold; velour covered
Samsonite, bronze frame; fiberglass seat and
   back in white or gold
TABLET ARM CHAIR
KIDDIE CHAIR

TABLES
Bridge—30 inches by 30 inches
Cocktail Table—round 24 inches
Cocktail Table—round 30 inches
Cocktail Table—round 36 inches
Round 48 inches (Seats 6-8)
Round 60 inches (Seats 8-10)
Round 72 inches (Seats 10-12)
Banquet—30 inches by 72 inches (Seats 8)
Banquet—30 inches by 96 inches (Seats 10)
42 inches Metal mesh table w/umbrella
Formica Top Schoolroom
   Table—18 inches by 72 inches
Snack Table
Quarter-round table (Smorgasbord)

Child's Table w/12 chairs
Poker Table

CHINAWARE—White w/Gold Rim
Bread and Butter plate
Salad plate
Dessert plate
Fruit plate
9-inch Luncheon plate
11-inch Dinner plate
Cup
Saucer
Soup Dish
Snack plate w/cup
Sugar and Creamer (per set)
Gravy Boat
Vegetable Dish
Large Platter
Small Platter
Pickle Dish

FLATWARE
Silverplate (Flowertime pattern)
  Forks
  Knives
  Spoons
  Silver Serving Spoons
  Silver Serving Forks
Deluxe Stainless
  Forks
  Knives
  Teaspoons
  Oyster Forks
  Butter Spreaders
  Sugar Spoons
  Serving Spoons
  Serving Forks
  Steak Knives
  Lobster Crackers
  Ice Tongs

GLASSWARE
Flat Bottom
  Water, Hi-ball, Whiskey Shot, Beer, On-the-Rocks, Old Fashion, Punch Cups, Sherbet
Stemware
  Champagne, On-the-Rocks, Cocktail, Cor-dial, Parfait, Wine, Beer Goblets, Whiskey Sour, Old Fashion
Beer Mugs
Salt and Pepper
Ashtrays
Pitchers—glass or plastic
Bud Vases
Supremes

AMUSEMENT EQUIPMENT
Pop-Corn Machine, Cotton Candy Machine, Snow Cone Machine, Carnival games, Booths, Prizes

BARS
4-foot Deluxe
Rolling

CANDELABRAS
Silver
  3 Branch
  5 Branch
Glass
  Single Crystal
Gold
  Bridal

CHAFING DISHES
Silver
  1–2–3 quarts
  6 quarts
Stainless
  4 quarts Square
  8 quarts Oblong

COFFEEMAKERS, Automatic
36 Cups
60 Cups
125 Cups
175 Cups

DANCE FLOORS
12 feet by 12 feet
12 feet by 18 feet

ELECTRIC FANS
Adjustable Height
Floor Model

GARMENT RACKS
40 Hangers

GRILLS, Barbecue
Large, Big John
Rotisserie
L. P. Gas 30 inches

LAMPS
Hurricane Table

LIGHTS, Outdoor

DISPOSABLES

Disposables have become indispensable in many areas of catering; they are not only pleasing, but extremely functional. Moreover, disposables can generate additional income because they make it feasible for even the most elegant catering and eating establishments to sell their foods for take-out. To some, it is a status symbol to boast that their "tailgate party food" at the football game or the polo match came from a prominent caterer. This is made possible by the availability and quality of disposable dishes, cloths, napkins, "cutlery," and "glassware."

There are disposable napkins in all colors, sizes, and textures. Disposable tablecloths are plasticized to prevent moisture penetration. The proliferation of colors and designs guarantee many beautiful settings and combinations. A close examination of the product can still leave doubt as to whether the product is synthetic or not.

Sturdy, reinforced disposable platters are now used at clambakes. The weight of heavy clams, oysters, and lobsters does not cause the platter to buckle and the sauces do not soak through.

Many disposables have excellent thermal qualities for heat and cold retention so that complete meals can be packaged in your kitchen and delivered for group consumption. If necessary, these meals can be reheated in radar ranges or in conventional ovens, in the original containers.

Composition, plastic, paper, or styrene trays and containers can be used effectively for display and for decorated no-return food trays.

Disposables can be manufactured to meet the needs of any product sale. Imprinting a company message on the containers is a valuable method of low-cost advertising.

Quantities of disposables can be stored in comparatively little space. Handling them requires much less exertion than handling similar quantities of glass, metal, clay, or fabric items.

Safety is another factor as disposables do not shatter and leave sharp edges. Theft is greatly reduced because disposables have no value to souvenir hunters. And, finally, the repetitive chore of dishwashing can be eliminated or reduced.

Quantity dumping of disposables is less expensive as they can be compacted to one-sixth of their volume. Large volume establishments can install special machinery to incinerate or pulp their throwaways and thus eliminate unsightly, bulky, and smelly containers.

CHAPTER SIX

FOOD-TRANSPORTING EQUIPMENT

As an off-premise caterer providing foodservice in a variety of locations, your menus and service ware must be sufficiently flexible to fit in with the varied facilities at each location. It is essential, therefore, that careful consideration be given to the types of food-transporting equipment required to handle the wide variety of demands.

VEHICLES FOR TRANSPORTING PEOPLE, FOOD, EQUIPMENT

Station Wagons

A station wagon probably has more aesthetic than utilitarian value, at least from the standpoint of equipment-carrying ability. A six-passenger wagon allows some deck space, but after checking the interior height from the deck floor to roof, you will find that this space rarely exceeds 36 inches. If it is a nine-passenger wagon, deck-carrying capacity is reduced to nearly zero. This lack of space should be carefully considered before you purchase a station wagon.

Vans

Unquestionably, the most practical vehicle for small catering purposes is the van, which can carry nine passengers, or more, and still have ample room for equipment. In addition to rear doors, many vans have side doors that slide or fold open to more than half the vehicle length; they permit easier loading of large and bulky pieces of equipment. Most vans also have side windows, and this is definitely an asset.

Requirements

A FEW WORDS OF CAUTION ON WAGONS AND VANS: Instead of number of passengers or cubic-feet capacity, you should be interested in *how much weight can be carried.* Remember, dishes, silverware, and equipment are heavy; in addition, you must also consider the weight of any passengers.

Get a heavy-duty motor that is capable of carrying more than the rated capacity, at a sustained speed for any distance, without breaking down or burning up.

Find out if additional leaves can be added to springs in order to distribute weight over a greater area, and use oversize tires. Although heavy-duty springs and oversize tires cause a rougher ride when the vehicle is empty, they assure a safer, surer ride when it is fully loaded.

TRUCKS

Purchasing

Purchasing a truck requires a substantial cash down payment, as well as monthly payments over a period of several years. Before making this investment, consult your accountant to determine whether your liquid cash is sufficient to meet this obligation, and to learn the appropriate dollar depreciation and other tax advantages of such an acquisition.

Owning your own truck has many obvious advantages, but you must be prepared to accept the responsibility for proper maintenance. Trucks must be mechanically sound, and kept in top-notch condition—immaculately clean and always "at the ready."

Do you have a dependable garage man to whom these responsibilities can be delegated? Does he have a towing service that can be used in the event of a late night or early morning breakdown? If catering services are offered at distances more than 25 miles from your commissary, provide your drivers with a list of garages in those areas that can be called on for towing and service.

Features. If you decide to purchase a truck, thought should be given not only to engine capacity but to the size and type of body and its appearance. The body should have a side door and should be *insulated* against adverse and extreme weather conditions.

In extreme cold, foods can freeze during transit. Dishes, glasses, and silver will "sweat" when taken from a cold truck into a warm room, and handling will leave fingermarks. In hot weather, the interior truck temperature is intensified, rapidly increasing the possibility of food spoilage. Unless mandated by law, it may be possible to avoid buying an expensive refrigerated truck, providing you have adequate and modern heat and cold retention equipment (refer to chapter 2).

The size of the truck body depends on the volume of business anticipated. What is the largest party you are equipped for and capable of handling? How many times during the course of a year would you be handling such large parties? It might be advisable to rent a larger truck for these few occasions rather than "drag around" unused and wasted space. The larger the body, the more expensive the initial cost, license fees, and insurance; the more weight, the more motor drag and the more expensive the energy requirements. Longer truck bodies are more difficult to maneuver and access to home driveways could sometimes be impossible. Dual rear wheels, even on the shortest body, are a prime requisite.

Step-in or platform trucks are a personal choice. A step-in has the advantage of accessibility, but more expertise must be used in loading to prevent top-heaviness. In windy conditions, step-ins are more difficult to control.

Trucks must be impeccably clean, both inside and out, at all times and must give a favorable impression. Have a graphic artist design the message you want on the truck and suggest the colors. This is an important one-time investment that can yield gratifying returns if your truck ad is effective. (Many art schools and colleges give courses in graphic design. Contact the department heads about possibly sponsoring a design contest.)

Leasing

Leasing is beneficial because the small down payment required leaves additional cash on hand for other purposes, and maintenance problems are reduced. There are also tax advantages to leasing, but they vary according to the profitability of each business.

There are two basic types of leases—open-end and closed-end. An open-end lease calls for small payments each month, but, at the end of the lease (usually three years) the "balloon payment" for the remaining value of the car or truck is due *all at once*. Also, a maximum mileage stipulation may be part of the lease and if this is exceeded, there is a mileage penalty that costs at least 5 to 7 cents per mile.

Most leasing companies will not contract for less than a two-year period. Termination of this contract can be expensive because repainting, removing dents, and other work must be paid for by you *at the submitted price of the lessor.* Remember, leasing is a purchased service, and the rental concern is in business to make money too.

A closed-end lease requires larger monthly payments but no balloon payment at the end of the contract. The vehicle is returned to the leasing agency, which disposes of it—*probably selling it back to you at a price.* Caveat emptor, let the buyer beware before signing for either of these options.

Renting

If there is a reputable truck rental agency in your area, one that has trucks available on demand, renting trucks as you need them might be a very wise move. In fact, it could be exactly what you need. If you do rent, check costs every few months to determine, from a cost point, whether you should continue to rent or whether you should lease or buy your own vehicle.

There is one very important fact to keep in mind. *Trucks rented or leased for food transportation must be refrigerated and used only for transporting food.* It is illegal, as well as hazardous, to transport food in a rented truck previously used to move household goods or other merchandise.

If using a rented truck, spray its interior with a non-toxic (to humans) insect spray after the completion of each job, but prior to your return. This spray will work while you are in transit to your commissary, and greatly reduce the possibility of transferring roaches and other insects to your facility. All the equipment you used and carried in the truck should be thoroughly washed and sterilized before being covered and placed in storage.

PORTABLE EQUIPMENT

Your operation will often be judged by the type of equipment you use. In view of this, as well as sanitation hazards and your desire to have food arrive at its destination in the best possible condition, you should use the best possible food-carrying equipment.

Many excellent, insulated metal, food-carrying cabinets are on the market today. Some can be hand carried and have drop handles. Larger ones may require either two persons to carry them, or they may be mounted on neoprene wheels; companion dollies can be used for moving and stacking. These square and solidly constructed containers pack beautifully in the delivery truck. Because they are enclosed on all sides, food is well protected from foreign contamination. They will also hold standard sheet and hotel pans

 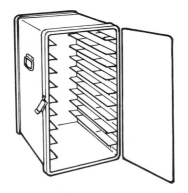

Figure 6.1. Enclosed food carriers with or without dollys. Available insulated and in various sizes.

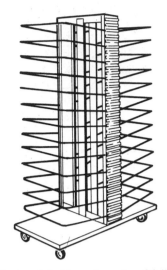

Figure 6.2. Insulated food service or banquet cabinets. Some have built-in heat-and-hold facilities.

Figure 6.3. Butterfly racks of full sheet-pan capacity. Effective for cooling and storing. (Also, an aid in sorting and packing for off-premise presentations.)

securely, assuring that food will arrive at the point of service in good condition.

Corrugated cardboard boxes should be used only in emergencies and *should never be stored or packed on the floor of the truck*. If the truck floor is wet, the bottom of the boxes may fall out when they are lifted, which could cause a loss of merchandise and take extra time for clean-up and repacking. Furthermore, the glued areas of corrugated cardboard boxes can be a haven for roaches.

There are disadvantages to wooden tote or carrying boxes. They retain moisture, have a tendency to mold, are difficult to clean, and may have slivers that can cause injuries to the handler.

Foot lockers, the type available in Army-Navy stores, are excellent carriers of silver trays and other valuable pieces of equipment. They have reinforced corners, and are sheet-steel jacketed and vinyl-covered. However, it would be wise to install a hasp so the locker can be padlocked.

All carrying containers, as well as other equipment, should have your name or some identification conspicuously painted, burned, engraved, or indelibly marked on them.

There are a limited number of manufacturers of institutional utensils and equipment, and the possibility always exists that duplicate ware may be stocked in the facility where you are catering. Therefore, it is *imperative* to properly identify your equipment as soon as you buy it. A good engraving tool is an inexpensive investment. Its use will save you embarrassment and will help your employees identify your equipment when on a job.

When purchasing equipment that may be transported to a job, consider the following:

1. How easy is it to store?
2. Can it be disassembled and stacked without marring?
3. Is it lightweight but rugged? Will it show abuse?
4. Do vulnerable parts protrude in a hazardous manner?
5. Are locking devices easy to use?
6. Are companion dollies available to facilitate handling?

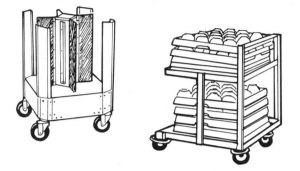

Figure 6.4. Dish dolly dividers can adjust to hold any size of dishes, eliminating back-breaking toting. Enclosed models, or see-through plastic covers are available from the manufacturer.

Portable Coffee Urns

Although some locations at which you will be catering will have coffee urns in their kitchens, you cannot assume they will be adequate for your needs. Therefore, you should plan to have enough portable urns in inventory to provide two (2) cups of coffee for each guest you anticipate serving at any affair.

There are many new, portable coffee urns available today. They not only make good coffee, but are decorative and easy to clean and handle. For catering in private homes, a 30- to 50-cup coffee maker is generally adequate.

Rolling Bars

In making a purchasing decision, scrutinize a rolling bar carefully. How well constructed is it? Does it have ample capacity? Are the legs strong enough and properly anchored? Is the bar transportable? Does it have large wheels? Since most dining areas are carpeted, it is very difficult to push a bar unless the wheels are large.

CHAPTER SEVEN

CONTRACTING FOR CATERED SERVICES

Because of the varied circumstances under which off-premise catering is performed, many factors must be considered in setting your price for an affair. They include:

1. Food
2. Condition and location of the dining/service areas
3. Required equipment
4. Distance from your commissary
5. Labor and overhead costs.

DETERMINING CHARGES

The following suggestions are only a guide, modify them to suit the requirements of your own operation.

Get a minimum number guarantee for guests.

This is a major factor. If guests are few in number, your charges must, of necessity, be much greater. If too few guests are anticipated, it may not pay you to book the party.

Take, as an example, a Sunday dinner at a private home for 20 persons. If there is a $12.50 per person charge for food and service, your gross receipts would be $250 (20 × $12.50). Deducting 33 percent for food costs and 38 percent for payroll costs (a total of $177.50) would leave you with $72.50 to cover costs for transportation, laundry, china, equipment, rent, light, heat, insurance, and other related items. Consider, too, the time spent negotiating for the party, plus the fact that you may have made a few costly phone calls for additional details. As a result, you might well feel that you had wasted a day and worked for practically nothing.

Judge each party on both its gross and net profit. In social catering, do not count on large parties carrying smaller ones. Each affair must be treated separately and each must be profitable.

What will food costs be?

At the time of this writing (1981), accountants specializing in foodservice estimate that a realistic food cost figure for off-premise caterers should not be more than 35 percent. Although restaurants, hotels, and other eating places may safely spend up to 42 percent, the profit spread for social caterers must be greater.

Catering business is sporadic; moreover, the work is much more physically demanding than work in fixed eating areas. Unlike many other foodservice operators, a caterer cannot reuse leftovers for subsequent luncheon or dinner menus.

Determine your labor charges.

Since you are emphasizing service as well as food, you must analyze the personnel requirements of each function. How many employees and how much time will be needed for food preparation? How much time is required for travel? Service? Setup and breakdown?* With all these points to consider, a 38 percent payroll cost is realistic.

Think in terms of distance.

How far is the party location from your commissary? How long will the round trip take?

If using your vehicles for transporting food and equipment, incorporate their per-mile cost into your total charges. To determine a fair charge, check with local car and truck rental agencies for their rates.

Compute charges for your personal services.

Too many caterers forget to charge for their personal services, which can be a costly omission. Skill and ability must be rewarded, and the value of your personal services should be double that of your highest paid employee.

Since *you are the leader* and must organize each part of the event to produce successful results, your true worth would become obvious immediately if you were unable to handle a scheduled affair due to illness or an emergency. Someone else would have to replace you and this

person would, of course, have to be paid. However, if your estimate did not include a charge for your services, then your profit would be reduced substantially.

Set a use charge for dishes, glasses, and other equipment.

Check your packing list for the quantity of dishes, glasses, and other units required for the job and charge for their use. You cannot afford to ignore the costs involved in packing, transporting, washing, storing, and replacing damaged equipment. To figure equipment use charges, contact local rental agencies. Compare quality and cost, and if your dishes and other equipment are of higher quality, your charges should be greater.

Review factors in delivery.

This factor is often overlooked in computing charges. Consider such labor- and time-consuming factors as: a location inconvenient for loading or unloading; inaccessible driveways; and not being able to "dolly" equipment and, instead, having to carry it up and down steps. Since it costs *you* more to set up and break down, these costs must be passed along to your client.

Is there an elevator?

If the party is to be held in an area accessible only by elevator, allow extra time for equipment delivery and return. Elevator space is limited and, if the elevator must be shared with tenants or other freight, the wait between loads can be agonizing and expensive.

When an elevator must be used, notify the building superintendent beforehand to be sure it will be available when you need it. (To express appreciation and thanks for assistance, you may wish to give a gratuity to the superintendent.) To prevent scratching the elevator or damaging your equipment, insist that the elevator be "padded." (Padding simply means that buffer blankets are hung from hooks screwed into the walls near the ceiling of the elevator.)

*Some union contracts stipulate a lower rate for setup and breakdown time and a higher rate for actual service time. When in effect, this contract works on a rotating basis so that all employees have an opportunity to put in extra time on setup and breakdown.

What is the duration of the party?

When guests insist on "hanging around" after a party is over, it generally indicates that the affair was successful. However, these guests can prevent you from cleaning up and removing equipment, as per contract or understanding, which can cut sharply into your profits.

Therefore, prior to the affair, make it clear to the host, either orally or in writing, that you will serve only a specified number of hours. If the host subsequently asks you to remain longer, you must be paid for that time.

A home cocktail party usually lasts from three to four hours. A formal dinner should not last more than four hours, including speeches and entertainment. Considering setup and breakdown time, as well as commissary return time, you and your employees will still spend more than one-third of a day at a party.

In summary, to estimate the cost of a catered meal, it is necessary to determine the costs of the following:

1. Total amount of raw food to be used
2. Personnel required for food preparation service, setup and breakdown, transporting, and clean up. Include a charge for your personal services.
3. Equipment usage
4. Overhead—utilities, rents, insurance, etc.
5. Party service time—mileage, delivery, service
6. Expected profit

To obtain the per-person, per-meal charge, divide this total figure by the number of guests to be served. (See Table 7.1.)

CONTRACTS AND DEPOSITS

Practically every business activity involves a contract—a *binding agreement* between two or more parties. This is also defined as *an agreement creating an obligation.*

In other words, the caterer is obligated to supply the food and service implied or detailed.

The client, on the other hand, is obligated to pay for food, and the specific/implied services, *if satisfactory!* If either party fails to fulfill its obligation, then the other party may have the right to legal recourse.

Each and every job, unless intended as a gift, *must have a contract,* even if it is done for a close friend or relative. You should not be embarrassed to require execution of a contract. You can explain that it is your firm business policy, and that you consider it inadvisable to digress from established procedure.

Furthermore, putting agreements in writing assures smooth and pleasant client relationships. A contract, written in even the faintest ink, is tangible and more readily acceptable than the most indelible memory. (A contract can be simple—see Figure 7.1—or complete and minutely detailed—see Figures 7.2 and 7.3.)

Contracts are also valuable business documents: they can be used as collateral if you wish to borrow money for your business, and are considered tangible assets in the sale of a business.

Under the terms of the contract, customer signing and acceptance requires (1) that the *host make a deposit,* which should be *no less than 25 percent of the anticipated bill,* and (2) that the balance of the bill must be paid upon completion of the affair. The reasons for this are sound. You, the caterer, incur considerable expense in properly completing your part of the contract. You must not only purchase, store, process, and deliver foods, but guarantee to perform a highly specialized service.

MENUS

Development

A caterer's menu should not be a chance offering. It should contain not only the traditional beef and chicken dishes, but also items that reflect your awareness of a changing world and its food preferences. These preferences may be fads, legitimate consumer movements to promote

Table 7.1. Factors in Determining Charges

CATERING INCOME		100 percent
DIRECT COSTS		
Food and supplies	26 percent	
Payroll	38 percent	
Payroll taxes	—	
Purchased services	6.2 percent	
TOTAL DIRECT COSTS		−70.2 percent
GROSS PROFIT		29.8 percent
OPERATING EXPENSES		
Advertising and promotion		
Auto and delivery expenses		
Bank charges		
Contributions		
Depreciation: auto and trucks		
Depreciation: furniture and fixtures		
Freight and express		
Gas		
Water		
Insurance		
Laundry and cleaning		
Light and heat		
Maintenance and repairs		
Permits, licenses, and fees		
Professional services: accountant, lawyer		
Refuse removal		
Rent		
Equipment rental		
Replacement of china, silver, etcetera		
Stationery and office supplies		
Taxes: property, state, and business		
Telephone		
Miscellaneous		
TOTAL OPERATING EXPENSES		−15 percent
NET INCOME		14.8 percent

SUMMATION:

Catering income	100 percent	
Minus direct costs	−70.2 percent	
Gross profit		29.8 percent
Operating expenses		−15 percent
NET PROFIT		14.8 percent

JOHN DOE CATERING COMPANY
45 Spring Street
Hyde Park, New York 12538
Phone: (914) 452-9600

CONTRACT

THIS AGREEMENT, made and entered into this _____ day of

_____ 19 _____ , by and between JOHN DOE, doing business

as the JOHN DOE CATERING CO. (hereinafter called "Caterer"), and

_____ of _____ , _____

(hereinafter called "Purchaser").   city   state

WITNESSETH

In consideration of this Agreement, the parties hereto agree as follows:

1) The Caterer agrees to cater an affair according to menus submitted

and mutually agreed upon on the day and date of _____ 19 _____

at _____ commencing at _____ A.M. _____ P.M.
              place
2) The Purchaser agrees to pay the sum of $ _____ per each

guest guaranteed. Guarantee for number of guests to be confirmed in

writing by the Purchaser at least five (5) days before the affair.

(Caterer will not accept guarantees for less than 100 guests.)

3) The Caterer will be prepared to serve 5 percent (5%) more

guests should the occasion warrant.

4) The Caterer acknowledges receipt of a deposit of $ _____

and the Purchaser agrees to pay the balance upon presentation of bill,

immediately upon the completion of service. Adjustments, if any,

either by the Purchaser or the Caterer will be fully made by either

party within 72 hours.

John Doe, for John Doe Catering Co. _____

Purchaser _____

Purchaser _____

Figure 7.1. Sample Contract

Figure 7.2. Sample Contract

CONTRACT
JOHN DOE CATERING COMPANY
Poughkeepsie, New York 12538

Banquet or Party Function Contract   Date: _____ , 19 _____

AGREEMENT between JOHN DOE CATERING CO., hereinafter called Caterer, and _____

_____ , hereinafter called Patron.

Full Name of Patron _____ Phone Number _____

          address _____ city _____ state _____ zip code _____

If club or organization, give name: _____

Principal address: _____

          Club president's name _____ Club treasurer's name _____

          address _____ address _____

          Committee representatives: Names/addresses

          name _____ _____ address _____

          name _____ address _____

          name _____ address _____

Guarantor: _____ Address: _____

Date of Function: _____ Hours: from _____ to _____

Area of Function _____

Minimum number of guests guaranteed _____ Price per guest _____

Extra charges as attached . . . . $_____

Anticipated total bill . . . . $_____

    1.) IT IS FURTHER AGREED as a condition precedent of the agreement that the patron will pay 25 percent (25%) of anticipated total bill as computed above upon acceptance of this contract.

    2.) All details of the Menu are set forth in letter dated _____ and attached extra charges which are made part hereof.

    3.) Patron agrees to inform Caterer at least 48 hours in advance, in writing, as to definite number guaranteed. Caterer will be prepared to serve 5 percent (5%) increase above guarantee.

    4.) This contract is subject to the terms and conditions printed on reverse side hereof and expressly made a part hereof.

Signature _____ Signature _____

Witness _____ Witness _____

REVERSE SIDE OF CONTRACT

1.) All federal, state, and municipal taxes applicable to this function shall be paid for separately by the patron, in addition to prices herein agreed upon.

2.) The caterer will exercise all reasonable care in security of liquor supplied by patron and will furnish bartenders to dispense such liquor. However, the patron will not hold caterer liable if theft, breakage, or vandalism should occur—or any other acts beyond reasonable care by caterer.

3.) Should affair be held in a facility with a liquor license held by the rentor, then all security and/or liquor service shall in no way involve the caterer.

4.) Patron agrees to begin function promptly at the scheduled time and to vacate premises at the closing hour indicated. The patron further agrees to reimburse the caterer for overtime wage payments or other expenses incurred by the caterer because of patron's failure to comply with these regulations.

5.) Patron assumes responsibility for any and all damages caused by any guest, invitee, or other person attending the function.

6.) It is understood that patron will conduct function in an orderly manner and in full compliance with all applicable laws, ordinances, and regulations (and any special requirements of rentor if set forth in contract).

7.) Patron agrees to reimburse the caterer for any extra meals requested for orchestra, entertainers, security, etc.

8.) Patron agrees to supply caterer with a tentative floor plan at least one week prior to the affair and a definite floor (and seating) plan no later than 48 hours before affair.

9.) In the event of breach of this agreement by patron, the caterer may keep the deposit and patron shall be obliged to reimburse caterer for any damage costs incurred by reason of breach thereof.

10.) This agreement is contingent upon the absence of strikes, labor disputes, accidents, or any causes beyond control. The caterer also reserves the right to make reasonable substitutions if unable to secure specified items... but will make substitutions upon explanation and notification to patron.

11.) This agreement is not assignable.

---

healthful foods, or special diets; they may enjoy short lives or they may become standards.

Eating trends are determined by studying present and past records that give accurate information on the popular and unpopular, the profitable and nonprofitable. Unit item records should be kept on the current menu, from appetizers to desserts, and the slow and/or non-sellers should be eliminated and other items substituted.

When introducing or listing a new dish, give it a chance. Favorable reaction could take months to develop.

If you offer an ethnic menu, it would be unwise to list only the foods of that group. Be aware that the client or guests are probably third, fourth, or fifth generation Americans. Their tastes have been weaned away from the foods enjoyed by their grandparents. True, some foods are traditional and necessary for ritual, and must be maintained; some foods should be offered for their nostalgic value. But if the caterer knows that certain foods are rejected, he should so inform the client who has requested them. If the client insists, satisfy him but prepare a small quantity. (Rejections should never be brought to the client's attention with an "I told you so" attitude.)

Promotion

People who are looking for quality and taste often rely on establishments that have a reputation for those characteristics. Your offerings, including such standards as chicken and roast beef, should be presented in such a way that the client cannot help but see the favorable difference. You should try to establish an identity and an image in your locale of offering the best for the price, the most artistic presentation, and the best tasting food. Make every effort to be consistent in quality, and to be dependable and honest in carrying out a client's wishes. If the affair has to be turned over

Figure 7.3. On-Premise Catering Contract

FUNCTION AGREEMENT FOR JOHN DOE CATERERS
Anystreet, Anywhere, U.S.A.
(This contract must be signed and accepted to guarantee function.)

Name of Company or Function _____

Address _____ City _____ Phone _____

Individual guaranteeing payment _____

Address _____ City _____ Phone _____

Tentative number of guests guaranteed _____

Room or facility or area for function _____

Day _____ Date _____ Time _____

Menu number _____

Extras, specify, and price for each _____

_____

_____

(   ) Cash bar _____ (   ) Open bar _____ (   ) Bottle price _____

Time _____

Cake price $ _____ Orchestra $ _____ Flowers $ _____

To be paid by: _____ (   ) Check _____ (   ) Cash _____ (   ) Certified check _____

Accepted by: (For John Doe Caterers) _____

Customer's signature _____

TERMS AND CONDITIONS (Please read carefully)

1.) A minimum deposit of $1.00 per person must be made—for each person.
2.) Guaranteed number to be served must be submitted within three days of function. (CHARGE WILL BE MADE EVEN IF LESS ATTEND.)
3.) ALL TAXES AND GRATUITIES MUST BE ADDED TO ALL PRICES QUOTED.
4.) Guaranteed number must be paid in full 3 days before affair.
5.) Contract must be signed and accepted to guarantee reservation. CREDIT CARDS ARE NOT ACCEPTABLE.
6.) Card-playing, gambling, or showing of objectionable films PROHIBITED.
7.) Guests attending function but not eating will be charged $1.00 each.
8.) Function running beyond specified time will be charged extra $1.00/guest.
9.) In the event of prohibitive weather, occurring within 24 hours of affair, you have the choice of:
   a.) Holding the affair and paying only for the food and liquor consumed by attending guests plus the miscellaneous items on the guaranteed minimum. (Examples: Flowers, linens, gratuities, service fees, music, check room, cake, printing, etc.)
   b.) Postponing the affair to a confirmed date within thirty (30) days, thereby incurring no additional costs.

to a subordinate, assure the client that the affair will receive the same meticulous attention that you would have given it.

Whether you meet at the client's premises or your own office, be fully prepared with appropriate types of menus that will interest your client. Have pictures or slides, even letters of appreciation, and have samples of your dishware, linens, glassware, and other service equipment.

For many clients that you interview, this could be their first experience in negotiating for a catered affair, and they may be naive regarding procedures. *Do not overwhelm them with a recital of unfamiliar menu terms or trade technology.* Try to put the client at ease immediately by patiently explaining the procedures necessary in this type of transaction. If you have preprinted menus, present them. Also, provide a fresh legal-size pad and sharp pencil so the client can make notes. Then proceed with your pertinent questions (refer to the Master Checklist later in this chapter.)

If you are an on-premise caterer, it might be opportune to show your facilities that will be required for the function (bar area, dining area, etcetera). Potential clients might even be invited to view this area when it is set up before a function—*never during a function,* as you will not be able to give them your undivided attention. Furthermore, you may be obviously anxious and the motion of personnel and guests could distract and overwhelm the client, who should be shielded from the mechanics.

If any of the menu items have a foreign name or are not self-explanatory, take the time to describe the dish and state whether you think it is appropriate to serve. After you have explained the menu, go into the ancillary services that may be required, such as, table decorations, special lighting, printed menus, or souvenirs. Explain the special services and charges for the orchestra, florist, photographer, and cloakroom attendant. Note any gratuities or other charges that are consistent with carrying out the activities.

At this point, issue the client a copy of your contract. Read each article to him and explain each item as to its fairness and equitability. Some of these interviews may tax your patience, but your annoyance must never be obvious. In dealing with committees, try to keep the group to a maximum of three; the larger the committee, the longer it may take to make decisions. With three persons, a majority decision is arrived at more quickly.

Salesmanship may be necessary in certain instances but within limitations. The high pressure approach of selling more than is reasonable—even when the client is willing to pay—can result in ostentatiousness and garishness. It can reflect unfavorably on your establishment or services. You are obligated to advise a client if you believe he is exceeding the boundaries of good taste and dignity essential to the proper conduct of any affair.

SCHEDULING A FUNCTION

Multi-unit or large volume catering firms have standardized forms for banquet estimates and contracts. When the contract is signed, copies are sent to all departments involved. Each department head then proceeds to fulfill his responsibilities, under the supervision of the catering manager.

A lesser volume or small operator has to assume many or all of the responsibilities. He may have to schedule or sell the affair, order all necessary supplies, and schedule the food production by the chef, whom he may also have to help. He frequently has to assume the head waiter's duties in the dining room.

Printed forms adapted to a caterer's specific needs will aid greatly in recording the details and in expediting the function (see Table 7.2). A packing list must be filled out regardless of whether the party is on or off premises, and a house check made to see that all equipment is available and in good condition.

The caterer should make a journal entry for each item ordered, or to be ordered, for each affair, and each item should be checked off when ordered. This system provides you with: (1) a

Table 7.2. Master Checklist for Catering (On and Off Premise)

1. Contact person in charge of party
2. Address and phone
3. Type of function
4. Date of function
5. Time of function
6. Name of room assigned
7. Number of persons
8. Minimum guarantee
9. Serving time
10. Contract signed
11. Bill made up
12. Cocktail reception
13. Dinner
14. Buffet
15. Dancing/band/entertainment
16. Head table/mike/lectern (podium if no head table)
17. Seating plan (floor plan)
18. Guest list/place cards
19. Ticket collection
20. Gratuities (included—not included)
21. Menu completed
22. Completed work "orders" and
23. Work "scheduled" to:

    a. Chef and kitchen crew
    b. Head waiter, captain and waiters—
       wine waiters—busboys
    c. Head bartender—bartenders—bar boys
    d. Food and beverage manager
    e. Steward
    f. Baker
    g. Butcher

    h. Housemen and porters
    i. Housekeeper
    j. Engineer
    k. Projectionist
    l. Electrician
    m. Parking lot attendants, drivers
    n. Mens and ladies room attendants
    o. Cloakroom attendants

24. Purchases—menu analyzed—broken down and ordered to purveyors and checked on arrival
25. Rentals—for extra equipment needed
26. Decorations—banners, flags, signs
27. Check if food and beverage ready to serve
28. Check if equipment ready
29. Check if rooms ready:

    a. Function room
    b. Reception room
    c. Meeting room
    d. Chapel
    e. VIP room

    f. Checkroom
    g. Dressing room
    h. Bridal room
    i. Suites
    j. Mens and ladies lounge

30. Directional signs
31. Draped tables for:

    a. Prizes/gifts (head table, bridal/cake table)
    b. Tickets/sign in
    c. Place cards

32. Printed tickets (liquor, checking, parking, dinner, raffle)
33. Direction cards

34. Stationary bars
35. Portable bars
36. Raffle drums
37. Parking and checking arrangements

OUTSIDE

38. Tents
39. Dance floors
40. Kitchen or preparation area
41. Stoves
42. Pantry area
43. Lavatory facilities or porto sans (outside bathrooms)
44. Dressing room for help
45. Storage area for equipment and supplies
46. Electrical outlets and hookup
47. Service area for trucks
48. Tables/work tables/cake tables
49. Chairs and tables
50. Catering equipment—visualize entire affair and make a packing checklist for entire affair (chinaware, silverware, pots, pans, linens, plus all equipment needed)
51. Entertainment (band with bandstand), platform
52. Sanitation (dumpster/waste containers, compactor, mops, brooms, soap, dust pan, pails, wringer, shovel, large plastic bags, work gloves)
53. Washing area
54. Air conditioning
55. Heating
56. Plate warmers
57. Plate chillers (ice)
58. First aid kit
59. Can and bottle openers
60. Coat racks, umbrellas, change and bills (tolls), petty cash
61. Ancillary services:
    a. flowers and accessories (fern, smilax leaves)
    b. photographer
    c. special lighting
    d. police (protection, security, traffic direction)
    e. audiovisual and sound equipment
    f. novelties
    g. souvenirs
    h. cake boxes
    i. limo
62. Printing:
    a. menus
    b. matches
    c. stirrers
    d. place cards
    e. directionals
    f. seating cards
    g. tickets
63. Make up schedule of events

record of items ordered so that they can be costed out; and (2) visual evidence that the items have or have not been ordered. This also prevents slip-ups or double ordering. *Do not depend on your memory to retain all this information.*

As food represents the largest dollar volume outlay, the purchase and control of raw or finished food must be on an exact per-need basis. This can be accomplished effectively by referring to the recipe file, which should be a priority source in determining quantities needed. Following recipes closely guarantees uniformity and is a most important component of quality control.

THE COMPOSITION OF A BANQUET

As acknowledged by the hospitality industry, a banquet is: (1) a feast, or (2) a category of a feast, or (3) a ceremonial meal, (4) with predetermined courses, (5) involving a specified number of guests, (6) at a specified place and time, (7) for a mutually established and accepted price.

1. A banquet is a feast—an elaborate meal, something that gives one unusual or abundant pleasure.
2. A category of a feast—a lesser degree of elaborateness dictated by occasion or financial limitations.
3. A ceremonial meal—integrating formal or conventional ceremonies as practiced by church, state, or tradition. Formalities include: introducing the bride, groom, and families at wedding meals; patriotic renderings; and grand entrances. Ritual invocations, special prayers, acknowledgments, and entertainment are often integral parts of each point of service.
4. Predetermined courses—all diners are to be served the same food. This helps with purchases, preparation, and control of food and related items. (Exceptions are guests whose food intake is restricted because of health or

religious reasons. Arrangements for such guests are made in advance, either by the host or by a committee.)
5. Involving a specific amount of guests—this determines the necessary physical space, personnel, and equipment required for each department involved. (Floor plans are discussed in later pages.)
6. At a specified place and time—this aspect is necessary in preparing the dining area chosen (for establishments having multiple dining rooms) and scheduling the proper personnel. This minimizes the possibilities of help "hanging around" or being rushed so that the proper attention cannot be given to details, or incurring overtime charges due to poor scheduling. (Some union contracts specify lower fees for setup and breakdown time than for actual service.)
7. For a mutually established and accepted price—price is determined beforehand and all details relative to agreed-upon surcharges because of ambience, type of food, and service are fully negotiated. Civic and charitable organizations are sometimes given special rates. WARNING—when giving special rates, *never* reduce portion sizes or lower the quality of food or service.

Basic Banquet Menu Construction

There are innumerable banquet presentation possibilities and various sequences. Deviations from the normal presentation and increases in the number of courses can add considerably to your profit picture. The standard dinner consists of four courses, called The Basic Four.

1. Starter Course—fruit, seafood, soup, small antipasto, etcetera
2. Main Course or entree—meat, fish, poultry, filled crepes, or even a substantial salad (with accompanying vegetables)
3. Dessert—cake, pie, ice cream, etcetera
4. Beverage—coffee, tea, milk, etcetera

Adjunct Courses

Basic Cocktail Reception. This normally precedes the meal by at least a half hour. Seating is restricted to chairs in strategic areas. The reception can consist of prepoured cocktails, such as, Manhattans, Martinis, Whiskey Sours, or an appropriate white wine, and an assortment of "finger-nibbles," such as, potato chips, peanuts, pretzels, bacon crisps, cheese cubes, etcetera. This type of service eliminates the additional charge for a professional bartender. It may require one server in the beverage area to keep the area clean and to handle refills. Another server may be assigned to the food area with similar duties.

In addition to the "nibbles," hot or cold hors d'oeuvre offered by a server from a (silver) tray, as a butler would do—hence the term *butler style*. Charges are computed on the cost of food and service involved.

Partial or Mini-Reception Also Preceding Dinner.

This reception involves a greater variety of finger and fork foods, dips, and at least one hot chafing dish item requiring the use of forks and dishes. Additional hors d'oeuvre may be passed butler style. The tables for displaying and serving the foods should be covered with good linens and display showpieces of ice, tallow, or butter. This kind of reception generally lasts about an hour. When computing the charges for this reception, take into consideration (besides the cost of food) the additional time required to set up the tables, extra personnel, linens, display pieces, dishwashing costs, fuel costs, and use-charges.* Charge for

---

*Use-charges are additional charges made for other than normal items that require special handling and preparation. Chafing dishes must be polished and cleaned after each use and they must be kept in good repair. Another example are candelabra with two, three, or five prongs. They are beautiful to look at but extreme care must be taken in handling. Repairs are expensive and replacements even more so. Extra charges must always be made for expensive flatware, crystal, and china.

personal services and take a generous markup on all items, as this falls into the category of a "production."

Full Reception. This type is generally served at lavish weddings, expensive fund-raising events, and VIP honorings. Buffet tables are set with expensive linens, a profusion of display showpieces, a wide diversity of expensive foods, plus four or more chafing dish items. In addition, one to three chefs are present to carve and slice hams, beef, turkey, pastrami, and smoked salmon or sturgeon, or to cook and serve filled crepes, omelets, and varied hot quiches. (This is called exhibition cooking.) Note that foods used for a reception must not be sweet—they should be salty, spicy, and drink inducing. There should be a complete bar setup, with an expensive inventory of appropriate liquor, attended by a ratio of at least one bartender to 40 guests. Small cocktail tables seating four should be placed in all available areas for the convenience of the guests. A reception of this type should last approximately an hour and a quarter; it is the time in which guests do their greatest amount of socializing. Once the guests are seated for dinner, the opportunities to visit with friends or relatives are curtailed.

Charges for this type of reception, which precedes the actual dinner, can be as much, and even more than, the charge for the basic dinner itself. Each component of this grand reception, including your planning time, use-charges for equipment, extra costs for expensive and unusual foods, extra costs for personnel engaged in carving or cooking at the buffet tables, must be taken into consideration when estimating charges. You must realize that when you borrow skilled kitchen help for the buffet presentation, you could be depleting the kitchen crew and jeopardizing the production of the dinner. Therefore, your kitchen crew must be augmented, at least for the time of the reception.

Liquor   Arrangements. The   method and charges for serving liquor quite often depend on the type of license you hold. If your facility holds no license, then your client may bring in liquor (if the law so permits). You supply the area of service, the bartender, all glassware, ice, and soft drinks necessary, and you charge what is known as *corkage.* The host either pays a flat rate for the entire affair, or the charge is set at so much per guest. You can charge extra for the services of the bartender(s), or include this price in corkage charges.

If your premises are licensed, then you have the following options:

1. A public cash or pay bar where guests purchase their own liquor and pay for their drinks individually
2. A limited bar where each guest is allowed a certain number of free drinks upon presentation of a tab or ticket for each drink (tickets furnished by the host to the guests)
3. An unlimited bar where guests may drink at no charge. Payment is made by the host at a flat rate per guest. A flat rate is the best arrangement for both host and licensee as it eliminates the possibility of "padding." In any case, there should be an understanding as to whether the liquor will be standard or premium quality.

Supplementing the Basic Four

Starter Course. This course is enhanced by the use of crystal glasses or silver coupes. Juices and fruit cocktail may be surrounded by crushed and/or colored ice and decorated with a fresh flower. For a wedding dinner, you could use a large, fluffy, white ribbon bow or little gold-colored wedding bells. Affairs of state could have appropriate tiny silk flags. The possibilities are limited only by your imagination and resourcefulness.

Mini Course or First Entree. This course would follow the starter course. It might be a small portion of seafood en pattie or cocotte, a small roulade of sole, ravioli with sauce, beef tidbits in burgundy, or any other food not in the same category as the main course.

Salad or Soup. It is now proper to serve a salad or soup following the mini course or first entree, if the client so desires.

Intermezzo. At this point in a banquet, a most impressive dish can be offered. It is called *Intermezzo* and, as the term implies, it offers an intermission—a pause before the main course. This is the time to cool and prepare the palate for the fine food to follow by serving a dish of water ices, slightly granular in texture and slightly tart in flavor (lemon, raspberry, etcetera). The ices are topped with a generous dollop of green creme de menthe. Many gourmets insist on this service when making their own arrangements. If handled properly, this course adds a weighty percentage to your profit picture. Intermezzo SHOULD NEVER BE SERVED FOLLOWING THE STARTER COURSE. It must be preceded by at least two courses.

Main Course. If the food for the main dish is preplated in the kitchen, the service is called *American service.* It is a quick method but it lacks a certain elegance, which some people desire and are willing to pay for. That extra touch, which requires really skilled help, can be achieved with the following types of service.

1. French Service—Attendants serve each guest from a gueridon (a rolling wagon) which may have a Rechaud burner (a little stove used to keep foods hot). The attendants display a great deal of personal flair in each aspect of the service. Each guest is made to feel that this show is just for him or her. The attendants must know the anatomical construction of seafood, meat, and poultry in case tableside filleting or carving is required. Attendants must use the proper tools in a skillful manner. Persons with these skills must be compensated accordingly.

2. Russian Service—Waiters serve the food to guests from hand-held and artfully decorated trays. The trays may contain the main entree plus the appropriate garniture, or another waiter may follow with the garniture of vegetables, etcetera. It is not uncommon to find waiters serving this type of meal wearing white cotton gloves. Russian service requires a great deal of skill and dexterity on the part of the waiter; one hand holds the tray while the other hand is used for serving. (Never employ an inexperienced or clumsy server for this type of service as guests may be injured by hot liquids or tipped trays.)

3. Flaming Service—Foods are flamed with the use of warmed brandy or trademarked liquids made especially for this purpose. Flamed foods can be served as main courses or as desserts. This procedure must also be handled skillfully and carefully. When prepared properly, it is a thrilling sight and worth the extra charges entailed. WARNING: FLAMING SERVICE SHOULD NEVER BE ATTEMPTED IN LOW CEILING AREAS—flames and smoke could activate the sprinkler system. Your insurance agent should be notified that you may use this type of presentation on occasion, and coverage for possible related accidents should be provided.

Bread Station or Bread Cart. One way of elevating the meal presentation is to have a bread station(s) in a conspicuous area of the dining room. This is a fixed and decorated table offering a variety of breads (guests slice their own), rolls, and crackers. Guests often enjoy choosing their own breads and rolls. A bread wagon may also be rolled tableside.

Relish Station or Relish Wagon. A variety of relishes may be offered in the same manner as the breads.

Cheese and Fruit Presentation. A popular and profitable course for a supplemental dessert (or as THE dessert) are individual trays containing a variety of cheeses, fruits, and nuts for each table. A gueridon cheese service is also effective but much slower to dispense. It might require a number of gueridons and additional waiters, which could increase labor costs considerably.

Viennese Dessert Table. It requires superlative adjectives like dazzling, overpowering, overwhelming, and awe-inspiring to properly describe a real Viennese dessert table. A Viennese table is a magnificently decorated table(s) often containing as many as 50 different varieties of desserts! Some examples are petite French and Danish pastries, layer cakes, pies, gelatin molds, ice cream with a variety of sauces, Strawberries Romanoff, Crepes Suzettes, Baked Alaska, Cherries Jubilee, watermelon balls, cantaloupe slices, simmered pears in chocolate sauce, petits fours, and cookies. The table is filled with carvings of ice, butter, sugar, and wax. The food is displayed on silver stands and in compotes of various heights. The cherries used for the Jubilee are contained in chafers and constantly flamed; concealed blocks of dry ice are set in water baths to produce clouds of vapor. These exquisitely draped tables must remain out of sight during the meal—they may be kept behind screens or wheeled in for presentation. Tables that are integral parts of the presentation can be so arranged to "break away"—they can then be rolled over to individual guest tables. At the moment of presentation, these tables should be brilliantly spotlighted and the rest of the room temporarily darkened. The orchestra can be called on for a trumpet fanfare and a roll of drums. When the excitement diminishes, an announcement should be made by either the maitre d' or the orchestra leader inviting guests to go to the Viennese table, when notified, to select their own desserts. This will eliminate long lines and result in proper crowd control. There should be sufficient attendants behind the table to assist the guests.

All pastries presented should be smaller than usual, and all cakes and pies should yield at least

50 percent more per unit. You should estimate that each guest will take at least three units. The cost of producing this extravaganza often runs into double figures per guest. It takes a tremendous amount of planning and preparation. It is time consuming to set up each tray in a beautiful manner. Some showpieces can only be prepared and finished off at the last moment.

Storage up to the time of service can also be a problem. The help required to set up the table in an artistic manner requires premium compensation. Your charge should include a most liberal markup for each item you have produced or purchased. Fragile pieces of ice, sugar, or butter should be charged for at a rate at least three times your cost to compensate for possible breakage or replacement. You personally should be liberally reimbursed as the architect for the project.

Beverages. The coffee served at the end of a banquet should be brewed a little stronger. There is little opportunity to sell additional foods or services at this point, but some additional revenue may be gained by selling coffee laced with brandy and orange peel or Irish coffee. It could provide a gracious final touch.

After Dinner Brandies. An effective finale can be offered at this point with the service of brandy. A European touch is the service of brandy in chocolate cups instead of glass ponies. The guests may sip their brandy and then eat the chocolate container. This type of cup is available from fine restaurant supply companies.

CANCELLATIONS

Pre-printed contract forms with blank spaces for firm name, date, and terms are available from hotel stationery supply firms. However, some caterers prefer to print their own forms and insert specific stipulations. They may state that cancellations for whatever reasons (such as illness, broken engagement, or death) will permit the caterer to

retain the deposit plus penalty payments for "damages." *The contract must conspicuously disclose the cancellation fee and it must be reasonable!* (See Figure 7.4.)

If the caterer is brought to court, the item of "damages" must be thoroughly detailed on the contract and fully substantiated by the caterer in order to be collectible. In New York State, judges are empowered *not to enforce* contracts that are unconscionable and one-sided. (Section 2-302 of the States' Uniform Consumer Code.) In one court case, a cancellation occurred four months before the scheduled date and the caterer refused to return the deposit. The caterer could not prove an actual loss and his claim was refused. The presiding judge ruled that "Failure to re-let the premises is just another business hazard to be faced in the type of business the caterer conducts." (Excerpted from an article in *New York* magazine [July 23, 1979] entitled "Legal Aid for Cancelled Parties.")

Cancellation of a party within weeks of the scheduled date can justify a caterer's demand for total compensation as he will have already made costly arrangements and scheduled employees. He will be obligated to pay employees' salaries and benefits even though they will not work. It would be highly unusual for him to re-let the premises at such short notice.

Cancellations have occurred because of tragedy involving the principals. If time and other considerations favor the caterer, then he has every legal right to be compensated for his loss. But there is a moral issue involved! Allow a reasonable length of time to elapse and if family, survivors, attorney, or executor have not taken the initiative, then the caterer should try to arrange a meeting so that an equitable settlement can be negotiated. Such a meeting can result in goodwill of inestimable value—even if it results in a financial loss to the caterer.

One of the axioms of the catering business is that the success and longevity of each establishment is determined by the amount of goodwill associated with that company. Reputation has

DEPARTMENT OF CONSUMER AFFAIRS

CODE OF CONSUMER PROTECTION LAW REGULATIONS

REGULATION 518.   CATERING CONTRACTS

(a) *Definition.* "Caterer" means any person or business engaged in serving food or beverages for private functions in New York City.

(b) *Cancellation.*

(1) If a consumer cancels a catering contract and the caterer can re-book the date, the caterer's cancellation fee may not exceed 5 percent of the total contract price or $100, whichever is less, plus actual expenses reasonably incurred.

(2) If a consumer cancels a catering contract and the caterer cannot re-book the date, the caterer's cancellation fee may not exceed the difference between the total contract price and the cost of performance, plus actual expenses reasonably incurred. The caterer must be able to show diligent efforts to re-book and must fairly calculate the cost of performance.

(3) It will be presumed that a caterer who receives notice of cancellation six months or more before the scheduled date of the function will be able to re-book.

(4) Cancellation occurs:

(A) when the customer mails the caterer a notice of intent to cancel; or

(B) when the caterer has actual notice of the consumer's intent to cancel.

(c) *Refunds.* As soon as reasonably practicable after cancellation (and never later than 30 days after re-booking) the caterer must return to the consumer any sum received which exceeds the permissible cancellation fee.

(d) *Contract Forms.* Contract forms must conspicuously disclose the caterer's cancellation fee.

(e) *Delegation of Performance.* A caterer may not delegate performance of any contract to another caterer without the consumer's consent. This consent may be obtained only after the caterer advises the consumer of its inability to perform under the contract.

Effective: October 30, 1980.

Figure 7.4.

concrete dollar value and can be traded as a commodity; it is often of greater intrinsic value than the physical assets.

An act of God such as flood, blizzard, hurricane, tornado, catastrophic fire caused by lightning, or volcanic eruption can often relieve either the client or the caterer (or both), from any legal responsibility. (If the caterer is covered by Business Interruption Insurance, his loss will be minimal or none at all.)

SAMPLE FORMS

Figure 7.5. Suggested Snow
Clause for Off-Premise Caterers

A.   In the event of such unusual weather conditions that local or state police agencies prohibit travel or public transportation of any kind, then the patron will be relieved of payment for guaranteed number of guests. Patron, however, is obligated to pay for any dated printed matter or such perishable items that have been specifically ordered for the affair (flowers, highly perishable fruit or berries, etcetera).

B.   If travel is possible and only travel warnings issued, and affair is delayed for no more than one and one-half (1½) hours, then THERE WILL BE NO OVERTIME PENALTY.

C.   If guaranteed number of guests do not arrive then the caterer will only hold patron responsible for half of the difference between arrived guests and guaranteed number. Full payment must be made for printed dated items and/or flowers or items specifically ordered for this affair.

D.   Caterer will freezer-pack for patron (upon caterer's return to commissary and at his discretion) such food items that will not have deteriorated and that would have been served to guests paid for but who did not arrive.

Figure 7.6.

	Month	Year

BOOKING REQUEST FORM

☐ DEFINITE   Copies ☐ File — White

☐ TENTATIVE/HOLD TILL _____   ☐ F.O. MGR. — Pink

                                              ☐ Sales Dir. — Blue

   BOOKED BY _____   DATE _____

NAME OF GROUP _____

CONTACTS NAME _____ TEL. NO. _____

ADDRESS _____

CITY _____ STATE _____ ZIP _____

Figure 7.6. (continued)

Day of Week	Date	Type Function	Start	Close	Room	Attendance	Rent
							$

REMARKS _____

_____

SLEEPING ROOMS   BLOCK OF _____ (TOTAL)

Arrival: Day _____ Date _____   _____ Singles @ $ _____

Depart: Day _____ Date _____   _____ Twins @ $ _____

                                                _____ Suites @ $ _____

REMARKS _____

                        RECAP: Room Nites _____

            Food Covers: Breakfast _____

                           Lunch _____

Entered by _____   Dinner _____

Date _____   RENTALS $ _____

Figure 7.7.

ESTIMATE

Contact's Name: _____
Name of Organization

_____

Address _____
City _____ State _____ Zip _____

Tel. No. _____

FUNCTION: TIME: ROOM:

DATE OF FUNCTION: _____ _____ _____

NO. OF PERSONS _____ _____ _____ _____

_____ _____ _____

_____ _____ _____

_____ COCKTAIL HOUR PKG. PLANS _____ @ (T) $ _____ $ _____

_____ DINNER PKG. PLANS _____ @ (T) $ _____ $ _____

_____ EXTRAS: _____ *@ (T) $ _____ $ _____

_____ _____ *@ (T) $ _____ $ _____

_____ 17% GRATUITIES ON EXTRA (ITEMS ONLY) * $ _____ $ _____

_____ COATROOM CHECKING @ (T) $ _____ $ _____

_____ LOUNGE ATTENDANTS @ $ _____ $ _____

_____ PIECE BAND FOR FOUR HRS. @ $ _____

_____ PIECE BAND CEREMONY/RECEPTION @ $ _____

_____ FLORAL AISLE BASKETS FOR CEREMONY @ (T) $ _____ $ _____

_____ FLORAL CANOPY FOR CEREMONY (T) $ _____

_____ _____ @ (T) $ _____ $ _____

_____ _____ @ $ _____ $ _____

_____ _____ @ $ _____ $ _____

_____ _____ @ $ _____ $ _____

8% State Tax (on Taxable items only) (T) $ _____
=============

MUSIC BY: EDDIE LANE   DON JOSEPH   TOTAL $ _____
            PL3-5800   352-0174

FLOWERS BY: AVENUE J FLORIST
               ES7-2002   _____

ESTIMATE BY

Figure 7.8.

BANQUET CONTRACT

Nature of Function: _____

Name of Room: _____

Day & Date: _____ Time: From _____ To _____

Name of Organization _____

Address _____

Name of Representative _____

Address _____

Telephone: Home _____ Business _____

No. Expected _____ No. Prepared for _____ No. Guaranteed _____

Cocktail Hour: From _____ To _____ Room _____	
— FOOD —	— LIQUOR —
Type of Service: _____	Type of Service: _____
	Bartender Charge: _____
Price (per person) $ _____	Price (per person) $ _____
Menu: Service Time: _____	— WINES/LIQUORS/BEVERAGES —
Type of Service: _____	Type of Service: _____
Price (per person) $ _____	Price (per person) $ _____

(continued)

Figure 7.8. (continued)

Linen _____ Napkins _____ Lace _____ Candles _____

Flowers _____

Cake _____ Filling _____

Vienesse Table _____

Room Rental _____

Music _____ Pieces For _____ Hrs.: From _____ To _____ Name _____ Price $_____

Show _____ Price $_____

Photographer _____ Price $_____

Checkroom _____ Lounges _____

Parking _____ Security _____

Cigars/Cigarettes _____ Mints/Nuts _____

Ice Carving _____

Special Uniforms _____

Special Decorations _____

Carpeting _____

Corkage _____

Overtime Charges _____

Gratuities (Incl./Not Incl.) _____

State and City Tax _____

Remarks _____

_____

_____

(Reverse Side) _____

Copies to:

____ HOSPITALITY OFFICE   ____ PUBLIC RELATIONS

____ BLDG/MAINTENANCE   ____ BANQUET KITCHEN   ____ RECEPTIONIST

____ SANITATION   ____ CATERING DEPARTMENT   ____ INSTRUCTIONAL MEDIA DEPARTMENT

____ STOREROOM   ____ BAKING DEPARTMENT

____ COOKING DEPARTMENT   ____ CONTROLLER   ____ BUFFET CATERING DEPARTMENT

____ SECURITY   ____ F&BS DEPARTMENT   ____ PURCHASING

— DETAILS AND REMINDERS —

___ Floor Plan	___ Blackboard/Chalk/Eraser	___ Dance Floor	___ Printed Menus
___ Table Numbers	___ Pointer	___ Piano	___ Printed Matches
___ Registration/Card Table	___ Amplifiers	___ Organ	___ Printed Tickets
___ Collection of Tickets	___ Motion Picture Projector	___ Flags	___ Printed Direction Cards
___ Microphone	___ Screen	___ Food for Band	___ Signs
___ Podium	___ Spot Lights	___ Printed Invitations	___ Favors
___ Lectern	___ Lighting Effects	___ Printed Place Cards	___ Bulletin
___ Easel	___ Platforms	___ Printed Seating List	___ Other

— CONDITIONS OF CONTRACT —

ALL RESERVATIONS AND AGREEMENTS ARE MADE UPON, AND SUBJECT TO, THE RULES AND REGULATIONS OF THE MANAGEMENT, AND THE FOLLOWING CONDITIONS:

1. The quotation herein is subject to a proportionate increase to meet increased costs of foods, beverages and other costs of operation existing at the time of performance of our undertaking by reason of increases in present commodity prices, labor costs, taxes or currency values. Patron expressly grants the right to the management to raise the prices herein quoted or to make reasonable substitutions on the menu and agrees to pay such increased prices and to accept such substitutions.

2. In arranging for private functions, the attendance must be definitely specified 5 days in advance. This number will be considered a guarantee, not subject to reduction, and charges will be made accordingly.

3. All federal, state, and municipal taxes which may be imposed or be applicable to this agreement and to the services rendered by the management are in addition to the prices herein agreed upon, and the patron agrees to pay them separately.

4. No beverages of any kind will be permitted to be brought into the premise by the patron or any of the patrons, guests or invitees from the outside without the special permission of the management, and the management reserves the right to make a charge for the service of such beverages.

5. Performance of this agreement is contingent upon the ability of the management to complete the same, and is subject to labor troubles, disputes or strikes; accidents; government (federal, state or municipal) requisitions, restrictions upon travel, transportation, foods, beverages or supplies; and other causes whether enumerated herein or not, beyond control of management preventing or interfering with performance.

6. Payment shall be made in advance of the function unless credit has been established to the satisfaction of the management, in which event, a deposit should be paid at the time of signing the contract and a substantial additional payment will be required forty-eight hours before the function. The balance of the account is due and payable at the conclusion of the function. A service charge of one and one-half percent per month is added to any unpaid balance over thirty days old.

25% of total payment due on the signing of this contract. Total balance is due at the conclusion of the affair.

Name of Salesman	Date	Signature of Engager

(This Contract is subject to the terms and conditions stated.)

Figure 7.9.

FINAL BILL

ORGANIZATION _____   TYPE OF FUNCTION _____

CONTACT _____   DATE _____

ADDRESS _____   TIME _____

PHONE _____   NO.: GUARANTEED _____

ITEM	COST	TOTAL COST	SUMMARY	
FOOD			FOOD	_____
BEVERAGE			BEVERAGE	_____
LIQUOR			EQUIPMENT	_____
BEER			ADDITIONALS	_____
WINE			SUB TOTAL	_____
SODA			TAX _____ %	_____
LABOR			LABOR	_____
EQUIPMENT			TOTAL	_____
ADDITIONALS			LESS DEPOSIT	_____
FLOWERS			BALANCE DUE	_____
PHOTOS				
PRINTING				
MUSIC				
LIMO				
ETC.:				

PREPARED BY _____

DATE _____

Figure 7.10. WORK ALLOCATION AND SCHEDULE OF DUTIES. This is an excellent example of work detail, which can be adapted by operators to suit their particular establishment. The Escoffier dinner is a classical and prestigious event; the participants are considered gourmands. Not only must the meal be perfect but the service must be impeccable and served with eclat.

The kitchen brigade and the dining room personnel have overwhelming responsibilities. A great deal of time must be spent in planning, planning, planning! The chefs must perfect their recipes and predetermine cooking and service time precisely. Dining room attendants must have exact knowledge of their duties also. There is no room for assumptions or error. Each guest is presumed to be an expert who anticipates that the service will be on the same plateau of perfection as the food to be served.

Even if top professionals are employed, the chronology of service and the accoutrements for each course must be thoroughly explained. A "dry run" is an effective way to attain the perfection sought.

ESCOFFIER DINNER
April 26, 19____

Uniform For All Service Personnel

> White shirt or blouse
> Black slack or skirt
> Black shoes (shined)
> Black bow-tie
> Gold coats
> White apron
> White service gloves

Number Of Service Personnel

> 20 Waiters
> 10 Sommeliers
> 5 Bus Boys
> 5 Captains

Service Instruction

> Reception: Time   (S) 5:00 p.m._____   (F)_____
>
> Place: Student Lounge
>
> Set Up: Two (2) bars each to serve the following:
>> Moet et Chandon Brut Imperiale
>> Beaujolais Blanc
>> Lillet Blanc
>> Kir (Cocktail)
>> 1/3 Glass of white wine
>> 2 Drops of Creme de Cassis
>
> Equipment for Bars: 75 each   Champagne Tulips
>   75 each   White Wine Glasses (8½ oz.)
>   1 pkg.   Cocktail Napkins
>   Ashtrays (not displayed)

(continued)

Figure 7.10. Service Instruction (continued)

Instructions:
   1) All glassware is to be steam cleaned.
   2) Bars are to be set up on Friday, April 25, 19_____ .
   3) Champagne and wine should be placed in cooler on Friday, April 25.
   4) All beverage served from bar only.

Student Bartenders:

(1) _____   (3) _____

(2) _____   (4) _____

Buffet Setup

   Location of Table: Center of room

   Type: Two-station buffet (see floor plan)

   Draping done by: Mr. Steve Beno and crew

   Buffet served by: Mr. Fritz Sonnenschmidt and crew

   Maitre d': _____

   Waiters assigned:

   _____   _____   _____

   _____   _____   _____

   Instruction:
      1) Set up small round tables with four (4) chairs at each around room (see diagram)—12 tables.
      2) Alternate table cloths red and white.
      3) Supply 150 7"-plates for buffet table; also supply 150 salad forks. (Be sure all items are spotless.)
      4) Have a supply of ashtrays (but, do NOT display).
      5) Supply 100 linen napkins displayed on tables.
      6) All food will be served from buffet table. (No item on table to be passed.)
      7) All waiters are to clear soiled dishes and glasses during reception—Cork Bar Trays.

Dinner

   Time: (S) 6:00 p.m.   (F) _____

   Number of Covers: 100

   Floor Plan: See Diagram

   Number of Tables: 10 ten-covers per table

   Linen: Alternate tables with red and white cloths—90 × 90 size. Red tables will have white napkins; white tables will have red napkins.

   Table top: (in order of placement)
      1) Show Plate
      2) To right of show plate, knife and consomme spoon
      3) Next to the show plate, Escoffier Room
         (a) White wine glass   (b) Red wine glass   (c) Red wine glass   (d) White wine glass
      4) To left of show plate, dinner fork

5) Napkin center of plate (top)

6) Menu displayed on show plate for each cover

Centerpiece: Bouquet of vegetable flowers—one per table

Side Tables: A side table will be placed in each alcove and will contain the following items in the order of requirement:

        a) Dinner fork (Lamb)

        b) Dinner knife (Lamb)

        c) Teaspoon (Granite)

        d) Butter knife (Cheese)

        e) Teaspoon (Souffle)

        f) Teaspoon (Coffee)

        g) Ashtrays

        h) Sugar packs (Raw from Escoffier Room)

        i) Extra napkins

        j) Water pitcher (in case requested)

        k) Water goblet

Procedure of Service

Instruction:

1) There will be two (2) waiters per table, one (1) sommelier per table, one (1) bus boy per two tables and one (1) captain per two tables.

2) All waiters, bus boys, and sommeliers will receive instruction from their captain.

3) When not involved in the act of service, waiters/waitresses will stand by assigned station, feet slightly apart, arms behind back.

** THERE IS ABSOLUTELY NO TALKING AMONG CO-WORKERS DURING THE SERVICE.

Procedure:

	Step 1.	Waiters will assist guest when seating begins.
SOUP served from Gueridon.	Step 2.	Upon command from captain, waiters will proceed to hot cart and pick up hot soup cup and saucers.
	Step 3.	Upon command from captains, waiters and bus boys will clear soup cup and saucer and spoon.
	Step 4.	Sommelier upon command from captain will pour first wine, Corton Charlemagne, in white wine glass nearest the plate. 1/3 of the glass is to be poured.
FISH course plated by Chef.	Step 5.	Upon command from captains, waiters will proceed to entrance of Great Hall and pick up fish course, five plates each, which will be plated; bus boy to pick up sauce and pass.
		"Sommelier Check Wine Glasses"
	Step 6.	Upon command, waiters are to clear show plate and fish plate all in one step, along with fork and knife; bus boy to take tray to dishroom.
2nd WINE served.	Step 7.	Sommeliers to pour second wine, Chateau Lafite Rothschild, in glass (b), upon command.
	Step 8.	Waiters are to place dinner knife on right side of guest, and dinner fork on left side of guest.
LAMB plated by Chef.	Step 9.	Upon command, waiters are to proceed with captain to service area, pick up and serve main entree, making sure lamb faces guest; bus boy to pick up additional jus and serve from left of guest.
		"Sommelier Check Wine Glasses"

(continued)

Figure 7.10. Procedure of Service (continued)

Step 10. Bus boy and one (1) waiter clear white wine glass *used;* bus boy takes glasses to dishroom.

Step 11. Upon command, waiters and bus boy are to clear dinner plates; bus boy takes plates to dishroom.

Step 12. Waiters to place show plate in front of guest and teaspoon on right side of show plate.

Step 13. Waiters to pick up Granite, five each, and place on show plate.

Step 14. Waiters to clear all plates, upon command from captain; bus boys remove to dishroom.

Step 15. Waiters place butter knife on right side of guest.

Step 16. Sommelier to serve next wine, Bonnesmares, in remaining red wine glass.

CHEESE served from Gueridon. Step 17. Waiters to pick up plates for cheese, captain to pick up cheese, cut and plate from Gueridon.

DO NOT REMOVE WINE GLASS FROM LAST COURSE.

"Sommelier Check Wine Glasses"

Step 18. a. Upon command, waiter to clear cheese plate and knife; bus boy removes to dishroom.
b. Waiter to crumb the table.
c. Waiter to place two (2) teaspoons to the right of the guest.
d. Bus boy to remove centerpiece—put in Pantry area.

Step 19. Sommelier to pour last course wine, Chateau Climens, in white wine glass.

Step 20. Waiters to pick up Souffle Glace and serve, five each waiter; Captain to pick up sauce and serve one spoon over souffle.

Step 21. Sommelier and waiter to remove BOTH RED WINE GLASSES.

Step 22. a. Captains designated will prepare Gueridon for liqueurs and cordials; there will be four Gueridons serving; one (1) waiter to assist each captain.
b. Waiters to place coffee cups and saucers to right of guest, sugar and cream center of table, serve coffee.
c. Bus boy to pick up Corbeille de Mignardises (Pulled Sugar Baskets with sweet goodies) and place in center of table.

Step 23. Waiters clear dessert plates.

Step 24. STAND BY STATIONS.

Instruction for Sommelier

1. All wines will be issued from Pantry 2 in order of service.

2. All empty or partially used bottles must be returned to the Pantry and given to wine stewards.

3. When serving wine, fill glass 1/3 full only.

4. Keep an eye on the tables that you are assigned to in case the guest might require more of the wine being served.

5. a. When serving all wines, make sure that each guest has seen the label.
b. Remember!! (Four steps when serving)
(1) Pour
(2) Stop
(3) Twist
(4) Retrieve

6. The white wine glass that the Corton Charlemagne was served in is removed once the main course (Lamb) has been served, NOT BEFORE.

7. Both RED WINE GLASSES, the one with the Chateau Lafite Rothschild and the one with the Bonnes Mares, will REMAIN ON THE TABLE until the dessert has been served.

8. All commands for wine service will come from the captain assigned to your station.

9. ABSOLUTELY NO DRINKING BY ANYONE BEFORE OR DURING DINNER.

10. a. All wines to be decanted will be done under my supervision.
    b. Wines and time of decanting will be discussed at a later date.

11. ORDER OF WINES SERVED

    1st.... Corton Charlemagne—Served after soup is cleared and before fish is served.
    2nd... Chateau Lafite Rothschild—Served after fish is cleared and before lamb is served.
    3rd... Bonnes Mares—Served after the Granite is cleared and before cheese is served.
    4th....Chateau Climens—Served after the cheese is cleared and before the dessert is served.
    REMEMBER, COMMAND WILL COME FROM CAPTAIN.

Instruction for Wine Stewards

1. You will be responsible for all wines, liqueurs, and champagne.

2. All white wines must be refrigerated by Friday night, April 25, 19_____ .

3. Cork screws will be supplied by myself.

4. All wines will be issued by you and emptied or partially full bottles will be returned to you.

5. If you should issue ten (10) bottles of Corton Charlemagne, make sure you receive ten (10) bottles back.

6. YOU ARE NOT TO DRINK, nor are you to serve any wine to any staff, to include instructors.

7. All beverages used during the reception should be returned to you by the assigned bartenders.

8. A list of all beverages issued and returned must be kept. A form is attached for this purpose.

9. Wine for the Dinner to be issued in the following order:
    (1) Corton Charlemagne
    (2) Chateau Lafite Rothschild
    (3) Bonnes Mares
    (4) Chateau Climens

WINE STEWARD CHECK LIST

RECEPTION

ITEM	No. on Hand	Issued	No. Returned
Moet et Chandon Brut	_____	_____	_____
Beaujolais Blanc	_____	_____	_____
Lillet Blanc	_____	_____	_____
Creme de Cassis	_____	_____	_____

(continued)

Figure 7.10. Wine Steward Check List (continued)

DINNER

Corton Charlemagne	_____	_____	_____
Chateau Lafite Rothschild	_____	_____	_____
Bonnes Mares	_____	_____	_____
Chateau Climens	_____	_____	_____
V.E.P. Chartreuse	_____	_____	_____
Cognac Hennessy Bras d'Or	_____	_____	_____
Liqueur de Poire	_____	_____	_____
Creme de Menthe	_____	_____	_____

Assigned Wine Stewards

_____ Group # _____

_____ Group # _____

TABLE ASSIGNMENTS

Maitre d':	Mr. _____	Tables 1, 2, 3
	Mr. _____	Tables 4, 5, 6
	Mr. _____	Tables 7, 8, 9, 10

Captains:	Mr. _____	Tables 1 and 2
	Mr. _____	Tables 3 and 4
	Mr. _____	Tables 5 and 6
	Mr. _____	Tables 7 and 8
	Mr. _____	Tables 9 and 10

Bus Boys:	_____	Tables 1 and 2
	_____	Tables 3 and 4
	_____	Tables 5 and 6
	_____	Tables 7 and 8
	_____	Tables 9 and 10

Table 1

W _____

W _____

S _____

Table 2

W _____

W _____

S _____

Table 3

W _____

W _____

S _____

Table 4

W _____

W _____

S _____

Table 5

W _____

W _____

S _____

Table 6

W _____

W _____

S _____

Table 7

W _____

W _____

S _____

Table 8

W _____

W _____

S _____

Table 9

W _____

W _____

S _____

Table 10

W _____

W _____

S _____

CHAPTER EIGHT

ACCOMMODATOR SERVICE (IN-HOME COOKING AND SERVING)

This type of business, as stated earlier, has often been the starting point for many successful caterers. (The accommodator is not to be confused with In-Home Catering, which is detailed in another chapter.)

The client supplies the facilities, food, and equipment, while the accommodator prepares and cooks *all* food *on* the client's premises.

Therefore, you need not equip a commissary; obtain Board of Health permits; register with the State Sales Tax Department; own trucks or other expensive rolling equipment; get involved in complex bookkeeping procedures; or have compensation and liability insurance.

The only investment required is a set of good working tools, baking necessities, two or three sets of working "whites" (uniforms), and a polyurethane cutting board.

FEES

Accommodator catering can be done on a part-time basis to provide you with a second income, or it can develop into a full-time occupation.

As an accommodator, you can charge a flat rate or charge by the hour. If charging an hourly rate, your fee for consultation, preparation, and cleanup should be less than the charge for time spent during the actual function.

EXAMPLE: (Figures given are for this illustration only.)

Consultation with host or committee for planning function	2 hours @ $6.00	12.00
Preparation on day of function	4 hours @ $6.00	24.00
Time spent on service during function	3 hours @ $9.00	27.00
Cleanup	1½ hours @ $6.00	9.00
	TOTAL FEE FOR FUNCTION	$72.00

The host/client pays the accommodator the full rate without deductions. You, the caterer, are then obligated to report this amount on your federal and/or state income tax returns.

RECOMMENDATIONS

The following recommendations are of value, if you intend to specialize in in-home cooking and serving as an accommodator:

1. Discuss the menu for the affair in the home of the host, or in the area where you will be doing the cooking. In this way, both you and your client will be aware of limitations in the service and production areas.

2. After deciding on the menu, determine the quantities of food you will need, and what additional dishes and equipment must be secured. Insist, if possible, that the host/client handle all rentals and purchases. Thus, you cannot be accused of padding the bill or of giving short weights. In addition, you will not have to use your car or spend your time on shopping. Time is money, and it is costly to operate a car. Therefore, if you must do the purchasing, be sure to charge for the time involved, as well as for the use of your car.

3. When your client purchases the food, it will be his or her responsibility to provide refrigeration and storage.

4. Any breakage or other loss that occurs from the time of purchase until the time of the actual event is also the responsibility of the host, if she or he makes the purchase.

5. Liability for injuries incurred on the client's premises is not the responsibility of the accommodator. It is generally covered by the host's homeowner's policy.

6. If you need extra help for the party, have the host hire workers on a direct basis. In this way, the host assumes liability and you are absolved from legal responsibility.

7. Do not transport additional help to the party location, and then charge them for transportation. If you do this, you could be in violation of local transportation ordinances. This could possibly lead to prosecution, or be in violation of your personal automobile coverage. Therefore, you would be wise to discuss this point with your attorney, the local public utility authority, and/or your insurance company.

8. *Remain until the party is over and assist with final cleanup.* You should not only make certain that your own work area is left in immaculate condition, but should also assist the host with total cleanup. This will be appreciated, and could lead to repeat business in the future.

9. *A word of caution* is needed regarding liquor. Liquor laws are strict in many communities, and you must exercise great caution. If there are to be alcoholic beverages at the function, have the host purchase and bring them to the place of service. Do not pick it up "on your way." There can also be a great deal of unpleasantness in the handling and dispensing of liquor. Thus, *never serve liquor to someone who is under the legal age, or to someone who obviously has already had too much.*

10. When arranging the menu, do not let yourself be talked into preparing part or all of the food in *your own home.* If you prepare food in your home for eventual sale, you are breaking the law. Your home is strictly residential and is not zoned for business—no matter how small and insignificant the business. From a safety standpoint, preparing food in your home could create a potentially hazardous situation. Should you have a fire, your regular household insurance carrier will not honor your claim because of this technicality. (Look at your insurance policy. It specifically states that your premises are covered as *residential* property only.)

Also, if you are transporting home-prepared food to the job and are involved in an auto accident, your claim *may not be honored.* Your automobile insurance policy probably states that your car is specifically insured for pleasure purposes only and *not* for business purposes.

ESTABLISHING YOUR CREDENTIALS

Accommodators do not have established and out-fitted commissaries, nor do they operate from furnished offices or storefront business establishments. Their contacts originate primarily from word-of-mouth recommendations and/or local newspaper advertisements or spot radio commercials. Accommodators are really free-lance food specialists. A single line, heavy type listing in the telephone directory, or a small ad in the yellow pages, could be the largest ongoing fixed expense. The phone is the primary means of contact and negotiation.

Accommodators are engaged by individuals or organizations to assist with or take over completely the preparation of food and service at functions *held on the host's premises*. Thus, an accommodator is an employee rather than an employer, and becomes exempt from many responsibilities, such as, collecting sales taxes where applicable, carrying employee insurances, and making other mandated obligatory deductions.

Being an accommodator can be lucrative, whether one devotes himself exclusively to this business, or branches out to own an off-premise or on-premise business. As an accommodator, you can establish a reputation and acquire a viable and prominent identity.

It is important that accommodators do not assume responsibilities they cannot fulfill. Understate your abilities rather than overstate them. If you are expert in one area—cooking, for instance—then isolate your duties and responsibilities to that specific area. If asked, offer suggestions for other areas, but do not be ashamed to inform your client of your limits. Faking a skill will show you off to disadvantage and will denigrate your real talents.

Assert your professionalism by setting up your station in a workmanlike manner, whether in the kitchen, at the bar, or at the serving area. Maintain orderliness and impeccable cleanliness at all times, not only at your station but on your person. Be proud of your work tools and always have an extra uniform in reserve.

If you are assisting in the bar area, you should make a preliminary check of the facilities. How much space is allotted to you? Will the host supply all or any of the necessary working tools? (An experienced bartender always brings a kit of tools—corkscrew, bottle opener, measures, stirrers, strainer, shakers, sharp paring knife, small cutting board, and TOWELS.)

Check the supply of appropriate glasses, and plan to avoid rinsing as much as possible. Use disposables if allowed. Check the supply of ice cubes. Unless the bar is already in a fixed area, place the temporary bar in a space that will not cause a traffic bottleneck, as far away from the entrance area as possible. Try to keep the variety and combinations of liquor to be served within the bounds of your ability to dispense them quickly. Other guests do not like to wait while exotic combinations are being concocted.

If you are involved in serving guests, determine what linens, silverware, dishes, and glassware will be needed. Any needed items should be purchased or rented *by the host*.

Determine the *exact* seating area to allow for the comfort of guests and the convenience of the server. Do not attempt French or Russian service in a crowded area—there could be disastrous accidents. DO NOT ATTEMPT, UNDER ANY CIRCUMSTANCES, to flame any dish in crowded surroundings. If an inconsiderate host insists on such a procedure, and is willing to take the chance, YOU MUST STILL REFUSE. You have too much to lose. Better to go without employment one day than hazard the possibility of a disaster.

Once the affair is over, return all equipment to its proper place and cleanup thoroughly. Have the host inspect the results of your efforts and do not leave until you have complete approval.

CHAPTER NINE

OFF-PREMISE CATERING

The most important primary step in off-premise catering is the preparation of a proper packing list. An itemized packing list should be prepared for each off-premise job. This list then serves as a guide for assembling items to be used or packed for the upcoming event.

PACKING LISTS

A packing list is much more essential to an off-premise caterer than to an on-premise operator, whose equipment is always on hand. Setting up for a party some distance from the commissary and discovering that some essential equipment was short-packed, or omitted entirely, could cause considerable confusion, embarrassment, and even trauma if time does not allow sending to the commissary for the needed items. Purchasing substitutes could be impossible if stores are closed or substitutes are unsuitable. (An off-premise caterer should always carry substantial pocket money as credit cards are not always accepted.)

Making out the list requires a concentrated and methodical approach. Carelessness can be expensive and, therefore, must be eliminated!

An effective system in making out the list is to study each course on the menu and decide exactly what and how much service equipment it requires. Examine each line of the menu in succession and, on a blank sheet of paper, make the appropriate heading (the equipment required) and list the amounts needed for that service (see Figure 9.1). Skipping around or using preprinted forms leads to unnecessary detail and confusion.

Enter the needed amounts under the appropriate headings and if a subsequent course uses a dish or piece of equipment previously listed, simply add to the number needed (see examples 12, 13, and 14 in Figure 9.1). Continue this process until the menu has been completed and then RECHECK FOR ACCURACY! Total the amounts under each heading and transfer the numbers to the packing sheet (see Figure 9.2).

The scheduler must have a knowledge of the number of items in each unit, box, rack, cabinet, etcetera. He should always schedule for packing *full* racks, even if they reasonably exceed the actual number needed. Full racks allow for safer transport and easier tallying when packing for the return trip. There should also be an allowance

Figure 9.1. Menu Service Equipment

14" ROUND TRAYS (#1) IIII (4)	5" DOILIES (#11) (1 BOX)	BUTTER KNIVES (#21) IIII (4 BAGS)
COCKTAIL NAPKINS (#2) I (1 BOX)	7" UNDERLINERS (#12) THL THL THL THL THL II (27 DZ. OR 324 COUNT)	DESSERT FORKS (#22) IIII (4 BAGS)
FRILLED PICKS (#3) I (1 BOX)	10" PLATES (#13) THL THL (10 DZ.)	REVERE BOWLS (#23) I (1 BOX)
10" DOILIES (#4) I (1 BOX)	TEASPOONS (#14) THL III (8 BAGS)	SERVICE SPOONS (#24) I (1 BOX)
HI-BALLS (#5) IIII (4 RACKS)	FORKS (#15) IIII (4 BAGS)	COFFEE CUPS (#25) THL (5 RACKS)
LO-BALLS (#6) II (2 RACKS)	ALL PURPOSE WINES (#16) THL (5 RACKS)	SAUCERS (#26) THL IIII (9 DZ.)
WATER GOBLETS (#7) III (3 RACKS)	TULIP CHAMPAGNES (#17) III (3 RACKS)	BRANDY PONIES (#27) I (1 CASE)
SUPREMES (#8) THL II (7 RACKS)	DINNER KNIVES (#18) IIII (4 BAGS)	SALT-PEPPERS (#28) 2 (2 BOXES)
SUPREME INSETS (#9) IIO (110)	RELISH DISHES (#19) I (1 BOX)	SUGAR BOWLS (#29) I (1 BOX)
SUPREME RINGS (#10) IIO (110)	BREAD TRAYS (#20) I (1 BOX)	CREAMERS (#30) II (2 BOXES)
		ASH TRAYS (#31) I (1 BOX)

Figure 9.2.

PACKING LIST
(This list is intended only as a guide)

Job no. _____ Supervisor _____ Packed in truck _____

To be packed by, day _____ Date _____ Scheduled by _____

ABC CATERERS, CENTRAL CITY, N. Y.

PACK		RET'D	PACK		RET'D
	Service plates			Serving forks	
120	10″ Dinner plates			Tongs	
324	7″ Plates				
	Bread and butter		3	Water goblets	
	Monkey dishes		4	Hi-balls	
5	Coffee cups		2	Lo-balls	
108	Saucers			Pilsner	
	Bouillon cups		5	All purpose wines	
1	Relish dishes, china			Sherry glasses	
	Silver _____ 1 BOX			Manhattans	
	Casseroles, type			Whiskey sours	
	Gravy boats, china			Champagnes, saucer _____	
	Silver _____		3	Tulip	
	Individual salad bowls		1	Cordials	
	Demi tasse combos				
7	Supremes		1	Silver bread trays	
110	Rings for supremes		1	Silver crumbers	
	Insets, glass _____		1	Ash trays	
	Silver _____ 110			Lg. round silver trays	
				Lg. square silver trays	
8	Teaspoons			Lg. oval silver trays	
	Bouillon spoons		4	Med. ovals _____ 14″ Small _____	
	Salad forks			Russian service trays	
4	Dinner forks				
4	Dessert forks			Stainless bowls _____ size	
	Oyster forks			Stainless pans _____ lg. small	
4	Dinner knives			St. serving ladles	
4	Butter knives			Ice cream scoops, size	
	Demi tasse spoons				

(continued)

Figure 9.2. (continued)

PACK		RET'D	PACK		RET'D
1	Chef's tools (1 _____) (2 _____)			Large Mahogany salads	
1	Bar tools			Small Mahogany salads	
1	All purpose tool box		1	Silver water pitchers	
1	First aid kit		1	Silver coffee pitchers	
4	Stainless bar pitchers		2	Silver creamers	
	Gueridons		2	Silver sugar bowls	
	Portable bars _____1 _____2 _____3			Silver candy dishes	
1	Stirrers			Silver coupes	
1	Coasters		1	Revere bowls, size _9"_	
2	Waste baskets — Garbage cans NONE		1	Silver ice bowls	
	Garbage liners			Silver compotes	
1	Table numbers		1	Silver coffee urns	
	Portable fry pots			Silver punch bowls	
	Silver chafing dishes		1	Silver candelabra	
	Stainless chafers			Silver ladles	
	Marmite stands and insets			Silver vegetable dishes	
	Rechaud burners				
	Sterno, lg. small				
	Electric extensions		1	Frill picks	
	Westinghouse ovens			Plain picks	
	Gas grills _____ Tank gas		1	Ferns	
1	Skirts, color _BLUE_		1	Smilax	
4	Lace overlay		1	Flowers	
	White cloths, size _____				
	Napkins, color _____ size _____		1	Cocktail napkins _BLUE_ color	
18	Colored cloths _BLUE_ size _96_		1	Doilies _10"_ size _BLUE_ color ADD 1 BOX 5"	
16	Silence cloths			Place mats	
	Lace tablecloths			Punch cups	
4	Chef's coats			Styrofoam cups	
10	Aprons, bib _____ half _____			Folding table tops	
12	Side towels			Ice carving pans _____ tongs	
2	Bar jackets _____ Waiters			Ice carving tools _____	
1	Corsage pins			Light wheel _____ foil _____	
1	Stapler			Round tables _____ long _____	
1	Candles _1 DZ._ color _BLUE_			Serpentine _____	

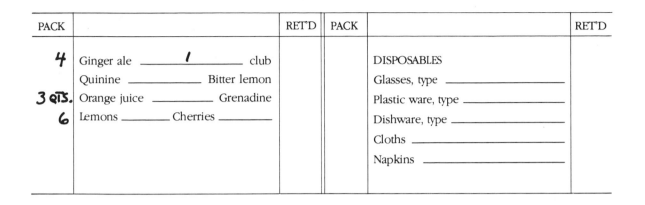

PACK		RET'D	PACK		RET'D
4	Ginger ale _____ *1* _____ club			DISPOSABLES	
	Quinine _____ Bitter lemon			Glasses, type _____	
3 QTS.	Orange juice _____ Grenadine			Plastic ware, type _____	
6	Lemons _____ Cherries _____			Dishware, type _____	
				Cloths _____	
				Napkins _____	

made for extra guests, breakage at the point of service, or rejection because of damage. (The author finds it expedient to pack thirty count pieces of silver in heavy-duty plastic bags. They are sanitary, easy to handle, and not excessive in numbers for parties of 50, 100, or more.)

Finally, check every item on the packing list that will be needed for ancillary services—water pitchers, coffee pitchers, creamers, candelabra (for head table), cloths, napkins, work tools, ice buckets, baskets, etcetera.

If dishwashing facilities are available, you probably will not need to pack as much equipment. As an example, if you are serving a party of 150, you will probably need highball glasses, which are normally packed 6 by 6, or 36 glasses to a rack. Where washing facilities are available, you could safely pack five (5) racks of glasses, a total of 180 glasses, knowing that you can keep glasses clean as needed. When dirty glasses are returned, accumulate them until you have enough for one rack, at which time they can be washed and returned to the bar. By the time they are ready to be used again, they will be clean and cool enough so that beverages can be poured into them.

Without dishwashing facilities, you would have to pack at least 10 racks of glasses, which would take up more truck space and require additional packing time.

This same principle applies to other items. For example, the underliner used in the starter course can be used again, after washing, for the dessert course.

The packing list also serves as a record of where equipment was previously used. It pinpoints time and place and, if a particular piece of equipment is missing, can make the task of getting it back much easier.

Make notations on each packing list as to its accuracy, missing items, condition of equipment, and all other pertinent comments. *Do not destroy* the packing list but keep it with other permanent records of that particular affair.

Miscellaneous Pointers

- Each truck should always have a broom, shovel, dust pan, mop, pail with squeegee, and a number of large heavy-duty plastic bags.
- Carry two pairs of work gloves for use in the event of mechanical breakdowns, or for handling garbage cans and other such items.
- A good first aid kit is a wise investment. It should be carried at all times, and include pamphlets explaining what to do in emergencies. These pamphlets are readily obtainable from all Red Cross offices.
- As an off-premise caterer, you may work in sparsely traveled areas or in unusual facilities (fairgrounds, isolated beach areas, picnic groves, and party boats). Thus, a *portable*

oxygen inhalator would be a valuable addition to the first aid kit.

- Your catering tool box should be equipped with at least TWO can openers, which can be mounted or hook-fastened on a board or in a specific container. Remember, since electric power is not always available, include at least one manually operated opener together with the portable electric model. Nothing is more frustrating than having to open a can and learning you do not have a usable opener.

- Many caterers find it advisable to carry several sturdy 30-inches square, folding tables. Those with 1-inch plywood tops are useful as extenders for regular 6- and 8-foot tables. They are also useful for displaying wedding cakes and as extra work tables.

- Carry a hardware tool box containing a hammer, screwdriver, pliers, wrenches, extension cords (heavy-duty), fuses, assorted nails, and screws.

IN-HOME CATERING

In-home catering differs in size, scope, and responsibilities from in-home cooking and/or serving by an accommodator. Unlike the services provided by an accommodator, which are usually limited to the preparation and the service of the party, in-home caterers assume *total responsibility* for supplying the food, equipment, and *all* personnel crucial to the successful functioning of the affair. The caterer relieves the host of all responsibilities, other than menu decisions and securing and furnishing the alcoholic beverages (in most states, a caterer cannot supply liquor).

In-home catering can constitute a favorable percentage of the aggregate business of an off-premise caterer. On-premise caterers who perform in-home catering are governed by exactly the same procedures in scheduling and performance as off-premise operators.

Entertaining at home is becoming increasingly popular, not only because of the rising costs of dining out but because homes offer more privacy. There is more leisure and comfort and the opportunity for intimate conversation. There can also be an elegance that is not always available in public areas. Moreover, the host has the pleasure of doing something special for his friends—an exhilaration results when his guests appreciate his efforts in creating a function for their pleasure and well-being.

Visit the Site

Catering in a home has many more areas of concern than catering in a public facility where the furnishings are constructed to withstand heavy and rough usage, and where there are built-in facilities for quantity food preparation and service.

In-home catering parties should never be negotiated "blindly." You must visit the home to familiarize yourself with the (limited) kitchen facilities and to study the layout of the dining areas. Another essential aspect of this visit is to check the loading and unloading facilities, which can create a time-consuming factor, plus the parking areas available for equipment delivery and help.

Take more than a superficial glance at the home furnishings. They could be fragile and delicate and incapable of withstanding the demands of numerous guests. The dining room table may not be substantial enough to hold the quantities of proposed food and tableware. The furnishings may be so luxurious that possible damage to them by your help or the guests could be devastatingly expensive to repair or to replace. If the furnishings are bulky, bringing in supplementary seating or tables may be impossible.

You must also be aware that standard, quantity preparation, serving and holding equipment, such as used in your commissary, IS NOT APPROPRIATE OR SIZED for home service. The home heating and cooking facilities will not accommodate large pots, which could injure stove surfaces. Nor will your pans fit into home ovens. You must supply your own properly sized units, in good quality and impeccable condition.

Guests, who cannot be gracefully restricted, will visit your area either out of curiosity, to compliment you, or to discuss a party of their own.

If you are bringing in auxiliary equipment for cooking or heating, make certain that it will be located in a safe and secure area and will not present a fire hazard. If they are electric powered units, make certain that the home wiring and wattage can handle the extra current requirements and not cause outages of lighting, air-conditioning, heating, refrigeration, and freezing. (It is always a good policy to carry extra screw-in and cartridge-type fuses.) If electric disruption occurs, once the energy is restored CHECK WITH THE HOST to see that all facilities (reefers, freezers, laundry equipment) are once again functioning normally. Some appliances require manual activation of starter buttons.

Menu

The choice of the menu requires studied deliberation. It need not be French haute cuisine, but it must not lack richness in the presentation. It can offer the most ordinary or peasant foods, or complicated ethnic dishes. But they all require resourcefulness and creativity to enhance not only their taste but their visual appeal. Remember, the wrapping is just as important as the gift it encloses.

Although you may have your own repertory of food specialties—and this is one of the reasons you were engaged—there is nothing wrong in adding a specialty or dish that the host may want you to prepare according to his own recipe. Try it out first. If it has merit, offer it to the guests with kudos for the host. This will reinforce his pleasure and importance and add to your reputation for cooperation. You may also be able to add this dish to your own inventory.

Buffet presentations can be made more effective and even spectacular by tabletop cooking of omelets, crepes, or pasta. The slicing of beef, poultry, or fish, by one of your employees, at the buffet table adds a touch of the theatrical, and his dexterity may even become a topic of con-

versation. This demonstrates again that the host has been attentive to the entertainment and enjoyment of his guests.

Bar Facilities

If there is a fixed bar facility in the home, then you have no alternative but to use it. Otherwise, you have the option of placing the bar where it interferes least with room-to-room traffic. Because of the probable limited storing and serving facilities, the burden on the bartender should be reduced as much as possible to facilitate his production and serving effectiveness.

You need not duplicate the variety of liquors available at the neighborhood bar. And do not offer an overwhelming array of brands that will delay decisions and confuse the guests.

At a house party, it is acceptable to use a stemmed, 10 ounce, all-purpose glass for on-the-rocks, highballs, cocktails, and all soft drinks—also, wine. "White wine has become the all-purpose liquor of the moment with vodka a close second. Vodka leaves no odor on the breath and mixes with anything from strawberries to tomatoes. Scotch, gin, bourbon, rye or a blended whiskey, sweet vermouth, and dry vermouth should sate most drinkers. One would be safe to stock twice as many bottles of white wine, vodka, and Scotch as he would of the other liquors. The adjuncts of orange and tomato juice, plus (diet) ginger ale, colas, etcetera should also be available." (Food and Wine Supplement, *N. Y. Times*, 28 October 1979.)

If you are involved with the service of a formal party, it would be advisable to make martinis and whiskey sours ahead of time and keep them refrigerated. Punches are NOT appropriate for cocktail or dinner parties. Their place is at festive occasions, such as weddings or late night dances.

After-dinner drinks are not crucial. You need not present a boggling array of flavored cognacs and liqueurs—this will seem ostentatious. One good brandy and one sweet liqueur should suffice.

Remember, simplicity is the key to providing an efficient and well-stocked bar. There should always be a plentiful supply of ice (a 10 pound bag of ice cubes is ample for 12 guests).

There are certain people who are concerned with diet and prefer to eat and drink "light." White wine satisfies this preference. It is really an all-purpose liquor that serves as a cocktail and table beverage. Sparkling water greatly enhances this presentation. Red wine is never meant to be a cocktail—it goes with dinner.

One note of advice—the caterer, whether on- or off-premise, must be conditioned and have the ability to handle excessive drinkers. At a house party, it is the host and perhaps a family member or friend who must assume this responsibility, with the moral and sometimes physical support of the caterer. At a public function, committee chairpersons must handle this unpleasantness and, if assistance is required, it may be necessary to call in house security personnel. Unfortunately, these situations, while infrequent, do happen and often the caterer is the only one sought out to resolve it with discretion and subtlety.

Leftovers

There should be a definite understanding, preferably as part of the contract, regarding the disposition of leftovers and what actually is considered leftovers. Any food that has been on display, any food that is in the chafers, and any food that is being or has been heated should be left for the host. Food or pastries that show obvious surface deterioration, or will not be in *prime* condition for your next presentation, can be left. Unused reserve foods (refrigerated, frozen, or canned) obviously are not part of your generosity.

Special Touches

The subject of music at home parties is controversial. If offered at all, it should occur early or very late in the party as it will either be drowned out by or intrude on the conversation. The interplay of personalities and good conversation are the only entertainment advisable at small home parties.

Candles are virtually essential to the party spirit, as are flowers. If guests are seated, candles and flowers must be kept below eye level.

There are unlimited opportunities to express personal taste; whimsical porcelain figures, appropriate holiday decorations, and any unusual accessories can be incorporated into table arrangements. There is no reason for all table arrangements at a home party to be the same. Your resourcefulness and creativity will add to the guests' appreciation of the setting, particularly those with artistic sensibilities. They can even add a sense of opulence!

Brillat-Savarin, the nineteenth century French gastronome, in his *Physiology of Taste,* wrote "To invite people to dine with us, is to make ourselves responsible for their well-being as long as they are under our roofs."

Traffic

If the party is large and many guests are expected, street parking may be necessary. In this case, tell the host to notify the Police Department and give both the beginning and ending times for the affair. This, no doubt, will please the police, neighbors, and guests by easing problems of traffic control.

For such a party, it may be necessary to have an officer direct the flow of traffic. If the police can "work-in" the traffic control as part of an officer's regular duty, there may not be a charge. But if a special officer must be assigned to the task, a fee will, in all probability, be charged. In either case, be certain to provide the policeman on duty with food and beverage.

Bad Weather Procedures

In rainy weather, provide umbrellas for guests, and assign one of your employees the task of escorting them to and from their cars. If there is snow or slush, put a rubber or manila mat in front of the door leading to the house, as well as a carton at the protected entranceway for rubbers and boots. You should also provide a broom or a brush so that guests can remove snow from footwear.

Clothes Racks, Coat-Hanging Areas

You can provide serviceable folding clothes racks at a price that will cover their use, as well as your transportation and setup costs. However, with the permission of the client, you also can use a specific room where clothing apparel can be hung or simply placed on a bed.

Guests should be responsible for their own apparel. If one of your employees takes the guest's coat to the "coatroom," then you, the caterer, have given *an implied assumption of responsibility*. When guests take care of their own coats, you cannot be held for any liability.

Food and Equipment Storage Area

This area should be located where it will not interfere with guest traffic. Store everything in an orderly, systematic manner—food in one stack, linens in another, china in yet another. By doing this, you will not have to search through all of your equipment to find what you need.

Food Preparation and Service Area

All personnel, but especially those who work in the kitchen, must wear impeccably clean uniforms, and keep their stations clean at all times. Plenty of clean side towels and extra uniforms should also be available.

A bag or other garbage receptacle should be in an *inconspicuous place.* Thus, if curious guests wander into the kitchen to see who you are, and how you manage to serve so much food from such a confined area, your operation will present a neat and orderly appearance.

It is *inadvisable* to use your client's garbage disposer. Most home units are not built to withstand heavy-duty use, and the extra strain you put on it could do serious damage to the unit.

Food Display Area

Advise your client to remove fragile crystalware, china, show plates, and other small valuable pieces from food-serving or other areas where guests gather. In such areas, crowding could conceivably result in an accident.

If these pieces cannot be removed, they should at least be pushed out of the way or displayed in an area less exposed to the hazards of guest traffic.

If you use your client's dining table, buffet credenza, or other pieces of furniture for food display or dispensing, *place pads or buffers under trays and chafing dishes to prevent surface damage.*

Avoid rearranging furniture as much as possible because:(1) it will completely change the character of the room that your client has spent considerable time and effort in creating; and (2) furniture can be damaged when moved from one place to another.

Toilet Facilities

Remind your client to have additional reserves of toilet tissue and towels on hand. Toilet facilities are usually taxed to capacity during a party, and much embarrassment can be avoided simply by having ample supplies of these necessities.

Help Assignments

Give each employee specific assignments and areas of responsibility. In addition to specific duties, they should be encouraged never to go to the kitchen empty-handed; they should pick up dirty dishes and glasses.

Make certain that at least one employee is responsible for keeping ashtrays clean. Be sure to inform all personnel that they are to remain in the area(s) where they perform their duties. *They must not wander around the house to inspect rooms and furnishings.*

Following the party, thoroughly clean all areas. Check all rooms for glasses, dishes, or any other property that belongs to you. Even though a disposal area may be provided by the host, *remove all garbage* so that the client will have sufficient space until the regular collection time.

Before leaving, inspect storage and service areas. In this way, any damage incurred during the party will be noticed immediately, thus reducing the possibility of a delayed claim or a dispute by either party at a later date.

CATERING IN RENTED FACILITIES

When catering in a hall or large dining room, which is an integral part of a club, church, temple, or fraternal organization, do not automatically assume that the kitchen or preparation area is of standard institutional construction and design or that furnishings are standard. You must make a personal inspection of the premises to see what facilities are available and their condition.

Negotiations for the rental of facilities are generally taken care of by the client, who informs the superintendent or rental agent of the institution that the organization will bring in its own caterer. However, *the renting agent has the option of refusing to lease the premises* to any individual or organization using a catering firm with whom the lessor has had previous difficulties. Such a refusal is usually based on a caterer's previous disrespect and abuse of the facilities or because of late or nonpayment of accrued fees.

Some facilities charge one fee for the use of the hall and the kitchen. Other facilities charge the client a rental fee for the hall and the caterer a separate fee, or per diem rate, for the use of kitchen/cooking facilities.

You may also have to pay for the use of the dishwashing machine and, perhaps, for the use of refrigerators, freezers, and for garbage removal. Some kitchens permit you—for a fee—to use their pots, pans, and other utensils. They may even allow you to use their dishes, glassware, and silverware. If you do use them, be certain they are returned to their proper place and are in perfect condition and clean. Should you inadvertently take any of these items back with you to your own premises, immediately notify the manager of the facility and then return them at the earliest pos-

sible moment. If breakage of facility items occurs, promptly report and assume responsibility for it.

Following these rules will assure your welcome for subsequent events at the facility and may even result in party referrals by the lessor. Expressing appreciation to the superintendent of the facility with a pre-affair gratuity will encourage cooperation and increase the possibility that all equipment will be available and functioning properly when needed.

Since some dining areas are rented without tables or chairs, your client will expect you to know where to obtain these items. In this case, refer your client *directly to the proper agency.* Let the client make arrangements for rental, delivery, and payment. Avoid, when possible, transporting tables and chairs; they are bulky and heavy, and take up much needed space in trucks. Furthermore, rental agencies have the special equipment for handling and delivering these items.

Your client may ask you for a floor plan showing table placements and numbering, so that some persons can be assigned to certain seats or reserved areas. If the lessor cannot provide a floor plan, you will have to measure the area and make scale templates to plan the table layout (see chapter 2). Keep a copy of that floor plan for your permanent records because you may work in that facility again (see Figure 9.3). Also, make out a detailed work sheet for the use of your key people and the person(s) in charge of the affair, so that everyone will be aware of party details (see Figure 9.4).

Liquor Arrangements

Some public halls may rent all facilities *except the bar.* The lessor may have a liquor license and not allow liquor to be brought in because it could jeopardize the license. If this is the case, the lessor would probably offer you one of the following options:

1. *Public or Pay Bar.* This would be open to all guests, who would then pay for liquor or drinks individually.

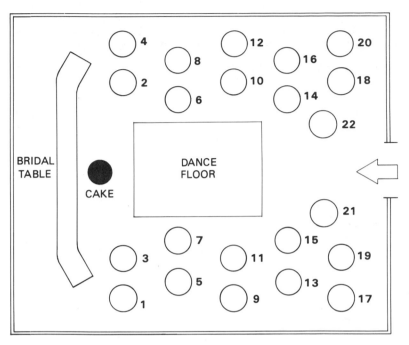

Figure 9.3. Schematic drawing submitted by an off-premise caterer for an infrequently used facility. (A 200-guest wedding dinner; ten guests per table maximum.)

2. *Limited Bar.* The client would furnish tickets to guests, and they would have to present a ticket for each drink.
3. *Unlimited Bar.* Guests could order as many drinks as they wished. Payment would subsequently be made by the client, based on a predetermined charge per bottle.

If the facility in question does not have an on-premise licensed bar, and if liquor is to be served, you must furnish bartenders and portable bars—the client supplies the liquor. This arrangement is similar to home-catering liquor dispensing, but since it is on a larger scale, the quarters may be roomier and, therefore, you can serve a greater variety of drinks.

It is not uncommon for halls without a liquor license to raise the rental fee by offering the well-known "Bring your own bottle" (BYOB) option, with the lessor sometimes supplying ginger ale, ice, and glasses, and setting a corkage charge for each guest.

Organization Affairs

Since many organizations hold affairs on limited budgets, you may not make your deserved profit. Furthermore, if you assume these affairs will be of great advertising value, you could be wrong. *It could, in fact, have the opposite effect!*

To illustrate, in order to accommodate an organization's limited budget, you set a lower rate for the party, which may necessitate "cutting corners." Such economical measures might include reducing portion sizes, eliminating a course, serving foods of lesser quality, using fewer serving personnel, or substituting paper for linens.

If any of these practices are deviations from your standards, your reputation will be harmed irreparably. Guests are not concerned about whether or not you are making or losing money on an affair. They are concerned with enjoying the service and satisfying a personal, aesthetic sense.

If you want to be a public-spirited citizen and serve these affairs, knowing full well that your

Figure 9.4. Work Plan

JOHN DOE CATERERS — HYDE PARK, NEW YORK

DETAILED WORKSHEET (SPECIMEN)
(To be issued to person in charge of affair)

NAME OF CLIENT:	State Historical Association
ADDRESS:	149 Oregon Street, E. Chicago, Illinois
AREA OF PARTY:	First Hungarian Church
ADDRESS:	1595 Sunrise Highway, E. Chicago, Illinois
PERSON(S) IN CHARGE:	Mrs. D. R. Jones Mr. F. G. Hussen
DAY AND DATE:	Saturday, January 18, 1983
TIME:	Reception — 5:00 P.M. Dinner — 6:30 P.M.
NUMBER OF GUESTS:	250 persons
GUARANTEED NUMBER:	245 persons
SPECIAL ARRANGEMENTS:	Use two church bars, but we supply two additional portable bars and supply four bartenders. Association will provide all liquor, carbonated beverages, soft drinks, and ice. Our bartender will inventory all liquor at setup; breakdown. During dinner, our portable bars will be wheeled into the dining room, and each will be attended by one or more of our bartenders. Association member in charge is Mr. F. G. Hussen.
RECEPTION: (One of our persons in charge.)	In reception area, set up two 8-ft. tables (belonging to facility) with equal amounts of Wisconsin and New York cheese, celery sticks, carrot sticks, and cocktail rye slices (as packed) on each. (One waitress will be assigned to each table.) Drape tables in blue and use 5-in. plates, service knives, and cocktail napkins. *PASS BUTLER STYLE*—400 speared cocktail franks, 300 rondelles of lobster, and 300 cocktail meatballs (all as packed).
COAT ROOM:	Attendants to be supplied by church. (We feed.)
PARKING:	Handled by policemen provided by the organization. (We feed them and all other personnel.)
ORCHESTRA:	Provided by the organization. Band leader is Hy Williams; our coordinator is Bob White. (We supply sandwiches only; it is our treat.)
CENTERPIECES:	Floral centerpieces will be provided by the organization. (Guests will not be permitted to take centerpieces, which will be sent to Shriner's Hospital. Orchestra will announce.)
CIGARETTES:	Organization to supply—one package (in cups) each table, plus matches at each place setting.
LECTERN:	Tabletop, center head table, two mikes.
HOUSE COUNT:	Before soup course, check with organization's Mr. Hussen. Check program with Mrs. Jones of the organization.
HEAD TABLE:	12 guests, blue table top, gold lame front skirt, gold napkins, 2/3-tier candelabra, blue candles, and dagger ferns across front.

DINING ROOM:	According to floor plan submitted. Organization to set out table cards. (Retain master guest list.)
DINNER:	6:30 P.M. *sharp,* blue cloths, and gold napkins. (Edith and captain left side of dining room; Norman and captain right side of dining room.)
MENU:	Fresh Fruit Cocktail, Supreme, Garniture of Strawberries (Silver coupes). In ice: Ripe and Green Olives, Radishes, Celery Hearts, Iced Butter Curls; bread and butter plates at each setting. From tureens: Potage Mongole Russian service: Chicken Kiev, Escoffier of Vegetables Preplated: Wedge of Cheese Cake, pass warm Blueberry Sauce; 12 Petits Fours per table. Coffee, self-poured; one pitcher per table, on candle warmer. (Following coffee service—one dish mints and nuts per table.)
GENERAL DIRECTIONS:	Wash dishes and glasses as used, two church crew members and two of our regular crew members. (Pay church crew minimum wage and tip at your discretion.) Following dessert service, one hour of dancing. All tables must be cleared, leaving only cloths and ashtrays. All dishes and glassware must be washed and truck-packed. *DISPOSABLE GLASSES TO BE USED AT BAR DURING LAST HOUR OF SERVICE.* Broom-sweep dining room only, with brushes to be supplied by church. Thoroughly wash kitchen floor, clean work tables, stoves, and reefers (refrigerators). Check garbage dumpster; make certain no garbage on ground. Check with church superintendent to make certain all areas meet with his/her complete satisfaction. Give superintendent gratuity check.

profit will either be reduced or eliminated entirely, do so *WITHOUT COMPROMISING YOUR STANDARDS OF QUALITY OR SERVICE.* You will gain greater respect for doing this, and adhering to high standards will enhance your reputation.

TIPS FOR A SUCCESSFUL FUNCTION

In addition to good food and service, you should pay careful attention to the following items:

1. Coordinate the timing and service of the meal with the client's plans for speeches, entertainment, or ceremonies. Determine in advance at what time, or place, or by what cue, service should cease or continue.
2. Do not serve a course while guests are dancing. Food served before guests are ready for it will either cool, get warm, or wilt.
3. Caution waiters and other employees *not to move place settings from one table to another*

without permission from the client or committee chairperson.

4. While the program is in progress, do not allow waiters to gather in groups in any part of the dining room.
5. Make sure water goblets are kept at the 7/8 level during the meal and are filled to this level prior to the departure of waiters at the start of the program.
6. Have all unused glasses, dishes, and unnecessary items removed from the tables as soon as possible. It is not pleasant for guests to be forced to sit at a cluttered table.
7. Keep ashtrays clean at all times.
8. Keep the client's or committee's original guest and seating lists accessible for ready reference.

RENTING OR LEASING A TENT

On some occasions, a client may want to hold the party in a tent. You should know which companies in your locality specialize in tent erections. Awning makers generally are a good source for tents.

Once you have collected this information, pass it along to your client, who should then consult these companies to determine the feasibility of erecting a tent in the desired area.

For your purposes, the surface covered by the tent should be hard-topped or a *perfectly level* grass area. However, it may be necessary to place shims under table legs to keep the tables from rocking. Should the tables be inadvertently moved, it may be necessary to have them re-shimmed.

Comparisons should be made between the price of renting a tent, along with the tables, chairs, dance floors, and other necessary platforms, and the price of renting a fully enclosed, air-conditioned facility.

If a tent will be used, you, the caterer, will have many problems to resolve. For example, where should you set up your preparation or kitchen facilities? Can you get field cooking ranges? Will ample refrigerating facilities be available? What can you do about bugs, flies, and mosquitoes, and how will you handle garbage disposal? Will your operating costs be increased considerably? And, finally, under such conditions, will you be able to maintain the standards for which you are known?

While the preceding are all negative factors, there are some positive ones:

1. Tent affairs can be gala and festive events.
2. A tent offers protection from the sun.
3. Generally, there is more elbow room for both the guests and the employees.

GENERAL CLEANUP
Cleanup following any party should be a systematic procedure. All glasses and dishes of the same type should be removed at one time from all tables. This speeds handling and packing in the dishwashing area and minimizes the number of packing cases needed at the exit end of the washing table.

Keep forks, knives, teaspoons, and other utensils in individual containers, each having a specified number of utensils, and then label each by contents and number.

When packing silverware, be methodical. With forks, pack all tines in the first row close together and facing the same way; tines in the second row should also all face the same way, but rest on the handles of those in the first row. Repeat this same procedure for the third and fourth rows and do the same thing with spoons.

When packing knives with hollow handles, place the flat side down, one row at a time. But remember to reverse the handles on every other row so that knife blades in one row will rest on knife handles in the row below.

Remove napkins separately and count before tying in a soiled but dry tablecloth. Leave tablecloths on two tables and, as the other cloths are removed, *shake them out onto one of the cloth-covered tables.* This has two purposes: (1) it keeps dirt off the floor; and (2) it enables you to discover quickly any valuables that have been inadvertently left behind.

After shaking the cloths, thoroughly examine remnants before discarding. Cloths already shaken out can then be thrown onto the second of the clothed tables, counted, and tied.

Keep wet and damp cloths separate, and, after returning to your commissary, spread them out to dry. This will prevent mildewing, which may not wash out.

Figure 9.5. Logistics of Off-Premise Catering

LOGISTICS OF OFF-PREMISE CATERING

Determining dining room items necessary to be truck-packed (for hypothetical party of 100 guests to be held at local Community Center).

DISHWASHING FACILITIES AVAILABLE. Center will supply 12 72-inch round tables plus all necessary chairs. Permanently fixed bar with ice, liquor storage, and glass display area. WE supply all linens, china, silverware, glassware, and all other service equipment.

RECEPTION — Butler Style — To be operational for ONE HOUR ONLY.

TINY POTATO PANCAKES (speared)	On 14″ round silver tray
COCKTAIL FRANKS (speared)	On 14″ round silver tray
SWEDISH MEATBALLS (speared)	On 14″ round silver tray
FRIED CHICKEN WINGS (pick up)	On 14″ round silver tray

Trays to be damp-wiped after each use.   4 silver trays required (#1)
1 pkg. cocktail napkins, 1000 to pack (#2)
1 box — 500 frilled toothpicks (#3)
10″ doilies — 25 required (#4)

AT BAR — Rye, Scotch, Vodka, Bourbon
　　　　　Hi-balls in 10 oz. glasses, 36 to rack　　　Pack 5 racks — 180 glasses (#5)
　　　　　Low-balls (wide mouth),
　　　　　25 to rack (8 oz.)　　　　　　　　　　　　Pack 4 racks — 100 glasses (#6)

As this is "stand-up," most guests will retain their glasses for refill. (Bartenders will bring their own work tools, such as pourers, stirrers, etc.)

DINNER — NO BAR SERVICE — Wine, champagne, and brandy to be poured at table.

　　　　　Water goblets (36 to rack)　　　　　　　Pack 3 racks — 108 units (#7)

FRESH FRUIT COCKTAIL
(In silver supremes — 16 to rack)　　　　　　Pack 7 racks — 112 units (#8)
Insets to hold fruit　　　　　　　　　　　　　Pack 9 dozen — 108 units (#9)
Rings to hold insets　　　　　　　　　　　　　Pack 9 dozen — 108 units (#10)
Supreme rests on doily　　　　　　　　　　　　Pack 1 box — 500/5″ doilies (#11)
　on 7″ underliner　　　　　　　　　　　　　　Pack 9 dozen — 7″ underliners (#12)
This rests on 10″ SHOWPLATE　　　　　　　　　Pack 9 dozen — 108 units (#13)
Teaspoon to be used　　　　　　　　　　　　　Pack 4 bags teaspoons — 120 units (#14)
　(All silverware packed 30 to a bag)

"MINI" ENTREE — STUFFED FLOUNDER
On 7″ plate　　　　　　　　　　　　　　　　　Add 9 dozen to above — 108 units (#12)
Fork required for this service　　　　　　　　　Pack 4 bags — 108 units (#15)

WHITE WINE TO BE POURED
(Before above service)
25 all-purpose wine glasses to rack　　　　　　Pack 5 racks — 125 units (#16)

(continued)

Figure 9.5. (continued)

ROAST PRIME RIBS OF BEEF — Preplated in kitchen
  Fresh asparagus   Rissole potatoes

This service on 10″ dinner plate   Pack 10 dozen dinner plates — 120 units (#13)

CHAMPAGNE TO BE POURED
(Before above service)
"Tulip" champagne glasses — 36 to rack   Pack 3 racks — 108 units (#17)
  Knife and fork required   Pack 4 bags knives — 120 units (#18)
                                                        Add 4 bags forks — 120 units (#15)

At each table: SILVER RELISH DISH
  Celery hearts   Olives   Burr gherkins   Pygmy egg plants

  Silver relish dishes — 18 to box   Pack 1 box silver relish dishes (#19)

At each table: SILVER BREAD TRAY LINED WITH 5″ PAPER DOILIES
  Use doilies as packed for fruit cocktail

  Silver bread trays — 18 to box   Pack 1 box silver bread trays (#20)

At each placesetting: 7″ Bread and butter plate   Add 9 dozen 7″ plates — 108 units (#12)
                                                        Pack 4 bags butter knives — 120 units (#21)

DESSERT — ICE CREAM FILLED ECLAIRS
  On 7″ plate   Add 9 dozen 7″ plates — 108 units (#12)
  Dessert fork required   Pack 4 bags dessert forks — 120 units (#22)

Pass HOT FUDGE SAUCE from Revere bowls — 9″
  (5 passers needed)
  Bowls — 12 to box   Pack 1 box Revere bowls (#23)

  10 Service spoons needed for fudge sauce
    and whipped cream — 24 spoons to box   Pack 1 box service spoons (#24)

COFFEE
  25 cups to rack   Pack 5 racks — 125 units (#25)
  Saucers   Pack 9 dozen — 108 units (#26)
  Teaspoons required   Add 4 bags teaspoons — 120 units (#14)

BRANDY TO BE PASSED AT THIS POINT
  1 oz. Brandy "ponies" — 12 dozen to case   Pack 1 case — 144 units (#27)

On each table: 2 sets salts and peppers
  Pack 24 sets to box   Pack 1 box — 24 each salt, 24 each pepper —
                                                          48 units (#28)

On each table: 1 sugar bowl — 18 to a box   Pack 1 box — 18 units (#29)

On each table: 2 creamers — 18 to a box   Pack 2 boxes — 36 units (#30)

On each table: 4 ashtrays — 48 to a box   Pack 1 box — 48 units (#31)

POTATO PANCAKES	Use 10 lbs. potatoes and recipe on file. Cook on job. Serve with 1 pint appleberry sauce.
COCKTAIL FRANKS	Take 8 lbs. (30 to lb.). Spike 1 pt. mustard with 1/2 cup horseradish and few drops Tabasco.
COCKTAIL MEATBALLS	Prepare 10 lbs. (30 to lb.). (Omit garlic from recipe.) Make 2 qts. sweet/sour pungent sauce.
FRIED CHICKEN WINGS	Finish in Commissary. Reheat on job. Make 1 pint duck sauce.
FRUIT COCKTAIL	Use base of 2 gal. chilled citrus sections. Ball out 6 cantaloupes, dice 6 apples with skin, split 3 lbs. black grapes, 4 lbs. strained blueberries. Garnish with 6 pts. strawberries and 2 bunches mint.
STUFFED FLOUNDER	110 portions* according to recipe. Reheat on job. Pack in low, covered hotel pans. (*This will allow for "imperfects" and feeding of help.)
RIB ROASTS	Prepare 7 ribs, oven ready. Cook on job. Slice 17 to rib (this will also allow for feeding of help.) Pack in square covered roasting pans.
ASPARAGUS	Steam 25 lbs. in Commissary. Reheat on job. Make 1 gal. Hollandaise (recipe on file). Take 4 7-oz. cans pimientos; "strip" on job. Take 5 bunches washed watercress.
RISSOLE POTATOES	Prepare 250 "sized" potatoes (2 to portion) in Commissary and finish on job with roast beef drippings. (Allow for breakage and feeding of help.)
ICE CREAM ECLAIRS	Bake 10 doz. eclair shells 4″ long. Split and fill fully with pistachio ice cream. Pack 24 to plastic covered containers in portable freezer. Cover with 10 lbs. sliced dry ice when shipping.
HOT FUDGE SAUCE	Make 2 gallons as recipe indicates. Pack in gallon, clear plastic containers and take double boiler for reheating.
CELERY HEARTS	Please check that kitchen man scrapes and *thoroughly washes* (3 to 4 times) all celery hearts and cut thinner.

Figure 9.6. Chef's Instructions (For Hypothetical Party of 100 Guests at Local Community Center)

Figure 9.7. Schematic floor plan of kitchen for off-premise caterer. Note generous space for packing and dolly storage.

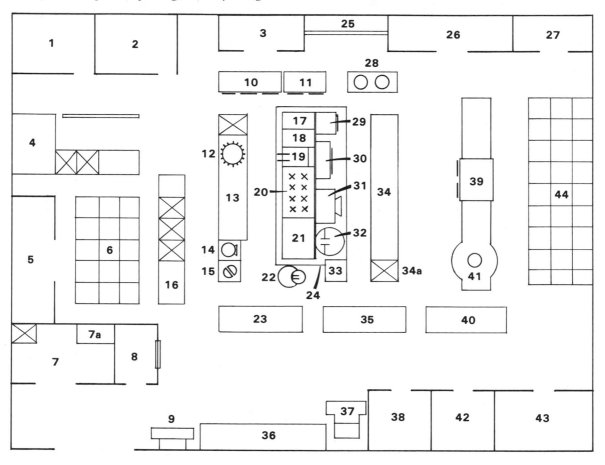

1. Men's dressing room	17. Broiler	32. Steam stock kettle
2. Ladies' dressing room	18. Re-con oven	33. Meat grinder
3. Chef's office	19. Fryer	34. Work tables
4. Pot washing area	20. Surface burners	Shelves under
5. Cart washing area	2 ovens under	34a. Hand sink
6. Cart storage	21. Deck oven	35. Assembly table
7. Trash room with sink	22. Mixer	36. Receiving and sorting table
7a. Compactor	23. Assembly tables	37. Ice machine
8. Receiving office	Also #35 and #40 (for cart	38. Merchandise stores
9. Receiving scale	packing)	39. Dishwasher
10. Reach-in refrigerator	24. Exhaust canopy over	Hot-water booster under
11. Reach-in freezer	25. Vegetable-fruit storage	40. Food assembly tables (for
12. Suspended pot-pan hooks	26. Walk-in refrigerator	cart packing)
13. Chef's work table	27. Walk-in freezer	41. Disposal
Shelves and bins under	28. Coffee makers	42. Storage, dishes, silver, props
14. Chopper	29. Radar oven	43. Storage, linens, etc.
15. Slicer	30. Oblong tilt steam kettle	44. Glasses, cups, dishes, storage
16. Work sink with	31. Vegetable steamer	in mobile racks
drainboards		

1. Get $30.00 in small bills from Helen in office.
2. Take Mike as helper—*leave no later than 2 P.M.*
3. Stop off at Fusco Ice Co. for 4 bushels ice cubes as ordered. Pay cash and get receipt. (Our ice machine is temporarily out of commission.)
4. Stop off at Wolfe Bakery and pick up special breads and sheet cake as ordered. Retain invoice and leave in office with truck keys upon return.
5. Destination: Community Center in West Haven—Proceed to South Avenue Turnpike Entrance North, rather than usual Park Avenue North Turnpike Entrance as there is a football game in the Stadium and traffic could be backed up.

Pay toll at Cumberland Avenue and *get receipt.* Get off at 27A to Lindley St. (one-way traffic) and continue to Capitol Avenue (also one-way traffic). Continue to third light, Howard Avenue, and MAKE A LEFT TURN to middle of second block—white marble building with tall iron fence. Park in front of building and go into office (to right of entrance). Ask for Mr. Reo, the Super-intendant, who will open gate and direct you backing into driveway to loading platform. Circular driveway is a little tricky. Loading platform leads directly into kitchen. Kitchen crew will help unload.

Lock cab of truck, lower roll-down door and also lock it. *Do not leave any items on loading platform unattended* as youngsters from neighborhood have been known to scale back fence and make off with items left there. (In the event of any type of truck breakdown, call 276-4367, Bernie's Garage.)

Figure 9.8. Instructions to Sam Cooper, Driver

Figure 9.9. Accident Report

BANQUET ORGANIZATION
ACCIDENT REPORT

NAME: _____   DATE: _____

ADDRESS: _____   TIME: _____

_____

TELEPHONE NO.: _____

Give description of accident: (Describe what, where, and how the accident occurred. Give full details that led to accident.)

_____

_____

(continued)

Figure 9.9. (continued)

_____

_____

_____

_____

_____

_____

_____

_____

What action was taken in handling the accident:

_____

_____

_____

_____

Date of Report: _____

Prepared by: _____

Position: _____

_____

CHAPTER TEN

ON-PREMISE CATERING

According to estimates, customers spend two-thirds of their total foodservice expenditures in restaurant and hotel/motel dining rooms. The remaining one-third is spent in drive-ins and fast food establishments. Public eating places, individually and company-owned, represent the greatest number of United States retail outlets.

In vying for their share of the market, many restaurants and hotels use special promotions, which offer lower prices for certain foods on set days. Children's birthday parties, which are encouraged, include such special offers as birthday cakes, party favors, and menus that can be converted into carry-out toys (often displaying the restaurant's name in some conspicuous spot.)

These promotions are nearly always aimed at *basic daily meal periods*—breakfast, lunch and/or dinner.

However, after peak periods, the average restaurant or hotel dining room is usually empty. Although they are attractive, comfortable, and air-conditioned eating places, they are nearly devoid of customers.

This presents a serious difficulty. The facility must be maintained, lighted, and heated. Furthermore, it is staffed with cooking and baking specialists who are not busy. With imagination and by greater utilization of working tools, these difficulties can be converted into assets by promoting on-premise catering.

Getting Your Operation Known

To start, you might attach clip-ons to regular daily menus explaining that your facilities are available for wedding breakfasts, bridge parties, sales meetings, service/fraternal club banquets, etcetera. Table tents at each table can elaborate on your on-premise catering or cite special prices. You can also have professionally lettered posters made up and posted in prominent positions. If you have to make space for them, often you have only to remove signs installed by cigarette and beverage salesmen and *PUT UP YOUR OWN SIGNS,* which *advertise your products and services.*

If you use floor stanchions to control traffic while guests wait to be seated, use part of them as a message board to display pictures of your buffet presentations, or a fully set guest table for a catered party. A handsomely decorated wedding or birthday cake (with dummy layers) placed in an appropriate location can be worth more than a thousand words.

Another possibility is to have a sign painter make an extra panel for your outdoor sign. The panel should contain, in addition to the word catering, a strong, positive adjective or a descriptive phrase, but not just a single word. Some examples include: Distinctive On-Premise Catering, Unexcelled Catering Facilities, Attractive Rates For Catering, Celebrate Your Next Happy Occasion With Us, or Ask About Special Rates.*

BANQUET HALL/ROOMS

Because of initial costs involved in building or renting and equipping a facility, most on-premise caterers were originally successful off-premise caterers before they expanded their services and moved into banquet hall/rooms operations.

A banquet-hall caterer can offer the same services as a restaurant/hotel catering department. In addition to a commissary/kitchen, the caterer's facilities will include at least one large, tastefully decorated, air-conditioned room containing a stage or raised dais. He or she might also have several smaller rooms, which can be offered to small, informal groups for bridal showers, ladies' luncheons, business luncheons, and other such functions.

FUNCTION ROOM FURNITURE

The equipment used for public functions held in hotels, restaurants, catering halls, and clubs is known collectively as *function room furniture*. As these institutions are host to business functions, community, and social events, the furniture must be structurally sound to withstand mishandling and abuse, and aesthetically pleasing.

*For additional ideas, see "Developing A Market" section in Chapter 1.

Furniture purchased to outfit these areas should meet the following criteria:

1. Strength and durability—The use of household-grade furniture in a commercial establishment is foolhardy and can lead to disastrous incidents. Furnishings should have built-in ruggedness to withstand transport from one area to another, and to withstand being pushed, rolled, setup, knocked down, stacked, and stored. The roughest handling should still leave the equipment relatively unscathed and totally functional.
2. Ease of handling—The equipment must be easy to move and arrange, and not too heavy or too bulky to handle. It should require a minimum of personnel to load and unload on transport dollies and trucks.
3. Ease of storing—Equipment should fit in available storage areas and through standard openings without having to be dismantled. Chairs should stack high, one on the other, without marring or toppling. Tables should have underframes wide enough to totally enclose folded legs; stacking will then be firm and solid, and dangerous slide-offs will be avoided. (The wishbone style leg offers the most comfortable knee and foot room. See Figure 10.1.)
4. Flexibility—It is advisable to purchase furniture that can serve two or more purposes, for example: a *schoolroom* table can be incorporated into an elevated buffet setup (see Figure 10.2); and, center column and heavy base cafe tables can be used as cocktail tables (a large round top can be added to convert it to a dinner table and a square top can convert it to an extender for an oblong table).

Tables

There are folding tables that come in many sizes and shapes. Standard rounds range in size from 24 inches to 108 inches; oblong tables range from 15 inches to 30 inches in width and up to 10 feet in length. Larger tables are available on special

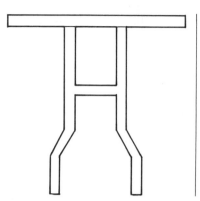

Figure 10.1. Wishbone-style table leg. Comfortable because of minimal knee contact.

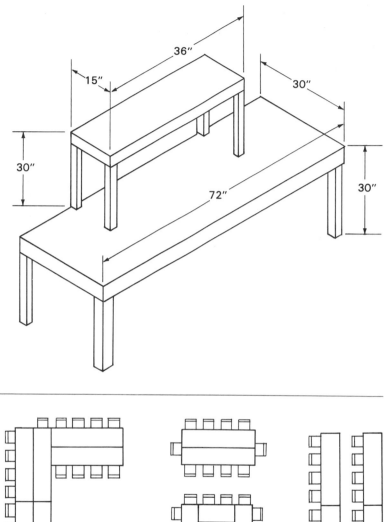

Figure 10.2. Placing a school room table on top of a standard oblong table can make a two-height buffet table.

Figure 10.3. Suggested uses of schoolroom tables in 15 to 18 inch widths.

order, but such oversize tables are bulky to handle and to manipulate.

The 12-to-15 inch wide oblongs are called *schoolroom* tables. Two widths together equal a standard 30-inch table. They are suited to crowded meeting halls (but not convenient for meal service) and make excellent display tables for merchandise shows, etcetera. (See Figure 10.3.)

Folding tables come with various shaped tops—oblong, round, serpentine, oval, quarter-round, half-round, and trapezoid (see Figures 10.4 and 10.5). Serpentine tables are shaped like arcs, which makes them part of a circle. Butted in reverse, they make an S-shaped setup. (See Figures 10.4 and 10.5.) Serpentines can be used to form round, half-round, S-shaped, and horseshoe groupings. They can be used to make graceful buffet and head table setups. Used in conjunction with oblong tables, they round off a rectangular buffet into half-round projections.

A quarter-round table makes a rounded corner for two tables placed at right angles; half-round tables can be used to round out rectangular ends (see Figures 10.4 and 10.5). This unit makes a particularly effective raised center for buffet or spotlighted presentations.

There is a folding trapezoid table that makes a solid hexagonal table when two are placed together on the longer sides. Many other variations

and effective combinations are possible with this table.

Regardless of the type of table purchased, make certain that the *locking devices are strong, simple, and effective.* The element of human error in properly locking complicated devices should be eliminated.

Stack and Folding Chairs

Stack chairs, whether they are framed in aluminum, steel, chrome, or iron, are easier to handle than folding chairs. They can be set up with greater ease, with less noise, and in less time. They eliminate the worry of infirmly locked legs. The seats and backs of stacks can be upholstered more luxuriously than folding chairs. Good stack chairs have "wall-saver" legs that extend beyond

Figure 10.4. Suggested configurations using schoolroom, serpentine, round, trapezoid, quarter-round, and half-round tables.

Figure 10.5. Suggested table configurations that can make unique and effective buffet table layouts.

the back, thus preventing it from marring the walls.

In expensively formal and luxurious dining areas, the chairs may be massive with arms, backs, and seats upholstered in rare materials. This type of ambience is usually indicative of a successful operation.

Folding Platforms

These are fabricated in many sizes and styles to suit numerous needs, and they are extremely flexible. Some have two sets of folding legs that afford varying heights. They can be used to elevate banquet tables or can be set up in tiers for distinguished guests. They can also be used as runways for fashion shows, or as elevated platforms for musical groups. (Reliable manufacturers furnish liability insurance with each sale.)

Portable Dance Floors

Portable dance floors offer several advantages. They do not require an initial permanent and expensive installation, nor do they require zip-out sections of rugs to make them functional.

Portables can be set in any room-area arrangement and, therefore, do not restrict guest setups.

MODULAR UNITS

An exciting development in buffet catering now offers a myriad of possibilities for unusual and effective food presentation—MODULAR UNITS.

The profusion of uses offered by modular equipment is limited only by one's sense of innovation. The units, which are from 30 inches to 72 inches long, can be interlocked to form a continuous display or used independently as serving

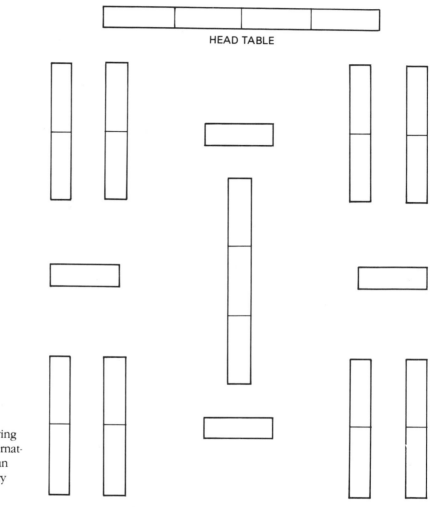

Figure 10.6. Schematic drawing using only oblong tables. Alternating table positioning creates an atmosphere of greater intimacy and interest.

islands in various parts of the dining area. They can be rolled directly to guest tables or locations to create an atmosphere of special and intimate dining.

They are beautifully constructed and covered in grained mica, leather, metal, or tufted luxury fabrics. Their maneuverability makes them equally valuable and effective for the on- or off-premise caterer. They are comparatively light and can be rolled on or off trucks via portable ramps or mechanical tailgates.

They are particularly effective for beef carving as infrared lamps keep food at the proper temperature and lend warmth and beauty to the dining environment. Mechanically, they retain heat or cold at the degree programmed. Total efficiency is achieved when used as a salad bar as built-in and surface spaced units only require filling, eliminating the need for decorative show-pieces and saving labor.

There are built-in and interchangeable and sized hot wells that retain constant heat without the use of liquids or solid fuels. Crushed ice displays retain their volume and effectiveness even in the hottest and most humid weather, which makes these units totally efficient for chilled fruits and frozen desserts.

There are some negative features to modulars. They offer limited opportunities to express decorative capabilities. (This can be a plus factor as many operators lack skilled display help.) Displays must be contained within the square or rectangular areas, and display height is limited because of mandatory sneeze or dust guards. This does not allow for spectacular carvings of ice or tallow, or special fruit displays. Flower arrangements must be separate or on tables alongside. (Free-standing buffets have practically no size restrictions and flowers can be integrated with carvings to create spectacular arrangements.)

Trays of all sizes and shapes with masterful decorations can be set on stands of varying heights, creating interest and attractiveness. Many interesting table configurations can be achieved (see Figures 10.3, 10.4, and 10.5). that are impossible with modulars.

Skirting and theme drapings, ready-made or not, accent and add beauty to the presentation.* However, modulars can be effectively combined with free-standing tables to form functional and aesthetic groupings.

SERVICE STANDS

Service stands are essential in every fixed dining area. Their locations should be strategically available to the station that they service.

Supplying and maintaining the stand should be delegated to one individual in each station.

Off-premise caterers will not find these stands practical as they are not constructed for mobility. Off-premise stands, if needed, will have to be improvised, or a small table set up and used for that purpose.

---

*Modulars are available with frame bottoms that allow personalized draping.

CHAPTER ELEVEN

ARRANGEMENTS FOR VARIOUS FUNCTIONS

SERVICE CLUB MEETINGS

Service clubs, such as Rotary, Lions, Chamber of Commerce, Kiwanis, and others, who meet at regularly scheduled times and at the same dining area, should be given the consideration of a rate reduction. There is no doubt that the establishment gains prestige through their patronage.

The host establishments can count on a specified and guaranteed number of guests and can forecast, fairly accurately, the food production amounts and the number of service and satellite personnel required.

In this era of energy conservation, you can eliminate wasteful lighting and air-conditioning since you know the exact time to make these units operational. Another residual is that some members will patronize the bar and lobby shops.

The most valuable residual is the amount of free advertising generated by their meetings. Newspapers, radio, and TV usually detail the time and place of such meetings. If a notable is to be featured at a meeting, interviews and pictures are printed and broadcast, and the location is always mentioned.

The lectern at the speaker's table should always bear the name of the establishment—or an easily recognizable logo in a "discreetly conspicuous" place.

Roadside signs (maintained by the Club) inform travelers when and *in what place* the luncheon or dinner meetings are being held. Strangers seeking a place to eat are influenced by these signs and often decide in your favor.

BANQUET AND GROUP SALES

Banquet and group sales can result in additional revenue for many restaurant and hotel facilities. Banquet business was once the sole province of hotels and catering halls. This exclusivity has been splintered off to independent restaurant operators and even to private clubs. This is evident from the restaurant ads in daily papers and the display ads in the *Yellow Pages*. Many operators feature their catering facilities rather than the specialties de maison.

Catering and group sales are profitable! Henry Sgrosso, the owner of the successful Once Upon a Stove in New York, NETS 15 percent on banquets! (The Chart P. & L. of a Successful Caterer listed in Table 7.1 details a duplicate profit.) McMullen's and Tarfos, also of New York, report similar nets. (*Restaurant News* 17 December 1979.) *New York Magazine* notes that Vincent Sardi of Sardi's, one of the city's nationally known and respected independent operators, is pursuing this aspect with greater intensity than heretofore. His justified confidence has resulted in the construction of additional space to be used exclusively for catering. As noted in the chapter on kosher catering, prominent New York hotels report that catering accounts for 40 percent of gross income. Independent operators seem to be making a greater thrust in this direction than chain operators.

There are very few establishments that do not have slow periods. These periods should be utilized for this potential income. Operators should make a complete overview of their day-by-day, hour-by-hour traffic count and income. Labor expenditures in relation to income should be analyzed, along with employee productivity and employee potential—would they be proficient and capable of producing the desired end product?

This study will give an accurate picture of the feasible hours that could be utilized for extra income.

Dining areas that open at 5 P.M. daily are booking weddings and group luncheons that terminate at 3:30 P.M. Many are featuring Sunday brunches and communion breakfasts. Weekday fashion shows for department stores and specialty shops are another source of income. Organizations involved in political and fund-raising activities can be given the exclusive use of the facilities during these periods.

The progressive operator of Little Dicks Night Club in Portchester, New York, rents out his complete facilities on Saturday nights (9 P.M. to 3 A.M.), to organizations only, for up to 250 guests for $4,000, including meals and liquor. Mr. Richard Gildersleeve, the owner, claims that his sales are not necessarily better but his NET is better because of greater cost control—the plus feature for banquets (*Restaurant News,* 17 December 1979).

Senior citizen promotions can add to revenues. Do not assume they are financially deprived. Newspaper articles detailing their many activities—trips, show buses, holiday banquets, and educational participation—attest to their numbers and projects. Some of their business could possibly be siphoned off to the area of catering.

There are government funds that pay for nutritionally balanced meals furnished to the elderly in churches, centers, and community halls. In general, these meals are bulk-produced in a central area and delivered to the feeding points, where they are individually portioned. Given the superior, quantity food production abilities of restaurants and catering halls, it would be feasible to acquire the lucrative contracts for this food production. Practically all of these programs operate five days a week.

If the restaurant or catering hall is in an historic district or theme park area, it might be possible to arrange with tour operators to make special feeding arrangements for their groups. Athletic events or tournaments involving team participation could be a profitable source of additional income if you arrange to feed the teams, coaches, and other essential personnel.

Takeout foods can add materially to income. The only additional expense would be for packaging. Available disposables have excellent temperature-holding qualities that simplify packing. The full retail price received yields greater than normal profit as extra serving personnel (with their expensive benefits) are almost eliminated.

Sales and profits can be increased by adapting the operation to meet the preferences of the clientele. Most people value good taste and appearance, and avoid cheap, shoddy, and tasteless items. All people want sound quality and value for their money. Many can afford better things because their discretionary incomes have increased. People are better educated and informed, and appreciate good taste—what is beautiful, appropriate, and in good proportion.

Excellence and good taste are more important than price when such people shop. They desire superior quality products and presentations, and *are willing to pay for it!* Naturally, the higher the markup, the higher the profit.

You will find receptive listeners when you highlight the quality of the food you serve. In addition, emphasize that you have trained personnel who are *alert to the needs of the guests at all times.*

Try to become more knowledgeable in your food, beverage, and service areas so that you will be regarded as an authority on what you sell. You will also be able to advise and assist your clients in indulging their epicurean tastes. Finally, remember that a well-executed banquet or party can trigger repeat business from satisfied customers who never patronized your place before.

SIGNATURE ITEMS

A caterer should attempt to develop an unusual food offering or a surprise presentation that will generate favorable table conversation. Your establishment then becomes identified with this *signature item.*

It should, if possible, be an exclusive recipe development and not easily duplicated (for example, cranberry, strawberry, and walnut relish). Or, it could be the service of an extra, fancy item (whole spiced peaches) or a generous dish of Hungarian or Turkish pastries accompanying the dessert.

The signature item can be presented during any part of the meal, but it must be visually and tastefully impressive. Memorable signature items can be the deciding factors when catering contracts are awarded. The following are some examples:

Complimentary cheese and fruit tray
Oversize popovers with sweet butter
Cannister of penny candies with dessert
Crock of minced salmon and whipped cream cheese
Whole spiced peaches as table relish

Cornmeal batter-dipped cocktail franks on lollipop sticks
Table bowls of cranberry dotted sauerkraut and burr gherkins
Banana bread and pecan honey buns
Pizza-flavored, toasted miniature bagels
Dollar-sized German potato pancakes with appleberry sauce
Lazy Susan of individual antipastos on each table
Frosted seltzer bottle with a carafe of house wine
Unlimited soup or chowder tureen per table
Super-supreme black olives with pygmy eggplants
Center table arrangement of provolone cheese, whole tomatoes, green pepper, celery hearts, and sesame bread sticks
Crisp oven-browned ravioli
Individual 10-inch salad bowl per guest as an intermediate course
Takeout soft ice cream in cups at dining exit
Logo-decorated, take-home beverage glass
Bowl of matzo balls in chicken-mushroom gravy with main course, per table
Breaded mushroom caps with bourbon dip
Bubbling rarebit on candle stand with skewered crusty bread
Maitre d's and captains offering to pour brandy in guests' black coffee, as a house treat.

RENTALS

Some clients may want a little more artifice and dazzle to make their parties memorable extravaganzas. The following is a list of such items that can be rented from many metropolitan agencies:

Hot dog stands with red, white, and blue umbrellas
Neon sculpture

Hand-painted or plain canopies

Huge papier mache Buddhas

Silver-plated place mats

Candy-striped ice cream wagons

Bumper pool tables

Cots for extra guests

Grand pianos

Tents (from 12 ft. square to 50 × 200 ft.)

Heaters for tents

Palms—exotic plants and flowers

Yucca trees

Ficus trees

Terra cotta urns and vases

Clear glass cubes for seating or decoration

Votive candles in vases filled with blue irises

Hand-painted "fat" pillows for floor seating

Boughs of flowers in vases of molded ice

Antique hay wagons

Split rail fences

Victorian gazebos

Vintage cars

Penants

Pom-poms

Football bleachers

Lucite pillars with crystal bowls of flowers on top

Banquettes

Disco floors and lights

Mirrored balls

Sound systems

Soap-bubble machine

Neon-lit fish tanks

Helium-filled balloons.

Many special linen items are also available. For example:

Gold or silver lame

Chocolate and cream batik

Emerald and ruby paisley

Pristine white eyelet

Black and white taffeta

Lavender moire

Mauve mohair cloths

Navy cloths with hand-painted borders, topped with white linen ones.

You can also consider such special party entertainment as:

Rollerskate disco

Astrologers or palm readers

Belly dancers

Caricaturists

Children's entertainment—puppets, clowns

Mobile discotheque

Disc jockey

Magic ESP

Handwriting analyst

Hypnotist

Parody pianist

Mechanical robots.

THE BUFFET

The buffet, where foods are presented so guests can serve themselves, is not only popular for receptions and cocktail parties, but can also be a spectacular means for presenting an entire meal. It is particularly appropriate in homes, where space is limited and a large number of people are to be served. The buffet can be elaborate and elegant enough to suit the most sophisticated gourmet tastes, or can add a special flair to the simplest of breakfast, lunch, or dinner menus.

Successful buffet catering must use the basic principles of merchandising, since *well-displayed merchandise sells itself*. Your food display, the garnitures, and the service ware all enhance the appearance of the table, and act as attention-getters. As supplementary showpieces, use ice carvings, flowers, tallow or butter molds, or sugar or nougat work. These are "come-ons" that attract guests to the table.

The buffet table is a miniature market place because its charm, magnetism, excitement, flavor, and food are geared to stimulate the shopper's appetite. As guests approach the table, their minds subconsciously photograph the entire display; if it is artistically and attractively presented, they are entranced with the picture. Tempted by a wide choice of food, beautifully offered, they become impulse buyers.

No matter how beautiful the table may be, its appearance will be enhanced by either mechanical or human animation. Having employees serve food from chafing or other service dishes is not only ·a gracious gesture, but one that assists in speeding up the service. A chef carving a roast or slicing a salmon has great customer appeal, but one actually cooking a variety of omelets, crepes, or deep-fry specialties kindles a curiosity that is hard to resist, and practically all onlookers are intrigued by the action.

Table-top or "exhibition cooking" should be used when practical. That means giving serious consideration to such elements as price, time, equipment, and safety.

Price

The costs involved in table-top cooking are higher because the person selected to do specialized cooking has to spend the entire time at the buffet. Since this person's skill is great, his or her wage rate will be higher. Therefore, consider whether your monetary return is sufficient to warrant this service.

Time

Table-top foods should not take too long to cook because waiting guests could create a traffic jam, interfering with service to others. Small crepes should be prepared in the kitchen, then taken to the buffet for final touches. Each pan should contain at least a dozen crepes so that a number of guests can be served within a short time. Filled omelets should be made large enough to be cut

into 12 fork portions. Eggs Foo Yung, made in a 12-inch pan, will yield approximately 25 appetizer portions.

Small table-top grilles, heated by propane gas tubes, can cook from 40 to 60 cocktail franks or 40 cocktail hamburgers, which can be served on finger rolls or cocktail breads. A cheese fondue in a 2-quart chafing dish or fondue pot is enough for at least 50 bread cubes. These suggestions are but a few of the different items that can be prepared quickly, but in quantity.

Equipment

In addition to small table-top grilles, other cooking equipment, such as, electric fry pans, waffle irons, chafing dishes, fondue pots, and deep fryers, can be also used effectively for buffet catering.

Table-top deep fat fryers are excellent for exhibition frying. The most effective and convenient are stainless steel-clad of 4-quart capacity *(do not use a larger one for buffet service)*, with a rating of no more than 110 volts and 1500 amps. The 1500 amps is important because the electrical system must be able to carry the load, which includes a large number of lights and/or other electrical equipment, without blowing fuses or tripping switches. Before using the fryer at a party, give it a dry run. Also, remember that great care and proper precautions must be taken to guard against accidental spillage.

When using, firmly set the fryer on a table, fill it to the factory-suggested line, using *homogenized shortening,* which is easier to carry and reduces the possibility of spillage.

Products to be deep fried must be free of water and lowered *carefully* into the shortening. Avoid overcrowding; this allows the product to cook faster and eliminates overflowing of hot grease.

Some items that lend themselves well to table-top frying are: cocktail franks in beer batter; tiny potato puffs; ravioli; breaded shrimp; corn puffs; tiny apple fritters; eggplant fingers; fillet of sole fingers; batter-dipped bologna cubes; and boneless chicken wings.

Fondue cooking on a buffet is a surefire attention getter, and fondue is a comparatively simple dish to prepare. A cheese fondue is the most popular type. To prepare, shred or dice cheese into small squares. Place them in the fondue pot, which is over a small fire, add wine, a touch of garlic and seasoning, and stir occasionally to prevent sticking or scorching. When the cheese begins to bubble, reduce the fire so that cheese bubbles only intermittently. Crusted French bread or croutons—each speared by a long bamboo skewer or a two-pronged fondue fork—are placed on a tray so guests can dip their own. Large paper napkins and 4-inch plates should be available. An attendant should be nearby to replenish fondue or bread.

Space is an important consideration. Can traffic move freely? Is there enough space or room on the table to present this service effectively? Will there be sufficient open space around the preparation area so that the heat generated by the unit will not adversely affect other foods?

Safety

Safety is a paramount consideration at all times. Since table-top cooking involves hot liquids, cooking apparatus must be *firmly anchored or tied* to table legs or sides, and set on a tray that is at least one-third larger than the unit used. *The table must be rigid and stand steadily on the floor. Never, never use a wobbly table.*

If using a "knockdown" or collapsible table, make certain that leg hardware is firmly locked in place. *Then take the additional precaution of tying or wiring the leg hardware* to avoid the possibility of table collapse. When electric wiring is used, *tie the utensil's cord to the table leg* so that if anyone trips over the wire, the grille or fryer will not slide or move. When an extension cord must be on the floor—whether in a traffic area or not—cover it with 4-inch adhesive firmly fastened to the floor; thus, the wire cannot be kicked and no one can trip over it.

Careless Employees

All precautions will be nullified if you permit a careless employee to do table-top cooking. The efficiency, skill, and adeptness of a qualified employee will add greatly to the effectiveness of your presentation.

DECORATIVE PIECES FOR THE BUFFET

Whether a simple affair or a spectacular showcase, the buffet provides you and your staff with an opportune setting for displaying artistic and culinary talents. Ice carvings, tallow work, decorated foods, colorfully garnished food trays, speciality cakes, spun sugar, and nougat designs can be used singly or in combination to dramatize and individualize buffet tables.

Ice Carvings/Molds

Because of their size and the effort needed to execute and move them, ice carvings are generally used only for very special occasions, and those held in hotels, clubs, and banquet halls. Furthermore, large unique ice carvings can be done only in an icehouse, or where there is a large walk-in freezer. Smaller ice molds, however, can be made in a commissary/kitchen.

Caviar on Ice. Caviar lends a touch of elegance to a reception or cocktail party buffet. It is most frequently presented in the original can on an ice mold (see Figure 11.1).

To make an ice display for caviar, fill a large gelatin mold, round bowl, or saucepan with water to a depth of 4 inches. Place in a freezer until solidly frozen (from two to three days).

To unmold, set pan in hot water for a moment or two, then invert quickly on a tray covered with a plastic doily. (The diameter of the tray should be at least 8 inches greater than the mold.)

Using hot water, half fill a can or pan having approximately the same diameter as the caviar can. Place container of hot water in the center of the ice mold for a few minutes so the ice will melt sufficiently to accommodate the caviar tin.

Figure 11.1. Decorative presentation of caviar using a simple, pan-made ice mold as the base.

Figure 11.2. Styrofoam base, anchored with florist's clay, used in making fruited centerpiece.

Figure 11.3. Fruited centerpiece. (Stand may be eliminated.)

Before placing the caviar on ice, fold a small white napkin and place it in the melted area. This will prevent the can from rolling or sliding. At this point, decorate the mold with lemon leaves, watercress, or parsley. Hollowed-out serrated lemons, filled with finely chopped, hard-cooked egg whites, or finely minced onions in sour cream, make a very effective garnish. Add lemon wedges or arrange them in a separate dish next to the mold.

Keep a large dry sponge and small pan nearby. About once every half hour, use the sponge to absorb the melted ice and squeeze the water into the pan. (Do this as unobtrusively as possible.)

Fruited Ice Molds for Punch Bowls. In the bottom of a heart-shaped pan, loaf pan, or ring mold, arrange sliced fruit, or mint leaves with strawberries or cherries. Pour in plain or tinted water, gingerale, fruit juice, or lemonade to a depth of 1/4 inch, and freeze. When frozen, fill the mold with additional liquid and refreeze. To unmold, dip the pan in hot water to the rim, and invert over punch bowl.

Edible Centerpieces

Edible, or partially edible, centerpieces can highlight different sections of the table, or can be most attractive as the focal point on the buffet. For a large elaborate buffet table, they may be supported by an elegant floral arrangement or an ice carving.

Fruited Centerpiece. With florist clay, anchor shaped styrofoam (see Figure 11.2) inside a medium or large silver or glass bowl. Insert bamboo sticks or club toothpicks in the styrofoam and "hang" leaves, grapes, pineapple stems, melon balls, strawberries, etcetera, from them. Fill the bottom of the bowl with shredded coconut, walnut or pecan meats, lemon leaves, or other greenery (see Figure 11.3).

Melon Pieces. Melons, particularly watermelons, can be made into eye-catching centerpieces. Because of their size and shape, watermelons can be arranged either vertically or horizontally, depending on the amount of display space allowed and the effect desired.

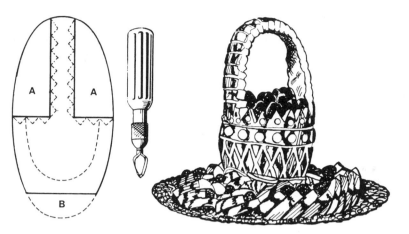

Figure 11.4. Vertical melon basket and gouging tool used to create patterns.

Melon basket (vertical)—Scrub entire melon and dry it well. Scabs and blemishes can be removed by gently scraping the surface. Cut off the bottom (see B in Figure 11.4) so that the melon will stand firmly by itself. Cut away two sections (see A in the same illustration) and reserve for slices to surround the base of the melon.

Use an ice cream scoop or large spoon to scoop out the melon flesh to within 2 inches from the bottom, and about 1/2 inch from the walls. Smooth off inner walls before filling with melon balls and more fruit.

Score patterns on the melon surface with a gouging tool (see illustration) available in hobby shops or art stores. Use French ballers of various sizes to cut "buttons" from the rind. Reverse the buttons in each hole for a pleasing effect, or cut buttons from orange and/or grapefruit rinds and place these cutouts in the watermelon rind holes. If the melon must be made far in advance, shrinkage could occur; in this case, the cutouts should be anchored with toothpick points.

Serrate handles and edges of melon in any manner desired. Fill the basket cavity with cut melon pieces or balls, and any additional fruit desired. Make certain that the melon rind surfaces are perfectly dry, then polish with a soft cloth lightly coated with salad oil.

Melon basket (horizontal)—Follow the same procedure as the one used for a vertical basket, but work with the melon placed horizontally. If part of the handle breaks off while cutting, just even off the broken sides, and add a few decorative finishing touches to make it appear that the design was intentional.

Melon head—Wash the watermelon thoroughly, and let it dry. Using a magic marker, outline the nose, eyes, and lips. Cut through the rind around the marked areas, and carefully pull away the unwanted rind with a paring knife. Smooth off all exposed surfaces, then decorate as desired. For the hat, use a pineapple stem on a center cut of pineapple. For the ears, position

Figure 11.5. Horizontal melon basket.

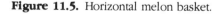

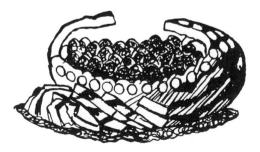

Figure 11.6. Melon head.

Figure 11.7. One passenger melon mobile is an effective showpiece.

pineapple rings with toothpicks. Fill centers with red cherries (optional).

One passenger automobile—

1. Wash and dry melon thoroughly.
2. Cut as shown in Figure 11.7, slicing a piece of the rind from the bottom of the melon so it will rest steadily on a tray.
3. Slice a piece from the thinner end of the melon, and attach a pineapple stem with toothpicks.
4. For the windshield, fit a wedge-shaped slice of melon into a groove prepared in front of the center cut.
5. For the bumper, fit a wedge-shaped slice of melon into a prepared groove in the front end of the automobile.
6. For the head, use a small orange, and cut out features.
7. For the hat, use half of a large orange; scallop the edges, cut out pulp, and top with a cherry button.
8. For the steering wheel, use a thick, round slice of orange.
9. For backrests and doors, wedge a slice of fresh pineapple into place.
10. For large wheels, use fresh pineapple slices.

11. For smaller wheels or hub caps, use small slices of canned pineapple, and fill centers with cherries.
12. For the headlights, use sliced oranges or lemons with cherries in the centers.
13. Use a scoring tool to add finishing touches. Display on a decorative tray.

Decorated Food Presentations

Hot foods require only the very simplest garnishes—sprigs of parsley, crisp fresh watercress, paprika-dipped celery curls, pickle fans, carrot curls, parsley-dipped lemon wedges—that are added quickly.

Radish Roses. Using a small, sharp knife, remove the tail from each radish. With the point of a knife, make six or eight thin, deep cuts in each from top to stem. *Do not cut off.* Place radishes in cold water, and refrigerate for several hours to open rose petals (see illustration). For speed in preparing large numbers of radish roses, you may prefer to partially push the radishes through the center of a ten-section apple corer.

Figure 11.8. Radish rose and celery curl.

Figure 11.9. Carrot curl.

Celery Curls. Cut celery into 3- or 4-inch lengths. Slash lengthwise to within 1/2 inch of leaves or end of celery piece. Or slash both ends, leaving 1/2 inch in center. Place in cold water and chill until slashed ends curl (see Figure 11.8). Before serving, shake water from celery curls and dip ends in paprika.

Carrot Curls. Select large crisp carrots. Pare or scrape off outer skin. Using a vegetable peeler, cut carrot lengthwise into paper-thin strips. Roll the strips lightly and fasten with a toothpick. Chill for at least an hour in ice water in the refrigerator. Remove toothpicks before serving (see Figure 11.9).

Pickle Fans. Cut sweet gherkins into thin lengthwise slices almost to the end of each pickle. Spread slices carefully and press uncut end so fan will hold its shape (see Figure 11.10).

Accordion Pickles. Slice ends from sweet gherkins. Make thin, crosswise slices almost but not quite through each pickle. Bend pickle gently so the slices separate at the top (see Figure 11.11.)

Turnip/Potato Lilies. To make each lily, cut two thin turnip or potato slices, and fold to shape flower. Place a carrot stick in the center and fasten with toothpicks (see Figure 11.12). Chill in cold water in the refrigerator.

Cold foods by their nature, permit more time for garnishing and decorating than do hot foods. At times a simple garnish may be all that is needed. But, for special occasions and certain types of foods, you will want to use more creative and decorative designs.

Meat Presentations

Christmas ham, chaudfroid, can be displayed on a mirrored tray with garnishes of stuffed cherry

Figure 11.10. Pickle fan.

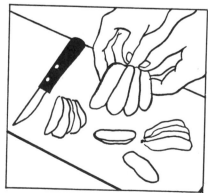

Figure 11.11. Accordion pickle.

Figure 11.12. Turnip or potato lily.

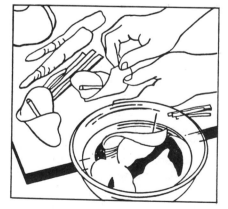

Figure 11.13. Ham with chaudfroid and decorations. Effective buffet presentation.

Figure 11.15. Cold, sliced roast beef offering.

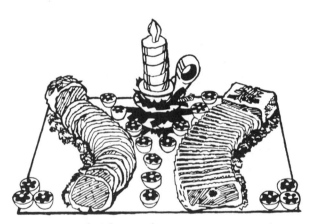

Figure 11.14. A ham and tongue pate presentation.

Figure 11.16. Turkey chaudfroid with sliced turkey breasts and poached pears.

tomatoes and wedges of large tomatoes, spread with cheese, reshaped, and glazed with aspic. (See Figure 11.13.)

Sliced ham and tongue pates are arranged on a mirrored surface and garnished with decorated and glazed hard-cooked eggs and chopped aspic. The candle and holder are of tallow. (See Figure 11.14.)

Roast beef and slices of beef can be presented around a parsley and cherry tomato "tree" and garnished with glazed salami cones on artichoke

bottoms. The "tree" is made from cone-shaped styrofoam. Toothpicks are used to hang the parsley and secure the cherry tomatoes. (See Figure 11.15.)

Slices of turkey breast encircle a whole roast turkey, chaudfroid. Poached pears with fresh mint or lemon leaves make an attractive garnish. (See Figure 11.16.)

Pastry Presentations
Pastry and other desserts arranged on mirrored trays make beautiful displays. If you make your

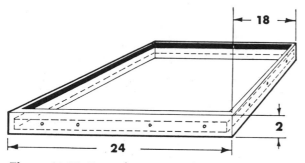

Figure 11.17. Frame for a mirrored tray.

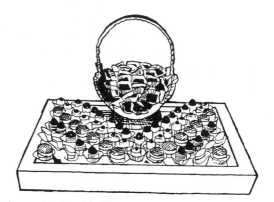

Figure 11.18. An effective arrangement of petit fours in a nougat basket, on a mirrored tray.

Figure 11.19. Marzipan-covered sliced cake roll with nougat showpiece.

own mirrored trays, you not only lift the presentation out of the ordinary, but individualize it as well. (See Figure 11.17.)

1. Make an 18- by 24-inch frame using 2- by 1/2-inch wood.
2. Fit in a 1-inch plywood sheet to within 1 inch from the top. Nail.
3. Cover entire area (exterior sides, inside, top of plywood) with velvet.
4. Measure the inside dimensions of the frame, and have a 1/4-inch-thick mirror cut to fit.

Although the following pastry displays are expensive to execute, they can serve as patterns for less elaborate affairs.

The handled basket filled with miniature brownies is made of nougat, a type of brittle. The petits fours, consisting of three to four layers, totalling not more than 1-1/4 inch in height, and topped with glazed apricots, cherries, and strawberries, are symmetrically arranged on a mirrored tray (see Figure 11.18).

The heart-shaped box is made of nougat, and topped with ribbons and a rose, both made of spun sugar. The rolled cake slices are filled with butter cream or melba jelly, and covered with a thin layer of patterned and flavored marzipan (see Figure 11.19).

Anyone who has mastered the fundamentals of cooking can develop the skills needed to dramatize foods effectively. One intent of this chapter is to stimulate interest in the art of food decoration and presentation. To further develop your skills and techniques, practice is necessary. Additional ideas for varying food displays can be found in the many foodservice industry magazines, and books such as *The Art of Garde Manger, The Book of Buffets,* and *The Professional Chef.**

CATERING CLAMBAKES AND BARBECUES

Dating from the days of the American Indian, clambakes or steams are traditionally a New England happening. Originally a seashore func-

*Published by CBI Publishing Company, Inc., Boston.

tion, they are now held in backyards, parks, and other picnic areas.

To prepare a clambake for 100 or more guests, dig a pit about 3 feet deep and 4 to 5 feet in diameter, and line it with large rocks. (In Rhode Island, bakemasters require rocks "as big as a man's head.")

Next, place cordwood on top of the rocks and allow it to burn until it is *white hot.* Depending on the size of the stones, pit, and type of cordwood, this procedure could take up to three hours. But from here on the process requires speed.

Embers should be removed and the stones swept clean of ashes. About 6 inches of seaweed should then be put on the stones. If seaweed is not available, wet leaves and ferns can be substituted. Next, place a layer of heavy wire mesh over this.

For every 50 guests, add a bushel of well-washed, soft-shell clams. With these place one live lobster and two ears of corn for *each guest.* Remove only the silk from the corn. Washed but not pared sweet and/or white potatoes may be added, if desired. As a "topper," add chicken quarters or halves that have been parboiled, buttered, and wrapped in foil. Gutted trout, mackerel, bluefish, or chunks of cod may also be foil-wrapped and used with, or in place of, the chicken.

Top the food with a thick layer of seaweed; then cover the entire area with wet canvas. Weigh down the canvas securely with large rocks or heavy planks, and allow the food to steam from one to two hours.

Although this can be a gala and exciting presentation, it calls for detailed planning and meticulous follow-through. Since all seafood items spoil quickly, they must be properly refrigerated and given priority attention.

In determining charges for a clambake, a number of unusual conditions must be considered.

1. Do you have the proper tools and personnel available to dig the pit? (This takes considerable time and requires the services of individuals who are physically able. Remember that at the end of the clambake, the pit must be refilled, smoothed over, and all excess stones and dirt carted away.)

2. Where are you going to get the proper stones? How will you get them to the site of the clambake?

3. Will you be able to get sufficient quantities of seaweed, leaves, or ferns?

4. Will you personally have to pick up the cordwood? Since your order will probably be small, the company from whom you purchase it may not make a delivery.

5. Do you have heavy wire mesh for the base, as well as heavy canvas for the top?

6. If the bake is to be held on public land, is a permit required? If it is to be held on private property, will you need written permission from the owner?

7. Ample space must be provided for dirty dishes, as well as for scraping and rinsing (if possible). Because of the informality of this event, be prepared for greater dish loss and breakage. Also, remember that because of the large area to be covered and the unevenness of the terrain, your employees will tire more easily and become more careless with equipment.

8. If disposable dishes must be used for the main course, then select *heavily coated and rigidly constructed* 10- to 12-inch oval plates. This is necessary because clams, lobsters, corn, and chicken are heavy, hot, and juicy.

9. The most inexpensive stainless steel forks, knives, and spoons should be used. Plastic ware can be substituted if it is the heavy-duty type that will not snap or break while in use.

10. Rugged paper or plastic tablecloths are particularly appropriate for a clambake. Provide *mountains of paper napkins* because these foods are wet and sticky. Also, have a sufficient supply of rubbish bags, and use the heavy-duty type that will not rip when lobster

shells, clam shells, and corn cobs are packed in them.

Barbecues

Barbecuing, a form of outdoor cooking, involves both preparation and presentation skills. Like other types of showmanship, the more flourishes and props there are, the more effective and impressive the service.

Props can include showy grilles, decorative and oversized tongs, giant salt and pepper shakers, colorful sauce bowls, gaudy aprons, extra large padded gloves and hot pads, plus a beautiful but functional carving knife, fork, and sharpening steel. These props should be displayed prominently and used with flourishes to add to the guests' enjoyment.

When catering a private home barbecue, you can very effectively use any of the many fabricated barbecue grilles available on the market. However, their production capability is limited, and the number of guests that can be served is, therefore, necessarily limited.

In catering home barbecues, you have the advantages of refrigerators, freezers, water, gas, and electricity. And in some homes, you may find permanently installed grilles, a situation that works to your advantage.

Home barbecues add much pleasure and diversity to home entertaining. In parts of the country where weather conditions are favorable and predictable, barbecues are held throughout the year. As a result, there is a greater variety of equipment available for both the home and for you, the professional caterer.

Building Your Own Equipment. In some areas, outdoor cooking and dining are only possible about four months out of the year. Thus, you may not want to buy special barbecuing equipment. But you can improvise or build your own, which will then be suited to your particular needs. Even if you do this, remember that household grilles can be used as *auxiliary units*

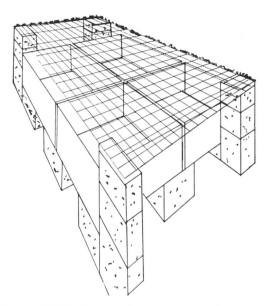

Figure 11.20. Homemade temporary outdoor barbecue for quantity production. The size is flexible, and it may be easily assembled and disassembled.

for producing or holding side dishes, hors d'oeuvre, or small quantities of food.

To build a large, effective charcoal grille, visit a scrapyard or a steel supply house and purchase an iron or steel cellar door grille (or the kind used to protect glass store doors). This grille should have horizontal, vertical, or diamond-shaped spaces no larger than three quarters (3/4 in.) of an inch (see Figure 11.20).

Next, place two, three, or four pans of equal size, such as old roasting pans or squareheads, on cinder blocks arranged in a shape suited to the size of your grille. The corners of the grille can rest on cinder block or brick columns placed on the outside corners of the pan arrangements—at whatever height is desired.

Line pan bottoms and sides with heavy foil to reflect heat, speed up cooking, and make them easier to clean. Place one or two inches of gravel (depending on the height of your pans) in the pans and top with the coals. The gravel, which allows even heat penetration and distribution,

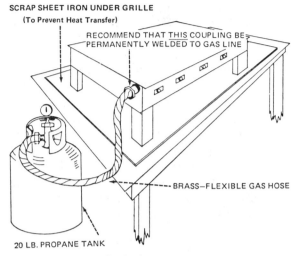

SCRAP SHEET IRON UNDER GRILLE
(To Prevent Heat Transfer)

RECOMMEND THAT <u>THIS</u> COUPLING BE
PERMANENTLY WELDED TO GAS LINE

BRASS—FLEXIBLE GAS HOSE

20 LB. PROPANE TANK

Figure 11.21. Method of converting standard gas griddle for outdoor or off-premise use.

can be washed after repeated uses, dried thoroughly, and used again.

The quantity and type of briquettes needed will differ, based on the amount and kind of food to be served. Thick steaks or roasts need a deep bed of coals, whereas franks or burgers call for shallow fires.

Prior to cooking, rub fat trimmings or bacon over grille rods or wire baskets to prevent sticking. If drippings flare up during the cooking process, sprinkle lightly with water from a plastic squeeze bottle.

Portable Griddles. An average size (18- by 42-in.), gas-fired restaurant griddle is capable of producing more than 100 orders of griddle cakes or more than 500 orders of franks or hamburgers per hour, and makes an excellent portable cooking unit surface for outdoor barbecues. Secondhand models are often available from restaurant supply houses.

Have a plumber connect a 4- to 6-foot *flexible brass gas hose* to the gas line on the griddle. If necessary, have it permanently brazed to that spot. The coupling on the opposite end can be fastened

to a 20-pound portable propane gas tank, available from most suburban gas companies. Chain an appropriate wrench to this hose so that it will be readily available (see Figure 11.21). Buy a sheet of scrap steel larger than the griddle dimensions, and set up the unit on it before placing it in the working area. When completed, test the griddle. Changes in valve openings may be required because they were not originally intended for use with propane gas.

This same procedure can be used for setting up a cooking range and oven on a mobile base. Mount the range on a steel-bottomed dolly with heavy capacity wheels. Thus, it can be platform-lifted on or off a truck and wheeled to the desired area. Using a range in this way will require a portable auxiliary chimney.

When using propane gas with portable equipment, it is always advisable to carry a spare tank with a gauge showing the amount of gas remaining. If there is no gauge, weigh the tank when full. Then, after each use, weigh it again and mark that weight on a piece of masking adhesive taped to the side of the tank. To better gauge this figure, check with a propane dealer in your area to find out how much the tank weighs when empty.

Building the Fire. When using large barbecue grilles for quantity production, it is essential that you give the fire area constant and undivided attention. In this type of setup, you do not have fingertip heat controls, so you cannot get the immediate heat elevation or reduction responses possible with conventional ranges.

Because of the many variables in outdoor parties, cooking time can only be estimated. Charcoal or compressed fuel packages can take as long as 45 minutes to reach the proper temperature. If you try to rush them, you either burn the food or undercook it.

To achieve that special "barbecue" flavor in food, you can: (1) brush the food with liquid flavoring; (2) scatter *impregnated* wood shavings on the fire at the proper time; or (3) wrap *dry* shavings in foil that is generously perforated at the top, and place the foil-wrapped shavings on the fire in the hope that the resultant smoke will produce the "smoky" flavor.

Remember, all meat cookery calls for *glowing coals—no flame!* And the fire should burn until a gray ash film covers the charcoal or briquettes. In home barbecues equipped with crank handles, the proper heat can be achieved by adjusting the grille to a high or low position.

If no thermometer can be placed on grille racks to determine the temperature, you will have to resort to the "field-mess detection method." To do this, hold your open hand a couple of inches above the grille and count one and two, two and three, three and four, and so on.

If you must remove your hand by the end of the one and two count, you know that the fire is very, very hot. In other words, the higher the count, the lower the temperature.

Determining the temperature in ovens without a thermostat can be done in the same way. Insert your hand halfway between the deck and the top of the oven and count, in the same manner, up to eight. If you must remove your hand before reaching the count of eight, you can be certain that the oven is hot enough and ready for roasting.

Starting a good barbecue fire requires practice and skill. The following methods are both workable and practical.

1. If using an electric starter, follow the model directions *explicitly*. If liquid starter fuel is used, sprinkle it on the coals *at least a full minute before* applying the starter.

   Never, never, never use gasoline or kerosene. And remove all aerosol cans—bug sprays, air fresheners, or other such units—from the vicinity of the grilles.

2. If using canned heat, empty the contents of a small can into a cup fashioned from aluminum foil. Then place it in the fire box, heap charcoal over it in a mound, and ignite. Allow it to burn through and then spread coals over the area desired.

3. Take an empty, 2-pound coffee can and cut off the bottom. With a triangular beverage opener, punch holes around the bottom rim in a straight line about 1-1/2 inches apart; bend the tip of the triangles down to form legs and to allow for draft. Half fill this with charcoal and place it in the center of the fire box. Pour a generous amount of starter liquid over it and cover lightly with charcoal. Allow it to stand for 15 minutes and then ignite *at base*. After it is burning well, add a number of untreated briquettes to nearly reach the top and allow to burn. Next, carefully remove the can and rake the coals over the area desired.

Transporting Equipment. Barbecue and grille equipment require care in packing for transport to and from your commissary. Heavy padded canvas tarpaulins should be used for cover and protection *only* because soot and odors from the equipment can be transferred to other equipment.

Preparing barbecue and grille equipment for return to the commissary is a time-consuming and dirty job. All coal and ashes must be removed from the fire boxes and disposed of properly.

Furthermore, *the equipment must be absolutely cold before handling.* Numerous layers of soaking wet newspapers can be placed on grilles to cool them down, and additional water can be poured over them to speed up the process. Access to a hose would be very helpful.

To clean pots, skillets, and wire grilles, soap-moistened abrasive pads are a great aid. However, after returning to the commissary, you should again thoroughly clean all equipment, steaming it, if possible. Then, and only then, can you inspect and repack it for future use.

In catering barbecues, as with other types of parties, proper sanitation and refrigeration cannot be overlooked. All work and serving areas should be inspected, and must be scrupulously clean. While flying and creeping insects may not be bothersome in the barbecuing area, since smoke and heat will drive them away, they could be a source of great annoyance in the service areas. If you must use an insect repellent, do it very carefully; spray it as close to the ground as possible and *do not spray it near food.*

If the truck you are using does not have refrigeration facilities, then keep all foods in portable foam or fiberglass coolers, using canned freezing pellets or dry ice to retain the desired temperature.

Unless proper refrigeration and refrigerated serving facilities are available, it would be inadvisable to serve any of the following foods at a warm weather barbecue: egg and milk mixtures, custards, eclairs, cream puffs, cream-filled cakes, and foods heavy with mayonnaise, such as, potato salad, tuna salad, and deviled eggs. These items are particularly sensitive to spoilage.

If you must use salads or dishes containing mayonnaise, take all the ingredients to the job location in separate containers, under refrigeration, and mix them on the job.

Destroy immediately any leftover foods. Do not be bighearted and give foods to guests or your client to take home. Strict adherence to this procedure will not only enhance your reputation, but will also protect you from the danger of illness resulting from possible food contamination.

Equipment List for Barbecue Parties

Asbestos gloves
Assortment of wood/bamboo skewers
Brushes—two: one for butter, one for sauce
Canvas gloves—for use in setup and cleanup
Cloth towels and aprons
Fancy carving knife, fork, and steel
Fire extinguisher
First aid kit with burn ointment
Heavy frying pans—cast iron is the most functional material
Hibachis—for use as supplementary grilles for appetizers, side dishes, or small items
Hot pads
Large metal-shielded skewers
Large/showy pepper mill and salt shaker

Large wooden spoons
Long tongs—two: one for meat, one for coals
Long-handled fork, spoon, and turner (spatula)
Meat thermometer
Paper towels
Paring knives
Roast beef slicer
Sturdy work table with cutting boards for food preparation and service
Wire basket grilles—adjustable for the thickness of meat, fish, etcetera; and having long handles for ease in holding over heat

VARIATIONS IN MEAL PRESENTATION

There are innumerable meal presentation possibilities to offer for your client's consideration. While some of these affairs provide normal profit returns, others offer larger profit opportunities. Presentation ideas vary with personal tastes, and although some people are financially able to indulge their desire for extremely lavish affairs, most clients select parties that have standard fare and are served with a modest amount of flourish.

THE AMERICAN MATRIMONIAL BUSINESS

The American matrimonial business generates in excess of $8 billion annually (*N. Y. Times,* 31 May 1974). Despite the more casual attitude toward marriage today, it is estimated that 8 out of 10 young women still prefer formal weddings. And many of these young women and their parents will be seeking your services!

In discussing plans with prospective clients you will determine the location of the affair, the time of service, number of guests expected, food preferences, general arrangements as well as be prepared to answer any questions concerning etiquette and protocol for the affair the clients may have. You should then prepare and submit a proposal for the menu and desired services for the clients' approval (see Figure 11.22).

Figure 11.22. Sample Wedding Menu Proposal

JOHN DOE CATERING COMPANY * 454 MAIN STREET *** HYDE PARK, N.Y.**

Menu proposals: Reception and dinner (Wedding)
Mr./Mrs. Joseph Bell
25 Cartright Street
Hyde Park, New York 12394

To be held at: Knights of Columbus Hall, North Road
New City, N.Y. 00965

Saturday, June 15, 19 ____
Reception at 3:00 P.M.
Dinner 4:30 P.M. (End by 8:30 P.M.)

To be served from Buffet Table: Choice of four

Deviled Eggs a la Russe	Salmon Roe Caviar	Coronets of Ham and Cheese
Rolled Anchovies on Rye	Pate of Calf's Liver	Shrimps on Horseback
Guacamole Dip	Celery Stuffed with Roquefort Cheese	

To be passed Butler style: Choice of three

Clams Casino	Oysters Rockefeller	Barquettes of Maine Lobster
Cocktail Franks in Batter	Chicken Livers en Brochette	Quiche Lorraine

To be served from Buffet Table: Choice of two

Bite-size Glazed Corned Beef (sliced to order) on Rye Bread
Chicken a la King on Rice Pilaf   Stuffed Cabbage Rolls (bite-size)
Smoked Turkey (bite-size, sliced to order) on Honey-Nut Bread
Smoked Irish Salmon (sliced to order), Sweet Onion Rings, Capers in Dill

Bar beverages: Unlimited drinks per guest at bar and at tableside during dinner,
including one champagne drink per guest, to toast newlywed couple,
according with private arrangements with management of K.C. Hall.

DINNER—Choice of one:

Fresh Shrimp Cocktail, Supreme	Fresh Fruit-Filled Cantaloupe	Pineapple Basket
Fresh Crabmeat en Avocado	Broiled Grapefruit with Clover Honey	

*

Choice of one: Vichyssoise with Fresh Chives   Consomme of Peacock with Game Quenelles
Boneless Brook Trout Filled with Salmon Mousse
Crabmeat-Stuffed Fillet of Sole with Truffles, Fish Veloute, and Wine Sauce

*

Optional Courses ($1.00 extra):   Intermezzo; Fresh Lemon Sherbet, Green Creme de Menthe
Salad prepared table side, House special

MAIN COURSE—Choice of one, served Russian style:

Saddle of Veal, Prince Orloff   Thick-Cut Roast Rib of Beef

Chicken Kiev on Wild Rice, Brandied   Beef Wellington, Giant Mushrooms

Filet Mignon (presliced), Bearnaise Sauce

*

Bouquetiere of Fresh Vegetables

*

Iced Revere Bowl of Celery Hearts, Colossal Olives,
Radish Rosettes   Watermelon Rind Pickles

*

Choice of Dessert: Listed on separate sheet submitted.

*

House Special   Coffee   Tea   Decaffeinated Beverage

WEDDING CAKE: An attractively decorated, 6-tier wedding cake on 4 sets of columns. Will be tied with tulle bows and ornamented on top layer by 3 styrofoam bells (all white). Cake will be served from rolling carts, will be made of pound cake with dark chocolate filling, almonds, and rum flavoring. Entire surface to be decorated with Royal Icing. The price as tentatively agreed upon, plus tax.

CIGARETTES: We will provide 2 packages of assorted popular brand cigarettes per table of 10 guests.

DECORATIONS: We will set up a very attractive display for the center of the main reception table. It will be an illuminated ice piece with two love birds in a heart ring, flanked by fresh flowers. All other reception tables will have appropriate tallow molds and/or butter molds. Each table will have a very attractive arrangement of fresh pink flowers set into a 4-candle candelabrum with 12-inch pink candles.

LINENS: All tablecloths will be pale pink as will the napkins. Ecru lace cloths over regular cloths, if desired, each table extra.

GRATUITIES: Included for waiters. Included for checkroom and restrooms; "No Tipping" signs to be displayed.

FLOOR PLAN: Floor plan, based on 150 guests, will be sent on acceptance of menu items and deposit, as defined on contract.

TABLE CARDS: Will be hand written, in authentic Spencerian script (extra), or will supply cards typed on I.B.M. Selectric at no extra charge. Guest list must be received no later than one week before affair.

SERVICE ARRANGEMENTS: Waiters, (waitresses) will wear red jackets. Beverage waiters will wear wine chains, and all waiters will wear white gloves.

MUSIC: Your own orchestra; we will coordinate service with leader.

MATCHES AND COCKTAIL NAPKINS: Personalized, and as tentative choice. Charges determined by amount ordered.

PRICE: $ per person; extra charges where so accepted, and initialed by you.

CONTRACT—DEPOSIT: Contract must be signed, and deposit acknowledged, by 14 days from date or by January 15th of 19 ____ .
Our representative, Mr. John Doe, will be very happy to discuss this entire procedure with you, either at your home or at our office, at your convenience.

Although a social caterer is usually not involved in the selection of a florist, orchestra, or photographer for a wedding, your client may ask for your recommendations. Certainly, to insure the success of the affair, you should be able to suggest people you know and with whom you will be able to work smoothly.

Some establishments (hotels, clubs, etc.) may not permit just any florist, orchestra, or photographer to work in their facility. Their reasoning is usually based on past experience—poor performance, abuse of house rules, lack of cooperation. Therefore, they may insist that a "house" florist, etcetera, be used. You should be aware of such conditions before making any recommendations to your client.

The Music

If music is to be used in public halls, hotels, and similar operations, union musicians must be employed. The union determines the size of the orchestra for the occasion, also. Rules vary across the country, so check with the local musicians' union before hiring any orchestra or musical group.

The music is an important and integral part of the wedding and reception. The leader announces the "grand entrance" of the newlyweds, their first dance together, and then the first dance of the newly married couple with their parents. The protocol of a religious ceremony before, during, or after the "feast," the cutting of the cake, and the music associated with this ritual, are also the orchestra leader's responsibility.

Lively and entertaining music contributes immeasurably to the total enjoyment of the affair. It is essential, however, that the orchestra leader coordinate his musical selections with the meal service. Dance music should *not* be played during the service of a food course. The musical selections to be featured during the meal should be planned with the host.

Unless specifically requested by the client, you are not required to serve food to the orchestra. However, if you can afford the expense, it might be prudent to provide a snack for them during one of their breaks.

The Flowers

Flowers for the wedding and reception are the responsibility of the wedding party. However, you should discuss with the client and the florist the flowers to be used on the buffet and/or head table.

A skilled florist will be able to tint flowers to match or harmonize with the bride's color scheme. Also, he will be able to provide wedding canopies and aisle markers, construct reception and head table backgrounds, and arrange plants and flowers in a variety of decorative settings.

All of the constructed pieces and floral decorations must be removed by the florist following the function, or at a time determined by the florist and the caterer. His area must be cleaned to the complete satisfaction of the supervisor of the premises. If a host-engaged florist neglects his cleanup responsibility, all related cleaning costs will probably be added to the host's bill.

The Photographer

A photographer of merit and ability should be employed to record the highlights of the affair. He should be skilled first in spotting, then in capturing on film, those special moments of joy so precious and evident at weddings.

A good photographer works without being too conspicuous or obtrusive. He can pick out suitable backgrounds for posed shots, and is knowledgeable about wedding customs and religious protocol.

Be sure the photographer supplies you with several good pictures of your part of the function: the buffet table, the bride and groom cutting the cake, the head table, and similar activities. These can be invaluable sales promotion tools for both you and the photographer.

The Wedding Invitation

Although your services as a social caterer are not required in the selection and issuing of wedding

Figure 11.23. Wedding cake using plastic columns to add height and eye-appeal.

invitations, you must point out to the client that an RSVP is essential if food is to be served. You must know how many guests will attend in order to prepare the proper amount of food.

The Menu

If your client wishes a printed menu, you must provide your client with a correct and clearly written menu for the printer. Formal menus are usually written in French; however, English is acceptable.

The Wedding Cake

The wedding cake is not only the focal point of the buffet or dessert table, but the cutting of it is one of the featured events of the affair. It is important that you work out the details of the cutting ceremony with the host and the photographer so there will not be any last minute confusion to spoil the event.

Although there are many wedding cake designs, traditionally, a wedding cake is always a tiered cake. The tiers are arranged either one on top of the other, or separated by dividers; inverted plastic or glass champagne glasses, or plastic or floral columns may be used as dividers.

Posed photos of the bride and groom cutting the cake may be taken without disturbing the side of the cake that guests see, or affecting the delicately balanced top layers on a tiered cake. Before the photographer actually takes the picture, the caterer should cut two pieces of cake from the rear of the bottom layer, and place them on a small plate. Conceal these until the bridal cake-cutting pose is photographed. Then photographs of the bride and groom sharing the pieces of cake may be taken. Your staff will then take over the cutting and serving of the cake.

Cutting the Cake. In certain areas of the country, it is customary to use the wedding cake as the main dessert item for the wedding menu. It is served either by itself or topped with ice cream and such sauces as vanilla custard, pineapple, fruit salad, black cherry, butter pecan, or any other that appeals to the client.

Other customs dictate that pieces of the cake be bagged or boxed, then given to the guests to take home as a memento (or for single girls to "dream on"). Special bags, with grease resistant liners, appropriately decorated for use as wedding cake souvenir containers, are available in stores selling party goods.

Traditionally, the top layer of the cake and the ornament are not cut, but are removed, boxed, and given to the newlyweds to be saved for their first anniversary celebration. The exposed second tier is then sliced and served, before cutting into the next lower tier. The tiers may be cut in a variety of ways to obtain the number of portions needed (see Figure 11.24).

DECORATING A HEAD TABLE

The head table is *the* focal point of the entire dining room. Not only should it have the most effective appearance, but whenever possible, it should be elevated on either a platform or a dais.

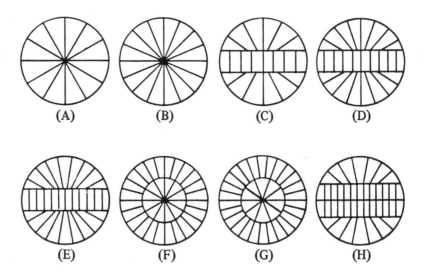

Cutting guide for tiered wedding cake. (A) 8-in., 2-layer cake; yield: 12 servings. (B) 9-in., 2-layer cake; yield: 16 servings. (C) 10-in., 2-layer cake; yield: 20 servings. (D) 11-in., 2-layer cake; yield: 26 servings. (E) 12-in., 2-layer cake; yield: 30 servings. (F) 12-in., 2-layer cake; yield: 36 servings. (G) 13-in., 2-layer cake; yield: 36 servings. (H) 14-in., 2-layer cake; yield: 40 servings.

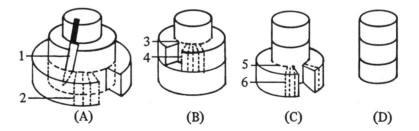

Cutting tiered cakes. (A) Cut vertically through bottom layer at edge of 2nd layer as indicated by dotted line No. 1; then cut out wedges as shown by 2. (B) Follow same procedure with middle layer; cut vertically through 2nd layer at edge of top layer as indicated by dotted line No. 3; then cut wedges as shown by 4. (C) When entire 2nd layer has been served, cut along dotted line 5; cut another row of wedges as shown by 6. (D) Remaining tiers may be cut as desired.

Figure 11.24. Cutting guide for tiered cakes.

(Reprinted with permission from the American Institute of Baking, *Catering Handbook*, p. 142.)

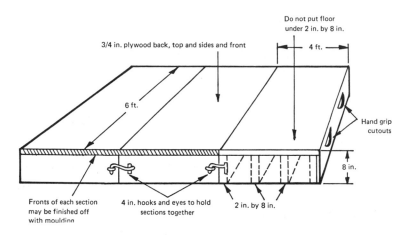

Do not put floor
under 2 in. by 8 in.

4 ft.

3/4 in. plywood back, top and sides and front

6 ft.

Hand grip
cutouts

8 in.

Fronts of each section
may be finished off
with moulding

4 in. hooks and eyes to hold
sections together

2 in. by 8 in.

Figure 11.25. Homemade portable risers for dais or head table.

Prefabricated platforms are available, and can be built in as many "steps" or rows as you desire. These are often worthwhile investments for permanent establishments, such as hotels and public banquet halls. Before purchasing any of these collapsible platforms, however, be certain to make provisions for storage. And, remember, when elevated arrangements are requested, you are entitled to an additional charge for setup, use, and breakdown.

If a dais is needed, but the facility in which you are serving does not have one, you should be able to supply it. Homemade ones are easy to build, to store, and transport, and can be set up with the services of just two persons. This equipment also represents a plus factor in terms of the services you can offer. And by charging a fee for use and transportation, your construction costs will be self-liquidating; you may, in fact, even show a profit on your investment.

Head Table Construction

Five portable (4- by 6-ft.) platform sections will hold two 8-foot by 30-inch tables end to end, seating from 8 to 10 persons, with sufficient room behind chairs so that waiters can serve comfortably.

These portable platform sections should be hooked together for safety (see Figure 11.25), and be covered with removable rugs or painted a glossy black, probably the most practical color. Keep in mind that neither the chairs nor the tables should extend to the very edge of the platform.

As a safety feature, and for aesthetic value, place two upright stanchions, at least 36 inches high, screwed into flanges bolted to the floor, at the front ends of the platform (see Figure 11.26). A plumber or a plumbing supply house can build these in short order.

Brass pipe, chrome, or even plain black pipe (painted gold, aluminum, or any other desired color) are also effective, but they should be capped with the same metal as the base. Insert screw eyes into each stanchion to hold decorative gold rope or ribbons (available from fabric and trimming stores).

Head tables *should always be draped or skirted.* To serve as a base for the skirts, a "silence cloth," similar to a lightweight blanket, should be positioned first to cover the entire table. This cloth reduces service noise and acts as an anchor for table drapes.

When draping the table, have the following items on hand (see Figure 11.27):

Roll of 1-1/2- or 2-inch masking tape
"T" pins of both the 1-1/2- and 2-inch size
Corsage pins (2-inch size)
Thumb tacks with 1/2-inch heads (*do not use a stapler*)

Steam iron

Draping material

Procedure for Draping Tables

Cover the table with the silence cloth, folding it under the table top and taping it securely. Before draping, fold the material to be used in half to find its center; then, pin the center into the middle of the table. Pin the right-hand end of the drape cloth to the table corner at the extreme right; repeat this procedure on the left side (see Figure 11.28).

The amount of loosely hanging material will determine how generous you can be with pleats. Pleats must all face in the same direction, and be of equal size. To maintain uniformity, and to mark off pleat widths, use a ruler or a piece of heavy cardboard; then tape or pin each fold to the silence cloth (see Figure 11.29). When using pins, do not leave points exposed.

In order to sharpen the folds, use a hot steam iron at the end of the table where the horizontal and vertical lines meet. To relieve pull on the silence cloth while draping, place several upended chairs or other heavy objects on the table opposite the part being draped. Make sure the skirt bottom is even all along the floor. *Do not allow the skirt to touch the floor;* it should be elevated enough so that it will not brush the shoes of anyone standing in front of the table. As a guide for uniform drape lengths, use a heavy piece of cardboard properly marked for that pur-

Figure 11.26. Stanchions for ends of head table dais indicate caution when stepping down, and can also be used for traffic control.

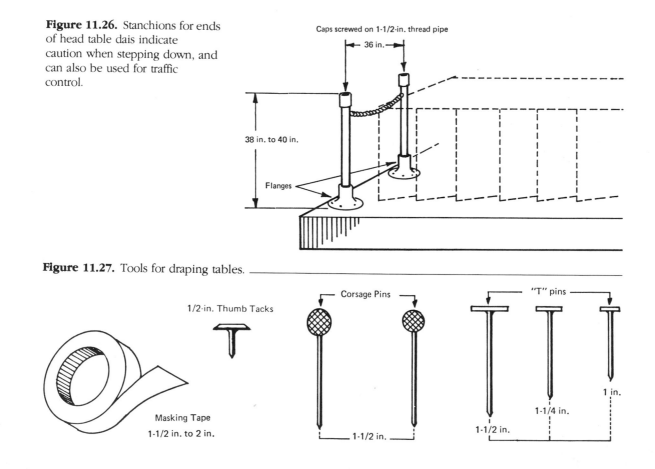

Caps screwed on 1-1/2-in. thread pipe

36 in.

38 in. to 40 in.

Flanges

Figure 11.27. Tools for draping tables.

1/2-in. Thumb Tacks

Corsage Pins

"T" pins

Masking Tape
1-1/2 in. to 2 in.

1-1/2 in.

1-1/2 in.

1-1/4 in.

1 in.

pose, adjusting to the proper height as you pin or tape.

Table skirts or drapes can be made of synthetic fabrics, but should be of subdued, solid colors rather than patterns. Additionally, remember that the fabric should be:

1. Lightweight, so that its weight will not pull down the anchor cloth

2. Opaque, closely woven, and easy to wash or clean

3. Wrinkle-resistant or crushproof, so it can be rolled, folded, or hung on skirt hangers

4. Preferably flameproof, a mandatory requirement in some areas.

If you know someone who is handy with a sewing machine, have that person hem the edges

Figure 11.28. Method of draping, using bulk cloths.

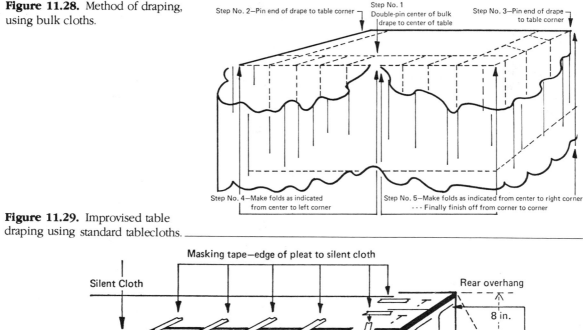

Step No. 2—Pin end of drape to table corner

Step No. 1
Double-pin center of bulk
drape to center of table

Step No. 3—Pin end of drape to table corner

Step No. 4—Make folds as indicated
from center to left corner

Step No. 5—Make folds as indicated from center to right corner
- - - Finally finish off from corner to corner

Figure 11.29. Improvised table draping using standard tablecloths.

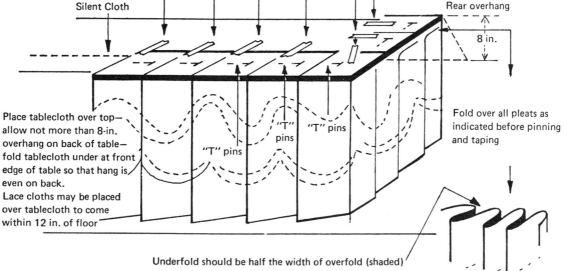

Masking tape—edge of pleat to silent cloth

Silent Cloth

Rear overhang

8 in.

Place tablecloth over top—allow not more than 8-in. overhang on back of table—fold tablecloth under at front edge of table so that hang is even on back.
Lace cloths may be placed over tablecloth to come within 12 in. of floor

"T" pins

"T" pins

"T" pins

"T" pins

Fold over all pleats as indicated before pinning and taping

Underfold should be half the width of overfold (shaded)

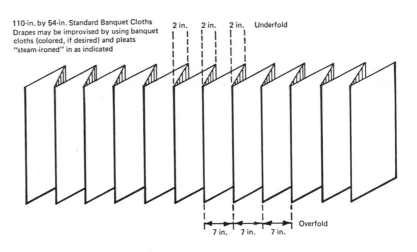

110-in. by 54-in. Standard Banquet Cloths
Drapes may be improvised by using banquet
cloths (colored, if desired) and pleats
"steam-ironed" in as indicated

2 in.   2 in.   2 in.   Underfold

Overfold

7 in.   7 in.   7 in.

Figure 11.30. Effective pleating can be ironed-in beforehand.

of one side of the draping material, and put a drawstring through it. Anchor-pin the string ends at the right and left corners closest to the back of the table, and be sure the resulting ruffles are evenly distributed.

To provide for graceful ruffling, as well as for convenient handling, have these units made in 5-yard lengths. This will result in luxurious ruffling at the front and on the ends of either 6- or 8-foot tables.

After the drapes are in place, put the top tablecloth over the table. Since seamed edges are not always straight, fold under the front edges to form a perfectly straight fold; or bring the regular seam of the top cloth to the table edge, then pin a 3- or 4-inch ribbon over it from one table corner to the other.

The cloth drop on the guests' side of the head table should be no longer than 8 inches. Longer drops interfere with seating and can get tangled with guests' clothes.

Lace cloths, which are placed over the tablecloth and allowed to hang beyond the front skirts to within a foot or so of the floor, will give an air of elegance to the entire head table. They will also save the time involved in trying to match top edges, because the lace cloth hides the slight unevenness.

If an occasion calls for a particular color scheme and your drapes are inappropriate, simply order additional tablecloths. Take a cloth, place it on a flat surface and press in folds or pleats with a steam iron (see Figure 11.30). Hang this as a prepleated drape, using the regular draping procedure. Since these emergency drapes are shorter, it is advisable to overlap edges from 4 to 4 inches to prevent gaps between cloths.

Figure 11.31. Contrasting colored napkins can highlight the pleating of a head table.

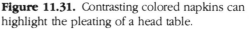

Colored napkin   Fold opposite corners   Reverse napkin and place between folds as indicated

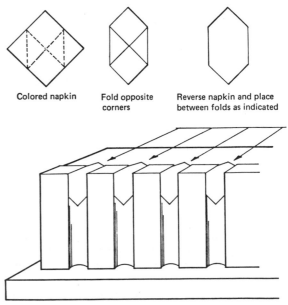

Figure 11.32. Four ways to fold a napkin. (A set of twelve glossy cards with assorted possibilities in napkin folding is available from Patricia Dann Willow Shop, Painted Post, NY 14870.)

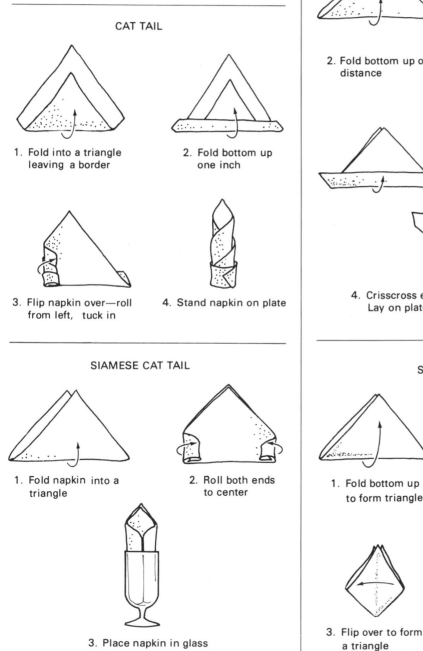

CAT TAIL

1. Fold into a triangle leaving a border

2. Fold bottom up one inch

3. Flip napkin over—roll from left, tuck in

4. Stand napkin on plate

SIAMESE CAT TAIL

1. Fold napkin into a triangle

2. Roll both ends to center

3. Place napkin in glass

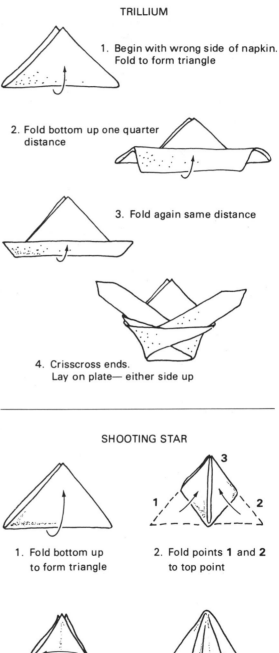

TRILLIUM

1. Begin with wrong side of napkin. Fold to form triangle

2. Fold bottom up one quarter distance

3. Fold again same distance

4. Crisscross ends. Lay on plate— either side up

SHOOTING STAR

1. Fold bottom up to form triangle

2. Fold points **1** and **2** to top point

3. Flip over to form a triangle

4. Stand on end

Another very effective way of adding interest to the head table is to fold napkins (see Figure 11.31) and, then, turn them over and put them in between each fold. You can use cloths and napkins of contrasting colors to make an intriguing arrangement.

The front of the head table can be garlanded with ferns, smilax, lemon, or huckleberry leaves, or natural string smilax, all of which can be obtained from your florist. Natural string smilax is,

of course, the most elegant. However, permanent string smilax of plastic or other synthetic material is now available; it is of very fine quality, decorative, delicate, and very difficult to distinguish from the natural.

Napkins can add interest and beauty to the head and guest tables particularly when they are folded into interesting shapes as illustrated in Figure 11.32. The colors should match or be complementary to the overall color scheme.

CHAPTER TWELVE

KOSHER CATERING

Tradition and heritage play important roles in the food preferences of most groups, but this is especially true for Jewish people. Thus, if you decide to specialize in kosher and Jewish foods, many opportunities will be available.

First, you can be assured of a "ready-made" clientele who will automatically seek you out. Also, since Americans are willing to try new and unusual foods, you have an additional opportunity for promoting these specialties among the non-Jewish population.

To operate a kosher establishment, you must know and follow the dietary regulations of the Jewish people. These laws concerning the preparation, selection, and service of food—even though they were delivered to Moses more than 3000 years ago—are so deeply woven into Jewish religious and family life that they remain virtually unchanged today. They still also govern, to differing degrees, the eating habits of many Jewish patrons.

NECESSARY REQUIREMENTS

In order to operate a strictly kosher operation, you must have an authorized orthodox rabbi or his representative, a *Mashgiach,* on your premises at all times. The Mashgiach, who is normally assigned by the area rabbi, must be a man whose character is beyond reproach, and one thoroughly knowledgeable in all aspects of the dietary laws. In addition, you, the caterer, should also be thoroughly familiar with Jewish dietary laws.

However, since only about one-half of the Jewish population is orthodox (requiring strict kosher food preparation), you might consider serving the Jewish patron who prefers Jewish-type foods, but does not require that they be in full compliance with all dietary laws. This is the case in many operations featuring so-called Jewish-style food, which is much less complicated in terms of preparation.

PROCESSING AND PURCHASING

In serving Jewish patrons, considerable care and emphasis must be given to purchasing procedures. For example, laws governing the use of meat—the main commodity for many foodservice operations—prohibit the use of pork and pork products, wild birds and game birds of prey, and seafood without scales and fins, such as, shellfish, lobster, crab, scallops, etcetera. Furthermore, the method of slaughtering animals, as well as the procedure for preparing them, is subject to very rigid controls.

Hindquarters of meat may not be used unless blood-carrying veins are properly removed. This operation is not only very complex and expensive, but it destroys the merchandising value of the meat and, in most instances, makes it unfit for commercial use. Therefore, meat selection is generally limited to forequarters of cattle, sheep, goats, and deer, and the internal organs of the forequarter; in the poultry classification, only the domestic varieties of chicken, turkey, duck, geese, Cornish hens, and squab pigeons are permissible.

These limitations are further complicated by the fact that the foods must be ritually prepared, or *koshered,* within 72 hours of slaughter.

The koshering process is designed to remove all excess blood from the meat. After the various blood vessels are removed, the meat is put in cold water for a half hour. It is then removed, rinsed, sprinkled generously with coarse sodium chloride (salt), and placed on a slanted drain board for one hour. After that, the meat is again washed in cold water—by hose or faucet—to remove the surface salt. Only then is it ready to be cut up for cooking, aged, frozen, eaten in a raw preparation, such as Steak Tartare, or to be cooked to the rarest degree of doneness.

This soaking and salting process, as well as the slaughter date, does not apply to liver, which is koshered only by *broiling.* Liver must be sliced, salted, and then broiled with the salt until it has turned color, or is edible. The salt is then washed off, and the liver processed in any desirable manner. Liver may also be frozen for future use, without regard to the date of slaughter.

It is a misconception that kosher meat has "several strikes against it" for the caterer. Koshered and aged meat can be just as tender as nonkosher meat. The koshering process *does not* impair the taste or quality. Variety in production, however, is limited because only the forequarters may be used.

However, if meat is soaked and salted within the 72-hour period, it is fit for kosher consumption, and may be stored frozen for an unlimited period, and/or shipped to any part of the country. But to have a really flavorful finished product, it is most important to purchase top quality meats, and to prepare them skillfully.

To be certain that all regulations have been followed, you should use the services of a certified kosher butcher, whose name can be supplied by an ordained, orthodox rabbi. Once the butcher has been certified as kosher, you can make future purchases from him without concern or rechecking.

In addition to meats, poultry must also be bought from an approved kosher butcher. It can also be purchased from an out-of-town source, which has properly slaughtered and koshered it before freezing and shipping.

Purchase of other foodstuffs—salt, condiments, soup bases, cheeses, etcetera—is not as critical as meat, but does require alertness if errors are to be avoided. Cheese is a good example. As a dairy food, there would seem to be no question as to its use on a kosher menu. However, since it may be prepared with rennin from a non-kosher animal, it must carry the rabbi's stamp of approval, certifying that it has been kosher prepared.

The rabbi's stamp does not make the product kosher. It merely testifies to the fact that it was prepared in strict adherence to kashruth regulations (Jewish dietary laws).

Fruits and vegetables, both canned and frozen, are not ordinarily covered by rules of the rabbinical council, and provide no special problems insofar as purchasing is concerned.

PREPARATION AND MENU PLANNING

Preparation of foods for a strictly kosher operation must conform to another dietary law of the Jewish religion. Restrictions in preparation arise from the fact that Jewish laws list three classes of food (meat and meat by-products; milk and all dairy products; and neutral foods, which are purely chemical and vegetable in origin), and stipulate that food items from the first two classes (meat and milk) can never be prepared in the same dishes, or served at the same meal.

Obviously, with these restrictions, menu planning can be very limited and quite a problem. If you are using meat as the main menu item, the rest of the meal is governed by a great many restrictions. Desserts, breads, and other items must all be prepared without the use of milk, butter, or cream. By the same token, meatless menus can be rather bland, unless you use considerable ingenuity.

These problems are obvious ones, but deeper, more far-reaching ones are discovered when, for example, you prepare a dish such as creamed turkey. The sauce for the creamed turkey must be made with either chicken fat or vegetable shortening, flour, and turkey stock. The use of cream, milk, or butter is prohibited. On the other hand, vegetable soup for a dairy meal cannot contain meat stock, but must rely on vegetable stock and seasonings for flavor.

To cover these criteria, most caterers and foodservice operators dealing in kosher foodservice have devised special recipes and/or rely on special commercial products. However, you can readily see that menu planning can and often does present many special and unique problems.

One menu planning aid not yet mentioned is neutral or parve foods—anything that grows on the land or in the sea (subject to dietary law), and all chemical-based foods or derivatives, such as monosodium glutamate or meat tenderizers. Parve foods can be served at either dairy or meat meals, depending on their method of preparation. They include jams, cereals, fish, eggs, grains, sugars, syrups, fruits, vegetables, vegetable oils and shortenings, and seasonings, including the whole gamut of herbs, spices, and flavorings—as long as no part of either a meat or dairy product is incorporated in their manufacture.

Therefore, while Jewish dietary laws exclude many foods and combinations of foods, there is still room for imagination and a challenge in developing new uses for the approved foods, thus providing pleasing menus. The emergence of dairy, meat, and seafood substitutes on the food scene has also led to a whole new era in kosher food development. It is now an accepted and seldom questioned custom to serve coffee whiteners (of parve vegetable origin), whipped toppings, and ersatz ice cream. Of course, you must make certain that these substitutes do carry a symbol of kosher certification.

Reading the listing of ingredients on packages, and interpreting technical terms, can be time-consuming and frustrating. It can also cause you to reject a food product that meets all requirements, or, on the contrary, accept a product that might be *trefe,* or forbidden. Therefore, many food manufacturers whose products meet dietary requirements, and who wish to take advantage of this captive and lucrative market, employ the services of the Union of Orthodox Rabbis. This group will only give its endorsement if the entire production process is under its constant supervision, and if the product meets kashruth standards. (See list of food additives in Figure 12.5.)

Products endorsed by the group carry the letter "U" enclosed in a circle, thusly Ⓤ. In many cases, there will also be information alongside the symbol as to whether the product is *milchig, fleishig,* or *parve.*

The letter "K" enclosed in a circle, thusly Ⓚ, signifies that a product has been endorsed by another respected group, the O. K. Laboratories or Organized Kashruth, which is composed of, and administered by, rabbis.

There is no hierarchy in the United States rabbinate. Rabbis may organize into groups or societies for religious or civic reasons, or for whatever reason(s) they wish. An ordained rabbi—with his own congregation—is the leader of his members only, and authority and parochial duties vary from synagogue to synagogue, and from city to city. For this reason, some processed kosher foods may show only the freestanding letter "K" alongside the brand name. This shows that the endorsement of kashruth has been given by only one individual rabbi.

Since Jewish dietary law prohibits dairy and meat foods from being prepared in the same dishes, many caterers plan and serve only one type of menu—meat, for example. However, caterers and foodservice operators serving three meals a day must, of course, prepare and serve both dairy and meat meals. Under these circumstances, they must have two separate, completely equipped kitchens or, at least, one large kitchen with a double set of ranges, ovens, broilers, fryers, cookers, mixing bowls, etcetera, as well as two complete sets of china and silver.

Glatt Kosher

Glatt kosher refers to a bovine whose lungs are smooth and whose kosher status does not have to be determined by testing the lungs for disease and/or wounds. Glatt kosher refers only to bovines, because in other animals the lungs are not inspected. Approximately one out of six kosher carcasses fall into this glatt category. The others are still kosher, but do not have the distinct glatt kosher status, which some people seek.

Much confusion has arisen over the use of this term. Many consider this a necessary criterion for the kashruth of a product. In reality, it is a specific criterion observed by Chassidic groups and by other very religious Jews. Glatt kosher has erroneously become synonymous with the term strictly kosher, but the two are distinctly separate concepts. Something may be strictly kosher, yet it need not be glatt kosher.

Glatt kosher products are generally more expensive than similar kosher products. This kosher category is not a criterion for kashruth, and it is only observed by certain ultrapious people. To apply this term to any other item, besides meat, is foolish and false.*

*Condensed from an article in a monograph by Marianna Desser, Cornell School of Hotel Administration.

MAINTENANCE

Two sets of utensils and dishes cause a problem— that of keeping meat dishes separate from dairy dishes. China is fairly easy since two distinct patterns can be used. However, utensils represent a great difficulty, and you must develop a system that works well. Some operations find that welding a plaque to the dairy utensils is the answer.

But, other than keeping dishes separated, maintenance presents no really large problem for the kosher operation. Of course, as soaps are ordinarily made with animal fats, a special kosher soap or chemical detergent must be used. Also strict adherence to kosher laws requires that articles of food preparation, and service, as well as the kitchen, be kept scrupulously clean.

PROFIT

As the owner of a kosher establishment, your profit range will be comparable to that of a non-kosher operation, providing all other factors are equal. Although the cost of food and preparation will be somewhat higher, the selling price will also be correspondingly higher.

COMBINING KOSHER AND NON-KOSHER OPERATIONS

Up to this point, only the operation of a strictly kosher establishment has been discussed. If you wish to combine both kosher and non-kosher foodservice, you will probably find that a great deal more planning is required in order to meet Jewish laws.

Storage space would, of necessity, nearly double since preparation and serving of both types of food cannot be combined. While it is permissible in some instances to use the same utensils, the scouring process involved in cleanup must be so thorough that it is usually not practicable; therefore, distinctly identifiable utensils should be purchased.

Although foodstuffs and items for dry storage can be stored with the non-kosher foods, meat must be held under separate refrigeration. With all these inconveniences, it would seem that operating a combination kosher/non-kosher establishment is impracticable.

However, large operations, such as hotels serving a mixed clientele, report that catering to Jewish banquets and special celebrations has proved to be very profitable, and that the added initial cost and extra storage space really is a minor consideration.

Hotel, motel, and club managers with attractive dining facilities often make them available for kosher affairs. Since the caterer prepares and serves the affair, using all of his or her own kosher dishes, equipment, and experienced personnel, the facilities' operator need not be knowledgeable in this area, or have the specialized personnel. The facility is reimbursed by a percentage of the gross, a per guest charge, or a separate kitchen and dining area charge—any arrangement equitable to both parties. As a result, the facilities' operator not only retains the bar operation, clothes checking, and parking facilities, but gets added revenue, since most kosher affairs are held on Saturday nights or on Sunday, when dining room counts are down or nonexistent in many areas. (See sample "use" charges in Figure 12.1.)

TRADITIONAL MEALS

Sabbath

The Fourth Commandment admonishes man to remember and keep holy the Sabbath. Thus, to the observant Jew, Sabbath is a day of special holiness, and one devoted to the soul. It is also a day of complete rest for both man and animals. All weekday cares and work must be completed before nightfall on Friday.

Since the home is considered a temple, and the table an altar, special preparations are made for the Sabbath meal. Twists of fine white bread, called challahs, are baked, and meals are planned so that "warming or reheating" of food will not reduce its good taste. Typical of these dishes are gefilte fish, chicken, chicken soup, brisket of beef, tzimmes, cholents, noodle pudding, and sponge and honey cakes.

The Sabbath meal is a leisurely one and includes many courses. Songs of peace, and of tribute to the ideal housewife (Ayshes Chail), are chanted. In addition, discussions of a spiritual nature and intellectual content are integral parts of this observance.

Passover

Passover, an eight-day holiday, is usually celebrated about the same time as the Christian observance of Easter. It celebrates the Israelites' release from bondage, which took place in Egypt more than 3000 years ago.

During Passover, rigid food regulations and restrictions are in effect. Forbidden are all cereals and their derivatives, leavening agents of any kind, and bread, biscuits, coffee substances derived from cereals, wheat, barley, oats, rice, dried peas, and dried beans.

Grain liquids such as beer, and grain alcohol derivatives, such as rye, vodka, scotch, bourbon, and gin, are prohibited. Wine and fruit-based cordials must be produced under rabbinical supervision, and carry a special Passover seal to be accepted beverages.

All fresh and frozen vegetables—except peas, corn, and beans—are permitted, as are all fresh and frozen fruits. These must be packaged in natural syrup. If they are sweetened with corn syrup, for example, they would be unsuitable. Special labeling is not required on sealed packages of bean coffee, sugar, salt, tea, and spices.

Matzohs, flat wafers made of a specific type of wheat mixed with water, and apple cider are sometimes used. Matzohs, baked immediately after forming, are used as a bread substitute.

Olive, peanut, and cottonseed oils are the only non-animal, neutral fats used. Milk, cream, cheese, and butter must be produced under special supervision.

Pots and pans, as well as the silverware and dishes used during the rest of the year, are put

Figure 12.1. Use Charges

ELEGANT HOTEL
NEW YORK CITY SUBURB

TO — Ladies Auxiliary of Anonymous Jewish Home for the Elderly

Charges for use of FACILITIES ONLY
Sept. 23, 19 ____

930 Guests	6.90	6417.00
930 Hat checks	.50	465.00
930 Mens and Ladies Room Attendants	.08	74.40
930 Mechanical Dept.	.06	55.80
	Total	7012.20

No tax as this is a bona-fide charitable organization
Meals furnished separately by a Kosher caterer

EXCLUSIVE COUNTRY CLUB
FAIRFIELD, CONN.

TO — Local branch of Israeli College Alumni Dinner Dance

Sept. 4, 19 ____   As per contract — Facilities ONLY

450 Guests	from 6 P.M. to 2 A.M.	
Use of main dining room		1500.00
4 Parking attendants	30.00	120.00
	Total	1620.00

No tax as this is a bona-fide charitable organization
Meals furnished separately by a Kosher caterer

HOLIDAY HOTEL
NEARBY CITY

TO — Ladies Auxiliary of Anonymous Jewish Organization

April 12, 19 ____

Use of dining room for 400 guests for
luncheon and fashion show   700.00

Use of main dining room until 4 P.M.
Meal furnished separately by a kosher caterer

No tax as this is a bona-fide charitable organization

---

away. Special dishes and utensils kept specifically for this holiday are used.

Stoves and ovens must be scrupulously cleaned before any Passover foods can be cooked on or in them.

The Seders, ceremonial meals on the first two days, are prepared with much symbolism. The table is usually covered with an ornately decorated cloth of rich material.

- Matzoh, unleavened bread, occupies a conspicuous place on the table. And a dish of salt should be readily available so it can be sprinkled on the matzoh before eating.
- A roasted lamb shankbone, symbol of the Paschal lamb sacrificed at the temple in ancient times, is placed near the matzohs. (A roasted chicken neck can be substituted for the shankbone.)
- A roasted egg—token of grief for the destruction of the temple—is also used.
- Bitter herbs, usually horseradish, are available as a reminder of the bitterness of slavery.
- Charosis—a mixture of chopped apples, nuts, cinnamon, and/or ginger—is moistened with wine to a pasty consistency. This symbolizes the mortar used by Egyptian Jews to hold bricks together.
- Also on the table are karpas—sprigs of parsley or celery leaves—and a dish of salt water in which the karpas can be dipped before eating. The salt water is a symbol of the tears of slavery.
- Wine is an essential part of the Passover Seder, and must be drunk four times during the meal.

The Passover meal is lavish and, by tradition, always includes fish, chicken soup with knaidlach, and poultry, and/or meat roasts.

Shevuoth

This two-day holiday is known as the Festival of the Torah. Usually celebrated in May, it commemorates the date upon which the Lord gave Moses the Tablets of the Law, which marked the beginning of the Jewish religion.

It is also known as the Feast of Weeks, and/or the Feast of the Pentecost. The former name comes from the fact that it is celebrated seven weeks after Passover, while the latter name means that it occurs the fiftieth day after the second day of Passover.

On Shevuoth in ancient times, the first fruits of the field were brought to the temple as an offering of thanksgiving. As a result, synagogues and homes are decorated with flowers and foliage symbolizing harvest.

Dairy meals are traditional during these days for two reasons. First, the Law is compared to milk and honey. Second, prior to receiving the Law, Jews did not eat kosher meats but, after receiving it, found that there was not enough time to prepare meals according to the new regulations.

Traditional Shevuoth dishes include: cheese blintzes and kreplach, pirogen, puddings containing cheese and fruit, fruit compotes, fruit tarts, and pastries rich with cream and butter.

Rosh Hashanah

Usually held in September, Rosh Hashanah is considered the "birthday of the world's creation," and is the Jewish New Year.

While these two days are essentially ones for rejoicing, they are also "days of awe" and, as such, are devoted to prayer. The ram's horn, known as the shofar, is sounded to arouse people to their spiritual shortcomings, and to encourage them to make worthy resolutions to improve their conduct.

Fish, symbol of fruitfulness and plenty, is one of the traditional dishes. Rich and sweet foods, which signify a wish for prosperity, and a sweet new year, are also served.

Challahs are braided and baked in round form to represent a wish for life without end. Years ago, the tops of the challahs were decorated with birds made of dough to indicate the "flying to heaven" of prayers for the new year.

Since bitter and sour foods are avoided, roast meats and poultry are accompanied by sweet vegetable compotes made from carrots, sweet potatoes, white potatoes, prunes, and honey. Taiglach, light dough nuggets cooked in honey and coated with nuts (possibly of Greek origin), are a staple holiday item, as is honey cake.

Yom Kippur

The Day of Atonement is the most solemn and awesome day of the year. This day, which is normally held in late September or early October, is one of penitence and prayer. Consequently, total abstinence from food and drink is required, and smoking is forbidden.

A pre-fast meal must be concluded before sundown the previous day. Since liquids, including water, are not permitted during the fast, the meal is normally underseasoned, and fish and other salty foods are avoided. Soup with kreplach, boiled chicken, simple vegetables, and bland desserts are standard fare. However, this meal must be substantial because it has to sustain an individual for the next 24 or 26 hours.

At the end of the fast, a very bountiful meal is served. It consists of pickled, cooked, and smoked fish variations, cheese blintzes, sour cream, salads, and rich yeast cakes laden with raisins and sweet spices. These foods are prepared the day before the fast so that, with a minimum of heating or other preparation, they can be eaten immediately.

Succoth

Succoth, also known as the Feast of Booths and Festival of the Harvest, is the Jewish Thanksgiving and usually takes place in October.

Booths, which denote the temporary shelters used by the Israelites in their wanderings, are lavishly decorated with fruits of the fields. Grapes, apples, figs, pears, and gourds are hung from the ceiling, or the open roof.

During this holiday, meals are eaten in the Sukkah (booth). In addition to fruits of the harvest, traditional fare includes stuffed cabbage in a sweet sauce, which is served for at least one meal. This symbolizes the products of the earth and the successful food—animal production.

On the ninth and final day, Simchat Torah (rejoicing of the Bible), the richest foods, the finest wines, luscious desserts, and candies are the order of the day.

Chanukah

The Festival of Lights is an eight-day holiday that is usually held in December. It was instituted by Judas Maccabeus to celebrate regaining of the temple, which the Maccabees then rededicated by burning a flask of oil for a full eight days. This led to the practice of lighting special Chanukah candles. Thus, the eight-branched candlestand is a frequent symbol for this holiday, during which gifts are exchanged.

Pancakes are traditionally served, due, no doubt, to the fact that they were the fare for the Maccabee warriors. Because of their thin, flat surface, the speed with which they could be cooked in hot oil, and their effectiveness as hunger quenchers, pancakes were a desirable dish for the warriors.

In various areas where Jews have settled, it has become customary to make the pancakes from rice, corn, and buckwheat—the latter being very popular with East European Jews.

Around the turn of the century, potato pancakes were quite popular with American Jews. Sociologists believe that this was due to the fact that the ingredients were inexpensive, and that the pancakes were an excellent means for warding off hunger. Applesauce and sour cream were later embellishments.

Purim

The one-day celebration of "Lots" is usually in March. It celebrates the deliverance of the Persian Jews from massacre more than 2500 years ago. Therefore, Purim is a day of jubilation, singing, dancing, and gift-giving. It is intended to show that, although wickedness may temporarily seem to succeed, freedom from persecution will come to those who have faith.

Hamantashen, a three-cornered fruit or poppy seed pastry, is traditionally eaten on this day. There is good-natured rivalry among culinarians to produce the best hamantashen and the best Purim dinner, and to show off their achievements.

Figure 12.2. Estimate for Kosher Catering

ESTIMATE FOR KOSHER CATERING

Function _____   Date _____

Name _____   Room _____

Address _____   Time _____

City _____ State _____ Zip _____

Telephone No. _____

NO.	ITEM	PER PERSON		TOTAL	
	Cocktail Hour ____ Butler Style ____ Buffet Style ____ Food Selections				
	Dinner				
	Cake				
	Chalah				
	Toast				
	Unlimited Liquor				
	Viennesse Hour				
	Extras:				
	Total Food & Beverage (t)				
	17% Gratuities				
	Kosher Charge				
	Rabbi				
	Cantor				
	Flowers: Floral Centerpiece Each Table (t)				
	Floral Centerpiece Head Table (t)				
	Floral Canopy (t)				
	White Runner (t)				
	Aisle Baskets (t)				
	Floral Sprays (t)				
	Checking at:				
	Lounge Attendants				
	Musician for Ceremony				
	( ) Piece Band for ( ) Hours				
	Yamulkas (printed)				
	Room Rental				
	Extras:				
	8% State & Local Tax				
	TOTAL:				

Estimate by: _____

Figure 12.3.

COMPLETE CUSTOMIZED BAR MITZVAH PACKAGE PLAN

For those who wish an
Elaborate Full Continental Smorgasbord!

during your Cocktail Reception — prior to your Dinner,
may we recommend: —
With your excellent selection of Hot Hors d'Oeuvres
and Fancy Cold Canapes the following:

1. **HORS D'OEUVRES** consisting of —
   Cold: Special decorated "Canapes Russe"
   which are varied, attractive and fancy
   formed Hors d'Oeuvres.
   Hot: Franks in Blankets, Potato Knishes, Liver
   Knishes, Kasha Knishes, Miniature Potato
   Pancakes, Stuffed Peppers, Fish Balls.

2. **CHAFING DISHES** consisting of —
   Chinese Prime Peppered Steak.
   Beef Stroganoff.
   Hungarian Stuffed Cabbage.
   Swedish Meat Balls.
   Barbequed Chicken.
   Veal Scallopine a la Marsala.

3. **DECORATED FORM MOULDS** consisting of —
   Chicken Liver Mould.
   Fruit Filled Gelatin Mould.

4. **SWEDISH TABLE** consisting of —
   Smoked White Fish.
   Nova Scotia Salmon.
   Assorted Imported Herrings.
   Gefilte Fish.

5. **FANCY DECORATED PLATTERS** consisting of —
   Sliced Tongue, carved and decorated.
   Sliced Turkey, carved and decorated.
   Potato Salad, garne.
   Cole Slaw, garne.
   Waldorf Salad.
   Celery, Olives, Radishes, and Pickles.

6. **CARVING TABLE** Our Chef will carve from his
   table:
   Glazed Hot Corned Brisket of Beef.
   Lean Hot Roumanian Pastrami.

7. **POLYNESIAN FRUIT DISPLAY** consisting of —
   An excellent variety of fresh fruit in season
   attractively displayed.

EXTRA TARIFF . . .$ **Per Person**

Hand Crafted, Ice Figures . . .$ **Additional**

— — —R— — —

*We appreciate your inquiry and assure you the finest
food preparation and service, a tradition that will be
extended to your Bar Mitzvah. It will be an affair long
remembered by your guests! Please contact our Banquet
Manager, as soon as possible, to assure you of your
preferred date.*

Thank You!

— For your COCKTAIL RECEPTION —

**We will serve UNLIMITED COCKTAILS, ALL
LIQUORS, Fruit Punch Fountain and Coke Bar
for the children.
Plus a delightful selection of Hot Hors d'Oeuvres
and fancy decorated Cold Canapes, Served Butler
Style on Sterling Silver Service.**

— — —R— — —

— DINNER SUGGESTIONS —
**Iced Hearts of Celery, Red Radish Rosettes,
Green and Ripe Queen Olives**

Your choice of Appetizer:
Fresh Florida Fruit Cocktail "Supreme"
Chilled Ripe Melon in Season
Fresh Chopped Chicken Livers
Fresh Pineapple Basket filled with
Assorted Fresh Fruit 1.00 extra

Your choice of Soup:
Matzo Ball Soup
Fresh Garden Vegetable Soup
Consomme Vermicelli
French Onion Soup
Petite Marmite Henry IV
Soup du Jour

Your choice of Entree:
Roast Prime Ribs of Blue Ribbon Beef, au Jus
Fresh Fish in Season — prepared to your taste

Your choice of Vegetable:
Fresh String Beans Amandine
Fresh Broccoli Maison
Fresh Cauliflower in Season
New Peas and Mushrooms
Grilled Tomato Provencale
Glazed Belgian Carrots
Fresh Vegetable in Season

Your choice of Potato:
Stuffed Baked Potatoes
Potato Croquettes
French Fried Potatoes
Lyonnaise Potatoes
Duchesse Potatoes
Rissole Potatoes
Allumette Potatoes

ALL Entrees served with Stuffed Derma!

Special Salad:
Fresh Tossed Mixed Garden Green Salad with Sliced
Tomato wedges and our Chef's Special Dressing

Dessert
Rainbow Sherbet Parfait served with assorted fresh
baked cookies

Coffee   Demi-Tasse   Tea

After Dinner Mints and Mixed Assorted Nuts

ALL these EXTRAS are included in your Package Plan!

BAR MITZVAH CAKE: A beautifully decorated Bar
Mitzvah Cake with Scroll and Bar Mitzvah's Boy's
Name. An impressive Candle Lighting Ceremony
will be conducted by the Captain and his Staff.

CHALAH: A fancy formed fresh baked Chalah.

UNLIMITED LIQUOR: Will be served throughout
your entire affair with only the finest premium
brands and assortment available.

FLORAL ARRANGEMENTS: Fresh cut Flowers for
each table plus extra large centerpieces for Dais
decorated with Table Ferns and Smilax. You select
the color of the Arrangements.

COLORED CANDLES: To match the color of your
table Linens.

COLORED TABLE LINENS & FINE SPANISH LACE:
For your tables plus a beautifully decorated Bar
Mitzvah Head Table with special Lighting effects.

STERLING SILVER SERVICE: Only the finest in
Silver service available, from the silver settings on
your tables, to our antique silver service trays, to
our beautiful Silver Candelabras.

MENUS AND MATCHES: Personalized menus and
matches for each guest to have their own souvenir.

CIGARS AND CIGARETTES: Will be presented to
your guests with our compliments.

**CHECKROOM & VALET PARKING "Free of
Charge":** Signs will be displayed to make sure
that no guest will be inconvenienced to tip.

ROLLING BARS WITH BARTENDERS: To service
your guests with the selection of drinks or liqueurs
they may desire during and after dinner.

A CAPTAIN: To conduct your affairs from beginning
to end and to be at your service for the entire event.

ALL GRATUITIES: For Captain, Staff, Waiters and
Bartenders are included in your Package Plan
Price.

PLUS AN EXTRA . . . . .

VIENNESSE HOUR!

An attractive Laced Viennesse Table decorated with
Fancy Cakes, Petit Fours, Miniature Pastries, Assorted
Tortes, Strudels, served with Viennesse Coffee and
Demi Tasse. An excellent selection of Cordials and
Dessert Wines will be served to those who wish them.

Price per person _____ .

Figure 12.4. Kosher Wedding
Menu

Tropical Whole Pineapple au Kirsch
Diced Pineapple Marinated in Kirsch—plate to be
decorated with galax leaves, small fruits
(cherries, green and red grapes, plum, peach)

Iced Hearts of Celery   Colossal Ripe and Green Olives
          Radish Roses   Sweet Gherkins   Spiced Watermelon Rinds

Salted Jumbo Peanuts and Almonds

Chicken Consomme Double with Mondels
Mock Cheese Straws

Baked Fillet of Sole with Supreme Sauce
Parisienne Potatoes

Roast Breast of Capon on Tongue, under glass, Mushroom Sauce
Wild Rice Croquettes

Cranberry and Orange Relish in Orange Baskets en Parade
(Orange baskets to be decorated with white ribbon
and orange blossoms)

Kishkie, to be passed on silver platters

Kentucky Limestone Lettuce with Hearts of Palm
Artichoke Bottoms, Pimiento Strips, Vinaigrette Dressing.

Pastry Swans, filled with mock ice cream
Brandied Peach Sauce

Petits Fours Glace

Black Coffee   or   Tea with Lemon

4-tier wedding cake to be all white with pale pink sugar ribbons and flowers.
Between first and second tier, place white gardenias. Upper tier to have
sugar swans.

All other items can be customized exactly as on Bar Mitzvah package
but wedding cake substituted for Bar Mitzvah cake.

Figure 12.5. Food Additives and Their Classification

A Milliken Market Research survey of 1000 Jewish families, chosen at random, showed that 85 percent of those that responded look for some type of Rabbinical endorsement on the product they buy.

Meaning of symbols:

K — Kosher	KF — Kosher Fleishig (meat)
KP — Kosher Parve	TR — Trefe — Totally Non-Kosher
KD — Kosher Dairy	RE — Rabbinical Endorsement Required

AGAR AGAR — Derived from seaweed .... KP

ARGOL — A crude cream of tartar — wine sediment derivative .... RE

CALCIUM CARBONATE — A white crystalline mineral .... KP

CALCIUM STEARATE — Compounded of calcium and stearic acid .... RE

CARAGHEEN — Extract of seaweed and moss .... KP

CASEIN — Protein found in milk .... KD

COCOA BUTTER — Derivative of cocoa bean .... KP

CREAM OF TARTAR — Wine sediment derivative .... RE

EMULSIFIERS — Most derived from non-kosher sources .... RE

ESTERS AND ETHYL OENANTHATE — Organic compounds formed by combining alcohol and
organic acids .... KP

GELATINS — Derived from animal bones .... RE

GLYCERINE (GLYCEROL) — Derived from oils and fat and petroleum .... RE

GLYCINE — A gelatin product derivative .... RE

GUM BASE — A glycerine derivative .... RE

GUM TRAGACANTH, GUM ARABIC, GUAR GUM, VEGETABLE GUM, LOCUST BEAN GUM — Derivative
from plant sources .... KP

LACTIC ACID — When found among the ingredients of olives and soft drinks it is usually made from
corn and molasses and is KP. Lactic acid used in the manufacture of cream cheese is derived from milk ... KD

LACTOSE — A cheese by-product .... KD

LECITHIN — Synthetic derivative or from soy beans and corn oil .... KP

LIPIDS — Fats of animals or vegetables .... RE

MAGNESIUM STEARATE — Compounded of magnesium and stearic acid .... RE

MONOCALCIUM PHOSPHATE — Derived from phosphate rock and limestone, or from bone meal ... RE

MONO- AND DI-GLYCERIDES — Similar to glycerides and most are of animal sources ... RE

MONOSODIUM GLUTAMATE — Vegetable and chemical in origin .... KP

NATURAL AND ARTIFICIAL FLAVORS — Extracted from plant and animal sources .... RE

NIACIN — Chemical in origin (member of "B_1" complex of vitamins) .... KP

PECTIN — Derived from fruits and vegetables .... KP

PEPSIN — Obtained from the secretions of animal stomach linings — particularly from hogs ... TR

POLYSORBATE 60 or 80 — Possible non-kosher derivative .... RE

POTASSIUM CHLORIDE — Composed of chemicals or minerals .... KP

POTASSIUM SORBATE — Synthetic chemical .... KP

PYROPHOSPHATE — Synthetic chemical .... KP

PYRODOXINE HYDROCHLORIDE — Synthetic chemical .... KP

RESINOUS GLAZE — Insect secretions .... RE

RENNET — Obtained from lining of calf's stomach .... RE

(continued)

Figure 12.5. (continued)

RIBOFLAVIN — VITAMIN B — Synthetic	KP
SODIUM CASEINATE — A soluble form of casein	KD
SHORTENING — Animal or plant source derivative	RE
SODIUM PROPIONATE — The sodium salt of propionic acid	KP
SOFTENERS — Mostly used in chewing gum and derived from either animal or vegetable	RE
SORBITAN MONOSTEARATE — Either animal or plant source	RE
SORBITOL — Synthetic	KP
STEARIC ACID — Extracted from tallow and other hard fats	RE
SULFUR DIOXIDE — A mineral derivative	KP
SODIUM BISULPHITE — Chemical	KP
SODIUM IRON PHOSPHATE, SODIUM HEXAMETAPHOSPHATE AND TRI CALCIUM PHOSPHATE — Inorganic chemicals and mostly of mineral derivatives	KP
TARTARIC ACID — Similar to cream of tartar	RE
THIAMINE, MONO NITRATE — Either vegetable or synthetic (water soluble form of Vitamin B_1)	KP
VANILLIN — An extract of vanilla bean or from glycerine	RE
VEGETABLE OILS — Vegetable oils and even "pure vegetable oils" may contain some animal derivatives. The Food and Drug Administration stated "Such statements as 'pure' or '100% pure' have no special meaning under the law. The use of the term 'pure' is, in our opinion, inappropriate on the label of any food product since it may have different meanings such as 'free from bacteria,' 'not contaminated with anything harmful,' etc., and in some cases it is misleading." It is necessary to ascertain the source used.	RE
VITAMINS — Many processed foods are vitamin-enriched with synthetically produced vitamins. However, Vitamin A and D are obtained from fish livers — possibly from shark liver, which is not kosher.	RE

*Condensed from a monograph by Marianna Desser of the Cornell School of Hotel Administration.

CHAPTER THIRTEEN

WINE AND BAR SERVICE

Every state (and many counties) has its own rules and regulations regarding the sale of alcoholic beverages. If wise, you will check with your local Liquor Control Board before purchasing liquor for resale.

A liquor license is required for all liquor service, except when it is served in a private home. In such a case, your client will purchase the liquor to be served to guests.

If you are an on-premise caterer, you can install a permanent bar in your banquet hall after getting a liquor license. When a liquor license is not obtainable, a special one may be available to permit the sale of beer and wine only. Whenever you are catering and alcoholic beverages are served, be very careful; do not sell or serve them to minors. If you do, you will not only jeopardize your license, but may find yourself in serious difficulty.

Although your client will supply the alcohol for a private home party, you must provide the bartender, a portable bar or a long table, the necessary glasses and bar service equipment, mixes, and ice. The number of glasses you will need will depend on the type and time of function, length of time the bar is to be open, and the type of guest

(age and sex) to be served. Generally, you should plan on providing approximately 10 to 15 percent more glasses than the number of guests expected, which will alleviate the need for on-the-job washing. Many attractive disposable "glasses" are available today, and you might consider using them for certain types of functions. However, be sure the client knows your intentions and agrees.

BASIC BAR EQUIPMENT

Your basic bar equipment should consist of:

Bar strainer

Bottle opener

Can opener

Cloth or absorbent paper towels

Corkscrew

Eight-inch round cutting surface

Glass stirring rod or long spoon for mixing, stirring

Large pitchers (with good pouring lips for water, juice, etc.)

Measuring spoons

One jigger measure—with an accurate scale for half and quarter ounces

Paring knife—for peeling and cutting fruit

Precision pourers to replace corks or caps

Sturdy mixing glass or shaker

Vacuum-type ice bucket with tongs

Waste basket

Wooden muddler—for mashing mint, herbs, and fruits

Zester—for cutting shreds of lemon, lime, or orange

BOTTLE INVENTORY

When liquor is delivered to the bar, you (or the bartender) and your client should inventory the number of bottles. Such an inventory can save embarrassment later, and avoid possible suspicions that some liquor is missing. At the end of the party, your client and the bartender should again count all bottles, including empty, unopened, and broken bottles. The number, of course, should be the same as originally inventoried.

THE COCKTAIL HOUR

In planning a cocktail hour/reception that precedes a dinner, your client and you must agree in advance as to when the bar will open and close. Do not prolong serving drinks beyond the agreed time, or your carefully planned dinner may not be up to your usual high standards.

During the cocktail hour, waiters can pass hors d'oeuvre or, if a buffet setup is used, they can replenish it as needed. These same waiters will also serve the dinner that follows.

An experienced bartender should be knowledgeable in the proper mixing and dispensing of drinks. Nevertheless, have a good basic bartender's guide book available for ready reference. In addition to dispensing drinks preceding the dinner, a bartender should pour the wine or champagne during the meal, and be available for bar service later in the evening, if the client so desires.

WINE AND CHAMPAGNE SERVICE

The selection of wines for any occasion is, of course, up to the client, but it is to your advantage to make suggestions whenever possible.

STANDARD BAR MEASURES

The following is a list of standard bar measures:

1 Dash	1/6 teaspoon (1/32 ounce)
1 Teaspoon (bar spoon)	1/8 ounce
1 Pony	1 ounce
1 Jigger (bar glass)	1-1/2 ounces
1 Wine Glass	4 ounces
1 Split	6 ounces
1 Cup	8 ounces
1 Miniature	1, 1.6, or 2 ounces
1 Half Pint	8 ounces
1 Tenth (4/5 pint)	12.8 ounces (1/10 gallon)
1 Pint (1/2 quart)	16 ounces
1 Fifth (4/5 quart)	25.6 ounces (1/5 gallon)
1 Quart	32 ounces (1/4 gallon)
1 Imperial Quart	38.4 ounces
1 Half Gallon	54 ounces
1 Gallon	128 ounces

Wine or Champagne Sizes
(NOTE: Called "pints" or "quarts" in the trade, but not true quantities)

Split	(1/4 bottle)	6 to 6-1/2 ounces
Pint	(1/2 bottle)	11 to 13 ounces
Quart	(1 bottle)	24 to 26 ounces
Magnum	(2 bottles)	52 ounces
Jeroboam	(4 bottles)	104 ounces
Tappit-Hen	(1 gallon)	128 ounces
Rehoboam	(6 bottles)	156 ounces (1.22 gallons)
Methuselah	(8 bottles)	208 ounces (1.625 gallons)
Salmanazar	(12 bottles)	312 ounces (2.44 gallons)
Balthazar	(16 bottles)	416 ounces (3.3 gallons)
Nebuchadnezzar	(20 bottles)	520 ounces (4.07 gallons)
Demijohn		627.2 ounces (4.9 gallons)

Figure 13.1. Guide for Determining Party Beverage Requirements

The following is a reference only. For safety purposes, use quarts instead of fifths.

Number of Guests	For Cocktails	Amount Needed	Buffet or Dinner	Amount Needed	After Dinner Party
4	10 to 16 drinks	1 fifth	8 cocktails	1 fifth	12 to 16 drinks
			8 glasses, wine	2 bottles	
			4 liqueurs	4/5 pint	
			8 highballs	1 fifth	
6	15 to 22 drinks	2 fifths	12 cocktails	1 fifth	18 to 26 drinks
			12 glasses, wine	2 bottles	
			8 liqueurs	1 fifth	
			18 highballs	2 fifths	
8	18 to 24 drinks	2 fifths	16 cocktails	1 fifth	20 to 34 drinks
			16 glasses, wine	3 bottles	
			10 liqueurs	1 fifth	
			18 highballs	2 fifths	
12	20 to 40 drinks	3 fifths	24 cocktails	2 fifths	25 to 45 drinks
			24 glasses, wine	4 bottles	
			16 liqueurs	1 fifth	
			30 highballs	3 fifths	
20	40 to 65 drinks	4 fifths	40 cocktails	3 fifths	45 to 75 drinks
			40 glasses, wine	7 bottles	
			25 liqueurs	2 fifths	
			50 highballs	4 fifths	

Rule of thumb for quick computation:
1 case/12 fifths whiskey—200 drinks; quarts—240 drinks per case
1 case wine or champagne (fifths)—96 to 100 drinks per case

The most commonly used guide is: red wine with red meats, game, and hearty dishes; and white wines with fish, seafood, omelets, chicken, and veal. Roses, champagnes, and other sparkling wines go with any foods—appetizers, the main course, or desserts.

Red wines should be served at a cool room temperature (60° to 65°F.). White wines, roses, and champagnes should be chilled to 50° to 55°F.

The amount of wine to be served depends on the size of the glass used. A large glass should not be filled more than half-full; a small glass should be filled to within one-half or three-quarters of an inch from the top of the glass. For champagne, a four- to five-ounce flute or tulip-shaped glass is often preferred to the traditional saucer-shaped glass, because it helps retain the wine's effervescence longer.

To pour wine, remove the foil or lead seal *just below the cork* so that it will not come in contact with the wine. Some wines have a ring on top of the cork; if this is the case, remove the ring, then twist and pull the cork from the bottle.

In wine bottles where the cork is inserted into the neck, and flush with the bottle top, a corkscrew will be required. Use the corkscrew gently and patiently to get a firm bite into the cork, then work the tip in without crumbling the cork. A good corkscrew is an essential component of your "tool box."

To pour champagne, remove the wire hood, but make sure the cork remains securely in the bottle. Grasp the cork in one hand, and hold the lower part of the bottle in the other hand at a 45-degree angle, and *away from you and any nearby guests. Twist the bottle, not the cork* (see illustration), to allow the internal gas pressure to push the cork out. Once the cork has been removed, keep the bottle at the 45-degree angle for a few seconds to prevent the champagne from bubbling over.

Champagne is poured in two motions. First, pour it into a *dry glass* (moisture will kill bubbles)

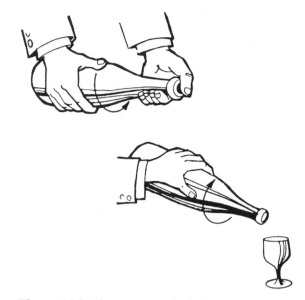

Figure 13.2. The proper method of handling a champagne bottle to remove the cork.

until the bubbles reach the brim of the glass. Stop pouring until bubbles subside, then fill the glass two-thirds to three-quarters full. Elevate the neck of the bottle slightly and turn it slowly, to prevent dripping (see Figure 13.2). Return the bottle to the cooler so that the champagne remains cold and retains its effervescence. Do not pour the champagne in advance and allow it to stand.

WINE PUNCHES

Wine punches (see chapter 16 for recipes) are popular for wedding and anniversary receptions, large tea parties, open houses, and similar occasions. Served from silver, glass, or decorated metal/plastic punch bowls, with matching ladles and trays, they can be very festive and less expensive than champagne. An ice ring or ice block decorated with fruit may be floated in the punch for added eye appeal.

Figure 13.3. This large champagne or punch fountain holds approximately six gallons, has concealed lights, and offers a constant flow from four attractive spouts. (Some Boards of Health prohibit this service because refills from used glasses can overflow into the bowl. Colored water may be substituted and the fountain used as a focal centerpiece.)

Punch cups should be used in serving wine and champagne punches. Be sure to have enough on hand to serve all guests expected to attend the affair.

Wine or champagne punches served from a flowing fountain make an elaborate display for a large party (see Figure 13.3). Keep the fountain filled and allow the guests to serve themselves.

FOUR STEPS IN PROFESSIONAL WINE TASTING

Enology. A science that deals with wine or wine making.

Enologist. A wine expert or professional taster.

To make an accurate evaluation of a wine, an expert looks for these four basic elements:

1. Appearance
2. Bouquet
3. Taste
4. Aftertaste

Appearance. The glass should be held against a white background and tipped slightly to the side. The wine should be crystal clear and the appropriate color. A white or red wine slightly off color signals deterioration. All wines turn brown in time. Wines under five years of age should not be off color. The brownish coloring develops as the wine reaches its tenth year.

Bouquet. An expert can detect with the first sniff whether the wine is sound. Sometimes a rotten odor or a sickening sweetness pervades wines that should be dry. The bouquet must be fresh and clean and reflect the type of grape used. A true enologist can even detect a slight wood scent from the barrel used in the first stages of wine making.

Taste. Mature dry wine must be clean to the taste without bitterness or pronounced acidity. Young red wines may be coarse naturally and slightly bitter to the taste. These are not objectionable traits. Beaujolais should be fresh and fruity to the palate and consumed while the wine is young.

Aftertaste. If after the wine is swallowed an aftertaste becomes evident, excess acidity is indicated. This often cannot be detected in the first three stages. Wine that is sound always has an enjoyable aftertaste, and if this taste lingers the wine has a "long finish."

CHAPTER FOURTEEN

MENUS

In planning menus for a catered affair, you must be flexible. Keep in mind such things as budget, facilities for service, season of the year, age and type of guest, and your own specialties. Menus should be designed to fit the occasion, and should offer as wide a selection as possible. This chapter offers some sample menus for your guidance.

One popular buffet menu contains the following items:

Iced Relish Trays—Celery, Olives, Carrot Sticks, Pickles, Radishes.

Assorted Cheese Platters—American, Swiss, Cheese Dip.

Salads—Jellied Rainbow Fruit Salad, Maraschino Dressing; Potato Salad; Old-Fashioned Coleslaw; Mixed Green Salad, Oil and Vinegar Dressing; Fresh Shrimp Salad.

Hot Dishes—Choice of two: Braised Tenderloin Tips; Swedish Meat Balls; Chicken Tetrazzini; Pan Fried Chicken Leg.

Cold Assorted Meats—Roast Beef; Corned Beef; Baked Ham; Liverwurst.

Condiments—Mustard Dish; Horseradish; Catsup.

Bread (with Butter)—Hard Rolls, Pumpernickel.

Beverage—Individual choice of: Milk, Orange, Coffee, Tea, or Iced Tea.

Choice of desserts.

Luncheon Menu (Minimum of 75 guests)

Choice of One

Supreme of Fresh Fruit   Spiced Tomato Juice
Soup du Jour   Eggs Romanoff
Miniature Antipasto
*

Sesame Sticks   Flaky Croissants   French Bread
*

Choice of One

Baked Karakas Ham, Champagne Sauce
Creamed Chicken and Mushrooms with Fleurons
Breast of Chicken a la Kiev
Yankee-Style Pot Roast with Potato Pancakes
Sliced Turkey over Wild Rice, Mushroom Giblet Gravy
Baked Boston Scrod, Lobster Sauce
Broiled English Sole, Creamy Tartar Sauce
Individual Chef's Salad Bowl with Julienne of
Stilton Cheese, Chicken, Ham, Garlic Croutons
*

Choice of Vegetable or Individual Small Salad
*

Choice of Potatoes

Potato Croquette in Corn Flake Crumbs
Baked, with Sour Cream and Fresh Chives, or with Crumbled Bacon
Duchesse Potatoes   Au Gratin Potatoes
Lyonnaise Potatoes
*

Celery Sticks   Carrot Curls   Cranberry Relish
*

Choice of Desserts

Three-Layer Strawberry Shortcake   Creme de Menthe Frappe
Linzer Torte   Warm, Deep Dish Apple or Blueberry Pie
Nesselrode Pie   Flaky Hungarian Strudel
Preserved Pear Halves with Chocolate Sauce and Pignolias
*

Choice of Beverage

Coffee   Tea   Milk   Decaffeinated Beverage

Luncheon Menu (For small groups of 20 to 30 guests)

Choice of Appetizer

Fresh Fruit Cup   Chilled Orange Juice
Soup du Jour   Chopped Liver on Tomato Slices

Choice of One Entree

Roast Half Spring Chicken, Dressing and Country Gravy
Sauteed Sirloin Tips of Beef, Mushrooms and Peppers on Pilaf
Fried Deep Sea Scallops or Stuffed Shrimp
Broiled Sirloin Steak (8 oz.)
Pot Roast of Beef, Jardiniere
Grilled Ham Steak, Pineapple Ring
Broiled Fresh Ground Sirloin, Mushroom Sauce, Onion Rings
Sliced Sirloin of Beef on Toast, Sauce Jardiniere
Broiled Halibut or Boston Scrod with Lobster Sauce

*

Tossed Green Salad, Bleu Cheese Dressing, or Choice of Vegetable

*

Choice of Potato

Baked Stuffed Potato, Bacon-Flavored Bits
Boiled Red Potatoes, Parsley Butter   French Fried Potatoes

Choice of Desserts

Cheese Cake, Graham Crust   Mint Frappe
Choice of Pies   Chocolate Eclair

Choice of Beverage

Coffee   Tea   Milk   Decaffeinated Beverage

Buffet Luncheons (Menu to be determined 5 days in advance—
100 guest minimum)

HOT FOODS

Choice of One   (Poultry)

Fried Chicken Tidbits   Stewed Chicken and Dumplings
Chicken a la Cacciatore   Chicken Creole

PLUS, Choice of One   (Beef)

Beef Bourguignonne   Beef Stroganoff
Beef Roulades   Salisbury Steaks (miniature)
Meat-Stuffed Cabbages
Hand-sliced Sirloin of Beef, or Baked Ham ($0.00 extra)

PLUS,   Choice of one Hot Vegetable in Chafing Dish

PLUS,   Choice of Au Gratin Potatoes, or Western-Style Fried Potatoes

(continued)

Buffet Luncheons (continued)

      PLUS,   Green Salad, with all the trimmings

      PLUS,   Sliced Cold, Poached Salmon or Halibut, Choice of Dressings, Combination Tray of Cold Corned Beef, Turkey, and Ham

      PLUS,   Assorted Cheeses, Crackers

      PLUS,   Fruit Bowl   Assorted Pastries   Three Varieties of Pie

      PLUS,   Slice-your-own breads and choice of sweet or salted butter

      PLUS,   Coffee   Tea   Milk   Decaffeinated Beverage

Women's Club Luncheon Menu (Menu to be determined 5 days in advance—50 guest minimum)

Choice of One
Fruit-Topped Grapefruit Half   Cranapple Juice
Fresh Shrimp Cocktail   Avocado Stuffed with Crabmeat
Vichyssoise

Choice of One
Chef's Special Salad   Fresh Fruit Cocktail with Cottage Cheese
Broiled Swordfish Steak
Crepe Filled with Chicken, Seafood, or Mushrooms
Pot Roast of Beef, Jardiniere   Breast of Chicken a la Kiev
Tuna Salad with Deviled Eggs
Grape Leaves Filled with Rice and Macadamia Nuts
*

Choice of Salad or Vegetable
PLUS, Choice of Potato or Additional Vegetable
*

Choice of One
Eclairs   Toasted Pound Cake
Bar-le-Duc with Crackers   Banana Cream Pie
Lemon Sherbet, Creme de Menthe Sauce
*

Choice of Beverage
Coffee   Tea   Decaffeinated Beverage

Mediterranean Buffet

Olives   Baby Eggplants   Feta Cheese   Relish Tray
Greek Salad   Marinated Chick-Peas
Hummus bi Taheeni (Sesame Chick-Pea Dip)
Moutabel (Sesame, Lemon Eggplant Dip)
Tabooley (Cracked Wheat, Tomato, and Fresh Mint Salad)
Tarator (Cold Cucumber, Yogurt, and Walnut Soup)
Spanakopetes (Spinach and Filo Pie)
Kreakopita (Lamb Pie)
Warak Mashi (Stuffed Grape Leaves with Garlic Mint Sauce)
Garides Me Saltsza (Shrimp in Tomato, Garlic, Feta Cheese)
Moussaka (Baked Eggplant, Tomato, and Lamb Cake)
Couscous a la Marga (Lamb, Chicken, and Vegetable Stew with Semolina)
Shish Tavuk (Skewered Marinated Broiled Chicken)
Souvlakia Mi Arni (Broiled Lamb Kabobs)
Sigari Bouregi (Feta Cheese Pastry)
Khobaz (Arabic Bread)
Baklava (Filo and Nut Rolls)
Gelato Boureka (Filo and Pastry Cream Rolls)
Coffee

French Buffet

FROID

Timbales de Sole, Sauce Aurore	Aloses ou Anguilles en Gelee
Maquereaux au Vin Blanc	Saumon Poche, Sauce Vincent
Homard en Bellevue	Rillette de Tours
Terrine de Lapin	Galantine de Canard
Pate Maison	Mousse de Foie de Volaille
Poulet Rose de Mai	Jambon de Bayonne
Salade Parisienne	Champignons a la Grecque
Salade de Concumbres	Celeri Remoulade

Salade d'Endives et Betteraves Rouges

CHAUD

Cassoulet Toulousain	Boeuf Bourguignonne

DESSERTS

Chocolate Sabayon Torte	Linzer Torte
Charlotte Russe	Petits Fours
Frangipane Tarts	Macaroons

Fashion Show or Dessert Bridge—Desserts and Beverages Only

DESSERT SELECTIONS—Choice of One

Assorted French or Danish Pastries (one tray per table)

Ice Cream Cake Roll (waiters to offer choice of sauces)

Choice of Parfait (served with cookies)

Assorted Petits Fours

Fresh Fruit Tarts (bowl of whipped cream on each table)

Large Fruit Cup (fresh fruits only)

Eclairs Filled with Whipped Cream (hot fudge sauce to be passed)

Cream Cheese Cake, Choice of Toppings

Strawberry Shortcake or Special Cream Pies

(will be made for a minimum of 60 portions)

*

Bottomless Carafe of Coffee (each table)

(Tea or Milk for individual requests)

*

Three-hour maximum. Host-supplied cards.

*

Mints, candies, cigarettes, if furnished, will be set out in our
dishes—no extra charge.

Service Club Luncheon Menu

APPETIZER—Choice of One

Fresh Fruit Cocktail	Tomato Juice	Soup du Jour

*

Variety Breads   Miniature Dinner Rolls

*

CHOICE OF ENTREE

Baked Virginia Ham, Champagne Sauce   Pot Roast of Beef, Jardiniere

Half, Batter-Fried Boneless Chicken   Chicken Pot Pie with Short Crust

Sliced Flank Steak with Mushrooms, Horseradish Sauce

Hungarian Beef Goulash, Noodles   Grilled Ham Steak with Prune and Raisin Sauce

Broiled Halibut Steak, Maitre d'Hotel   Baked Fillet of Sole Stuffed with Crabmeat

*

CHOICE OF ONE VEGETABLE

Broccoli Polonaise   Timbale of Spinach

Green Peas with Cocktail Onions   or   Cherry Tomatoes and Lettuce, Cream Dressing

*

CHOICE OF POTATO

Lyonnaise Potatoes   O'Brien Potatoes

Boiled Potatoes with Parsley Butter   Shoestring Potatoes

*

CHOICE OF DESSERT

Apple Pie with Stilton Cheese   Gruyere Cheese with Toasted Crackers
    Orange Sherbet with Mandarin Sauce   Baked Apple with Peppermint Sauce
                    Half Grapefruit
                        *

CHOICE OF BEVERAGE

Coffee   Tea   Milk   Decaffeinated Beverage

MICROPHONE AND LECTERN SUPPLIED
Remote mike supplied, if desired................ extra charge.
Dining area available from 11:30 A.M. Speaker and remainder of program must be completed by 1:45 P.M. or hourly penalty will be imposed.

Hors d'Oeuvre

HORS D'OEUVRE FOR COCKTAIL PARTY

Tiny Potato Pancakes with Applesauce
Cocktail Franks with Spiced Mustard
Swedish Meatballs
Barbecued Chicken Wings
Shrimp in Beer Batter
($0.00 extra per guest)

ASSORTED COLD CANAPE TRAY
$0.00 per tray of 72 units

(Above hors d'oeuvre items may be purchased by
the dozen at $0.00 per dozen.)

HORS D'OEUVRE FOR A RECEPTION

Barbecued Chicken Wings   Deep-Fried Won Tons
Swedish Meatballs   Shrimp in Beer Batter
Barbecued Pork Spareribs   Chicken Livers in Bacon
Quiche Lorraine   Pizza Slices
Deviled Eggs   Stuffed Celery
        ($0.00 per guest—minimum of 100 guests)

OPTIONAL
CHEDDAR CHEESE LOG WITH CRACKERS $0.00

CHEESE DIP WITH CRISPS . . . $0.00 per quart

Buffet Selections Preceding Formal Dinner or Wedding
(An excellent selection of hot and cold hors d'oeuvre)

Barquettes of Caviar
Tiny Roulades of Smoked Salmon
Sliced Smoked Sturgeon

Cocktail Frankfurters   Cocktail Meatballs

Clams Casino
Oysters Rockefeller
*

Bowls of Shrimp on Horseback, Spicy Cocktail Sauce
Glazed Virginia Ham (sliced to order, served on small slices of potato bread)
Diced, Imported Cheddar Cheese
Smoked Fancy Turkey

Cocktail Rye   New York Style Pumpernickel
with
Trays of Assorted Open-Face Canapes
*

Finest Imported Caviar
Presented on Illuminated, Sculptured Ice Socle
with full garniture consisting of
Blinis, Freshly Made Toast, Sour Cream, Chopped Onions, Drawn Butter
Sides of Smoked Sturgeon (sliced to order)

Dinner Menu

Relish Tray   Celery, Olives, Gherkins, Radishes, etc.

Choice of Appetizer

Fresh Fruit Cup   Chilled Orange Juice
Marinated Herring   Onion Soup au Gratin
Chilled Vichyssoise

Choice of One Entree

Yankee Pot Roast, Jardiniere   Broiled Fresh Halibut or Scrod
Boneless Breast of Capon, Gravy   Roast Turkey, Giblet Gravy, Jelly
Baked Stuffed Giant Shrimp   Sliced London Broil, Mushroom Sauce
Roast Sirloin of Beef au natural   Broiled Boneless Sirloin Steak
Roast Prime Rib of Beef au jus   Broiled Filet Mignon, Mushroom Sauce
*

Tossed Green Salad, House Dressing
(Fresh vegetable may be substituted)
*

Choice of Potato

Baked, with Sour Cream and Chives

French Fried   Lyonnaise   Roesti Potatoes

Potato Croquette in Corn Flake Crumbs
*

Bread Basket Consisting of

Sesame Seed Rolls   Dark Pumpernickel

Banana Bread   Mini-Bagels   Butterflake Rolls
*

Choice of Dessert

Old Fashioned Strawberry Shortcake   Choice of Pies

Chocolate Parfait   Orange Sherbet with Mandarin Sauce

Cheese Cake with Blueberry topping
*

Choice of Beverage

Coffee   Tea   Milk   Decaffeinated Beverage

Cub Scouts or Little League Menu

Fresh Fruit Cocktail
or
Soup du Jour

Fried Chicken, Cranberry Sauce
Broiled Chopped Steak
Spaghetti with Meatballs
Roast Turkey, Giblet Gravy
Fried Fillet of Sole
Baked Ham with Sliced Pineapple
*

Choice of Vegetable and Potatoes
*

DESSERTS—Choice of One

Apple, Peach, Cherry, Blueberry, or Pineapple Pie
Ice Cream with "Make Your Own Sundaes Fixins"
Strawberry Shortcake

Milk   Chocolate Milk   Fruit Drink

Three Budget Buffet Presentations (For 75 or more guests)

No. 1
Tossed Green Salad, Dressing
Celery Sticks, Radish Roses, Olives
Roast Sirloin of Beef, sliced to order
Baked Country Ham
Swedish Meatballs
Barbecued Chicken Wings
Deep-Fried Shrimp
Chinese Mushroom Chow Mein
Delmonico Potatoes *and* Potato Salad
Assorted Pastries *and* Pies
Tea, Coffee, or Milk

No. 2
Tossed Salad, Dressing
Celery Sticks, Radishes, Olives
Roast Sirloin of Beef, sliced to order
Roast Turkey, Sage Dressing
Fried Chicken Tidbits
Swedish Meatballs
Deep-Fried Shrimp
Chinese Mushroom Chow Mein
Delmonico Potatoes *and* Potato Salad
Assorted Pastries *and* Pies
Tea, Coffee, or Milk

No. 3
Tossed Salad, Dressings
Celery Sticks, Radishes, Olives, Gherkins
Steamship Round of Beef, sliced to order
Roast Turkey, Sage Dressing
Baked Virginia Ham, Champagne Sauce
Chinese Chicken Chow Mein, Long Grain Rice
Deep-Fried Shrimp
Poached Fillet of Sole, Lobster—Cream Sauce
Tiny Italian Meatballs with Pasta Shells, Marinara
Vegetable Gelatin Mold
Tiny Spiced Crabapples
Cauliflower Potatoes au Gratin
Three-Layer Strawberry Shortcake
Plus, Petits Fours and Cookies
Tea, Coffee, or Milk

CASH BAR SET UP IN THIS AREA (extra charge)
UNLIMITED CHAMPAGNE PUNCH OR BOTTLED BEER—extra charge of $0.00 per person

Special Buffet Dinner (Cash bar in area throughout the entire dinner)

AT BAR AREA

| | Onion Dips | | Cornucopias of Salami | |
| Pickled Eggs | | Cheese Cubes | | Pretzel Sticks |

*

AT PLACE SETTING FOR EACH GUEST
Choice of One

Fresh Fruit Cocktail

Mini-Shrimp Cocktail

Eggs a la Russe

Cold Icelandic Sea Trout, Mustard Sauce

*

FROM BUFFET TABLE

Seafood Creole

Fried Wickford Clams

Fried Chicken Tidbits

Cornish Hen Quarters in Orange Sauce

Chinese Pepper Steaks

Beef Bourguignonne

Baked Stuffed Pork Chops

Rice Pilaf

Noodles with Caraway Seeds

Paprika Fried Potatoes

Cold Sliced Turkey, Cranberry Relish

Cold Sliced Corned Beef, Horseradish Mustard

*

Assorted Pickles   Olives   Relishes   Gelatin Molds

AVAILABLE AT EXTRA COST—CARVED BY UNIFORMED PERSONNEL

Steamship Round, carved to order

Standing Prime Ribs of Beef, carved

Carved Skirt Steaks or Brisket Beef

*

DESSERTS

Individual French and Danish Pastries

An assortment of 5 Pies and 4 Layer Cakes

Fresh and Preserved Fruit Medley

*

BEVERAGES

Coffee   Tea   Decaffeinated beverage on request

NOTE: The above is *an organized buffet dinner.* Guests will be advised as to what tables they are assigned by the use of *table tent cards at the entranceway.* Their starter course will be on the table. Our Head Waiter will explain the procedure over the microphone. He will then call on *each table* to proceed to the buffet tables. This avoids long lines. *Beverages will be served at the tables.* When guests go to the buffet, waiters will clear their starter dishes.
This menu may also be used as a Prom Menu. House bars will only service guests with *proof of age* (identification card). Self-service areas will be furnished with wine or champagne punch during the entire affair. Colored linens at no extra charge.

Dinner Dance Menu

Celery Sticks   Ripe and Green Olives   Carrot Curls

*

Choice of One

Fresh Fruit Cocktail

Fresh Shrimp Cocktail

Avocado Half Stuffed with
Crabmeat

Soup du Jour

*

(continued)

Dinner Dance Menu (continued)
Choice of One
Double Breast of Boneless Chicken, Jubilee
Roulade of Turkey, Giblet Gravy
Roast Sirloin of Beef, Mushroom Sauce
Pot Roast of Beef with Red Cabbage
London Broil, Mushroom Sauce
Deep-Fried Half of Boneless Chicken
Broiled Swordfish Steak, Maitre d'Hotel
Rolled Leg of Veal en Croustade
Roast Prime Rib of Beef

*

Choice of Vegetable and Potato

*

Banana Bread   Mini-Muffins   Parker House Rolls

*

Choice of One
Black Forest Cake   Cheese Cake with Strawberry Sauce
or Two-tiered tray of pastries—(one tray per table)

*

Coffee   Tea   Milk   Soda

Bud vase of flowers supplied each table.

Wedding Breakfast (Minimum 50 guests)
(Available only from 8 A.M. to 11 A.M.—in private area.
Party must end by 11:00 A.M.)

Fresh Orange Juice

*

Scrambled Eggs

*

Choice of One
Canadian Bacon   Sausage Patties
Rasher of Bacon or Grilled Ham
OR, Poached Eggs and Ham On Muffins a la Brennan
($0.00 extra)

*

Hash Brown or Roesti Potatoes

*

Toasted   *AND*   White Toast,
Corn Cakes   Orange-Butter Spread

*

Warm Danish Pastries ($0.00 extra)

*

Coffee   Hot Chocolate   Tea   Milk

NOTE: The above breakfast may be served *Buffet Style, with
each and every item as listed,*
for *$0.00 extra* per guest.

ALSO AVAILABLE

Wine (for toast) @ $0.00 per glass
Champagne (for toast) @ $0.00 per glass
Bottles of Blended Whiskey, Scotch, Bourbon @ $0.00 per bottle

---

Wedding Package Plan (For 100 or more guests)

Choice of One

Fresh Fruit Cup, Grenadine   Chilled Orange and Grapefruit Sections
Chilled Melon   Sardines on Tomato Slices and Stuffed Egg Wedges

*

Nutted Fruit Breads   Butterflake Rolls

*

Choice of One

Soup du Jour   or   Onion Soup, Toast Points

*

Choice of One

Sliced Flank Steak, Sauce Jardiniere   Roast Stuffed Breast of Capon   Roast Turkey, Country Dressing

*

Individual Salad Bowl or Choice of Vegetable

*

Choice of One

Potatoes au Gratin   Baked Potato, Sour Cream   Potato Croquettes

*

COMPLIMENTARY HOUSE DRINK OF CHILLED SAUTERNE, CHABLIS, OR BURGUNDY
(Champagne in place of the above $0.00 extra)

Choice of Dessert

Three-Layer Strawberry Shortcake   Ice Cream Cake Rolls
Creme de Menthe Parfait

*

Coffee   Tea   Milk   Decaffeinated Beverage   plus, Tray of Cookies

(continued)

Wedding Package Plan (continued)

The above meal includes:

    WINE TOAST

    THREE-PIECE ORCHESTRA FOR FOUR HOURS

    WHITE WEDDING CAKE WITH ROYAL ICING AND *ORNAMENT*

    HOSTESS TO SLICE AND BAG WEDDING CAKE TO BE GIVEN TO EACH GUEST

    CANDELABRA AND FLOWERS FOR HEAD TABLE ONLY

    HOST OR HOSTESS TO SUPERVISE AND GIVE GUIDANCE

NOTE: ALL WEDDING PRICES APPLY TO THE FOLLOWING SCHEDULE

Day Weddings — 11 A.M. to 4 P.M.

Evening Weddings — 5 P.M. to 11 P.M.

If weddings overlap these two periods, there will be an added charge of $0.00 per person.

CHAPTER FIFTEEN

A COLLECTION OF RECIPES

A collection of standardized recipes is a must for every social caterer. The collection, in addition to the tried and true "basics," should include a variety of specialty dishes that have been thoroughly tested and individualized.

For handy reference have one or more good general cookbooks of family-size as well as quantity recipes always available in the catering office. An avid recipe collector, as all caterers should be, will find magazines and newspapers are good sources of recipes.

RECIPE FILE

Tested recipes should be typed on special cards (5- by 8-inch or 4- by 6-inch cards are good), with notations made as to preparation, yield, serving tips, costs. Any changes made in the recipe must always be noted on the recipe card.

For added convenience, file recipe cards alphabetically by category, that is, appetizers, breads, desserts, salads, etcetera.

STANDARD MEASUREMENTS

In testing or developing recipes, standard measurements should be used.

RECIPE CONVERSION

Modern technology has produced pocket-sized calculators that accurately resolve the most com-

Measurements		Scoops		Ladles	
3 tsp.	= 1 tbsp.	No. 6	= 2/3 cup	2 oz.	= 1/4 cup
4 tbsp.	= 1/4 cup	No. 8	= 1/2 cup	4 oz.	= 1/2 cup
2 cups	= 1 pt.	No. 12	= 1/3 cup	6 oz.	= 3/4 cup
2 pt.	= 1 qt.	No. 16	= 1/4 cup	8 oz.	= 1 cup
4 qt.	= 1 gal.	No. 20	= 3-1/5 tbsp.		
		No. 24	= 2-2/3 tbsp.		
		No. 40	= 1-3/5 tbsp.		

plicated problems. Assuming that a calculator may not be available when it is necessary to convert a recipe into greater or lesser quantities, the following formula can be used.

Assume that a standard pie crust formula for 50 units consists of the following ingredients.

FLOUR, sifted	3 lb. 12 oz.
SHORTENING	2 lb. 4 oz.
SALT	2 oz.
WATER	3/4 qt.

STEP ONE: Convert all of the units into ounces.

Flour, 3 lb. 12 oz.	= 60 oz. (16 oz. to 1 lb.)
Shortening, 2 lb. 4 oz.	= 36 oz.
Salt	= 2 oz.
Water, 3/4 qt.	= 24 oz. (32 oz. to 1 qt.)

STEP TWO: Assuming that only 32 crusts are needed, divide the required number (32) by the number of the original recipe (50).

$$
\begin{array}{r}
.64 = \text{(multiplier factor)} \\
50 \overline{\smash{)}32.00} \\
\underline{30.00} \\
2.00 \\
\underline{2.00}
\end{array}
$$

STEP THREE: Using .64 as the factor, multiply all ingredients by this number.

60 oz. flour × .64 = 38.4 oz. or 2 lb. 6-1/2 oz.
36 oz.
shortening ×   .64 = 23.04 oz. or 1 lb. 7 oz.
2 oz. salt ×   .64 =   1.28 oz. or 1-1/4 oz.
24 oz. water ×   .64 = 15.36 oz. or 15-1/2 oz.

As another example, the following recipe is for 25 portions of Roast Beef Hash.

ONION, finely diced	1 lb.	=	16 oz.
CELERY, finely diced	1/2 lb.	=	8 oz.
OIL	5 oz.	=	5 oz.
POTATOES, cooked, diced	6-1/2 lb.	=	104 oz.
ROAST BEEF, coarsely chopped	4-1/2 lb.	=	72 oz.
SALT and PEPPER			to taste

Number of portions needed = 110.

STEP ONE: DIVIDE

$$
\begin{array}{r}
4.4 = \text{multiplier factor} \\
25 \overline{\smash{)}110.0} \\
\underline{100.} \\
10.0 \\
\underline{10.0}
\end{array}
$$

STEP TWO:

Onion	16 × 4.4 =	70.4 oz.	or 4-1/2 lb.
Celery	8 × 4.4 =	35.2 oz.	or 2 lb. 3 oz.
Oil	5 × 4.4 =	22 oz.	or 1 lb. 6 oz.
Potatoes	104 × 4.4 =	457.6 oz.	or 28 lb. 6 oz.
Beef	72 × 4.4 =	316.8 oz.	or 19 lb. 8 oz.

For further conversion information, refer to the Appendix.

APPETIZERS

Dips, Hors d'Oeuvre, Punches

Anchovy Cocktail Dip

YIELD: 1-1/2 lb.

INGREDIENTS

CREAM CHEESE*	1 lb.
PAPRIKA	1/8 tsp.
CELERY SEED	1 tsp.
LEMON JUICE	2 tbsp.
ANCHOVY PASTE	4 tbsp.
CREAM	4 tbsp.
ONION, minced	4 tsp.

*Blue cheese thinned with a little yogurt may be substituted for cream cheese.

PROCEDURE

1. Cream the cheese until smooth.
2. Add remaining ingredients and blend until fluffy.

Hibachi Appetizers

YIELD: 12 appetizers

INGREDIENTS

CAESAR DRESSING MIX	1 pkg.
WATER	2 tbsp.
BURGUNDY or CLARET	1/4 cup
SALAD OIL	1/2 cup
SIRLOIN TIP STEAK, cut in 1-in. cubes	1-1/2 lb.
MUSHROOM CAPS	as needed
CHERRY TOMATOES	as needed
GREEN PEPPER, cut in 3/4-in. pieces	as needed

PROCEDURE

1. Empty Caesar dressing mix into screw-top, pint jar. Add water and shake well. Add wine and oil. Shake again, about 30 sec. Pour over cubes of meat and mushroom caps. Marinate about 2 hr.

2. Arrange meat cubes on skewers, alternating with mushrooms, cherry tomatoes, and green pepper pieces. Grill quickly over charcoal until meat is nicely browned, about 4 to 6 min.

Prawn Hors d'Oeuvre

PROCEDURE

Buy medium-sized prawns, shell, and devein. Insert anchovy fillet into deveined prawn cavity, wrap with a strip of bacon, and broil.

Codfish Cakes

PROCEDURE

Shape usual codfish cake mixture into tiny balls. Place in frying basket and fry in deep fat at 375°F. until golden brown. Serve as appetizers on toothpicks.

Pigs in Blankets

PROCEDURE

To make pigs in blankets, wrap oysters individually in thin half slices of bacon. Fasten with toothpicks. Bake at 425°F., about 20 min. or until bacon is crisp. Serve hot.

Caraway Cheese Wafers

YIELD: 8 doz. 2-in. wafers

INGREDIENTS

BUTTER or MARGARINE	8 oz.
FLOUR	1 lb.
SALT	2 tsp.
CHEDDAR CHEESE, grated	2 lb.
MILK	3/4 cup
CARAWAY SEEDS	as needed

PROCEDURE

1. Combine shortening with sifted flour and salt; cut in shortening until the particles are the size of peas.
2. Add grated cheese; mix well.
3. Add milk and mix until blended.
4. Form into rolls 2-in. in diameter and wrap in waxed paper. Chill.
5. Cut into thin slices; place on well-oiled sheet pans. Brush with milk; sprinkle with caraway seeds.
6. Bake at 375°F. for 12 min.

Cocktail Sauce

YIELD: approx. 1 qt.

INGREDIENTS

TOMATO CATSUP	2 cups
CHILI SAUCE	1 cup
LEMON JUICE	1/4 cup
HORSERADISH	1 tbsp.
WORCESTERSHIRE SAUCE	1 tbsp.
SUGAR	1 tbsp.
SALT	2 tsp.
LIQUID HOT PEPPER SEASONING	dash

PROCEDURE

1. Blend all ingredients. Mix thoroughly.
2. Pour into jar, cover, and place in refrigerator. Shake well before using.

Shrimp Canape

YIELD: 36 canapes

INGREDIENTS

SHRIMP, canned, or freshly cooked and shelled, chopped	1-1/2 lb.
ANCHOVY PASTE	2 tbsp.
LEMON JUICE	2 tbsp.
MAYONNAISE	1 cup
TOAST ROUNDS (2 in.)	36
EGG YOLKS, hard-cooked, sieved	8
SHRIMP, whole	36

PROCEDURE

1. Mix chopped shrimp, anchovy paste, and lemon juice with mayonnaise. Spread on toast rounds.
2. Top with grated egg yolk and one whole shrimp.
3. Serve with lettuce, tomato wedge, and celery heart for garnishes.

Bleu Cheese Log Roll

YIELD: 4 doz. appetizers

INGREDIENTS

CREAM CHEESE	8 oz.
BUTTER	3 tbsp.
BLEU CHEESE DRESSING MIX	1 pkg.
WALNUTS, finely chopped	1/4 cup

PROCEDURE

1. Blend softened cream cheese and butter with bleu cheese dressing mix. Form into a roll about 1-1/2 in. in diameter.
2. Roll in chopped nuts. Wrap in waxed paper; chill thoroughly.
3. Slice thin and serve on toast rounds or crackers.

Curried Meatballs

YIELD: 10 lb. of meatballs, approx. 2 gal. sauce

INGREDIENTS

MEATBALLS	10 lb.
SAUCE	
TOMATOES, canned whole	1/2 No. 10 can
BEEF GRAVY, thickened	2 gal.
CURRY POWDER	3 tsp.

PROCEDURE

1. Prepare meatballs using your regular recipe, but using only salt and pepper to season. Brown them.
2. Cook sauce ingredients for 2 hr.
3. Add meatballs to sauce, heat to simmer, and serve over hot rice.

Egg Canape Spread

YIELD: 1-1/2 cups

INGREDIENTS

EGGS, hard-cooked	4
CELERY, finely chopped	1/2 cup
GREEN ONIONS, chopped	2 tbsp.
SWEET PICKLE RELISH	2 tbsp.
SEASONED SALT	1 tsp.
SEASONED PEPPER	1/4 tsp.
MAYONNAISE or SALAD DRESSING	1/4 cup

PROCEDURE

Chop hard-cooked eggs and place in a small mixing bowl. Add remaining ingredients and mix thoroughly. Refrigerate for several hours. Serve with black or rye cocktail bread or crisp crackers.

Bean Dip Caliente

YIELD: 2-1/2 cups

INGREDIENTS

MEXICAN REFRIED BEANS	1 can (1 lb. 4 oz.)
DAIRY SOUR CREAM	1/4 cup
GARLIC SPREAD	2 tbsp.
SEASONED PEPPER	1/2 tsp.
SEASONED SALT	1 tsp.
CHILI POWDER (optional)	1 tsp.

PROCEDURE

1. Combine all ingredients in saucepan and heat until bubbly.
2. Keep hot over candle warmer or in chafing dish while serving.
3. Garnish with minced onion tops or parsley, if desired. (Excellent with corn chips or tostadas.)

Cheese Pate

INGREDIENTS

BUTTER	2 oz.
CREAM CHEESE	1 lb.
BLEU CHEESE	10 oz.
WORCESTERSHIRE SAUCE	1 tsp.
DRY MUSTARD	1 tsp.
SALT	to season
PEPPER	to season
PARSLEY	2 tbsp.
PIMIENTO, canned	2 whole
GREEN PEPPER, seeds and core removed	1
OLIVES, chopped	3/4 cup

PROCEDURE

    1. Cream butter. Blend in the cheeses. Mix well.

    2. Add Worcestershire sauce, dry mustard, salt, and pepper.

    3. Put parsley, pimientos, green pepper, and olives through chopper. Squeeze through cheesecloth to remove liquid. Add to cheese mixture and blend thoroughly.

    4. Shape into desired form. Refrigerate.

This is colorful enough to dispense with surface decorations. Garnish with carrot curls, pickle slices, and watercress.

Chili-Cheese Ball

YIELD: 48 servings

INGREDIENTS

SHARP CHEDDAR CHEESE, grated	3-1/2 lb.
INSTANT GARLIC POWDER	4 tsp.
CHILI POWDER	

PROCEDURE

    1. In large bowl combine cheese with garlic powder; mix lightly.

    2. Shape into 8 balls, pressing firmly. Roll each ball in chili powder until well coated.

    3. Serve with corn chips or crackers.

Stuffed Mushrooms

YIELD: 100

INGREDIENTS

MEDIUM MUSHROOMS, stems removed	100
LARGE ONIONS	2
RIBS OF CELERY	4
PARSLEY, full sprigs	4
MARGARINE or BUTTER	12 oz.
WORCESTERSHIRE SAUCE	2 tbsp.
GARLIC SALT	1/2 tsp.
POULTRY SEASONING	1/2 tsp.
SALT, as needed	
CRACKER MEAL, as required	

PROCEDURE

    1. Wash caps and stems thoroughly and dry.

    2. Grind stems, onions, celery, and parsley.

    3. Saute the ground ingredients in butter or margarine and add Worcestershire sauce, garlic salt, and poultry seasoning for 15 minutes.

    4. Stir with wooden spoon and gradually add cracker meal until it forms a soft mass, add salt if necessary, and cool.

    5. Stuff the mixture into each mushroom cap.

To serve, broil stuffed mushrooms and serve on bread rounds that have been toasted on one side.

Mushrooms Italiano

PROCEDURE

1. Prepare one 14-oz. jar Italian dressing mix for salads according to directions, using dry red wine in place of vinegar.

2. Rinse fresh mushrooms well under running water. Remove stems and drain thoroughly. Canned mushrooms may be used and should also be drained thoroughly.

3. Pour a sufficient amount of dressing over mushrooms to cover. Marinate several hours or overnight. Stir occasionally. Drain and reserve liquid.

4. Serve with cocktail picks.

Note: Use reserved liquid for salad dressing over greens.

Tuna-Cheese Dip

INGREDIENTS

TUNA	2 7-1/2 oz. cans
CREAM CHEESE	1/2 lb.
DRY WHITE WINE	1/2 cup
MAYONNAISE	1/2 cup
PARSLEY, chopped	2 tbsp.
ONION RELISH, well-drained	1/2 cup
LIQUID HOT PEPPER SEASONING	dash
SALT	1/2 tsp.
GARLIC SALT	1/2 tsp.

PROCEDURE

1. Drain tuna and blend with cream cheese.
2. Add remaining ingredients and blend well.

Adjuncts to Dips

For informal buffet-type presentation

1/2-in. rounds of crusty
  French or Italian bread
Swedish bread
Breadsticks
Crisp crackers
Toasted thin corn bread
Potato crisps
Raw carrot sticks
Fresh or canned pineapple
  chunks

Apple and pear wedges, dipped
  in lemon juice
Celery chunks
Radishes
Scallions
Cucumber fingers
Raw cauliflower buds
Avocado chunks, dipped in
  lemon juice

Celery Whirls

YIELD: about 18 slices

PROCEDURE

Carefully remove full-length individual stalks from fully trimmed bunch of celery. Clean each stalk thoroughly and drain on absorbent paper.

Mix together 1 cup crumbled blue cheese, a 3-oz. package softened cream cheese, and 1 tbsp. mayonnaise. Beat until mixture is smooth and creamy. Blend in 2 tsp. lemon juice, 1 tsp. onion juice, 1/4 tsp. garlic salt, 1/8 tsp. monosodium glutamate, and 1/2 tsp. celery or caraway seeds (optional). Beat until thoroughly blended.

Fill full length of celery strips and rearrange stalks into natural shape of celery bunch. Wrap tightly in aluminum foil or plastic wrap and refrigerate for several hours. Cut crosswise into 1/2-in. slices and arrange on tray.

Pickled Eggs

Excellent as "nostalgia"—keep in jar at bar area or display in liquid on buffet tables.

YIELD: 30 portions

INGREDIENTS

DRY MUSTARD	4-1/2 tsp.
CORNSTARCH	4-1/2 tsp.
WHITE VINEGAR	3 pt.
SUGAR	6 tsp.
TURMERIC	1-1/2 tsp.
EGGS, hard-cooked	30

PROCEDURE

1. Blend dry mustard and cornstarch with enough water to form a loose paste.
2. Add vinegar and spices, and boil 12 min.
3. Remove from heat and let rest 15 min.
4. Add shelled eggs and refrigerate overnight.

Deviled Eggs

YIELD: 12 halves

INGREDIENTS

EGGS, hard-cooked	6
MAYONNAISE	1/4 cup
SALT	1/4 tsp.
PEPPER	to taste
PREPARED MUSTARD	1/2 tsp.
ONION, minced	1 tsp.
LIQUID HOT PEPPER SEASONING	a few drops
MONOSODIUM GLUTAMATE	1/8 tsp.
YELLOW FOOD COLORING	2 drops

PROCEDURE

1. Split shelled eggs lengthwise. Carefully remove yolks (use stainless steel spoon).
2. Force yolks through strainer; blend in other ingredients.
3. Pipe blended yolks through pastry bag into hollows of egg whites.
4. Garnish with pimiento, olives, parsley, or capers.

To glaze: Place filled and garnished eggs on wire rack and pour cooled, liquefied clear gelatine over each. (This enhances the appearance and prevents discoloration.) Chill in refrigerator.

Deviled eggs may be served as an hors d'oeuvre in bar area, as salad, or as garnish on cold meat platter.

Variations

Eggs may be "topped off" with red or black caviar or strips of anchovy; fill cavities with flaked smoked whitefish and garnish with yolk puree; garnish with tiny shrimp or one large shrimp; sieve a few slices of smoked salmon or anchovy together with egg yolks; top hard-cooked egg halves with russian dressing or thick tartar sauce; blend a teaspoon of white horseradish with a little whipped cream and add to egg yolk mixture before filling whites.

Steak Tartare

YIELD: 50 little balls

INGREDIENTS

TOP ROUND of BEEF, lean, ground twice	2 lb.
ONION, minced	2 tsp.
PARSLEY, minced	2 tsp.
WORCESTERSHIRE SAUCE	2 tsp.
PREPARED MUSTARD	1/2 tsp.
SALT	1 tsp.
BLACK PEPPER, freshly ground	1/2 tsp.
LETTUCE, PARSLEY, or WATERCRESS	
ANCHOVY FILLETS, cut in half	
DILL PICKLE, thinly sliced	
PUMPERNICKEL or RYE BREAD, thinly sliced rounds	

PROCEDURE

1. Combine meat with onion and next 5 ingredients. Mix well; form into about 50 little balls.
2. Cover; refrigerate until well chilled.
3. Arrange on greens on serving plate.
4. Serve with rounds of bread. Provide additional chopped onion, anchovy, and dill pickle slices as accompaniments.

Antipasto Ingredients

Anchovies	Stuffed eggs	Celery
Sardines	Pickled artichokes	Chick-peas
Tuna	Sliced prosciutto	Pickled eggplant
Pimientos	Salami	Lettuce
Pickled mushrooms	Olives	Scallions
Cherry tomatoes or tomato wedges	Radishes	Ricotta cheese
Onions	Pickled beets	Cold sausage
Melon wedges	Bologna	
	Raw green peppers	

No less than 6 items should be used at one time. Remember to contrast flavors—spicy, sharp, bland—as well as color.

Cocktail Meatballs

YIELD: 75 tiny meatballs

INGREDIENTS

GROUND BEEF	1 lb.
GROUND PORK	1/2 lb.
EGG, slightly beaten	1
ONION, grated	1 large
SEASONED SALT	1 tsp.
BLACK PEPPER	1/4 tsp.
ALLSPICE	1/4 tsp.
CLOVES	1/4 tsp.
FLOUR	1/4 cup
MILK	1/2 cup

PROCEDURE

1. Have beef ground twice; grind beef and pork together.
2. Combine meat, egg, onion, and seasonings. Add flour and beat, using electric mixer, until thoroughly blended and fluffy.
3. Add milk slowly, 1 tbsp. at a time, beating well. Mixture should resemble a thick dough.
4. Shape into tiny balls with a melon ball cutter.
5. Fry in butter or salad oil until golden brown. Turn frequently for even browning.
6. Serve with prepared spaghetti sauce in chafing dish.

Note: These meatballs can also be made using all beef.

Shrimp On Toast Rounds

YIELD: 36 canapes

PROCEDURE

1. Drain canned jumbo shrimp and marinate overnight in French dressing.
2. With a small round cutter, cut bread rounds the size of the shrimp.
3. Drain shrimp and place on bread rounds; decorate with mayonnaise and a strip of ripe olive.

Bagels Galore*
When using miniature bagels, these make excellent appetizers for receptions.

Plain 'Ol Bagel Bliss

Cut bagels in half and toast. Top each half with 3/4 oz. cream cheese, 1 slice red onion, and 1 slice tomato. Garnish with a sprig of parsley.

Pizza Bagel

Cut bagels in half; top each half with 1 oz. pizza sauce. Sprinkle 1/2 oz. grated mozzarella cheese over each half; broil until bubbly. Garnish with spinach leaf.

*These recipes were developed by the Culinary Institute of America and are reprinted with permission.

Say Cheese Bagel

Cut bagels in half; spread each half with mayonnaise. Top each with 1 slice tomato and 1 slice American cheese; toast until melted. Garnish with parsley and one black olive.

Tuna Italiano

Cut bagels in half; top each half with 1 oz. tunafish salad (mixed with Italian seasonings—oregano, basil, thyme, garlic). Top each half with 1 slice American cheese; broil until bubbly. Garnish with parsley or spinach leaf.

Blushing Bagel

Cut bagels in half; toast each half. Spread each half with mayonnaise and top each half with 1 oz. thinly sliced turkey breast. Sprinkle 1 tbsp. of diced pimiento over the halves. Garnish with parsley or spinach leaf.

Bagel Reuben

Cut bagels in half; spread each half with Thousand Island dressing. Top each half with 1 oz. corned beef, 1/2 oz. sauerkraut, 1 tbsp. Thousand Island dressing, and 1 slice Swiss cheese. Broil until bubbly. Garnish with parsley or spinach leaf.

Bagel Teriyaki

Cut bagels in half; spread each half with butter. Top each half with 1 oz. thinly sliced roast beef. Sprinkle each half with 1 tsp. soy sauce, 1/2 tsp. toasted sesame seeds, and 1/2 tomato slice, chopped. Garnish with parsley or spinach leaf.

Curried Bagel

Cut bagels in half; top each half with 1 oz. chicken salad. Sprinkle with 1/3 tsp. curry powder; top each bagel half with 1 tbsp. shredded spinach. Garnish with pineapple slice and maraschino cherry.

Bombay Punch

YIELD: about 70 cups

To 2 cups lemon juice, add enough powdered sugar to sweeten; stir. Pour over large block of ice in punch bowl. Add 1 qt. brandy, 1 qt. sherry, 4-1/2 cups grenadine, 1/2 cup curacao, 4 qt. champagne, and 2 qt. club soda. Stir well; decorate with fruits in season.

Brandy Punch

YIELD: about 35 cups

To 2 cups lemon juice, add the juice of 4 oranges, 1 cup grenadine, and 1 qt. club soda. Add enough sugar to sweeten. Stir well. Pour over large block of ice in punch bowl. Add 1/2 pt. curacao and 2 qt. brandy.

Cardinal Punch

YIELD: about 45 cups

To 2 cups lemon juice, add enough powdered sugar to sweeten; stir. Pour over large block of ice in punch bowl. Add 1 pt. each brandy and light rum, 1 qt. champagne, 2 qt. claret, 1/2 pt. sweet vermouth, and 1 qt. carbonated water.

Claret Punch

YIELD: about 45 cups

To 2 cups lemon juice, add enough powdered sugar to sweeten. Stir well. Pour over large block of ice in punch bowl. Add 1/2 pt. curacao, 1 pt. brandy, 3 qt. claret, and 1 qt. carbonated water.

Vichyssoise

YIELD: 16 cups

INGREDIENTS

LEEKS	1 bunch
BUTTER	6 oz.
ONIONS, medium	3
SALT	to taste
PEPPER	to taste
CHICKEN STOCK	3 qt.
POTATOES, medium, thinly sliced	6
CREAM	1 pt.
CHIVES or PARSLEY	

PROCEDURE

1. Wash leeks and cut finely.
2. Add to hot butter with onions and seasonings. Cover and cook slowly without browning.
3. Add stock and potatoes. Cook until tender.
4. Put soup through foodmill or china cap. Adjust seasoning.
5. Stir in cream and sprinkle with chives or parsley when serving. May be served hot or cold.

MAIN DISHES

Beef Stroganoff

YIELD: 3 servings

INGREDIENTS

BEEF FILLET, cut in thin slices	1 lb.
SALT	as needed
PEPPER	as needed
ONION, diced	1/2 cup
MUSHROOMS, sliced	1 cup
SHORTENING, for braising	as needed
FLOUR	1 tbsp.
SOUP STOCK	1 cup
MONOSODIUM GLUTAMATE	1 tsp.
MOCHA MIX	1 cup

(continued)

Beef Stroganoff
(continued)

PROCEDURE

1. Season beef with salt and pepper and let stand 2 hr.
2. Braise onion and mushrooms in shortening for 10 min. Add flour, and blend together. Pour in soup stock and let simmer for 10 min. Add monosodium glutamate.
3. Saute beef in shortening until brown and add to sauce. Let simmer 10 min.
4. Before serving, add mocha mix. Serve with broad noodles or rice.

Grilled Salisbury Steak, Belmont

YIELD: 20 portions

INGREDIENTS

BEEF, finely ground	9 lb.
ONION, grated	1-1/2 cups
GREEN PEPPER, grated	1-1/2 cups
GARLIC, finely minced	3 cloves
PARSLEY, finely chopped	1/2 cup
PAPRIKA	1 tsp.
SALT	1 tbsp.
PEPPER	1 tsp.
THYME, powdered	1 tsp.
FLOUR	1-1/4 cups
SALT	1 tsp.
PEPPER	1 tsp.
OLIVE OIL	1/4 cup

PROCEDURE

1. Combine ground beef, onion, green pepper, garlic, and parsley. Season with paprika, salt, pepper, and thyme.
2. Blend well and shape into 20 steaks or 40 small steaks, 2 for each portion.
3. Sprinkle lightly with seasoned flour and brush with olive oil.
4. Broil 5 to 6 min. on each side, or until done.

Sauce

INGREDIENTS

BUTTER	2 cups
CATSUP	4 cups
LEMON JUICE	1/2 cup
WORCESTERSHIRE SAUCE	4 tbsp.
LIQUID HOT PEPPER SEASONING	3 to 4 dashes
PREPARED MUSTARD	3 tbsp.
MACE	pinch
SALT	to taste
PEPPER	to taste
DRY SHERRY	1-1/2 cups

PROCEDURE

1. Melt butter in a saucepan.

2. Add the catsup, lemon juice, Worcestershire sauce, hot pepper seasoning, mustard, and mace. Season with salt and pepper. Blend well.

3. Stir in sherry; heat just to boiling point.

4. Pour sauce over steaks at service time.

Chicken or Turkey Cacciatore

YIELD: 52 servings

INGREDIENTS

FRYER CHICKENS, quartered	13
ONION, sliced 1/4 in.	3 lb.
GARLIC CLOVES, minced	2
TOMATOES, whole	1-1/2 No. 10 cans
TOMATO PUREE	1/2 No. 10 can
OREGANO, crushed	2 tbsp.
CELERY SEED	2 tbsp.
BAY LEAVES	10
A LA KING SAUCE MIX	2-1/2 lb.
WATER, cold	1-1/2 gal.

PROCEDURE

1. Brown chicken until half done.

2. Saute onion and garlic; add to tomatoes and tomato puree. Add oregano, celery seeds, and bay leaves. Add chicken and simmer in oven at 350°F. for approx. 30 min.

3. Prepare A La King Sauce following package directions, using the 1-1/2 gal. water. Add sauce to chicken mixture and bake for 30 min. more, or until "forkdone."

4. Serve a quarter chicken per portion with sauce ladled over top.

Cauliflower Seafood Casserole

(Excellent for buffet receptions.)

YIELD: 25 to 30 portions

INGREDIENTS

CAULIFLOWER, large	1
BUTTER	1/2 cup
FLOUR	1/2 cup
MILK or HALF-AND-HALF	1 qt.
SALT	3 tsp.
LUMP CRABMEAT	4 cups
LEMON JUICE	1-1/2 tbsp.
FRENCH-PEAS	2 No. 2 cans
PARMESAN CHEESE, grated	1 cup
BREAD CRUMBS, fine	1 cup

(continued)

Cauliflower Seafood
Casserole (continued)

PROCEDURE

1. Separate cauliflower into flowerettes. Cook in boiling salted water for 10 min. Drain thoroughly.
2. Melt butter in saucepan. Stir in flour; when bubbly, slowly add milk and season with salt.
3. Stir over moderate heat until mixture thickens.
4. Add crabmeat and lemon juice. Blend and remove from heat.
5. Place cauliflower flowerettes in shallow baking dish. Add drained peas, and cover with crabmeat mixture. Sprinkle surface with grated cheese and bread crumbs. Bake 20 min. at 350°F.

Mushroom Seafarers Special

(May be used on buffet, or as main course, or one-dish luncheon with broccoli or asparagus.)

YIELD: 30 portions

INGREDIENTS

MUSHROOMS, fresh	5 lb.
FISH FILLETS (COD, SOLE, etc.)	4 lb.
CHICKEN GUMBO SOUP, condensed	1 No. 5 can
TOMATOES, crushed	3 No. 2-1/2 cans
SHRIMP, deveined	2 lb.
THYME, ground	1/2 tsp.
SALT	1/2 tsp.
LIQUID HOT PEPPER SEASONING	1/2 tsp.

PROCEDURE

1. Halve fresh mushrooms.
2. Cut fish fillets into 2-in. chunks.
3. In saucepan, bring soup and tomatoes to boiling point. Add mushrooms, fish, and remaining ingredients.
4. Simmer until fish and shrimp are cooked, about 10 min.
5. Serve over rice or extra-wide noodles.

Batter for Scampi Fritters

INGREDIENTS

FLOUR	1 lb.
SALT	1 tsp.
WATER, tepid	1-1/2 cups
SALAD OIL	6 tbsp.
EGG WHITES	8

PROCEDURE

1. Put flour and salt in a bowl and make a well in center.
2. Add water and oil alternately, whipping constantly until batter is smooth and light.
3. Just before using, add stiffly beaten egg whites.
4. Dip scampi in batter and deep fry until crisp. May be served with lemon wedges.

Banana Fritters

YIELD: 12 fritters

INGREDIENTS

FLOUR, sifted	1 cup
BAKING POWDER	2 tsp.
SALT	1-1/2 tsp.
SUGAR	1/4 cup
EGG, well beaten	1
MILK	1/3 cup
SHORTENING, melted	2 tsp.
BANANAS	3

PROCEDURE

1. Sift flour, baking powder, salt, and sugar together into mixing bowl.
2. Combine egg, milk, and shortening and add to dry ingredients. Mix until batter is smooth. DO NOT THIN BATTER.
3. Peel three firm bananas and cut each into 4 diagonal pieces. Roll in flour and dip into batter, completely coating banana.
4. Deep fry about 6 min. at 375°F., until well browned. Turn fritters to brown evenly.
5. Serve hot. These may be served as a main course or as a dessert with fruit sauce or whipped cream.

Cassoulet

"Menu Maker and Party Planner" by Elizabeth Hedgecock Sparks, Menu Maker, Kernersville, N.C.

YIELD: 10 servings

INGREDIENTS

NAVY BEANS, small, dried	1 lb.
SALT	2 tsp.
HERB BLEND (see procedure)	
ONION, chopped	3/4 cup
SMOKED SAUSAGE LINKS	1 lb.
BEEF or POULTRY, cooked, diced	2-1/2 cups
DRY WHITE WINE	3 cups
TOMATO SAUCE	1 8-oz. can
PARSLEY, minced	3/4 cup
BREAD CRUMBS, fine, dry	3/4 cup
BUTTER, melted	1/3 cup

PROCEDURE

1. Cover beans with cold water and bring to a boil. Remove from heat and soak for several hours.
2. Add salt and blend of herbs—a pinch each of basil, marjoram, thyme, oregano, mace, and savory. Cook until beans are almost tender, adding water as needed. All the water should be gone when beans are finished.
3. In a large casserole, arrange a layer of beans, onion, thinly sliced sausage, and meat. Continue until all ingredients are used.
4. Mix wine with tomato sauce and pour over the top. Mix parsley, bread crumbs, and butter and spread over the top.
5. Cover and bake at 325°F. for 2 hr.

Pocket Sandwiches

Creative Pocket Breads

YIELD: 10 pocket breads

INGREDIENTS

ACTIVE DRY YEAST	1 pkg.
WARM WATER	1-1/3 cups
ALL-PURPOSE FLOUR	3 to 3-1/2 cups
ENRICHED CORN MEAL	1/2 cup
VEGETABLE OIL	3 tbsp.
SUGAR	1 tbsp.
SALT	1 tsp.

PROCEDURE

1. Dissolve yeast in warm water. Stir in 1 cup flour, corn meal, oil, sugar, and salt. Add enough additional flour to make soft dough.

2. Knead on lightly floured surface 8 to 10 min. or until smooth and elastic. Shape dough into ball; place in greased large bowl, turning once to coat surface of dough. Cover; let rise in warm place about 1 hr. or until double in size.

3. Punch dough down. Divide into 10 equal parts; shape into balls. Cover; let rest 10 min. Roll out each ball on lightly floured surface to form 5-in. circle. Place on greased cookie sheet sprinkled with additional corn meal. Let rise in warm place about 1 hr. or until double in size.

4. Bake on lowest oven rack at 450°F. for 5 to 6 min. or until slightly puffed. Cool; cut breads in half. Carefully cut pocket in each half; fill.

Fillings

California Egg Salad

YIELD: 5 servings

INGREDIENTS

HARD-COOKED EGGS, chopped	4
AVOCADO, medium, chopped	1
TOMATO, medium, chopped	1
PLAIN YOGURT	1 cup
RIPE OLIVE SLICES	1/3 cup
SALT	1/2 tsp.
DILL WEED	1/4 tsp.
POCKET BREADS	5

PROCEDURE

1. Combine all ingredients, mixing well. Chill.
2. When ready to serve, spoon into pocket breads.

Tuna Waldorf Salad

YIELD: 5 servings

INGREDIENTS

APPLE, medium, chopped	1
CELERY, sliced thin	3/4 cup
TUNA, drained and flaked	1 can (6½ to 7 oz.)
MAYONNAISE	1/2 to 3/4 cup
WALNUTS, chopped	1/3 cup
LEMON JUICE	1 tsp.
POCKET BREADS	5

PROCEDURE

1. Combine all ingredients, mixing well. Chill.
2. When ready to serve, spoon into pocket breads.

Apple-Meat Pie

YIELD: 6 10-oz. portions

INGREDIENTS

GOLDEN DELICIOUS APPLES, cored, thinly sliced	2 cups
TURKEY or HAM, cooked, cut in 3/4-in. cubes	2 cups
ONIONS, small, whole, drained	1 16-oz. can
CARROTS, whole, tiny, drained	1 16-oz. can
MUSHROOMS, whole, drained	1 4-oz. can
BUTTER	3 tbsp.
FLOUR	3 tbsp.
LEMON PEEL, finely grated	1 tbsp.
ROSEMARY LEAVES, dried, crushed	1/4 tsp.
CHICKEN or TURKEY BROTH	1 cup
PASTRY, for 1 1-crust, 9-in. pie	
SHARP CHEDDAR CHEESE, shredded	1/2 cup

PROCEDURE

1. Combine apples, turkey, onions, carrots, and mushrooms; set aside.
2. Melt butter; stir in flour, lemon peel, and rosemary. Gradually stir in broth; cook and stir until thickened and bubbly.
3. Mix sauce into apple-meat mixture; spoon into 2-qt. casserole.
4. Prepare pastry, stirring cheese into flour mixture before adding water. Roll out to fit top of casserole; tuck edges in and flute. Cut vents in top. Bake at 400°F. 30 to 40 min. or until apples are tender.

**Rolled Turkey Cutlets
with Vegetables**

YIELD: 4 servings

INGREDIENTS

CARROTS, large	2
ZUCCHINI, medium	1
CHICKEN-FLAVOR BOUILLON CUBE, or envelope	1
WATER	2 cups
TURKEY CUTLETS, fresh or frozen (thawed)	1 16-oz. pkg.
SALT	3/4 tsp.
PEPPER	1/4 tsp.
ALL-PURPOSE FLOUR	2 tbsp.
BOTTLED SAUCE FOR GRAVY	1/4 tsp.
FONTINA CHEESE, shredded	1/4 cup
PARSLEY, minced	1 tbsp.

PROCEDURE

1. Cut each carrot lengthwise into 8 sticks. Cut zucchini lengthwise in half; cut each half lengthwise into 8 sticks. In 12-in. skillet over high heat, heat carrots, bouillon, and 2 cups water to boiling. Reduce heat to low; cover and simmer 5 min. Add zucchini; over high heat, heat to boiling. Reduce heat to low; cover and simmer 3 to 5 min. until vegetables are tender-crisp. With slotted spoon, remove vegetables to plate; reserve cooking liquid.

2. With meat mallet, pound each turkey cutlet until 1/8 in. thick. Sprinkle cutlets with 1/2 tsp. salt and 1/8 tsp. pepper; place a few pieces of carrot and zucchini crosswise on a narrow end of a cutlet. Starting at the end with vegetables, roll cutlet jelly-roll fashion. Repeat with remaining cutlets and vegetables.

3. Over high heat, heat reserved liquid in skillet, with 1/4 tsp. salt and 1/8 tsp. pepper, to boiling. Add rolled cutlets, seam-side down; heat to boiling. Reduce heat to low; cover and simmer until cutlets are fork-tender, about 5 min.

4. Mix flour, bottled sauce for gravy, and 1/2 cup water; gradually stir into liquid in skillet; cook over medium heat until slightly thickened, stirring.

5. To serve, arrange cutlets, seam-side down, on platter. Pour sauce over; sprinkle with cheese and parsley.

Bird and Bean Cassoulet

YIELD: 8 servings

INGREDIENTS

DRIED MARROW BEANS, PEA BEANS, or GREAT NORTHERN BEANS	1 lb.
CHICKEN or BEEF BROTH	4 cups
ONIONS, medium, diced	2
GARLIC CLOVES, chopped	2 to 3
HAM BONE or HOCK	1
ONION, small, studded with 2 cloves	1
BAY LEAF	1

PRE-BROWNED or ROASTED CHICKEN (or turkey, smoked pork or ham, garlic sausages, or a combination)	3 lb.
TOMATOES, or	1 8-oz. can
FRESH TOMATOES, cut up	2
CARROTS, diced	4
SALT	to taste
PEPPER	to taste

PROCEDURE

    1. Bring beans to boil in 2 qt. of water; simmer 20 min., covered. Let stand 1 hr.; drain.

    2. In large kettle, combine beans, broth, onions, garlic, ham bone, studded onion, and bay leaf. Cover and simmer slowly until beans are almost tender, about 1-1/2 hr. Remove bay leaf and studded onion.

    3. In a 4-qt. casserole, arrange in layers the beans, chicken, tomatoes, carrots, seasonings, and liquid from beans. If necessary, add broth or water to barely cover beans. Cover and bake at 350°F. until beans and meats are tender, about 1-1/2 hr. If beans become too dry during cooking, add more broth or water.

Reuben Meat Loaf

YIELD: 8 to 10 servings

INGREDIENTS

CONDENSED TOMATO BISQUE SOUP	1 11-oz. can
GROUND BEEF	1 lb.
CORNED BEEF, finely chopped	1 12-oz. can
SOFT BREAD CRUMBS	2-1/2 cups
EGGS, slightly beaten	2
PARSLEY, chopped	2 tbsp.
GARLIC CLOVE, minced, large	1
SAUERKRAUT, well drained, finely chopped	1 8-oz. can
SWISS CHEESE, shredded	1/2 cup
CARAWAY SEED	1/2 tsp.
PREPARED HORSERADISH	2 tsp.
SWISS CHEESE, slices cut in 8 triangles	2 slices (2 oz.)

PROCEDURE

    1. Mix thoroughly 1/4 cup soup, beef, corned beef, bread crumbs, eggs, parsley, and garlic.

    2. On waxed paper, pat meat firmly into rectangle 15 by 10 in.

    3. In small bowl, combine sauerkraut, shredded cheese, and caraway seed; press into meat to within 1 in. of edges. Roll meat tightly jelly-roll fashion, starting at short edge. Seal seam and ends.

    4. Place in 2-qt. shallow baking dish (12 by 8 by 2 in.). Bake at 350°F. for 30 min. Combine remaining soup and horseradish. Spoon over loaf; bake 15 min. more. Arrange cheese slices over top, overlapping slightly. Bake 1 min. more or until cheese just begins to melt.

Pork and Sauerkraut

YIELD: 6 servings

INGREDIENTS

PRUNES, pitted	18
PORK CHOPS, 1-1/2 in. thick	6
BACON STRIPS, diced	3
ONION, diced	1
SAUERKRAUT, drained and rinsed	1 1-lb. 11-oz. can
TART APPLE, cut in 12 wedges	1
CARAWAY SEEDS	2 tsp.
SALT	to taste
PEPPER	to taste
CHICKEN BROTH or WATER	1/2 cup

PROCEDURE

1. Soak prunes in red wine or boiling water for 1 hr.
2. Cut a pocket in each pork chop; stuff each pocket with 3 prunes.
3. Brown bacon in heat-proof casserole; remove and reserve. Brown pork chops on both sides in bacon fat; set aside. Cook onion in remaining fat until transparent.
4. Add sauerkraut, apple wedges, and seasoning; toss in fat. Add broth and reserved bacon.
5. Arrange chops in sauerkraut; cover. Bake at 350°F. until chops are tender, about 1 hr.

Beef in Red Wine

YIELD: 8 servings

INGREDIENTS

LEAN, BONELESS BEEF, cut in large cubes	2 lb.
FLOUR	1/4 cup
SALT	1-1/2 tsp.
PEPPER	1/2 tsp.
CLOVES, ground	pinch
OIL or BACON FAT	2 tbsp.
GARLIC CLOVES	2
WHITE ONIONS, small	1/2 lb.
CARROTS, cut in chunks	2
DRY RED WINE	2 cups
POTATOES, peeled, cut in large pieces	1 lb.
TURNIPS, cut in large pieces	1/2 lb.
BAY LEAF	1
THYME	1/2 tsp.
SALT	to taste
PEPPER	to taste
WATER or BEEF BROTH	
MUSHROOMS, quartered, browned in oil or butter	1/2 lb.

| GREEN BEANS, cut up | 1/2 lb. |
| PARSLEY, chopped | |

PROCEDURE

1. Shake beef cubes in a bag with flour, salt, pepper, and cloves. Brown well in oil. Add garlic, onions, and carrots; stir over heat until glazed.

2. Add wine, potatoes, turnips, bay leaf, thyme, salt and pepper to taste, and enough water to cover.

3. Cover and bake at 350°F. for 1-1/2 hr. Add mushrooms and green beans; bake another 30 min. or until meat is tender. Adjust seasonings and sprinkle with chopped parsley.

Bitki

(meatballs)

YIELD: 35 to 40 meatballs

INGREDIENTS

WHITE BREAD SLICES, crusts removed	4
MILK	1/2 cup
GROUND BEEF	1 lb.
ONIONS, minced	2
SALT	to taste
PEPPER, freshly ground	to taste
FLOUR, seasoned with 1/2 tsp. salt and 1/4 tsp. freshly ground pepper	1/2 cup
OIL	3 to 4 tbsp.
SOUR CREAM	2 cups

PROCEDURE

1. Soak bread in milk until soft; squeeze out excess moisture. Grind together bread, beef, and onions using fine plate of grinder or food processor. Season to taste with salt and pepper (mixture should taste highly seasoned).

2. Turn into medium bowl and beat with wooden spoon 1 to 2 min. until mixture comes away from sides of bowl and forms a ball. Shape into walnut-sized balls and coat evenly with seasoned flour.

3. Heat oil in large skillet over medium-high heat. Add bitki and cook, turning carefully, until well browned on all sides. Drain off excess fat.

4. Blend in sour cream, reduce heat; cover and simmer 5 to 10 min. Transfer to chafing dish with slotted spoon; strain sour cream sauce over.

Bittersweet Stew

YIELD: 6 servings

INGREDIENTS

BONELESS BEEF CHUCK, cut in 1-in. cubes	4 lb.
SALT	to taste
PEPPER	to taste
OIL	2 tbsp.

(continued)

Bittersweet Stew
(continued)

ONIONS, large, sliced	2
TOMATOES, undrained	1 16-oz. can
CARROTS, large, cut in 1-in. chunks	6
RAISINS	1/3 cup
SUGAR	1/4 cup
CIDER VINEGAR	1/3 cup
WATER	1/3 cup
SALT	1 tsp.
PEPPER	1/2 tsp.
ANGOSTURA BITTERS	1 tbsp.

PROCEDURE

1. Sprinkle beef cubes with salt and pepper; coat cubes lightly with flour.

2. Heat oil in Dutch oven and brown meat on all sides. Add onions, tomatoes, carrots, and raisins. Stir in remaining ingredients.

3. Cover tightly and simmer gently for 1 to 1-1/2 hr., or until beef is tender.

Lasagna Romagna

YIELD: 6 to 8 servings

INGREDIENTS

BUTTER or MARGARINE	6 tbsp.
ALL-PURPOSE FLOUR, unsifted	6 tbsp.
MILK	3 cups
SALT	1 tsp.
PEPPER	1/4 tsp.
PARMESAN CHEESE, grated	2/3 cup
PARSLEY, fresh, chopped	1/3 cup
GROUND BEEF, lean	1-1/2 lb.
ONIONS, chopped	1/3 cup
SPAGHETTI SAUCE	3 cups
MOZZARELLA CHEESE, shredded	2 cups
LASAGNA NOODLES	8 oz. (about 12)
PARMESAN CHEESE	garnish

PROCEDURE

1. Melt butter in medium saucepan; stir in flour. Gradually add milk. Cook and stir constantly over medium heat until mixture thickens and begins to boil; boil and stir 1 min.

2. Remove from heat. Add salt, pepper, cheese, and parsley; stir until smooth. Set aside.

3. Brown ground beef in skillet; add onions and cook until tender. Drain off excess juice. Stir browned beef into white sauce.

4. Cook lasagna according to package directions for 10 min.; drain well. Separate noodles and lay flat to prevent sticking together.

5. Spread a layer of spaghetti sauce, about 3/4 cup, on bottom of a 13- by 9- by 2-in. pan. Arrange 1/4 of the noodles over the sauce; layer with

1/3 of the meat sauce, 1/2 cup spaghetti sauce, and 2/3 cup mozzarella. Repeat the layers two more times. Top with remaining lasagna and spaghetti sauce.

6. Sprinkle with additional Parmesan cheese; cover with foil. Bake at 350°F. for about 30 min. Remove foil; continue to bake 15 min. more until bubbly and lightly browned. Serve with sprinkling of Parmesan cheese, if desired.

VEGETABLES

Asparagus with Cheese-Beer Sauce

YIELD: 6 servings

INGREDIENTS

PROCESSED AMERICAN CHEESE, diced	1/2 lb.
DRY MUSTARD	1/2 tsp.
CAYENNE	1/8 tsp.
COLD BEER	1/2 cup
ASPARAGUS STALKS, cooked	24
TOAST, crisp slices	6

PROCEDURE

1. Combine cheese, seasonings, and beer. Place over hot water. Cook slowly, stirring constantly, until smooth.

2. Arrange asparagus on toast. Serve with sauce.

Scandinavian Baked Beans

YIELD: 6 servings

INGREDIENTS

DRIED NAVY BEANS	1 lb.
SALT	1 tsp.
ONION, minced	2 tbsp.
DRY MUSTARD	1/2 to 1 tsp.
BROWN SUGAR	3 tbsp.
MOLASSES	2 tbsp.
SALT PORK	1/4 lb.
BEER	1 cup

PROCEDURE

1. Soak beans overnight in water to cover. Add dry salt pork and simmer beans in water to cover until tender.

2. Mix cooked beans with onion, salt (unless salt pork has seasoned beans sufficiently), dry mustard, brown sugar, and molasses. Dice cooked salt pork and mix with beans.

3. Turn into greased baking dish and add beer (to cover beans). Cover dish and bake at 350°F. about 1 hr., stirring twice during cooking. Remove cover for last 15 min. of cooking.

Potato Salad

YIELD: 6 servings

INGREDIENTS

NEW POTATOES, medium	6
VINEGAR	1 tbsp.
OLIVE OIL	2 tbsp.
SALT	1 tsp.
PEPPER	1/2 tsp.
ONION, finely chopped	1 tbsp.
CELERY, finely diced	1/2 cup
LETTUCE	

Dressing

MILK	1 cup
BUTTER	1 tbsp.
CORNSTARCH	3 tbsp.
COLD WATER	3 tbsp.
DRY MUSTARD	2 tsp.
SALT	1 tsp.
CAYENNE	dash
BEER	1/2 cup

PROCEDURE

1. Cook potatoes in rapidly boiling salted water until tender. Drain and peel. Cut into small cubes.

2. Make a marinade of remaining salad ingredients except lettuce. Pour over warm potatoes and let stand until thoroughly cooled. Heap in lettuce cups.

3. Heat milk with butter. Mix cornstarch to a paste with cold water; add to milk with seasonings. Cook over hot water, stirring constantly until thick. Cool.

4. Add beer slowly to milk mixture, beating until smooth. Force through a sieve if necessary. Serve on potato salad.

Kidney Beans Savory

YIELD: 18 servings

INGREDIENTS

KIDNEY BEANS	3 cans
CANNED TOMATOES	3 cups
BEER	1-1/2 cups
CORNED BEEF	3 12-oz. cans
ONIONS, medium	6
FAT	1/2 cup
BROWN SUGAR	3 tbsp.
WORCESTERSHIRE SAUCE	1-1/2 tsp.

PROCEDURE

    1. Combine beans, tomatoes, and beer in large casserole or bean pot. Cube corned beef and add to beans.

    2. Slice onions; separate into rings. Saute in fat until golden brown; add with brown sugar and Worcestershire sauce; mix well.

    3. Bake at 325°F. for 2 hr. May be served on split toasted rolls.

Sweet Potatoes and Beer

YIELD: 6 servings

INGREDIENTS

SWEET POTATOES, medium	6
BUTTER	2 tbsp.
SALT	1 tsp.
BEER	1 cup

PROCEDURE

    1. Cook potatoes in rapidly boiling salted water 30 min. or until tender. Peel and slice 1/4 in. thick.

    2. Place potatoes in casserole; dot with butter. Sprinkle with 1/2 tsp. salt; add beer.

    3. Cover and bake at 400°F. for 1 hr. or until beer is almost absorbed. Sprinkle with remaining salt. Serve hot with plenty of melted butter.

Cabbage Slaw

YIELD: 6 servings

INGREDIENTS

CABBAGE, medium head	1
CELERY SEED	2 tbsp.
GREEN PEPPER, shredded	1
ONION, minced	1 tsp.
SALT	1 tsp.
PEPPER	1/4 tsp.
MAYONNAISE	1 cup
BEER	1/2 cup

PROCEDURE

    1. Shred cabbage. Add celery seed, green pepper, onion, and seasonings.

    2. Thin mayonnaise with beer. Add to cabbage; toss thoroughly. Chill.

Savory Yam Pie

YIELD: 6 servings

INGREDIENTS

BUTTER or MARGARINE, softened	1/4 cup
LIGHT BROWN SUGAR	1 tbsp.
EGGS, separated	3

(continued)

Savory Yam Pie
(continued)

FLOUR	3 tbsp.
LEMON JUICE, freshly squeezed	2 tbsp.
SCALLIONS, chopped, fresh	2 tbsp.
PARSLEY, fresh, chopped	2 tbsp.
BASIL, dried	1/4 tsp.
SALT	1/4 tsp.
YAMS, cooked, mashed	2 cups
HAM, cooked, diced	1-1/2 cups
APPLE, large, cored, pared, and chopped	1 (1 cup)
PASTRY SHELL, 9-in., unbaked	1

PROCEDURE

1. In large mixing bowl, cream butter and sugar. Beat in egg yolks, flour, lemon juice, scallions, parsley, basil, and salt. Beat in yams. Stir in ham and apple.

2. Beat egg whites until stiff peaks form; fold into yam mixture. Turn into pastry shell.

3. Bake at 375°F. for 1 hr. or until a knife inserted in the center of pie comes out clean. Let stand 10 min. before serving.

Baked Stuffed Yams

YIELD: 4 servings

INGREDIENTS

YAMS, large	4
SPINACH, fresh	12 oz. (1 bag)
BACON, cooked	8 slices
MILK	3 tbsp.
BUTTER or MARGARINE	2 tbsp.
ONION, chopped	2 tbsp.
EGG	1
SALT	1 tsp.
PEPPER	1/4 tsp.
PARMESAN CHEESE, grated	1/4 cup

PROCEDURE

1. Wash and dry yams; prick several times with a fork. Bake at 400°F. for 45 to 55 min. or until soft.

2. Remove stems from spinach; rinse in cold water. Place in saucepan with 1/2-in. boiling salted water. Cover and cook until spinach wilts, about 3 to 4 min. Drain well and chop.

3. Immediately cut a slice from top of each yam. Carefully scoop out centers; mash in large mixing bowl.

4. Crumble bacon, reserving 2 slices. Add crumbled bacon, spinach, milk, butter, onion, egg, salt, and pepper to mashed yams; beat until smooth. Spoon mixture into yam shells.

5. Crumble reserved bacon; sprinkle over yams. Sprinkle with cheese. Bake at 350°F. for 15 min. or until heated through.

SALADS

Jellied Vegetable Salad

YIELD: 6 servings

INGREDIENTS

GELATINE, granulated	1-1/2 tbsp.
COLD WATER	1/4 cup
BOILING WATER	1 cup
BEER	2 cups
CABBAGE, shredded	2 cups
GREEN PEPPER, finely shredded	1
SALT	1/2 tsp.
LETTUCE	

PROCEDURE

1. Soften gelatin in cold water. Dissolve in boiling water. Add beer.
2. Place cabbage and green pepper in shallow pan 6- by 8- by 2-in. Sprinkle with salt. Cover with gelatine mixture. Chill until firm.
3. Cut into squares. Serve in lettuce cups and sprinkle liberally with salt. Do not serve with mayonnaise.

Rainbow Melon Cup

YIELD: 8 servings

INGREDIENTS

WATERMELON BALLS	2 cups
HONEYDEW MELON BALLS	1 cup
CANTALOUPE BALLS	1 cup
BEER	1-1/2 cups

PROCEDURE

1. Place melon balls in shallow pan. Add beer. Chill several hours.
2. Arrange in serving dishes. Add a little fresh, cold beer to each dish.

Bavarian Fruit Slaw

YIELD: 6 servings

INGREDIENTS

MAYONNAISE	1 cup
BEER	1 cup
LEMON JUICE	2 tbsp.
POWDERED SUGAR	2 tbsp.
APPLES, sliced	1 cup
BANANAS, sliced	2
CABBAGE, shredded	3 cups

PROCEDURE

1. Combine mayonnaise, beer, lemon juice, and sugar; beat with rotary beater until well blended.
2. Slice fruit into this dressing. Add shredded cabbage; toss with fork until thoroughly mixed.

Hot Potato Salad Tyrolean

YIELD: 6 servings

INGREDIENTS

ONIONS, medium, minced	2
POTATOES, cooked, sliced	6 cups
CIDER VINEGAR	1/3 cup
BEER	2/3 cup
SUGAR	1 tsp.
EGG, slightly beaten	1
SALAD OIL	1/3 cup
SALT	to taste
PEPPER	to taste
PARSLEY, chopped	garnish

PROCEDURE

1. Combine onions and potatoes. Heat vinegar and beer to boiling point; add sugar. Pour slowly on egg, stirring constantly. Add salad oil; beat vigorously. Pour over potato mixture and mix thoroughly with fork.

2. Pour into frying pan and heat piping hot. Season with salt and pepper. Garnish with parsley.

Chef's Salad

YIELD: 6 servings

INGREDIENTS

LETTUCE	1 head
ROMAINE	1 head
CUCUMBER	1
TOMATOES	3
STUFFED OLIVES, sliced	1/2 cup
SHARP CHEDDAR CHEESE, diced	1/2 cup
BEEF TONGUE, slivered	2 cups

PROCEDURE

1. Arrange crisp greens in salad bowl. Score and slice cucumber; add to bowl.

2. Cut tomatoes in wedges; add to bowl with remaining ingredients. Add dressing just before serving.

BREADS

Popovers

(Excellent to serve from baskets passed around during meals)

YIELD: 24 popovers

INGREDIENTS

FLOUR	2 cups
SALT	1-1/2 tsp.
OIL	2 tbsp.
EGGS	5
MILK	2 cups

PROCEDURE

1. Grease medium-sized custard cups (or foil cups) and place on baking sheets. Preheat oven to 375°F.

2. Into a mixing bowl, sieve the flour and salt. Add oil and stir until the mixture resembles corn meal.

3. In another bowl, beat eggs slightly and add milk. Add the flour mixture and beat until smooth.

4. Fill cups 1/3 full and bake for 50 min.

5. Remove from oven and quickly cut a slit in side of popover to let out steam; return to oven for 10 min. Remove from cups and serve at once.

Banana Tea Bread

YIELD: 1 loaf

INGREDIENTS

FLOUR, sifted	1-3/4 cups
BAKING POWDER	2 tsp.
BAKING SODA	1/4 tsp.
SALT	1/2 tsp.
SHORTENING	1/3 cup
SUGAR	2/3 cup
EGGS, well beaten	2
BANANAS, fully ripe, mashed	3

PROCEDURE

1. Sift together flour, baking powder, baking soda, and salt.

2. Whip shortening until creamy. Add sugar gradually and continue beating until light and fluffy.

3. Add eggs and beat well.

4. Add flour mixture alternately with bananas, a small amount at a time, beating after each addition until smooth.

5. Turn into well-greased bread pan (8-1/2 in. by 4-1/2 in. by 3 in.) and bake at 350°F. for about 1 hr. 10 min., until done.

Monkey Bread

YIELD: 20 servings

INGREDIENTS

YEAST	1-1/2 cakes
SUGAR	1 tbsp.
MILK	1 cup
BUTTER	1/4 lb.
EGGS, beaten	3
FLOUR, sifted	3 or 4 cups
SALT	1 tsp.

PROCEDURE

1. Soften yeast in small amount of lukewarm water. Add sugar.

2. Scald milk and add butter, allowing it to melt. Cool to lukewarm; add beaten eggs, then add yeast mixture. Add flour and salt and mix well. Place in greased bowl and allow to rise.

3. Roll out to 1/3-in. thickness, and cut with diamond cookie cutter. Place one layer in well-oiled ring. Spread with melted butter; add second layer and spread with melted butter. Continue adding layers and melted butter until mold is 3/4 full. Allow to rise until double in bulk.

4. Bake at 350° to 375°F. for 45 min.

DESSERTS

Chocolate Beer Cake

YIELD: 1 7-in. layer cake

INGREDIENTS

CAKE FLOUR, sifted	1-3/4 cups
BAKING POWDER	1 tsp.
BAKING SODA	1/4 tsp.
SALT	1/2 tsp.
BUTTER	1/3 cup
SUGAR	1 cup
EGGS, separated	2
UNSWEETENED CHOCOLATE, melted and cooled	2 squares (2 oz.)
BEER	3/4 cup

PROCEDURE

1. Mix and sift flour, baking powder, baking soda, and salt together three times.

2. Cream butter until soft. Add sugar gradually, beating after each addition until light and fluffy. Add egg yolks, one at a time, beating until well blended. Add chocolate; beat until smooth.

3. Add flour alternately with beer, a small amount at a time, beating until smooth after each addition. Fold in stiffly beaten egg whites.

4. Turn into 2 greased, 7-in. layer tins. Bake at 375°F. for 30 min. or until done. Cool.

Blueberry Pecan Coffee Cake

YIELD: 1 9-in. round cake

INGREDIENTS

BLUEBERRY COFFEE CAKE MIX	1 pkg. (16 oz.)
EGG	1
BEER	1/4 cup
MILK	1/4 cup
ORANGE RIND, grated	2 tsp.
PECANS, chopped	1/2 cup

PROCEDURE

1. Prepare coffee cake according to package directions using egg, beer, and milk. Fold in orange rind.

2. Spoon half the batter into well-greased 9-in. round cake pan. Mix topping from package with pecans and sprinkle half over batter.

3. Pour remaining batter in pan. Place blueberries from package over batter. Sprinkle remaining topping over blueberries.

4. Bake at 375°F. for 25 to 30 min. or until cake feels firm to the touch. Cut in wedges in pan and serve warm.

Candied Fruit Coffee Cake

YIELD: 6 servings

INGREDIENTS

COFFEE CAKE MIX	1 pkg. (10½ oz.)
EGG	1
BEER	1/2 cup
DATES, finely chopped	1/4 cup
PECANS, chopped	1/4 cup
CANDIED CHERRIES, finely chopped	1/4 cup

PROCEDURE

1. Combine all ingredients in plastic bag (may be provided with mix). Close top and mix as directed on package.

2. Pour dough into pan provided in mix. Bake at 375°F. for 25 min. or until cake feels firm to the touch. Serve warm.

Butterfly Fudge Cake

YIELD: 1 2-layer cake

INGREDIENTS

FUDGE CAKE MIX	1 pkg. (1 lb. 1½ oz.)
BEER	12 oz.
EGGS	3
ORANGE RIND, grated	1
CHOCOLATE FROSTING	
COCONUT, grated	

(continued)

Butterfly Fudge Cake
(continued)

PROCEDURE

1. Prepare cake mix as directed on package using beer (in place of water) and eggs. Beat in orange rind.

2. Pour batter into well-buttered layer cake pans. Bake at 350°F. for 30 to 35 min. or until cake springs back when touched lightly.

3. Cool on rack in pans; remove layers.

4. Frost bottom layer; place second layer on top. Cut cake in half and place round sides together to form butterfly shape. Frost top and sides of cake, swirling frosting to simulate wings. Decorate with grated coconut.

Pineapple Cheesecake

YIELD: 1 8-in. cake

INGREDIENTS

CHEESE CAKE MIX	1 pkg. (10½ oz.)
SUGAR	3 tbsp.
BUTTER or MARGARINE, melted	1/4 cup
MILK	1 cup
BEER	1/2 cup
PINEAPPLE, crushed, well drained	3/4 cup

Topping

DAIRY SOUR CREAM	1 cup
SUGAR	2 tbsp.
VANILLA EXTRACT	1/2 tsp.

PROCEDURE

1. Mix crumbs in package with sugar and butter. Press crumbs into ungreased 8-in. pie pan.

2. Prepare cheesecake filling according to package directions, using milk and beer. When filling is thick, fold in pineapple. Pour mixture into pan. Chill until firm.

3. Combine sour cream, sugar, and vanilla and spread over top of cake. Bake at 425°F. for 5 min. Chill for another hour or more.

Spicy Orange Cake

YIELD: 1 9-in. layer cake

INGREDIENTS

ORANGE CAKE MIX	1 pkg. (1 lb. 3 oz.)
BEER	12 oz.
EGGS	3
CINNAMON, ground	1 tsp.
NUTMEG, ground	1/4 tsp.
CLOVES, ground	1/4 tsp.
COCONUT, flaked	1/2 cup
PECANS, chopped	1/2 cup
FROZEN WHIPPED TOPPING, thawed	1 qt.
FROZEN ORANGE JUICE CONCENTRATE	2 tbsp.

PROCEDURE

1. Prepare cake mix according to package directions using beer (in place of water) and eggs. When batter is well blended, fold in spices, coconut, and pecans.

2. Pour batter into 2 well-greased and floured 9-in. layer cake pans. Bake at 350°F. for 25 to 30 min. Remove from pans and cool on rack.

3. Combine whipped topping with undiluted orange juice concentrate. Spread between layers and over top and sides of cake.

Apple Streusel

YIELD: 6 servings

INGREDIENTS

GOLDEN DELICIOUS APPLES	4
LEMON JUICE	2 tbsp.
BROWN SUGAR, packed	1/3 cup
FLOUR	1/3 cup
CINNAMON	1/4 tsp.
MACE	1/4 tsp.
BUTTER	2 tbsp.
WALNUTS, chopped	1/4 cup
SHREDDED COCONUT	1/4 cup
HALF AND HALF or CREAM	

PROCEDURE

1. Core and slice apples. Toss with lemon juice and layer in 9-in. round baking dish.

2. Blend together sugar, flour, spices, and butter with pastry blender or fork.

3. Add walnuts and coconut; mix well. Sprinkle evenly over apples.

4. Bake at 350°F. about 35 min. or until topping is golden brown and apples are tender. Let stand 5 min.; serve with cream.

L'Ile Flottante Pralinee

(floating island with hazelnuts)

YIELD: 5 servings

INGREDIENTS

Creme Anglaise

EGG YOLKS	6
GRANULATED SUGAR	1/3 cup
MILK, scalded	2 cups
VANILLA EXTRACT	2 tbsp.
HEAVY CREAM, very lightly whipped	1/2 cup

Hazelnut Praline

HAZELNUTS	1 cup
GRANULATED SUGAR	1 cup
WATER	1/4 cup
CREAM OF TARTAR	pinch

(continued)

L'Ile Flottante Pralinee
(continued)

Caramel Syrup

GRANULATED SUGAR	1/2 cup
WATER	1/2 cup
CREAM OF TARTAR	pinch

Meringue

EGG WHITES	10 (about 1¼ cups)
SALT	pinch
CREAM OF TARTAR	pinch
SUPERFINE SUGAR	3/4 cup
VANILLA EXTRACT	1-1/2 tsp.
HAZELNUT PRALINE, finely ground	3/4 cup

PROCEDURE

1. To make creme anglaise, beat egg yolks lightly in a bowl; sprinkle in sugar, beating until the mixture forms a ribbon. Stir in scalded milk.

2. Transfer mixture to a heavy saucepan and cook over moderately low heat, stirring constantly, until it thickens. Remove pan from heat and stir in vanilla. Chill the custard. Before serving, fold in the whipped cream.

3. To make the praline, roast the hazelnuts in a shallow pan at 350°F. for 25 min. or until nuts are lightly colored. Transfer nuts to a towel and rub briskly to remove skins.

4. In a skillet, combine sugar, water, and cream of tartar; bring mixture to a boil, brushing down any sugar clinging to the sides of the pan. Cook syrup until it is a golden caramel. Add hazelnuts and tilt the pan to coat the nuts. Pour the mixture onto an oiled marble or other smooth surface and let cool till brittle.

5. Break up the praline roughly and pulverize in a food processor or blender. There should be about 2 cups (leftover praline can be stored in airtight container in refrigerator).

6. To make caramel syrup, combine sugar, 1/4 cup water, and cream of tartar in small saucepan and bring to boil over low heat, brushing down any sugar clinging to sides of pan. Increase the heat and cook syrup until it is golden caramel. Remove pan from heat and pour in the remaining 1/4 cup water (that has been heated) to make a thick syrup.

7. Divide the syrup quickly among 5 1½-cup charlotte molds, tilting molds to coat the bottoms evenly. Set molds aside.

8. Preheat oven to 325°F.

9. To make meringue, beat egg whites with salt and cream of tartar in a bowl until they hold soft peaks. Add superfine sugar in a stream and the vanilla. Beat the mixture until it holds firm but shiny peaks. Fold in 3/4 cup of praline.

10. Divide the meringue among the caramelized molds, mounding it slightly. Arrange molds in a baking pan and add enough hot water to reach 2/3 of the way up the sides of the molds. Bake for 20 min. or until puffed and golden.

11. Remove molds from pan and let cool. Refrigerate, covered with rounds of waxed paper and their lids, until well chilled.

12. To serve, turn meringues out onto chilled dishes and surround with creme anglaise.

Tarte au Citron

(lemon tart)

YIELD: 12 servings

INGREDIENTS

TART SHELL, 12-in.	1 (see PATE BRISEE recipe)
EGGS, separated	6
GRANULATED SUGAR	1/2 cup
LEMON JUICE	1 cup plus 1 tbsp.
BUTTER, cut into pieces	5 tbsp.
SALT	pinch
SUPERFINE SUGAR	3/4 cup
CONFECTIONERS' SUGAR	garnish

PROCEDURE

1. Preheat oven to 425°F.

2. Roll out dough and fit inside a 12-in. tart shell. Line shell with sheet of waxed paper and add enough dried beans to cover the bottom. (This will prevent the shell from buckling during baking.)

3. Place the tart tin on baking sheet and bake for 10 min. Remove waxed paper and dried beans. Return to oven and bake 2 min. longer.

4. In mixing bowl, beat egg yolks and 1/2 cup sugar together until the mixture forms a ribbon. Stir in 1 cup lemon juice. Pour the mixture into a heavy saucepan and add the butter. Stir constantly over moderately low heat until it thickens. Pour mixture into a bowl, cover the top with a buttered round of waxed paper, and chill.

5. Preheat oven to 375°F.

6. In a large bowl, beat egg whites with a pinch of salt until they form soft peaks. Pour in superfine sugar in a stream. Add remaining lemon juice and beat until firm.

7. Combine chilled egg yolk mixture and meringue mixture and pour it into baked pastry shell. Put tart on baking sheet and place it on top level of the oven. Bake 15 min. or until puffed and golden. Remove tart from the tin and cool on a rack. Sift confectioners' sugar over the tart.

Pate Brisee

(rich pastry dough)

YIELD: 1 12-in. tart shell

INGREDIENTS

FLOUR	1-3/4 cups
SUGAR	1 tbsp.
SALT	pinch
BUTTER, very cold	12 tbsp.
ICE WATER	4-1/2 tbsp. approx.

PROCEDURE

1. Put flour, sugar, and salt in food processor. Process and add butter, cut into small pieces.

2. Continue processing and add water; add only enough so that dough comes away from sides of container. Gather dough into a ball and wrap in waxed paper. Chill for 30 min.

**Francis Lorenzini's
Roulade Ananas**
(pineapple cake)

YIELD: 1 cake

INGREDIENTS

Jelly Roll

EGG YOLKS	9
SUGAR	1 cup
UNBLEACHED FLOUR	2/3 cup
EGG WHITES	8
RED CURRANT JELLY	1 cup

Filling

HEAVY CREAM	1 qt.
CONFECTIONERS' SUGAR	1 cup
GELATIN STRIPS,* softened in cold water 5 to 7 min.	12
RUM	1/4 cup
GRANULATED SUGAR	1/4 cup
CANNED PINEAPPLE SLICES, drained and cut in 1/2-in. chunks	5

Glaze

APRICOT PRESERVES	1 cup

PROCEDURE

1. Preheat oven to 425°F.

2. Butter 2 sheets parchment paper and set on 2 12- by 16-in. jelly roll pans.

3. In a bowl, combine egg yolks with all but 2 tbsp. sugar. Beat mixture at medium speed with balloon whip until it forms pale yellow ribbons, about 3 min. Add flour to mixture but do not combine. Set aside.

4. Whip egg whites just until stiff peaks form. Add 2 tbsp. sugar. Beat until stiff and glossy. Gently fold egg whites into egg yolk mixture until combined. Do not overmix.

5. Pour equal amounts of batter into prepared pans. Spread gently. Bake 5 to 7 min. or until cake begins to brown.

6. Place a sheet of parchment paper on a counter and cover lightly with granulated sugar. Remove cakes from oven and turn out onto parchment paper. Peel off buttered paper from cakes and set paper aside. Using a spatula, spread a thin layer of red currant jelly across the cake surface.

7. Working from narrow end, roll cake into tight jelly roll. Wrap in buttered parchment paper; refrigerate 8 hr. or overnight.

8. To assemble roulade, carefully cut jelly roll into 1/4-in. slices. Using a round 9-in. diameter cake pan, 2-in. deep, line bottom and sides with jelly roll slices. The pan need not be buttered. There may be some leftover jelly roll.

9. To prepare filling, combine cream and confectioners' sugar in bowl. Mix with electric mixer at low speed for 1 min., then at high speed until soft peaks form. Refrigerate.

*Clear gelatin sheets are available at H. Roth, 1577 First Avenue, New York, N.Y.

10. Drain softened gelatin strips; melt in a pan over low heat, stirring continuously. As soon as melted, remove from heat and add rum and granulated sugar. Work rapidly. Add 1/2 cup whipped cream and stir to combine. Fold in remaining whipped cream and pineapple pieces. Add more rum or sugar if desired.

11. Spoon mixture over jelly roll slices. Work cream into crevices. Knock pan gently against table to settle mixture. Even surface with spatula.

12. Cover with foil. Refrigerate overnight or at least 6 hr.

13. When ready to use, unmold onto serving tray. If cake sticks, tap gently to release. To prepare glaze, warm preserves over low heat, then strain. Brush glaze on top and sides of roulade with pastry brush.

Note: The jelly roll must be prepared at least 8 hr. before assembling the cake. The entire roulade can be frozen, well wrapped, for up to 1 month, then thawed in the refrigerator for 1 day. Do not glaze until day it is to be served.

Gaston Lenotre's Tulipes
(tulip pastries)

YIELD: 8 pastries

INGREDIENTS

EGG WHITES, at room temp.	2
BUTTER, at room temp.	3-1/2 tbsp.
SUGAR	1/3 cup
VANILLA EXTRACT	1/2 tsp.
UNBLEACHED FLOUR	1/2 cup

PROCEDURE

1. Fill the bottom of a double boiler with hot, but not boiling water. When top of double boiler is in place, it should not touch the water. Work away from the heat to avoid cooking the egg whites. Place them in the top pan, allowing them to sit until they are lukewarm.

2. Rinse mixing bowl with very hot water and wipe dry. Place softened butter in bowl and beat until creamy. Add sugar and vanilla, beating constantly but slowly. Continue beating, adding the warmed egg whites a bit at a time. When whites have been added and the batter is homogenous, stop beating and sift flour into bowl, cutting and stirring into other ingredients with wooden spatula. Work quickly but gently when mixing flour.

3. The batter may be used immediately or refrigerated, for several hours, but should be used the same day it is prepared.

4. To prepare pastries, preheat oven to 350°F.

5. Using stiff cardboard, cut out an 8-in. diameter circle. Draw a smaller 6-in. circle in the center. Cut out the inner circle and discard. Place the cardboard ring in one corner of a baking sheet that has been lightly buttered and floured or lined with parchment paper.

6. Fill the hollow center of the ring with a tbsp. of tulip batter. Spread batter to completely fill the center of the circle. The batter should be thin and even. Carefully lift cardboard and repeat the operation 3 more times.

7. Bake 10 min. until edges are slightly brown and centers still cream colored.

(continued)

Gaston Lenotre's Tulipes
(continued)

8. Mold tulips immediately. To mold, take 8 small mixing bowls (each about 6-in. in diameter) and place 4 upside down on a table. Carefully remove tulips from baking sheet and place each circle on an upside-down bowl. Immediately cover with another bowl. Work quickly; as tulips cool, they become brittle.

9. Repeat procedure with remaining batter.

10. The tulip pastries can be stacked inside each other and kept in airtight container for up to 2 weeks. They must be stored as soon as they cool or they quickly become stale and rubbery.

Note: These pastries can be filled with a variety of mixtures, including a combination of one or more fruit sorbets. The sorbet may then be topped with fresh or preserved fruit. All except the final assembly may be done ahead of time.

Gaston Lenotre's Sorbet au Citron
(lemon sherbet)

YIELD: 1 quart

INGREDIENTS

Syrup

SUGAR	5 cups
WATER	4-1/4 cups

Sherbet

LEMON JUICE, freshly squeezed	1 cup
MINERAL WATER, noneffervescent	1 cup
SUGAR SYRUP	1-1/3 cups
EGG WHITE	1

PROCEDURE

1. The sugar syrup should be prepared in the given proportions, and to the letter, for a proper sorbet. The syrup can be stored for months in the refrigerator, and can be used in all sorbet recipes. To prepare, combine the water and sugar in a large saucepan. Place over high heat; stir with wooden spoon until sugar has dissolved. Bring to a full boil, remove from heat, and pour into a large jar to store. Cool completely before using.

2. To prepare sherbet, strain the lemon juice through a sieve directly into the ice cream freezer. Add mineral water and sugar; freeze according to manufacturer's directions.

3. About 10 min. before sherbet is ready (as it just begins to thicken—this will take 20 to 40 min. depending on the machine used) stop the machine and take out 2 tbsp. of the mixture. Place this in a bowl with the egg white and whisk vigorously until the mixture becomes thick and foamy. Then pour back into the ice cream freezer and finish freezing. Serve the day it is made.

**Albert Kumin's
Chocolate Truffles**

YIELD: 3 doz. truffles

INGREDIENTS

SEMISWEET CHOCOLATE	9 oz.
HEAVY CREAM	1 cup
UNSALTED BUTTER	1/4 cup
SUGAR	3 tbsp.
ORANGE LIQUEUR	3 tbsp.
COCOA POWDER	1/4 cup
INSTANT POWDERED COFFEE	1/8 cup

PROCEDURE

1. Cut chocolate in half-inch pieces. Melt in double boiler over warm water.

2. Combine cream, butter, and sugar in a heavy, medium-size saucepan. Bring to a boil over medium heat, stirring to dissolve sugar and blend ingredients. When mixture boils, remove from heat and gently stir in melted chocolate. Add liqueur. Set in pan of ice water and whip until mixture thickens.

3. When chocolate becomes thick and holds its shape, about 5 min., spoon into a pastry bag with a medium tip and pipe bite-size balls onto parchment or waxed paper. Truffles can also be formed using 2 teaspoons to mold mixture into balls. Refrigerate until set.

4. At this point, truffles can be refrigerated up to 2 weeks. Ideally, they should be stored at 63° to 65°F., but short of that refrigeration is best. Do not freeze or chocolate may crack.

5. To serve, mix cocoa and coffee powder and roll truffles in the mixture.

**John Clancy's Holiday
Mincemeat**

YIELD: filling for 2 large pies

INGREDIENTS

BRISKET OF BEEF, lean	2 lb.
BEEF SUET, chopped	1/2 lb.
SEEDLESS RAISINS	2 cups
CURRANTS	2 cups
APPLES, chopped	4 cups
CITRON, diced	1/2 cup
CANDIED ORANGE PEEL, diced	1/2 cup
CANDIED LEMON PEEL, diced	1/2 cup
SUGAR	1 cup
NUTMEG	1 tsp.
SALT	1 tsp.
CINNAMON	1 tsp.
ALLSPICE	1/2 tsp.
CLOVES	1/2 tsp.
BRANDY, to cover	1 qt.

(continued)

John Clancy's Holiday
Mincemeat (continued)

PROCEDURE

1. Cover brisket with salted water. Simmer, covered, until meat can be shredded with a fork, about 2 hr.

2. Combine shredded beef and remaining ingredients in large bowl or crock; cover with brandy. Cover and store at room temperature for at least 2 weeks. Check mincemeat every few days, and if becoming dry add more brandy, Scotch, or bourbon. Mincemeat will keep indefinitely at room temperature.

3. To assemble pie, preheat oven to 375°F.

4. To prepare filling, combine the mincemeat with equal parts freshly chopped apples, or pears, or a combination of both. Tart apples are excellent.

5. The mincemeat is best baked in a deep dish shell. Roll out the bottom crust and fit into pan, allowing an edge for fluting. Fill pie, then roll out top crust. Dough can also be cut in strips for a lattice top.

6. Place top crust in position and flute edges. Cut small air holes in top. Brush with glaze of egg yolk and water. Bake 40 to 50 mins. or until crust is lightly browned. If darkening too quickly, cover with foil. Serve warm, or reheat and serve with ice cream or whipped cream.

Cream Cheese Pastry

YIELD: pastry for 1 double-crust pie

INGREDIENTS

UNBLEACHED FLOUR	3 cups
SALT	1 tsp.
SUGAR	4 tsp.
UNSALTED BUTTER, at room temp.	12 tbsp.
CREAM CHEESE, at room temp.	12 tbsp.
	(about 6 oz.)

PROCEDURE

1. Place flour in a large bowl. Scatter salt and sugar over flour. Add butter and cheese. Using hands, combine ingredients by kneading until well blended. Shape pastry into 2 balls. Using palm of hand, flatten balls into thick cakes. Smooth out sides. Pastry may be rolled out immediately or, lightly dusted in flour, wrapped in plastic, and refrigerated up to 3 days.

Chocolate Sauerkraut Cake

YIELD: 1 8-in. layer cake

INGREDIENTS

MARGARINE or BUTTER	2/3 cup
SUGAR	1-1/2 cups
EGGS	3
VANILLA	1 tsp.
UNSWEETENED COCOA	1/2 cup
ALL-PURPOSE FLOUR	2-1/2 cups
BAKING POWDER	1 tsp.

BAKING SODA	1 tsp.
SALT	1/2 tsp.
COOL WATER	1 cup
SAUERKRAUT, rinsed thoroughly, drained, and well chopped	2/3 cup

PROCEDURE

1. Cream margarine and sugar. Beat in eggs and vanilla.

2. Sift dry ingredients and, in alternate thirds, add 1/3 dry with 1/3 water to 1/3 egg mixture.

3. Smooth and stir in sauerkraut. Turn into 2 greased 8-in. round baking pans. Bake at 350°F. for 30 to 45 min. until cake is done. Cool on racks.

Pineapple Mousse in Meringue

YIELD: 12 servings

INGREDIENTS

EGG WHITES, at room temp.	6
CREAM OF TARTAR	1/2 tsp.
SUGAR	
VANILLA EXTRACT	1/2 tsp.
SALT	
SKIM MILK	1 cup
EGG YOLKS	2
LEMON JUICE	2 tsp.
UNFLAVORED GELATIN	1 envelope
CRUSHED PINEAPPLE, in its own juice	2 8-oz. cans
FROZEN WHIPPED TOPPING, thawed	1 4-oz. container
CRYSTALLIZED VIOLETS, optional	garnish

PROCEDURE

1. Make meringue shell (at least 4-1/2 hr. before serving). Line a large cookie sheet with foil. Using an 8-in. plate, draw a circle on foil; set aside. Preheat oven to 275°F.

2. In small bowl, beat 4 egg whites and cream of tartar at high speed until soft peaks form. Beating at high speed, gradually sprinkle in 3/4 cup sugar, 2 tbsp. at a time, beating well after each addition until sugar is completely dissolved. Add vanilla extract and 1/8 tsp. salt; continue beating at high speed until meringue stands in stiff, glossy peaks.

3. Spoon about 1/4 of the meringue onto foil circle; spread evenly with metal spatula. Spoon remaining meringue into decorating bag with medium rosette tip. Pipe rosettes to make a high rim on top of meringue circle. Bake 1-1/2 hr. or until shell is lightly browned. With metal spatula, carefully remove shell to wire rack; cool.

4. While meringue is cooling, make filling. In heavy 3-qt. saucepan, whisk milk, egg yolks, lemon juice, 1 tbsp. sugar, and 1/2 tsp. salt until blended. Sprinkle gelatine evenly over mixture. Cook over medium-low heat until gelatin is completely dissolved and mixture thickens and coats a

(continued)

Pineapple Mousse in Meringue (continued)

spoon (do not boil or mixture will curdle), about 20 min., stirring constantly. Stir in pineapple with its juice. Refrigerate until mixture mounds when dropped from a spoon, about 1 hr.

5. In small bowl, beat remaining egg whites at high speed until stiff peaks form. Fold beaten egg whites and whipped topping into pineapple mixture. Spoon mousse into meringue shell; refrigerate until set, about 1 hr. Garnish with crystallized violets, if desired.

Tapioca-Plum Pudding

YIELD: 5 servings

INGREDIENTS

QUICK-COOKING TAPIOCA	3 tbsp.
SKIM MILK	2 cups
EGG, separated	1
SALT	1/8 tsp.
SUGAR	
ALMOND EXTRACT	1/2 tsp.
PURPLE PLUMS, drained and pitted	1 30-oz. can
GROUND CINNAMON	1/4 tsp.

PROCEDURE

1. In 2-qt. saucepan combine tapioca, milk, egg yolk, salt, and 1 tbsp. sugar; let stand 5 min. Cook over medium heat, stirring constantly, until mixture is very hot and thickens slightly (do not boil). Remove saucepan from heat; stir in almond extract; cover and refrigerate until well chilled, about 2 hr.

2. In covered blender at high speed, or in food processor with knife blade attached, blend plums and cinnamon until smooth; set aside.

3. In small bowl, beat egg white at high speed until soft peaks form. Gradually beat in 1 tbsp. sugar, beating until sugar is completely dissolved. (White should stand in stiff, glossy peaks.) Gently fold beaten egg white into tapioca mixture.

4. Spoon half of tapioca mixture into 5 6-oz. parfait glasses; top with half of plum mixture. Repeat. Refrigerate until ready to serve.

Chocolate Crepe Batter

YIELD: 24 5-in. chocolate crepes

INGREDIENTS

EGGS, large	3
ALL-PURPOSE FLOUR	1 cup
SUGAR	2 tbsp.
COCOA	2 tbsp.
MILK	1-1/4 cups
LEMON JUICE	1 tbsp.
KAHLUA	1 tbsp.
BUTTER, melted	2 tbsp.

PROCEDURE

1. Whirl all ingredients in blender; scrape down sides; blend until smooth, about 2 min.

2. Refrigerate several hours before using. Bake in the usual manner for crepes, being careful not to burn (chocolate burns easily).

Variations

Black Forest Peach Crepe

For each serving, fill 1 chocolate crepe with 1/3 cup sweetened whipped cream, flavored with 1 tsp. almond-flavored liqueur, 4 or 5 drained, canned peach slices, and 4 or 5 drained dark sweet cherries (brandied cherries are even better). Fold crepe and garnish with 1 tbsp. plain sweetened whipped cream, 1 peach slice, and 1 tsp. chocolate fudge topping.

Minted Fruit Sherbet Crepe

For each serving, place 1 chocolate crepe open-face on serving dish. Combine 1/3 cup drained canned fruit cocktail and 1/3 cup fresh fruit in season, such as cantaloupe and honeydew melon balls, diced banana, or strawberries. Top with 3 #60 scoops of pineapple, lime, and raspberry sherbet. Serve with 1 tbsp. creme de menthe liqueur on the side.

Fruited Yogurt Pie

YIELD: 6 10-in. pies

INGREDIENTS

CLING PEACH SLICES or FRUIT COCKTAIL	1 #10 can
PEACH-FLAVORED GELATIN	1 lb. 8 oz.
WATER, boiling	1-1/2 qt.
FROZEN ORANGE JUICE CONCENTRATE, thawed	1 cup
ALMOND EXTRACT	2 tsp.
VANILLA EXTRACT	2 tsp.
YOGURT, plain	2 qt.
PIE SHELLS, 10-in., baked	6

PROCEDURE

1. Drain peaches, saving syrup. Chop coarse.

2. Dissolve gelatin in boiling water; add reserved syrup, orange juice concentrate, and extracts. Chill until mixture mounds on spoon.

3. Beat gelatin mixture until fluffy and about double in volume. Fold in yogurt, then peaches. Chill until mixture mounds on spoon.

4. Turn 1-1/4 qt. into each pie shell. Chill until firm.

Mint Velvet Pie

YIELD: 6 9-in. or 72 3-in. pies

INGREDIENTS

MILK, cold	3-1/2 qt.
VANILLA EXTRACT	1 tsp.
VANILLA INSTANT PUDDING AND PIE FILLING	1 pkg.

(continued)

Mint Velvet Pie
(continued)

WHIP 'N CHILL DESSERT MIX, mint flavor	1 pkg.
PIE SHELLS, baked and cooled, 9-in. (or graham cracker crust or chocolate cookie crumb crust), or 72 3-in.	6

PROCEDURE

1. Combine milk, vanilla, pudding mix, and dessert mix in bowl. Blend at low speed of mixer for 1 min. scraping bowl as needed. Whip at medium speed for 1 min. Gradually increase speed to high and whip 5 min. or until light and creamy.

2. Ladle into pie shells, allowing 1 qt. per 9-in. shell or 1/3 cup (#12 scoop) per 3-in. shell.

3. Chill at least 2 hr. Garnish as desired.

BARBECUES AND GRILLS

Sirloin or Pinbone Sirloin
(from loin end just above hips)

Good for larger groups for open pit grilling. Should be no less than 1-1/2 in. thick. Sear both sides over white-hot coals to retain juices. Move to slightly cooler side of grill and continue cooking. Turn with tongs until proper degree of doneness has been reached. Slice in thin diagonal slices. Sauteed onions or mushrooms will greatly enhance presentation.

Salt Crust Steak

Spread one side of steak liberally with English or dijon mustard. Cover thickly with 1/4 in. of coarse or kosher salt. Dampen the salt and cover with piece of heavy brown paper. Roll firmly back and forth with rolling pin until salt is crusted. Turn steak over and repeat process. Place in wire grill and broil over fairly hot heat from 10 to 12 min. each side. Remove salt crust and drizzle butter mixed with steak sauce over surface. Slice diagonally.

Steak Marinade
(simple yet effective flavor improver)

Place steaks in shallow container and cover generously with olive oil, lemon juice, one or two finely minced garlic cloves and a few sprinkles of oregano. Allow to remain in marinade, turning occasionally, for at least 24 hr.

Steak au Poivre

Crack peppercorns coarsely with rolling pin or mallet. Use sirloin, porterhouse, or flank steak. Sprinkle both sides of steak generously with cracked peppercorns and press into meat using flat dish. Let rest for 1/2 hr.; broil.

Whole Fillet

5 to 8 lb. Trim well. If grilled on flat surface, fold thin ends under and tie securely. If open fire is used, do not tie, but cut off thin ends and save for another purpose. Rub well with butter or oil and allow to rest for 15 to 20 min. Broil over medium fire about 25 min.; turn frequently to keep color even.

Broiled Hamburger Steaks

4 lb. ground beef seasoned with salt and pepper and 1 tsp. monosodium glutamate. Add 2 eggs, a sprinkle or two of Worcestershire, 1/4 cup catsup, and enough bread crumbs to absorb moisture. Form into oval cakes 1-1/2 in. thick; broil over fairly high heat, turning to cook evenly.

Turkish Steaks with Garlic

5 to 6 lb. rump steak, 12 cloves of garlic, 3/4 lb. butter, 3 lb. sliced potatoes, and a No. 2-1/2 can of crushed tomatoes. Cut steak into long pieces about 3/4 in. thick. With point of paring knife make a hole near each end of slices. Insert half a clove of garlic. Place slices on top of each other to original shape and tie securely. Place meat in heavy stew pan with 3/4 lb. of butter. Cover and place over moderate charcoal fire for about 3 hr., turning occasionally. Partially fry the potatoes in butter, then add to beef together with crushed tomatoes. Salt and pepper to taste. Replace cover and continue to simmer until meat and potatoes are well done. A few bay leaves added during the last hour will add more flavor. Serves 10.

Garlicked Lamb Chops*

Cut chops about 1 in. thick. Mince 4 cloves garlic and 1 tbsp. chopped parsley. Soak this in 1/2 cup oil, 1 tsp. coarse salt, and 1 tsp. ground pepper. Rub this mixture well into chops and allow to marinate from 3 to 4 hr., turning once or twice. Broil slowly and, when ready, char quickly on hottest area of grill. (Lamb center should show pink!)
*Lamb steaks cut from shoulder or leg may be treated as above, but red wine should be added to marinade.

Pork

A rather hazardous dish for summer service. **MUST ALWAYS BE COOKED WELL DONE** and must be kept refrigerated until time to cook. Broil thick chops slowly and apply glaze several times during cooking. *Glaze:* Combine 2/3 cup honey, 1/3 cup of undiluted orange juice, and 1/3 cup brandy.

Pork Spareribs

1 lb. per person. Parboil or roast ribs about 3/4 hr. until just tender. Combine 1 cup honey, 1/2 tsp. lemon juice, and 1 tbsp. curry powder; brush each side of spareribs with this mixture and broil over medium-hot fire until highly browned and glazed.

Barbecue Menu

Choice of Two

Sirloin Steak   Turkish Steaks

Marinated Lamb Steaks   Broiled Hamburger Steaks

Pork Spareribs   Grilled Chicken

Grilled Fish   Grilled Canadian Bacon

Choice of One

Fresh Corn on the Cob   Foil-Baked Potatoes

Baked Yams or Sweet Potatoes   Baked Beans

Choice of Two

Assorted Relishes   Coleslaw

Tossed Green Salad with Assorted Dressings

Choice of Two

Hot Corn Bread   Hot Biscuits   French Bread

Choice of One

Chocolate Cake   Fruit Pie

Beverage

Coffee   Tea   Soft Drinks   Beer

Fish

More difficult to produce and requires, in many cases, more attention. It often requires "locking" each fish in a wire grill or wrapping in foil to retain form, shape, and flavor. Lobster tails and crab legs can be surface-grilled, using cooking techniques and recipes available.

Assorted Meats

Sausages, salami, Canadian bacon, kolbassa, pepperoni, knockwurst, and frankfurters are all excellent candidates for grilling. Cured slabs of pastrami also may be grilled. Creamed horseradish mixed with prepared mustard spread over the pastrami about 10 min. before removing from grill will add beautiful flavor. **COOKED** slabs of corned beef can be spread with a mixture of pineapple juice, honey, prepared mustard, and a little ground cinnamon, ginger, and cloves, which imparts a delicious flavor and surface to the corned beef. Slice thinly but "pile high" for service on pumpernickel or seeded rye. Foil-roasted potatoes are a good accompaniment.

Bear in mind that sauces and glazes can be individually compounded by combining complementary relishes such as mustards, soy sauces, liquefied jams, jellies, steak sauce, herbed butter, sliced or shredded cheeses, mayonnaise, and sour cream.

Poultry

Split six 2-1/2 lb. chickens; remove backbone and breast cartilage. Turn wings back to lock. Wipe chickens with towels moistened with lemon juice. For 12 servings, combine 3/4 cup peanut oil, 3/4 cup melted butter, 3 tsp. salt, 1-1/2 tsp. ground pepper, and 2 tsp. paprika. Brush with mixture and allow to rest for 15 min. Brush again and place bone-side down over white coals. Cook for 12 to 14 min. Turn and cook an additional 12–14 min. *Variations:* Chopped parsley, garlic, rosemary, oregano, shallots, or scallions may be added to "paint."

Grilled Chicken

Split 2 chickens of 3 lb. eviscerated weight, and remove all bones. Cut each into 4 parts and lay on flat surface. Cover with waxed paper or foil and flatten with mallet, cleaver, or rolling pin. Sprinkle with salt, pepper, and ground cinnamon; allow to rest for at least 1 hr. Broil over medium coals until nicely browned. Place in stew pan and add 3/4 lb. of prunes and 3 sliced raw carrots. Add chicken broth to depth of 1/2 in. over contents. (A little brown sugar or honey may be added if desired.) Cover pan and cook over moderate charcoal fire until tender.

Burgoo

YIELD: 1200 gal.

INGREDIENTS

SOUP MEAT, lean, no fat or bones	600 lb.
FAT HENS	200 lb.
POTATOES, peeled, diced	2000 lb.
CABBAGE, chopped	5 bushels
ONION	200 lb.
TOMATOES	60 No. 10 cans
PUREE of TOMATOES	24 No. 10 cans
PUREE of CARROTS	24 No. 10 cans
CORN	18 No. 10 cans
RED PEPPER	to taste
SALT	to taste
WORCESTERSHIRE, LIQUID HOT PEPPER SAUCE, or STEAK SAUCE	to season

PROCEDURE

Mix the ingredients a little at a time and cook outdoors in huge iron kettles, over wood fires, from 15 to 20 hr. Use squirrels in season—one dozen squirrels to each 100 gal. burgoo.

Barbecue Sauce for Basting

YIELD: 1-1/2 gal.

INGREDIENTS

SUGAR	2 cups
SALT	2 tbsp.
PAPRIKA	1 tbsp.
PEPPER	2 tsp.
GARLIC, minced	1 tbsp.

(continued)

Barbecue Sauce for
Basting (continued)

CIDER VINEGAR	3 qt.
TOMATO CATSUP	2 qt.
WORCESTERSHIRE SAUCE	1 5-1/4 oz. bottle
PREPARED MUSTARD	1/2 cup

PROCEDURE

1. Combine ingredients in a saucepan. Simmer 20 min., stirring occasionally.

2. Brush sauce over chicken, spareribs, or chops to be barbecued. Baste frequently. One pt. sauce should be used for every 5 lb. of meat. (If desired, meat may be salted during cooking.)

Sweet and Sour Sauce

YIELD: 16 gal.

INGREDIENTS

TOMATO SAUCE	6 No. 10 cans
TOMATO CATSUP	6 No. 10 cans
VINEGAR	2 gal.
WORCESTERSHIRE SAUCE	2 cups
SOY SAUCE	2 cups
DRY MUSTARD	1 cup
GINGER, grated	1/2 cup
PINEAPPLE, crushed	1 No. 10 can
SUGAR	32 cups
BROWN SUGAR	32 cups
SALT	2 cups
CORNSTARCH	3 cups

PROCEDURE

1. Combine all ingredients in suitable pot except sugar, brown sugar, salt, and cornstarch. When ingredients begin to simmer, add sugar, brown sugar, and salt.

2. Mix cornstarch with water and add slowly.

3. Let sauce simmer for 1 to 2 hr. Stir often from bottom with paddle.

Hot Beef Barbecues

YIELD: 48 sandwiches, 1 gal. 2 cups sauce

INGREDIENTS

INSTANT CHOPPED ONION	3 oz.
WATER	1 cup
CELERY, finely chopped	2 lb.
SHORTENING	4 oz.
TOMATO CATSUP	2 qt.
WATER	1 qt.

BROWN SUGAR, firmly packed	9 oz.
CIDER VINEGAR	1 cup
PREPARED MUSTARD	1 cup
WORCESTERSHIRE SAUCE	1/2 cup
LIQUID HOT PEPPER SAUCE	1/4 cup
CRUSHED RED PEPPER	2 tbsp.
WHITE PEPPER	1 tbsp.
GARLIC POWDER	1 tbsp.
TOP ROUND of BEEF, choice, roasted, thinly sliced	10 lb. 5 oz.
SANDWICH BUNS, toasted	48

PROCEDURE

1. Cover onion with water. Let stand 20 min.

2. Saute onion and celery in shortening until tender.

3. Add catsup and next nine ingredients; bring to a boil. Reduce heat; simmer 5 min.

4. Add sliced beef, simmer 10 min.

5. For each sandwich, serve 2-1/2 to 3 oz. meat with 2 tbsp. sauce on toasted sandwich bun, preferably hard-crusted French style.

Barbecued Shrimp

YIELD: 5 to 6 servings

INGREDIENTS

ITALIAN DRESSING, bottled	1 cup
CHILI SAUCE	1/2 cup
LEMON JUICE	1 tbsp.
PEPPER	to taste
MEDIUM SHRIMP, peeled, deveined, and well dried	1-1/2 lb.
ONION, cut in 2-in. pieces	1
GREEN PEPPER, large, cut in 2-in. pieces	1
PINEAPPLE, fresh, cut in 2-in. pieces	1/4
CHERRY TOMATOES	1 box

PROCEDURE

1. In 2-qt. bowl, mix dressing, chili sauce, lemon juice, and pepper. Add shrimp and stir to coat well. Cover and refrigerate overnight.

2. Drop onion and green pepper into boiling water for about 1/2 min. Drain and dry thoroughly.

3. Alternate shrimp, onion, green pepper, pineapple, and tomatoes on skewers. Brush with marinade. Place on barbecue and cook one side. Turn and cook other side until shrimp are pink and tender, about 10 to 15 min. total.

Lamb Brochette

(Excellent main dish for dinners, luncheons; serve mini portions as appetizers.)

YIELD: 48 portions

INGREDIENTS

OIL	3 cups
WINE or CIDER VINEGAR	12 oz.
LEMON JUICE	2/3 cup
ONION, minced	1/2 cup
PARSLEY FLAKES	2 tbsp.
SALT	2 tsp.
OREGANO, leaf	1-1/2 tsp.
BLACK PEPPER	2 tsp.
GARLIC POWDER	2 tsp.
LAMB LEGS, cut in 1-in. cubes	2
TOMATOES, firm, wedges	5 lb.
MUSHROOM CAPS	2 lb.

PROCEDURE

1. Combine first nine ingredients to make a marinade and mix well. Pour marinade over lamb cubes and refrigerate 5 to 6 hr., mixing 2 or 3 times.

2. Arrange lamb cubes, tomato wedges, and mushroom caps alternately on metal skewers or on disposable lamb skewers, and broil about 10 min., basting frequently with marinade.

3. Serve on bed of curried or saffron rice pilaf.

Note: Brochettes may be oven-baked at 375°F. for 40 min. in marinade that has been slightly thickened with cornstarch or beurre manie.* Cover with foil for first 20 min. Remove foil cover, turn brochettes, and finish baking.
*Beurre manie—2 tbsp. flour creamed with 2 tbsp. butter.

Barbecued Drumsticks

YIELD: 30 servings

INGREDIENTS

DRUMSTICKS, 5 to 6 oz. each	30
FLOUR	8 oz.
SHORTENING	1 lb.
SAUCE	
SALAD OIL	4 oz.
ONION, chopped	3/4 cup
GARLIC, minced	2 cloves
HOT PEPPER SAUCE	1/4 tsp.
LEMON JUICE	1/2 cup
WORCESTERSHIRE SAUCE	1/3 cup
SALT	1-1/2 tsp.
PEPPER	1/4 tsp.
MONOSODIUM GLUTAMATE	1 tsp.
SUGAR	2 tbsp.

CHILI POWDER	1-1/2 tsp.
OREGANO	1/2 tsp.
WATER	2 cups
CATSUP	1 cup

PROCEDURE

1. Flour drumsticks and brown in hot fat. Place in baking pans.
2. Saute onion and garlic in hot oil until transparent.
3. Add remaining ingredients. Cover and cook gently for 10 min. If necessary, more water can be added at the end of the cooking time.
4. Pour about half the sauce over the drumsticks. Cover and bake at 375°F. for about 30 min. Add remaining sauce and bake, uncovered, 20 min.

KOSHER RECIPES

The initials accompanying these recipes indicate kosher parve (KP), kosher dairy (KD), or kosher fleishig (KF). Refer to chapter 12 for more information.

Chopped Liver (KF)

YIELD: 50 portions as first course; 100 plus as spread

INGREDIENTS

CHICKEN FAT (rendered) or VEGETABLE OIL	2 cups
CHICKEN LIVERS or LIGHT COLORED STEER LIVER	8 lb.
ONIONS, medium sized, sliced	15
EGGS, hard-cooked	16
SALT	8 tsp.
BLACK PEPPER, freshly ground	1/2 tsp.
GARLIC POWDER	1/2 tsp.
MONOSODIUM GLUTAMATE	1 tbsp.
SUGAR	1 tsp.

PROCEDURE

1. Saute onions in fat or oil until light brown.
2. If chicken livers are used, saute them until they have lost color. Cover and steam 5 min. If steer liver is used, broil the liver until just done. Allow to cool.
3. Put liver, onions, and eggs through grinder three times.
4. Add all seasonings and monosodium glutamate, and mix thoroughly. Add a little oil if too dry. For a first course, serve with a No. 16 scoop on lettuce and garnish with cherry tomatoes or red radishes.

If used as a spread, the liver can be molded in any shape desired (as a pineapple or chicken). Chopped egg whites may be sprinkled generously over entire mold.

Meatless Chopped Liver (KP)

YIELD: 50 portions

INGREDIENTS

ONIONS, medium, thinly sliced	12
OIL	3 cups
MUSHROOMS, fresh	12 lb.
EGGS, hard-cooked, thinly sliced	18
MONOSODIUM GLUTAMATE	1 tsp.
SALT	to taste
PEPPER	to taste
GARLIC POWDER (optional)	

PROCEDURE

1. Saute onions until limp; add mushrooms and cook until tender and onions are browned.

2. Put onions, mushrooms, and eggs through grinder twice or put through Buffalo chopper until very finely minced.

3. Season to taste. Serve in the same way as chopped chicken or steer liver.

Knishes (KF)

INGREDIENTS

Dough

DRY YEAST	1 pkg.
WATER, warm	1/4 cup
FLOUR	2 to 2-1/2 cups
SUGAR	1 tbsp.
SALT	pinch
MARGARINE	2 sticks
EGG YOLKS, large	3

Fillings

CHOPPED LIVER (see recipe, p. 253)

POTATO

ONIONS, large, chopped	2
CHICKEN FAT	1/4 cup
POTATOES, mashed, hot	2 cups
EGG, large	1
SALT	to taste
PEPPER	to taste

Saute onions until brown; mix with other ingredients. Chill thoroughly.

Glaze

EGG YOLKS	2
EGG WHITE, lightly beaten	1 tsp.

Combine.

PROCEDURE

1. Dissolve yeast in warm water.
2. Mix the flour, sugar, and salt in a large bowl.
3. Cut the margarine into the dry ingredients until the pieces are tiny. Add the yeast and the egg yolks.
4. Knead the mixture by hand until it is smooth and holds together.
5. Wrap the dough in waxed paper and refrigerate overnight.
6. Divide the dough into 4 equal parts; refrigerate.
7. Place 1/4 of the dough on a pastry cloth and roll out into large rectangle, tissue paper thin. Use a well-floured cloth and rolling pin cover. Dough may be patched if it tears.
8. Place filling on dough in 1-in. strip along the long edge of the rectangle.
9. Pick up cloth and proceed to roll as a jelly roll, resting the seam side down. Cut into 1-in. diagonal slices and place on ungreased cookie sheet; cover. Allow to rest until all the dough has been used.
10. Glaze the knishes with the egg mixture.
11. Bake at 400°F. for about 20 min. until browned. Remove from sheet; cool.
12. To serve, bake at 400°F. for another 10 or 15 min.

Baked Gefilte Fish (KP)

(Serve sliced as first course, or cut into squares for hors d'oeuvre.)

YIELD: 30 portions

INGREDIENTS

WHITEFISH FILLETS	2 lb.
YELLOW PIKE FILLETS	2 lb.
WINTER CARP FILLETS	2 lb.
ONIONS, large	6
SALT	12 tsp.
PEPPER	to taste
EGGS, lightly beaten	24
ICE WATER (imperative)	4-1/2 cups
SUGAR	2 tsp.
MATZO MEAL	6 tbsp.

PROCEDURE

1. Grind fish and onions twice, using fine blade. Add remaining ingredients and mix thoroughly, seasoning to taste.
2. Turn mixture into very lightly oiled 9- by 5- by 3-in. loaf pans. Cover lightly with foil. Bake in water bath in oven preheated to 350°F. for 1 hr., or until tops are firm to touch.

This may be served hot or cold. Accompany with white or red horseradish, or with sliced hard-cooked eggs.

Matzo Balls (KP)

YIELD: 100 portions

INGREDIENTS

SHORTENING	3 lb. 8 oz.
MATZO FLOUR	4 lb.
EGGS	50
SALT	4 tbsp.
NUTMEG	a pinch
PEPPER	1 tsp.

PROCEDURE

1. Mix shortening in blender. Add matzo flour.
2. Gradually blend in the eggs. Add seasonings. Mix thoroughly.
3. Cover and let stand in refrigerator overnight.
4. On following day, form into balls slightly larger than golf balls. Place on waxed paper.
5. Bring a pot of salted water to a rolling boil. Add balls and cook, covered, approximately 20 min.

Quick Matzo Balls (KP)

YIELD: 12 balls

INGREDIENTS

FAT or OIL	2 tbsp.
EGGS, slightly beaten	2
MATZO MEAL	1/2 cup
SALT	1 tsp.
STOCK or WATER	2 tbsp.

PROCEDURE

1. Mix fat and eggs together. Mix matzo meal and salt, and add to eggs. When well blended, add stock or water. Cover mixing bowl and refrigerate for at least 20 min.
2. Bring 2 or 3 qt. of salted water to a brisk boil. Reduce heat, and drop walnut-size balls of mixture into slightly bubbling water. Cook 30 or 40 min., covered.
3. Lift out with slotted spoon and put into consomme. May be kept dry for hours in covered container. This recipe also freezes well.

Mushroom Barley Soup (KD)

YIELD: 24 7-oz. portions

INGREDIENTS

CARROTS, finely diced	2
ONIONS, finely sliced	2
CELERY STALK, finely diced	1/2
BUTTER	1/2 cup
WATER	1 gal.
PEARL BARLEY	2 cups
SALT	1 tbsp.

PEPPER	a pinch
MUSHROOMS, dried	4 oz.
WATER	1 pt.
MONOSODIUM GLUTAMATE	2 tbsp.
LIGHT CREAM	1 cup

PROCEDURE

    1. Saute carrots, onions, and celery in butter in hot skillet until tender and delicately browned.

    2. Add water, pearl barley, salt, and pepper. Simmer gently until barley is cooked.

    3. In the meantime, cook the dried mushrooms in the pint of water until soft—approximately 30 min.

    4. Drain off any excess liquid, and add mushrooms and monosodium glutamate to the barley mixture. Simmer just long enough to blend flavors.

    5. Just before serving add the light cream. Taste and adjust seasonings if necessary.

Braised Short Ribs of Beef (KF)

YIELD: 6 10-oz. portions

INGREDIENTS

SHORT RIBS (FLANKEN), STRIPS, 10 oz. each	6
MONOSODIUM GLUTAMATE	1 tbsp.
SALT	to season
PEPPER	to season
FLOUR, all-purpose, sifted	1 cup
SHORTENING, nondairy	1 tbsp.
ONIONS, large, coarsely cut	3
CARROTS, coarsely cut	3
CELERY STALKS, large pieces	8
BAY LEAF	1
GARLIC CLOVE, minced	1
SOUP STOCK	1 qt.
TOMATO JUICE	1 cup

PROCEDURE

    1. Rub short ribs with monosodium glutamate. Season with salt and pepper.

    2. Dredge with flour. Cut each strip in two.

    3. Brown on all sides in skillet in hot shortening.

    4. Place meat in pot with remaining 7 ingredients. Cover and simmer slowly 2-1/2 hr., or until meat is tender.

    5. Remove meat. Keep hot. Strain sauce.

    6. Serve on hot platter with sauce poured over the meat.

Note: Inviting accompaniments are peas, carrots, parsley bouquets, and red horseradish.

Potted Chicken with Vegetables and Matzo Ball (KF)

PROCEDURE

1. Simmer a 4- to 5-lb. stewing chicken with vegetables, such as, carrots, celery, knob celery, parsley, and leeks.

2. When fork tender, remove chicken, and season stock with salt, pepper, and monosodium glutamate.

3. In individual casseroles, place a bed of boiled noodles.

4. Add cooked vegetables, such as, carrots, green beans, and peas. Place a matzo ball in center.

5. Add cut-up stewing chicken and seasoned stock. Serve very hot.

Baked Eggs in Sour Cream (KD)

(May be used as a breakfast dish or light luncheon main course.)

YIELD: 8 portions

INGREDIENTS

SOUR CREAM	1 pt.
EGGS	16
CHIVES, chopped, or SCALLIONS, minced	2 tbsp.
PARSLEY, chopped	2 tbsp.
BREAD CRUMBS	2 tbsp.
BUTTER, melted	4 tbsp.
SALT	to taste
PEPPER	to taste

PROCEDURE

1. Pour cream in flat, (1-in. deep) oven dish and make indentations with back of bouillon spoon.

2. Break 1 egg into each indentation. Season lightly and sprinkle with chives, parsley, and bread crumbs. Pour melted butter over top.

3. Bake at 450°F. until eggs are set and top is browned. This may be served with a side dish of asparagus.

Palestine Lamb Casserole (KF)

YIELD: 50 servings (approx. 8 oz. ea.)

INGREDIENTS

ONION, sliced	2 lb.
OLIVE OIL or SALAD OIL	2 cups
LAMB SHOULDER, boneless, cubed	12 lb.
TOMATOES, fresh	6 lb.
OREGANO	2 tsp.
SALT	1 tbsp.
PEPPER	1/2 tsp.
SUMMER SQUASH, coarsely chopped	12 lb.
OLIVES, RIPE, GREEN or BLACK	100 to 150

PROCEDURE

1. Saute onion in hot oil in heavy pot or steam-jacketed kettle until soft. Add cubed lamb and saute until browned.

2. Dip tomatoes in boiling water for 1 min. Remove peel and cut in wedges. Add tomatoes and seasonings to lamb, cover, and simmer for 20 to 25 min.

3. Add squash and continue to cook until lamb and squash are tender.

4. Add olives. Ladle mixture into 8-oz. casseroles.

Piquant Stuffed Cabbage A La Thelma (KF)

(Named for the author's wife.)

YIELD: 36 portions

INGREDIENTS

CABBAGES, large	2
RICE, uncooked	3/4 cup
HAMBURGER	3 lb.
EGGS, large	2
SALT	1 tsp.
MONOSODIUM GLUTAMATE	1 tsp.
CATSUP	1/4 cup
ORANGE JUICE, frozen, thawed, undiluted	1 6-oz. can
TOMATOES, crushed	1 No. 2-1/2 can
TOMATO PUREE	1 No. 2-1/2 can
VINEGAR	1/2 cup
LEMON JUICE	1/3 cup
BROWN SUGAR	1/2 lb.
HONEY	2 lb.
CLOVES, ground	1/4 tsp.

PROCEDURE

1. Remove as much of core from cabbages as possible. Place cabbages in boiling water to soften outer leaves.

2. With a two-pronged fork, lift the cabbages from the water and remove as many leaves as possible.

3. Return cabbages to water and repeat process until all usable leaves are removed. Drain well.

4. Retain heart leaves and chop finely for use in sauce. Trim the ribs of each leaf until the entire leaf is the same thickness.

5. Cook the rice until soft; cool. Combine with hamburger and next 4 ingredients.

6. Line the bottom of the pan with the chopped cabbage (include finely chopped stems and any remaining cabbage not used for stuffing).

7. Flatten each cabbage leaf with palm of hand; fill each leaf with a No. 16 scoop of meat mixture. Roll up each leaf; place seamside down in baking pan, with sides touching each other. Do not pack more than 3 cabbage rolls high.

8. Mix orange juice and remaining ingredients; pour over cabbages. Liquid should be about 1/2 in. over top layer of cabbage rolls.

9. Cover and bake at 350°F. for 1-1/2 hr.

10. Adjust seasoning; continue baking for 1-1/2 hr. longer. In final stage of cooking it may be necessary to add catsup diluted with water to keep liquid to within 1 in. of top layer of cabbages.

Basic Crepe Recipe

YIELD: 16 crepes

INGREDIENTS

FLOUR, sifted	1 cup
SALT	1/3 tsp.
WATER	1 cup
EGGS	3

PROCEDURE

1. Sift together flour and salt.

2. Add eggs, unbeaten.

3. Add water gradually, beating and stirring until a smooth batter results. Strain.

Slightly grease a 6-in. frying pan, using a brush or paper napkin. Pour a small amount of batter to cover bottom of pan, tilting the pan so that the entire bottom is thinly covered. Turn with a spatula to cook both sides. Turn out to cool.

Salmon-Mushroom Filling for Crepes (KD)

INGREDIENTS

BUTTER	1/2 cup
OIL	1 tbsp.
ONIONS, large, diced	4
MUSHROOMS, sliced	1 lb.
GREEN PEPPER, finely diced	1
SALMON, cooked, cold	6-1/2 lb.
SALT	to taste
WHITE PEPPER	to taste
LIQUID HOT PEPPER SEASONING	to taste
DILL SEED, crushed (optional)	

PROCEDURE

1. Saute onions in butter and oil until limp. Add mushrooms and green pepper, and cook until onions are brown and mushrooms and green pepper are tender. Remove from heat.

2. Skin, flake, and bone the salmon and add to onion mixture. Add to cream sauce.* Season to taste. Chill.

Note: Cod or any boneless chunk fish may be substituted. It is not recommended that this product be frozen.

*Cream Sauce for Salmon-Mushroom Filling (KD)

INGREDIENTS

BUTTER	1 cup
FLOUR	1 cup
WHITE PEPPER	to taste
SALT	2 tsp.
PAPRIKA	dash
HALF-AND-HALF	1 qt.

PROCEDURE
1. Melt butter over medium heat.
2. Sprinkle flour over butter and whisk until smooth. Season and add half-and-half. Remove from heat.
3. Cover with waxed paper, and cool until ready to use.

Classic Crepes Suzettes (KD)

YIELD: 18 crepes

INGREDIENTS

SUGAR	3 tbsp.
ORANGE RIND, grated	1/2 tsp.
SWEET BUTTER, room temperature	5 tbsp.
LEMON JUICE, from	1 lemon
ORANGE JUICE	1/2 cup
COINTREAU, CURACAO, or GRAND MARNIER	1/2 tsp.
COGNAC or BRANDY (for flaming)	1/4 cup

PROCEDURE

For French service or exhibition cooking, the crepes should be made tableside in a chafing dish.
1. Place sugar in small bowl. Mix in grated orange rind and 2 tbsp. of the butter. Set aside.
2. Combine remaining butter with the lemon juice, orange juice, and liqueur. Stir over medium flame until butter melts. When it comes to a boil, stir in sugar mixture.
3. Add 4 crepes to sauce, stir. Turn crepes over and fold top one in half—spoon over liquid—fold half in quarter. Repeat until all are used.
4. Pour brandy over surface and ignite. Serve flaming.

Note: Crepes may be used as a main course at luncheon, serving 2 or more, or a single crepe may be served as a mini-entree before the main course.

Dessert Crepes or Blintzes (KD)
(Basic dessert crepes)

YIELD: 20 crepes

INGREDIENTS

FLOUR	3/4 cup
SALT	pinch
SUGAR	1 tbsp.
EGGS, whole	3
EGG YOLK	1
MILK	1-3/4 cups
BUTTER, melted, cooled	2 tbsp.
COGNAC or BRANDY	2 tbsp.
MELTED BUTTER for cooking crepes	

(continued)

Dessert Crepes or
Blintzes (continued)

PROCEDURE

1. Sift flour with salt and sugar in mixing bowl.
2. Beat whole eggs with egg yolk and add to milk. Blend with flour and whisk to a smooth batter.
3. Stir in melted butter and cognac. Cover and set aside at room temperature for at least 1-1/2 hr. before making crepes.
4. Heat 6-in. teflon fry pan or crepe pan. Use a pastry brush to grease pan lightly with butter.
5. Pour in about 2 tbsp. of batter and quickly rotate pan so that batter covers the bottom evenly. Cook until underside is lightly browned. Turn and cook second side for a moment or two. Remove from pan and set aside. Repeat until all batter has been used.

Note: Crepes may be made ahead and kept warm or reheated briefly in oven at 300°F. They should never be stacked while warm.

Traditional Cheese Filling
(For blintzes)

YIELD: 18 crepes

INGREDIENTS

FARMER'S CHEESE (COMPRESSED COTTAGE CHEESE)	1-1/4 lb.
CREAM CHEESE, softened	6 oz.
EGG	1
BUTTER, soft	3 oz.
SUGAR	3 oz.

PROCEDURE

1. Mix all ingredients until smooth.
2. Place a small quantity near the middle of each crepe and flatten.
3. Roll up and tuck in ends; keep seam side down. Slowly pan-fry each side until brown.

Dessert Filling

INGREDIENTS

WHITE RAISINS	1/3 cup
COGNAC	3 tbsp.
CREAM CHEESE, softened	1-1/2 lb.
SUGAR	1/2 cup
FLOUR	3 tbsp.
LEMON RIND, grated, from	2 lemons
EGG YOLKS	4
SOUR CREAM	3 tbsp.
BUTTER, melted	3 tsp.
VANILLA	3/4 tsp.

PROCEDURE

1. Marinate raisins in cognac 6 hr.
2. Mix cream cheese, sugar, and flour until fluffy.
3. Add remaining ingredients, except raisins, and mix well.

4. Add raisins, drained, and mix and chill for 2 hr.

5. Fill crepes and saute slowly in margarine or butter. When lightly browned, turn and fry second side. Serve hot "as is," or spoon a heavy dollop of sour cream or unsweetened whipped cream over top.

Note: Method used to "season" a black iron French crepe pan.
Scrub a No. 18 black iron crepe pan with a soapy fine steel wool pad. Dry well. Pour 1 in. of salad oil into it and place in oven at 300°F. Turn oven off after 2 hr. and keep pan in oven for about 12 hr. longer. Pour off oil and discard it. Wipe pan thoroughly with paper towels until no trace of the oil remains. This process seasons pan so that crepes will not stick. NEVER wash the pan after use, but wipe with paper towels until it is grease-free. Use pan only for crepes.

Quantity Baked Blintzes (KD)

YIELD: 60 blintzes

INGREDIENTS

BLINTZES, filled	5 doz.
CINNAMON-SUGAR	
EGGS	20
SOUR CREAM	2 qt.
ORANGE JUICE, frozen, undiluted	1/2 cup

PROCEDURE

1. Arrange blintzes on a greased sheet pan allowing 1/2 in. between each blintz. Sprinkle blintzes with cinnamon-sugar.

2. Beat eggs until fluffy. Add sour cream and undiluted orange juice and blend well. Pour over blintzes.

3. Bake at 350°F. for 45 min.

This is an excellent tea, luncheon, or Sunday brunch presentation.

Macaroon Fruit Slice (KD)

INGREDIENTS

Sweet Dough

BUTTER	8 oz.
SUGAR	4 oz.
EGGS, beaten	3
ORANGE, rind and juice	1
LEMON, rind and juice	1
SALT	pinch
CAKE FLOUR, sifted	1 lb.

Macaroon Mix

ALMOND PASTE	8 oz.
CONFECTIONERS' SUGAR	8 oz.
EGG WHITES	4

PROCEDURE

1. Cream butter and sugar; add eggs, fruit juices, and rinds. Stir in the flour and salt.   (continued)

Macaroon Fruit Slice
(continued)

2. Mix to a smooth dough. Turn out on lightly floured board. Roll out in two strips 5 in. wide and as long as the baking pan.

3. Place in baking pan and bake at 350°F. until only half cooked.

4. In meantime, combine ingredients for macaroon mix and mix to a smooth paste.

5. Remove pan from oven. Place a strip of macaroon mix along all four edges of each sweet dough strip. Return to oven until browned.

6. When cool, fill center with fresh stewed strawberries or any other colorful fruit.

Lukshen Kugel (KD)

YIELD: 8 to 12 portions

INGREDIENTS

BROAD EGG NOODLES	1 lb.
COTTAGE CHEESE	1 lb.
EGGS, lightly beaten	5
GOLDEN RAISINS	1-1/2 cups
SOUR CREAM	1 cup
BUTTER or MARGARINE, melted	1/4 cup
SUGAR	1/4 cup
CINNAMON, ground	4-1/2 tsp.
LEMON PEEL, grated	2 tsp.
SALT	1-3/4 tsp.
NUTMEG, ground	1/4 tsp.

Topping

CORN FLAKE CRUMBS	3/4 cup
BUTTER or MARGARINE, melted	1/4 cup

PROCEDURE

1. Cook noodles as directed. Drain, rinse, and place in large bowl.

2. Combine remaining ingredients except topping. Pour over noodles and mix gently but thoroughly. Spoon mixture into a buttered 13-1/2- by 9- by 2-in. pan.

3. Combine corn flake crumbs and melted butter; sprinkle over noodle mixture.

4. Bake in a preheated oven at 375°F. for 30 min. Remove from oven and let stand 10 min. before cutting.

Poire A L'Imperiale (KD) (Pears and Rice)

(Excellent buffet presentation)

YIELD: 25 portions

INGREDIENTS

RICE	12 oz.
MILK, warm	2 qt.
SUGAR	1-1/4 lb.
GELATINE, unflavored	2 oz.
HEAVY CREAM	1-1/2 pt.
PEAR HALVES, canned	24

COINTREAU	3 oz.
APRICOT JAM	as needed
RED CHERRIES	for garnish

PROCEDURE

1. Put rice in warm milk and cook for 20 min.; add sugar.
2. Dissolve gelatine in a little water, add to rice. Place in bowl and stir over ice until thick.
3. Whip cream until stiff and add to rice mixture, reserving some cream for decoration.
4. Add the cointreau; put into display bowl and chill.
5. Decorate surface with pears and glaze with warmed jam. Pipe whipped cream between pears; coat with a little apricot jam; sprinkle with cointreau. Red cherries may be used as a garnish.

Spiced Wine Passover Cake (KP)

YIELD: 8 to 10 servings

INGREDIENTS

MATZO CAKE MEAL	1-1/4 cups
SALT	1/2 tsp.
CINNAMON, ground	1 tsp.
ALMONDS, finely ground	6 tbsp.
EGGS, large, separated	8
SUGAR	1-1/2 cups
SWEET RED WINE	1/3 cup
ORANGE JUICE, fresh	1/3 cup
LEMON PEEL, grated	1 tsp.
CONFECTIONERS' SUGAR	

PROCEDURE

1. Mix first 4 ingredients together. Set aside.
2. Beat egg yolks until thick and lemon colored. Gradually beat in sugar and continue beating until thick and light colored.
3. Add wine, orange juice, orange and lemon peels and beat with an electric mixer set at medium speed for 4 min.
4. Fold in dry ingredients. Beat egg whites until they stand in soft, stiff peaks, and fold into the batter.
5. Turn into a 14-in. by 4-in. spring-form pan or a 10-in. by 4-in. round tube cake pan. Bake in a preheated oven at 325°F. for 1-1/2 hr. or until done.
6. Invert cake on a wire rack to cool. Remove from pan when cold.
7. Dust confectioners' sugar over the top.

Rice Pudding (KD)

YIELD: 35 portions

INGREDIENTS

RICE	12 oz.
MILK	2-1/2 qt.
SALT	1/2 tsp.
MARGARINE	10 oz.

(continued)

Rice Pudding
(continued)

SUGAR	1-1/4 lb.
EGGS, separated	15
LEMON, grated peel from	1 lemon
or VANILLA	1-1/2 tsp.

PROCEDURE

1. Simmer rice in milk with salt until soft. Cool.

2. Cream margarine, sugar, grated lemon peel, and egg yolks, and mix with rice.

3. Fold in stiffly beaten egg whites. Put into 6-qt. hotel pan and bake in water bath for about 1 hr. at 325°F.

Note: Drained canned fruit or raisins may be added.

Passover Sponge Cake (KP)

YIELD: 12 servings

INGREDIENTS

EGGS, large, separated	6
EGG, whole, large	1
SUGAR	1-1/2 cups
LEMON JUICE, fresh	1-1/2 tbsp.
LEMON PEEL, grated	1 tsp.
POTATO STARCH, sifted	3/4 cup
SALT	1/4 tsp.
GINGER, ground	1/2 tsp.
CONFECTIONERS' SUGAR	

PROCEDURE

1. Beat 6 egg yolks and 1 whole egg together until frothy. Gradually beat in sugar, lemon juice, and peel.

2. Sift potato starch with salt and ginger and add gradually, blending thoroughly.

3. Beat egg whites until stiff, but not dry. Gently fold into egg yolk mixture.

4. Turn batter into a 10-in. by 4-in. tube pan. Bake in a preheated oven at 350°F. for 50 to 60 min., or until cake is firm in the center. Cool in pan. Turn out on wire rack, top side up. Sift confectioners' sugar over the top.

Almond Tart Shells with Rum Chiffon Filling (KD)

YIELD: 32 individual tarts

INGREDIENTS

ALMOND TART SHELLS*	32
GELATINE, unflavored	1 oz.
WATER, cold	1 cup
EGG YOLKS	1-1/2 cups (approx. 12)
SUGAR	1 lb.

MILK	1 qt.
RUM	3/4 cup
EGG WHITES	1-1/2 cups
	(approx. 12)
SALT	1 tsp.
CREAM, whipped	1-1/2 cups
CONFECTIONERS' SUGAR	1/2 cup
SWEET CHOCOLATE, grated	1/2 cup

PROCEDURE

1. Soak the gelatine in cold water.

2. Beat the egg yolks and sugar; add the milk and cook over hot water, until thick. Remove from the fire and stir in the soaked gelatine, stirring until it is completely dissolved.

3. Add rum and allow the mixture to cool until it begins to congeal.

4. Fold in the egg whites which have been beaten with the salt.

5. Fill the baked tart shells and chill until the filling is firm.

6. Top with sweetened whipped cream and sprinkle with grated sweet chocolate.

Note: To make the almond tart shells, add 1/2 cup finely chopped, lightly toasted almonds for each pound of flour used in making the pastry. Add them after the fat has been cut into the flour but before the water is added. Bake as any tart shells.

Apple Strudel (KP)

YIELD: 24 servings

INGREDIENTS

Strudel

FLOUR, sifted	1 lb.
SALT	1/2 tsp.
SHORTENING	2 oz.
EGG	1
WATER, lukewarm	1 cup

Filling

STRAWBERRY JAM	1-1/2 cups
APPLES, fresh, sliced	6 to 7 cups
CINNAMON	2 tsp.
SUGAR	1-1/2 cups
RAISINS	1 cup
BREAD CRUMBS, toasted	1 cup

PROCEDURE

1. Sift flour and salt. Cut in the shortening. Add egg and water to form a soft dough. Let dough rest in oiled bowl for 30 min. Roll dough very thin.

2. Spread with strawberry jam. Add sliced fresh apples, raisins, and toasted bread crumbs. Combine cinnamon and sugar, and sprinkle over all. Roll up in long strips like jelly roll. Place in baking pan; bake at 400°F. for 25 to 30 min.

Pineapple Chiffon Pie (KP)

YIELD: 4 10-in. pies

INGREDIENTS

KOSHER GELATINE	3 oz.
PINEAPPLE JUICE	1 qt.
EGG WHITES	1 pt. (approx. 16)
SUGAR	3 cups
PINEAPPLE, crushed	1-1/2 qt.
PINEAPPLE JUICE	1 qt.

PROCEDURE

1. Hydrate gelatine by dissolving in hot pineapple juice. Cool.

2. Beat egg whites until frothy. Gradually add the sugar and beat until stiff enough to mound.

3. Combine gelatine mixture, pineapple juice, and crushed pineapple. Fold in egg whites. Pour into baked pie shells. Chill until filling is set.

APPENDIX A

PORTION CONTROL DATA

The following two conversion charts, one for ounces and one for pounds, have been designed to permit easy adjustment of basic recipes for the number of portions actually needed.

EXAMPLE: A basic 100-portion recipe calls for 7 ounces of a particular ingredient. When adjusting to 25 portions, find the column headed "100 Portions" and move down to the space reading "7 oz." Then move across this space, horizontally to the left, to the column headed "25 Portions." The figure "1-3/4 oz." appears as the number of ounces of the ingredient needed.

OUNCE CHART

25 Portions	50 Portions	75 Portions	100 Portions	200 Portions	300 Portions	400 Portions	500 Portions	600 Portions	700 Portions	800 Portions	900 Portions	1000 Portions
–	–	⅛ oz	⅛ oz	¼ oz	⅜ oz	½ oz	⅝ oz	¾ oz	⅞ oz	1 oz	1⅛ oz	1¼ oz
–	–	¼ oz	⅙ oz	⅓ oz	½ oz	⅔ oz	⅚ oz	1 oz	1⅙ oz	1⅓ oz	1½ oz	1⅔ oz
–	–	⅕ oz	⅕ oz	⅖ oz	⅗ oz	⅘ oz	1 oz	1⅕ oz	1⅖ oz	1⅗ oz	1⅘ oz	2 oz
–	–	¼ oz	¼ oz	½ oz	¾ oz	1 oz	1¼ oz	1½ oz	1¾ oz	2 oz	2¼ oz	2½ oz
–	–	⅓ oz	⅓ oz	⅔ oz	1 oz	1⅓ oz	1⅔ oz	2 oz	2⅓ oz	2⅔ oz	3 oz	3⅓ oz
–	¼ oz	⅜ oz	½ oz	1 oz	1½ oz	2 oz	2½ oz	3 oz	3½ oz	4 oz	4½ oz	5 oz
–	⅓ oz	½ oz	⅔ oz	1⅓ oz	2 oz	2⅔ oz	3⅓ oz	4 oz	4⅔ oz	5⅓ oz	6 oz	6⅔ oz
–	⅜ oz	⅝ oz	¾ oz	1½ oz	2¼ oz	3 oz	3¾ oz	4½ oz	5¼ oz	6 oz	6¾ oz	7½ oz
¼ oz	½ oz	¾ oz	1 oz	2 oz	3 oz	4 oz	5 oz	6 oz	7 oz	8 oz	9 oz	10 oz
½ oz	1 oz	1½ oz	2 oz	4 oz	6 oz	8 oz	10 oz	12 oz	14 oz	1#	1# 2 oz	1# 4 oz
¾ oz	1½ oz	2¼ oz	3 oz	6 oz	9 oz	12 oz	15 oz	1# 2 oz	1# 5 oz	1# 8 oz	1# 11 oz	1# 14 oz
1 oz	2 oz	3 oz	4 oz	8 oz	12 oz	1#	1# 4 oz	1# 8 oz	1# 12 oz	2#	2# 4 oz	2# 8 oz
1¼ oz	2½ oz	3¾ oz	5 oz	10 oz	15 oz	1# 4 oz	1# 9 oz	1# 14 oz	2# 3 oz	2# 8 oz	2# 13 oz	3# 2 oz
1½ oz	3 oz	4½ oz	6 oz	12 oz	1# 2 oz	1# 8 oz	1# 14 oz	2# 4 oz	2# 10 oz	3#	3# 6 oz	3# 12 oz
1¾ oz	3½ oz	5¼ oz	7 oz	14 oz	1# 5 oz	1# 12 oz	2# 3 oz	2# 10 oz	3# 1 oz	3# 8 oz	3# 15 oz	4# 6 oz
2 oz	4 oz	6 oz	8 oz	1#	1# 8 oz	2#	2# 8 oz	3#	3# 8 oz	4#	4# 8 oz	5#
2¼ oz	4½ oz	6¾ oz	9 oz	1# 2 oz	1# 11 oz	2# 4 oz	2# 13 oz	3# 6 oz	3# 15 oz	4# 8 oz	5# 1 oz	5# 10 oz
2½ oz	5 oz	7½ oz	10 oz	1# 4 oz	1# 14 oz	2# 8 oz	3# 2 oz	3# 12 oz	4# 6 oz	5#	5# 10 oz	6# 4 oz
2¾ oz	5½ oz	8¼ oz	11 oz	1# 6 oz	2# 1 oz	2# 12 oz	3# 7 oz	4# 2 oz	4# 13 oz	5# 8 oz	6# 3 oz	6# 14 oz
3 oz	6 oz	9 oz	12 oz	1# 8 oz	2# 4 oz	3#	3# 12 oz	4# 8 oz	5# 4 oz	6#	6# 12 oz	7# 8 oz
3¼ oz	6½ oz	9¾ oz	13 oz	1# 10 oz	2# 7 oz	3# 4 oz	4# 1 oz	4# 14 oz	5# 11 oz	6# 8 oz	7# 5 oz	8# 2 oz
3½ oz	7 oz	10½ oz	14 oz	1# 12 oz	2# 10 oz	3# 8 oz	4# 6 oz	5# 4 oz	6# 2 oz	7#	7# 14 oz	8# 12 oz
3¾ oz	7½ oz	11¼ oz	15 oz	1# 14 oz	2# 13 oz	3# 12 oz	4# 11 oz	5# 10 oz	6# 9 oz	7# 8 oz	8# 7 oz	9# 6 oz

POUND CHART

25 Portions	50 Portions	75 Portions	100 Portions	200 Portions	300 Portions	400 Portions	500 Portions	600 Portions	700 Portions	800 Portions	900 Portions	1000 Portions
4oz	8oz	12oz	1#	2#	3#	4#	5#	6#	7#	8#	9#	10#
5oz	10oz	15oz	1#4oz	2#8oz	3#12oz	5#	6#4oz	7#8oz	8#12oz	10#	11#4oz	12#8oz
6oz	12oz	1#2oz	1#8oz	3#	4#8oz	6#	7#8oz	9#	10#8oz	12#	13#8oz	15#
7oz	14oz	1#5oz	1#12oz	3#8oz	5#4oz	7#	8#12oz	10#8oz	12#4oz	14#	15#12oz	17#8oz
8oz	1#	1#8oz	2#	4#	6#	8#	10#	12#	14#	16#	18#	20#
9oz	1#2oz	1#11oz	2#4oz	4#8oz	6#12oz	9#	11#4oz	13#8oz	15#12oz	18#	20#4oz	22#8oz
10oz	1#4oz	1#14oz	2#8oz	5#	7#8oz	10#	12#8oz	15#	17#8oz	20#	22#8oz	25#
11oz	1#6oz	2#1oz	2#12oz	5#8oz	8#4oz	11#	13#12oz	16#8oz	19#4oz	22#	24#12oz	27#8oz
12oz	1#8oz	2#4oz	3#	6#	9#	12#	15#	18#	21#	24#	27#	30#
13oz	1#10oz	2#7oz	3#4oz	6#8oz	9#12oz	13#	16#4oz	19#8oz	22#12oz	26#	29#4oz	32#8oz
14oz	1#12oz	2#10oz	3#8oz	7#	10#8oz	14#	17#8oz	21#	24#8oz	28#	31#8oz	35#
15oz	1#14oz	2#13oz	3#12oz	7#8oz	11#4oz	15#	18#12oz	22#8oz	26#4oz	30#	33#12oz	37#8oz
1#	2#	3#	4#	8#	12#	16#	20#	24#	28#	32#	36#	40#
1#1oz	2#2oz	3#3oz	4#4oz	8#8oz	12#12oz	17#	21#4oz	25#8oz	29#12oz	34#	38#4oz	42#8oz
1#2oz	2#4oz	3#6oz	4#8oz	9#	13#8oz	18#	22#8oz	27#	31#8oz	36#	40#8oz	45#
1#3oz	2#6oz	3#9oz	4#12oz	9#8oz	14#4oz	19#	23#12oz	28#8oz	33#4oz	38#	42#12oz	47#8oz
1#4oz	2#8oz	3#12oz	5#	10#	15#	20#	25#	30#	35#	40#	45#	50#
1#5oz	2#10oz	3#15oz	5#4oz	10#8oz	15#12oz	21#	26#4oz	31#8oz	36#12oz	42#	47#4oz	52#8oz
1#6oz	2#12oz	4#2oz	5#8oz	11#	16#8oz	22#	27#8oz	33#	38#8oz	44#	49#8oz	55#
1#7oz	2#14oz	4#5oz	5#12oz	11#8oz	17#4oz	23#	28#12oz	34#8oz	40#4oz	46#	51#12oz	57#8oz
1#8oz	3#	4#8oz	6#	12#	18#	24#	30#	36#	42#	48#	54#	60#
1#12oz	3#8oz	5#4oz	7#	14#	21#	28#	35#	42#	49#	56#	63#	70#
2#	4#	6#	8#	16#	24#	32#	40#	48#	56#	64#	72#	80#
2#4oz	4#8oz	6#12oz	9#	18#	27#	36#	45#	54#	63#	72#	81#	90#
2#8oz	5#	7#8oz	10#	20#	30#	40#	50#	60#	70#	80#	90#	100#
2#12oz	5#8oz	8#4oz	11#	22#	33#	44#	55#	66#	77#	88#	99#	110#
3#	6#	9#	12#	24#	36#	48#	60#	72#	84#	96#	108#	120#
3#12oz	7#8oz	11#4oz	15#	30#	45#	60#	75#	90#	105#	120#	135#	150#
4#4oz	8#8oz	12#12oz	17#	34#	51#	68#	85#	102#	119#	136#	153#	170#
4#8oz	9#	13#8oz	18#	36#	54#	72#	90#	108#	126#	144#	162#	180#
5#	10#	15#	20#	40#	60#	80#	100#	120#	140#	160#	180#	200#
5#12oz	11#8oz	17#4oz	23#	46#	69#	92#	115#	138#	161#	184#	207#	230#
6#4oz	12#8oz	18#12oz	25#	50#	75#	100#	125#	150#	175#	200#	225#	250#

NOTE: The material in these charts was developed by the New York Department of Mental Health, and furnished through the courtesy of Mrs. Katherine Flack, Director of Nutrition Service.

AVOIRDUPOIS TO METRIC SYSTEM (LINEAR MEASUREMENTS)

INCHES	FEET	YARDS	MILLIMETERS	CENTIMETERS	DECIMETERS	METERS	KILOMETERS
1	0.0833	0.0277	25.4	2.54	.254	.0254	.00254
2	0.1666	0.0555	50.8	5.08	.508	.0508	.00508
3	0.2500	0.0833	76.2	7.62	.762	.0762	.00762
3.937	0.3280	0.1093	100.0	10.00	1.000	.1000	.01000
4	0.3333	0.1111	101.6	10.16	1.016	.1016	.01016
5	0.4166	0.1388	127.0	12.70	1.270	.1270	.01270
6	0.5000	0.1666	152.4	15.24	1.524	.1524	.01524
7	0.5833	0.1944	177.8	17.78	1.778	.1778	.01778
7.874	0.6561	0.2187	200.0	20.00	2.000	.2000	.02000
8	0.6666	0.2222	203.2	20.32	2.032	.2032	.02032
9	0.7500	0.2500	228.6	22.86	2.286	.2286	.02286
10	0.8333	0.2777	254.0	25.40	2.540	.2540	.02540
11	0.9166	0.3055	279.4	27.94	2.794	.2794	.02794
11.811	0.9842	0.3280	300.0	30.00	3.000	.3000	.03000
12	1.0000	0.3333	304.8	30.48	3.048	.3048	.03048
15	1.2500	0.4166	381.0	38.10	3.810	.3810	.03810
15.748	1.3123	0.4374	400.0	40.00	4.000	.4000	.04000
18	1.5000	0.5000	457.2	45.72	4.572	.4572	.04572
19.685	1.6404	0.5468	500.0	50.00	5.000	.5000	.05000
21	1.7500	0.5833	533.4	53.34	5.334	.5334	.05334
23.620	1.9683	0.6561	600.0	60.00	6.000	.6000	.06000
24	2.0000	0.6666	609.6	60.96	6.096	.6096	.06096
27	2.2500	0.7500	685.8	68.58	6.858	.6858	.06858
27.559	2.2965	0.7655	700.0	70.00	7.000	.7000	.07000
30	2.5000	0.8333	762.0	76.20	7.620	.7620	.07620
31.496	2.6246	0.8748	800.0	80.00	8.000	.8000	.08000
33	2.7500	0.9166	838.2	83.82	8.382	.8382	.08382
35.433	2.9527	0.9842	900.0	90.00	9.000	.9000	.09000
36	3.0000	1.0000	914.4	91.44	9.144	.9144	.09144
39	3.2500	1.0833	990.6	99.06	9.906	.9906	.09906
39.370	3.2808	1.0936	1 000.0	100.00	10.000	1.0000	.10000
42	3.5000	1.1666	1 066.8	106.68	10.668	1.0668	.10668
43.307	3.6089	1.2029	1 100.0	110.00	11.000	1.1000	.11000
45	3.7500	1.2500	1 143.0	114.30	11.430	1.1430	.11430
47.244	3.9370	1.3123	1 200.0	120.00	12.000	1.2000	.12000
48	4.0000	1.3333	1 219.2	121.92	12.192	1.2192	.12192
51.181	4.2650	1.4216	1 300.0	130.00	13.000	1.3000	.13000
54	4.5000	1.5000	1 371.6	137.16	13.716	1.3716	.13716
55.118	4.5931	1.5310	1 400.0	140.00	14.000	1.4000	.14000
59.055	4.9212	1.6404	1 500.0	150.00	15.000	1.5000	.15000
60	5.0000	1.6666	1 524.0	152.40	15.240	1.5240	.15240
62.992	5.2493	1.7497	1 600.0	160.00	16.000	1.6000	.16000
66	5.5000	1.8333	1 676.4	167.64	16.764	1.6764	.16764
66.929	5.5774	1.8591	1 700.0	170.00	17.000	1.7000	.17000
70.866	5.9055	1.9685	1 800.0	180.00	18.000	1.8000	.18000
72	6.0000	2.0000	1 828.8	182.88	18.288	1.8288	.18288
74.803	6.2335	2.0778	1 900.0	190.00	19.000	1.9000	.19000
78.740	6.5616	2.1872	2 000.0	200.00	20.000	2.0000	.20000
84	7.0000	2.3333	2 133.6	213.36	21.336	2.1336	.21336
90	7.5000	2.5000	2 286.0	228.60	22.860	2.2860	.22860
96	8.0000	2.6667	2 438.4	243.84	24.384	2.4384	.24384
98.425	8.2020	2.7340	2 500.0	250.00	25.000	2.5000	.25000
108	9.0000	3.0000	2 743.2	274.32	27.432	2.7432	.27432
118.110	9.8425	3.2808	3 000.0	300.00	30.000	3.0000	.30000
137.795	11.4829	3.8276	3 500.0	350.00	35.000	3.5000	.35000
144	12.0000	4.0000	3 657.6	365.76	36.576	3.6576	.36576
157.480	13.1233	4.3744	4 000.0	400.00	40.000	4.0000	.40000
177.165	14.7637	4.9212	4 500.0	450.00	45.000	4.5000	.45000
180	15.0000	5.0000	4 572.0	457.20	45.720	4.5720	.45720
196.85	16.4041	5.4680	5 000.0	500.00	50.000	5.0000	.50000
360	30.0000	10.0000	9 144.0	914.40	91.440	9.1440	.91440

In metric systems commas are not generally used. A space is used. Decimals are used rather than fractions.

AVOIRDUPOIS TO METRIC SYSTEM (VOLUME MEASUREMENTS)

FLUID OUNCES	CUPS	QUARTS	GALLONS	LITERS	MILLILITERS
2	0.250	0.063	0.016	0.059	59.1
4	0.500	0.125	0.031	0.118	118.2
6	0.750	0.188	0.047	0.177	177.4
8	1.000	0.250	0.063	0.237	236.5
8.448	1.056	0.264	0.066	0.250	250.0
10	1.250	0.313	0.078	0.296	295.7
11.264	1.408	0.352	0.088	0.333	333.3
12	1.500	0.375	0.094	0.355	354.8
14	1.750	0.438	0.109	0.414	414.0
16	2.000	0.500	0.125	0.473	473.1
16.896	2.112	0.528	0.132	0.500	500.0
18	2.250	0.563	0.141	0.532	532.2
20	2.500	0.625	0.156	0.591	591.4
22	2.750	0.688	0.172	0.651	650.5
22.544	2.818	0.705	0.176	0.667	666.7
24	3.000	0.750	0.188	0.710	709.7
25.357	3.170	0.793	0.198	0.750	750.0
32	4.000	1.000	0.250	0.946	946.3
33.814	4.227	1.057	0.264	1.000	1 000.0
40	5.000	1.250	0.313	1.183	1 182.8
42.269	5.284	1.321	0.330	1.250	1 250.0
48	6.000	1.500	0.375	1.419	1 419.4
50.723	6.340	1.585	0.396	1.500	1 500.0
56	7.000	1.750	0.438	1.656	1 656.0
59.178	7.397	1.848	0.462	1.750	1 750.0
64	8.000	2.000	0.500	1.893	1 892.6
67.629	8.454	2.113	0.528	2.000	2 000.0
72	9.000	2.250	0.563	2.129	2 129.1
80	10.000	2.500	0.625	2.366	2 365.7
84.538	10.567	2.642	0.660	2.500	2 500.0
88	11.000	2.750	0.688	2.602	2 602.3
96	12.000	3.000	0.750	2.839	2 838.9
101.446	12.681	3.170	0.793	3.000	3 000.0
118.355	14.794	3.699	0.925	3.500	3 500.0
128	16.000	4.000	1.000	3.785	3 785.2
135.261	16.908	4.227	1.057	4.000	4 000.0
169.079	21.135	5.284	1.321	5.000	5 000.0
192	24.000	6.000	1.500	5.678	5 677.8
202.893	25.362	6.340	1.585	6.000	6 000.0
256	32.000	8.000	2.000	7.570	7 570.4
320	40.000	10.000	2.500	9.463	9 463.0
384	48.000	12.000	3.000	11.356	11 355.6
448	56.000	14.000	3.500	13.248	13 248.2
512	64.000	16.000	4.000	15.141	15 140.8

In metric systems commas are not generally used. A space is used. Decimals are used rather than fractions.

MARKET LIST AND INVENTORY CONTROL SHEET[1]

Item	Unit	Unit Price
Artichokes	each	_____
Beans	lb.	_____
Beans, lima	each	_____
Beets	lb.	_____
Broccoli	bunch	_____
Brussels sprouts	pint	_____
Cabbage, green	lb.	_____
Cabbage	lb.	_____
Cabbage, red	lb.	_____
Carrots, cello	lb.	_____
Carrots, bulk	lb.	_____
Cauliflower	each	_____
Celery	bunch	_____
Celeryknob	lb.	_____
Chicory	each	_____
Cucumbers	lb.	_____
Dill	lb.	_____
Endive, Belgian	lb.	_____
Escarole	each	_____
Fennel		_____

[1]The author recommends that the operator copy on his own permanent market list any of the items that he uses and to refer to it when making out his purchase requirements.

Item	Unit	Unit Price
Garlic	lb.	_____
Kale		_____
Leeks	bunch	_____
Lettuce, iceberg	head	_____
Lettuce, Boston	head	_____
Lettuce, bibb	case	_____
Mushrooms	basket	_____
Olives, Greek	lb.	_____
Onions, green	lb.	_____
red	lb.	_____
Spanish	lb.	_____
Parsley	bunch	_____
Parsnips	lb.	_____
Peppers, green	lb.	_____
Peppers, red	lb.	_____
Peppers	lb.	_____
Potatoes, baker's	lb.	_____
chef	lb.	_____
Idaho	lb.	_____
sweet	lb.	_____
Radishes	each	_____
Rutabagas	lb.	_____
Romaine	head	_____
Shallots	each	_____
Spinach	lb.	_____
Squash, butternut	lb.	_____
yellow	lb.	_____
zucchini	lb.	_____
Tomatoes, cherry	pint	_____
Tomatoes	lb.	_____
Turnips, white	lb.	_____
Turnips	lb.	_____
Watercress	bunch	_____
Avocado	each	_____
Apples	each	_____
Apples, baking	case	_____
Apples, red delicious	case	_____

MISCELLANEOUS

Item	Unit	Unit Price
Applesauce	#303 can	_____
Applesauce	#10 can	_____
Barley	lb.	_____

Item	Unit	Unit Price
Base Beef Bouillon Paste	lb.	_____
Chicken	lb.	_____
French Onion		_____
Beans, green	#10 can	_____
kidney	#10 can	_____
kidney, red	lb.	_____
kidney, red	#303 can	_____
(navy) (pea)	lb. box	_____
Bread, frankfurter roll	package	_____
hamburger roll	package	_____
rye	loaf	_____
rye Wonder	loaf	_____
wheat	loaf	_____
white, sliced	loaf	_____
Wonder jumbo	loaf	_____
Cereal, ind.	case	_____
Coffee, instant	lb.	_____
Coffee, bean	14 oz. package	_____
Coffee, caffeine-free	lb.	_____
Flour	5 lb. bag	_____
Flour	25 lb. bag	_____
Juice, apple	6 oz. can	_____
apple	#5 can	_____
grape	#5 can	_____
grapefruit	#5 can	_____
orange	6 oz. can	_____
orange	#5 can	_____
pineapple	#5 can	_____
tomato	#5 can	_____
V-8		_____
Ketchup	14 oz. bottle	_____
Ketchup, ind.	case	_____
Ketchup	#10 can	_____
Lard	lb.	_____
Lentils	lb.	_____
Matzo meal	10 oz.	_____
Mayonnaise, ind.	case	_____
Mayonnaise	gal.	_____
M.F.B. (shortening)	50 lb. block	_____
Milk, evaporated	5 oz. each	_____
Molasses	1 qt.	_____
Molasses	1 gal.	_____
Mustard	4 oz.	_____

Item	Unit	Unit Price
Mustard	8 oz.	_____
Mustard, brown spicy		_____
Mustard, Dijon		_____
Mustard, dry	15 oz.	_____
Mustard, ind.	case	_____
Non-Dairy creamer	case	_____
Nuts, almonds, sliced blanched	#3 can	_____
almonds, whole blanched	4 lb. can	_____
peanuts	lb.	_____
pecans	#10 can	_____
Oatmeal	40 oz. box	_____
Oil, olive	gal.	_____
Oil, salad	gal.	_____
Oil, pure corn	gal.	_____
Olives, ripe pitted	#10 can	_____
stuffed Spanish	jar	_____
black	7-1/2 oz. can	_____
Onions, tiny whole	#10 can	_____
Oranges, mandarin	#2-1/2 can	_____
mandarin	#10 can	_____
Oysters (smoked)	4 oz.	_____
Pasta (cavatelli #120)	lb.	_____
dainties	8 oz.	_____
ditalini #40	lb.	_____
egg bows, small	12 oz.	_____
egg noodles, fine #133	12 oz.	_____
egg noodles, medium #131	lb.	_____
egg noodles, wide #130	lb.	_____
elbows #35	lb.	_____
fettuccine	lb.	_____
lasagne, curly #80	lb.	_____
linguine #17	lb.	_____
manicotta #90	8 oz.	_____
pastina egg	6 oz.	_____
rigatoni #27	lb.	_____
shells, jumbo #95	12 oz.	_____
spaghetti #8	lb.	_____
spaghetti #9	lb.	_____
spaghetti, vermicelli #10	lb.	_____
spinach noodles	lb.	_____
ziti #2	lb.	_____
Peas, split	lb.	_____
whole green	lb. bag	_____

Item	Unit	Unit Price
Pickles, dill	can	_____
dill kosher	jar	_____
Pimientoes	14 oz. can	_____
Potatoes, instant	#10 can	_____
Salt, table kosher		_____
Sardines	4 oz.	_____
Sauerkraut	#2-1/2 can	_____
Sauerkraut	#10 can	_____
Basil leaves	lb.	_____
Bay leaves	6 oz.	_____
Caraway seed	14 oz.	_____
Chili powder	lb.	_____
Cinnamon, ground	14 oz.	_____
Potato whitener	can or jar	_____
Saffron		_____
Snails, giant		_____
extra large		_____
shells	doz.	_____
Sugar, ind.	case	_____
Sugar	2 lb. bag	_____
Sugar	5 lb. bag	_____
Sugar, bar	lb.	_____
Sugar, brown	lb. box	_____
light brown	lb. box	_____
powdered	2 lb.	_____
Sweet 'N' Low	case	_____
Sweetex	50 lb. box	_____
Syrup, pancake, ind.	case	_____
Tea	box	_____
orange pekoe	box	_____
Darjeeling		_____
ice		_____
Tomatoes, diced-puree	6 oz.—#10 can	_____
paste	#10 can	_____
paste	6 oz. can	_____
pickled	#10 can—gal. jar	_____
plum	#10 can	_____
puree	#2-1/2 can	_____
puree	#10 can	_____
whole	25 oz.	_____
Trufflettes	13 oz. can	_____
Tuna	gal.	_____

Item	Unit	Unit Price
Vinegar, cider	bottle	_____
rice	gal.	_____
tarragon	12 oz.	_____
tarragon	gal.	_____
white	gal.	_____
wine	gal.	_____
Yeast, active dry	can	_____

FROZEN

Item	Unit	Unit Price
Asparagus, jumbo	2-1/2 lb. box	_____
med.	2-1/2 lb. box	_____
Broccoli spears	2-1/2 lb. box	_____
Brussels sprouts	2-1/2 lb. box	_____
Cauliflower	2-1/2 lb. box	_____
Green beans	2-1/2 lb. box	_____
Spinach	2-1/2 lb. box	_____
Kale	2-1/2 lb. box	_____
Peas	2-1/2 lb. box	_____
Peas, blackeyed	2-1/2 lb. box	_____

CHEESE

Item	Unit	Unit Price
American, sliced	lb.	_____
solid	lb.	_____
Bel Paese	lb.	_____
Blue, Danish	lb.	_____
domestic	lb.	_____
Stilton	lb.	_____
Boursin au poivre	lb.	_____
Camembert	lb.	_____
Cheddar, domestic	lb.	_____
Vermont	lb.	_____
Cottage	lb.	_____
Cream	lb.	_____
Emmenthaler	lb.	_____
Feta	lb.	_____
Gorgonzola	lb.	_____
Gouda, baby	lb.	_____
aged	lb.	_____
Gourmandise	lb.	_____

Item	Unit	Unit Price
Gruyere	lb.	_____
Parmesan, fresh	lb.	_____
grated	lb.	_____
Port Salut	lb.	_____
Provolone, domestic	lb.	_____
imported	lb.	_____
Ricotta	3 lb. tube	_____
Roquefort	lb.	_____
Romano, fresh	lb.	_____
grated	lb.	_____
Sap Sago	lb.	_____
Swiss, domestic	lb.	_____
Gruyere	lb.	_____
Jarlsburg	lb.	_____

CHINESE

Item	Unit	Unit Price
Bean sprouts		_____
Bean, curd, dry		_____
Cabbage, Chinese		_____
Celery, Chinese		_____
Soy sauce, superior	bottle	_____

BAKESHOP

Item	Unit	Unit Price
Almond paste	#10 can	_____
Apples, sliced	#10 can	_____
Baker's cheese	30 lb.	_____
Baking powder	#10 can	_____
Chocolate, bitter	10 lb. block	_____
Egg white solid	50 lb.	_____
Bread flour	100 lb.	_____
Cake flour	100 lb.	_____
Pastry flour	100 lb.	_____
Pumpernickel flour	100 lb.	_____
Rye flour	100 lb.	_____
Whole wheat flour	100 lb.	_____
Piping gel	5 lb. can	_____
Puff dough	40 lb.	_____
M.F.B. (shortening)	case	_____
Tastex	50 lb.	_____

Item	Unit	Unit Price
Sugar, granulated	100 lb.	_____
Sugar, powdered	100 lb.	_____
Voltex	30 lb. can	_____

FISH

Item	Unit	Unit Price
Bluefish	lb.	_____
Carp	lb.	_____
Cod fillets	lb.	_____
Cod, whole	lb.	_____
Crab, Alaskan King	lb.	_____
Crab meat, lump	lb.	_____
Crab, soft shell	lb.	_____
Dover Sole	lb.	_____
Flounder, fillets	lb.	_____
Flounder, IQF	lb.	_____
Flounder, whole	lb.	_____
Haddock	lb.	_____
Halibut steak	lb.	_____
C. Halibut	lb.	_____
Langostino gray	12 oz. package	_____
Mackerel	lb.	_____
Red snapper	lb.	_____
Silver salmon, whole	lb.	_____
King salmon	lb.	_____
Salmon steak	lb.	_____
Provincetown scallops	lb.	_____
Scallops, sea	lb.	_____
Sole, whole lemon	lb.	_____
Sole, IQF	lb.	_____
Sole, fillets, fresh	lb.	_____
Sole, fillets, frozen, non-IQF	lb.	_____
Gray sole fillets	lb.	_____
Shrimp, titti	lb.	_____
Shrimp, cooked Alaskan	lb.	_____
Shrimp, red	lb.	_____
Shrimp, U-10	lb.	_____
Shrimp, U-15	lb.	_____
Shrimp, U-20	lb.	_____
Shrimp, U-21/25	lb.	_____
Shrimp, U-26/30	lb.	_____
Scrod	lb.	_____

Item	Unit	Unit Price
Smelts	lb.	_____
Trout	lb.	_____
Trout, Idaho	lb.	_____
Trout, Idaho, frozen	lb.	_____
Turbot, IQF fillet	lb.	_____
French turbot	lb.	_____
White fish	lb.	_____

MEAT

Brisket, fresh	lb.	_____
Bones, beef	lb.	_____
Butt (top)	lb.	_____
Carcass	lb.	_____
Casing, beef	lb.	_____
Arm chuck	lb.	_____
Pastrami	lb.	_____
Corned beef brisket	lb.	_____
Frank steak	lb.	_____
Fore quarters	lb.	_____
Gooseneck	lb.	_____
Ground beef	lb.	_____
Hamburger patties	lb.	_____
Hind quarter	lb.	_____
Kidneys	lb.	_____
Knuckles	lb.	_____
Liver, (steer)	lb.	_____
Oxtails	lb.	_____
Ribs	lb.	_____
Short ribs of beef	lb.	_____
Rounds, standard	lb.	_____
Top round, choice	lb.	_____
Bottom round	lb.	_____
Boneless strip loin	lb.	_____
Corned tongue	lb.	_____
Beef tenderloins	lb.	_____
Tripe	lb.	_____
Tongue, beef, fresh	lb.	_____
Smoked tongue	lb.	_____
Pastrami	lb.	_____
Beef skin	lb.	_____
Shells strip choice	lb.	_____

Item	Unit	Unit Price
Veal breast	lb.	_____
Carcass, veal	lb.	_____
Calves feet	lb.	_____
Ground veal	lb.	_____
Calves head	lb.	_____
Brain, calf	lb.	_____
Bones, veal	lb.	_____
Kidney, veal	each	_____
Leg of veal	lb.	_____
Calves liver	lb.	_____
Loin of veal	lb.	_____
Rack of veal	lb.	_____
Shank of veal	lb.	_____
Shoulder of veal	lb.	_____
Sweet breads	lb.	_____
Veal cutlets	lb.	_____
Veal cubes	lb.	_____
Veal patties	lb.	_____
Turkey	lb.	_____
Turkey breasts, cooked	lb.	_____
Wings, chicken	lb.	_____
Squabs	lb.	_____
Bacon, Canadian	lb.	_____
Bacon, sliced	lb.	_____
Bacon, slab	lb.	_____
Pork bellies	lb.	_____
Pork butt, fresh	lb.	_____
Pork butt, smoked	lb.	_____
Caul pork	lb.	_____
Fatback	lb.	_____
Ground pork	lb.	_____
Hanks pork casings	lb.	_____
Jowls, pork	lb.	_____
Ham fleur de lis	lb.	_____
Fresh ham	lb.	_____
Ham hocks, fresh	lb.	_____
Ham hocks, smoked	lb.	_____
Link sausage	lb.	_____
Italian sausage, sweet/hot	lb.	_____
Canned pullman	lb.	_____
Smoked ham	lb.	_____
Genoa salami	lb.	_____

Item	Unit	Unit Price
Ham, Smithfield	lb.	_____
Sausage, sweet	lb.	_____
Breast of lamb	lb.	_____
Lamb carcass	lb.	_____
Casing lamb	lb.	_____
Chuck of lamb	lb.	_____
Ground lamb	lb.	_____
Hind saddle of lamb	lb.	_____
Kidney lamb	lb.	_____
Loin of lamb	lb.	_____
Leg of lamb	lb.	_____
Lamb rack	lb.	_____
Shank of lamb	lb.	_____
Breast of chicken	lb.	_____
Capon	lb.	_____
Chickens	lb.	_____
Chicken fat	lb.	_____
Cocks combs	lb.	_____
Cornish hens	lb.	_____
Duck	lb.	_____
Fowl	lb.	_____
Geese	lb.	_____
Giblets	lb.	_____
Chicken bones	lb.	_____
Chicken liver	lb.	_____
Chicken leg	lb.	_____
Partridge	lb.	_____
Pheasant	lb.	_____
Quail	lb.	_____
Roasters	lb.	_____
Skins, pork	lb.	_____
Cooked salami	lb.	_____
Boneless prosciutto ham	lb.	_____
Pork liver	lb.	_____
Pork loin	lb.	_____
Pepperoni	lb.	_____
Pigs feet	lb.	_____
Pigs head	lb.	_____
Bologna	lb.	_____
Salt pork	lb.	_____
Shoulder of pork	lb.	_____
Spareribs	lb.	_____

Item	Unit	Unit Price
Sausage roll	lb.	_____
Pork tenderloin	lb.	_____
Franks	lb.	_____
Kielbasa	lb.	_____
Franks, cocktail-regular	lb.	_____
Knuckles, pig	lb.	_____
Fishing ham	lb.	_____
Rabbits	lb.	_____
Venison legs	lb.	_____
Venison saddle	lb.	_____
Knockwurst	lb.	_____
Liverwurst	lb.	_____
Bratwurst	lb.	_____
Turtle steaks	lb.	_____

CULINARY TERMINOLOGY

GENERAL CULINARY TERMINOLOGY

A la broche (ah-lah-broch). Cooked on a skewer

A la mode (ah-lah-mod). In the style of

A la vapeur (ah-lah-vahper). Steamed

A l'etuvee (ah-l'ay-tu-veh). Stewed

Al'huile d'olive (ah-l-weel d'oh-leev). In olive oil

Aspic (as-pik). Any jellied dish or a jellied glaze

Au gratin (o-gra-tehn). Sprinkled with crumbs and/or cheese and baked brown

Au jus (o-zhu). Served with natural juice or gravy

Au lait (o-leh). With milk

Au naturel (o-na-tu-rehl). Plainly cooked

Aux champignons (o-shahm-peh-nohn). Cooked with mushrooms

Ballotine (bah-lo-teen). A rolled preparation of boned meat

Beurre (buhr). Butter; beurre fondu, melted butter; beurre noir, butter browned until it is almost black

Bien cuit (bian-kuee). Well done (meats)

Blanchi (blahn-shee). Blanched

Blanquette (blanh-ket). White meat in cream sauce

Bombe (bohmb). Fancy desserts made of ices, whipped cream, and various fruits

Bouilli (bu-yeeh). Boiled

Braise (breh-zeh). Braised. Food well browned in a little hot fat, then simmered in a little liquid, covered, until tender

Brouille (broo-yeh). Scrambled

Cafe noir (kah-feh-nwar). Black coffee

Chaud (sho). Hot

Chiffonade (shee-foh-nad). Any dish served with shredded vegetables

Coeur (kur). Heart

Confit (kohn-fee). Medium-size pieces of salted meat; goose, duck, turkey, or pork, simmered in and covered with their melted drippings

Cotelletes (kotlet'). Ground or chopped mixture fried in the shape of a cutlet

Coupe (koop). An ice cream dessert

Court bouillon (kur-bu-yohn). Liquid in which fish has been boiled

Cru (kruh). Uncooked, raw

FRANCAIS CULINAIRE

LA BRIGADE DE LA CUISINE	THE KITCHEN BRIGADE
CHEF	CHEF
SOUS CHEF	ASSISTANT HEAD CHEF
CHEFS DE PARTIE	STATION CHEFS
ROTISSEUR	ROASTING, FRYING, GRILLING
ENTREMETIER	EGGS, VEGS., FARINACEOUS
POTAGER	SOUPS
POISSONIER	FISH
SAUCIER	SAUCE, STEWED, AND SAUTEED
GARDE MANGER	LARDER
CHEF DE FROID	COLD BUFFET
TOURNANT	SUBSTITUTE
COMMUNARD	STAFF CANTEEN
PATISSIER	PASTRY
CHEF DE GLACE	ICE CREAM
COMMIS	ASSISTANT
STAGIAIRE	WORK STUDY COOK
APPRENTI	APPRENTICE
MISE EN PLACE	PREPREPARATION

UTENSILS		UTENSILS	
COUTEAU	Knife	BAIN MARIE	Steam Table Wells
SPATULE	Spatula	CHINOIS	Conical Sieve (china cup)
SPATULE EN BOIS	Wooden Spatula	FOUET	Whisk
FOURCHETTE	Fork	TAMIS	Sieve
MANDOLINE	Grater, Cutter	ETAMINE	Cheesecloth
CASSEROLE	Pots and Pans		

Diable (dyah-bleh). Deviled
Duchesse (duh-shes). Potatoes mixed with egg and forced through a pastry tube

En brochette (ahn-broh-shet). Broiled and served on a skewer
En coquille (ahn-ko-ki'ye). In the shell; in shell-shaped ramekins
En gelee (ahn-je-leh). In jelly
En papillote (ahn-pa-piyot). Baked in an oiled paper bag
Epice (e-pees). Spice

Farce (fars). Forcemeat. Stuffing with chopped meat, fish, poultry or nuts, well seasoned
Farci (fahr-see). Stuffed
Fines Herbes (feenz-airb). Mixture of herbs like minced chives, parsley, and tarragon or thyme
Flambe (flahm-beh). A food served with lighted spirits poured over
Foie (fwah). Liver
Fond (fohn). Bottom
Fondue au fromage (fohn-duh-o-fro-mahzh). A melted cheese dish
Fournee (furh-neh). Baked

DESCRIPTIVE CULINARY TERMINOLOGY

CRU	Raw	TENDRE	Tender
CUIT	Cooked	MOUX, MOLLE	Soft
BLEU, AU BLEU	Blue	SEC, SECHE	Dry
SAIGNANT	Rare	CROQUANTE	Crisp
A POINT	Medium rare	CROUSTILLANTE	Crunchy
BIEN CUIT	Well done	FUME	Smoked
TROP CUIT	Overcooked	EPICE	Spicy
FROID	Cold	SUCRE	Sugar(ed)
TIEDE	Warm	BEURRE	Butter(ed)
CHAUD	Hot	HUILE	Oil
BOUILLANTE	Boiling	” d'OLIVE	Olive Oil
FLUIDE	Fluid	” d'ARACHIDE	Peanut Oil
GELEE	Jelled	LARD	Bacon
CONGELEE	Frozen	SAINDOUX	Lard
DUR	Hard, tough		

SIZE AND SHAPE

MORCEAU	PIECE	BRUNOISE	No larger than 1/8″ cube
GRAND(E)	Big	DES	Dice
PETIT(E)	Small	BATONNET	1-1/4″ × 1/4″ × 1/4″
JULIENNE	2″ × 1/4″ × 1/4″	MINCE	Thin
PAYSANNE	1/2″ × 1/2″ × 1/8″	EPAIS	Thick

Frappe (fra-peh). Sweetened fruit juices frozen to a mush; iced drink
Fricassee (fri-ka-seh). Braised meats or poultry
Frit (fri). Fried
Froid (frwah). Cold
Fume (fuh-meh). Smoked

Galantine (gahl-lenh-teen). Boned poultry, game, or meat stuffed and pressed into a symmetrical shape. Usually with truffles. Served cold.
Garni (garh-nee). Garnished
Garniture (garh-nee-tuhr). Garnish
Gateau (ga-toh). Cake
Glace (glas). Ice; ice cream
Glace (gla-seh). Iced
Gras (grah). Fat
Grille (gree-yeh). Grilled or broiled

Hache (ah-sheh). Finely chopped or sliced
Jardiniere (zhar-di-niehr). Diced, mixed vegetables
Julienne (zhu-li-en). Match-like strips of meat, vegetables, or cheese

Lyonnaise (lee-on-ez'). Cooked with onions

Macedoine (mah-se-dwahn). Mixture of vegetables or fruits
Miettes (mee-yet). Flaked, bits, or crumbs
Mousse (moos). Light, airy dish, usually containing beaten egg whites or whipped cream, for dessert or main dish; meat, fish, or poultry, finely ground, served in a mold

Oeufs (oeh'). Eggs

Pain (pehn). Bread
Panache (pah-nah-shay). Mixed (usually two vegetables)
Pane (pah-neh). Prepared with bread crumbs
Pele (peh-leh). Peeled
Puree (pur-reh). Mashed

Quenelles (kuh-nell). Dumplings

Ragout (ra-gho). A stew with rich gravy
Raper (ra-peh). To shred or grate
Refroidi (reh-frwah-dee). Chilled
Revenir (reh-veh-nir). To fry lightly without actually cooking
Rillettes (ree-yet). Shredded meat and potted pork "deviled"
Roti (ro-tee). Roast

Rouleau (ru-loh). Roll of
Roux (ru). A mixture of butter or flour used for thickening soups or sauces

Sans aretes (sahnz-aret). Boneless
Sans peau (sahn-po). Skinless
Saute (so-teh). Fried lightly in a little fat
Souffle (su-fleh). A baked fluffy main dish or dessert made of milk and egg yolks into which stiffly beaten egg whites are folded

Tarte (tart). Tart or pie
Terrine (teh-reen). Earthenware crock (usually used for foie gras)

Vinaigrette (vee-neh-gret). A marinade or salad sauce of oil, vinegar, pepper, and herbs

INDEX